THE LEGAL HISTORY OF THE CHURCH OF ENGLAND

This book provides the first comprehensive analysis of the principal legal landmarks in the evolution of the law of the established Church of England from the Reformation to the present day.

It explores the foundations of ecclesiastical law and considers its crucial role in the development of the Church of England over the centuries.

The law has often been the site of major political and theological controversies, within and outside the church, including the Reformation itself, the English civil war, the Restoration and rise of religious toleration, the impact of the industrial revolution, the ritualist disputes of the nineteenth century, and the rise of secularisation in the twentieth. The book examines key statutes, canons, case-law, and other instruments in fields such as church governance and ministry, doctrine and liturgy, rites of passage (from baptism to burial) and church property.

Each chapter studies a broadly 50-year period, analysing it in terms of continuity and change, explaining the laws by reference to politics and theology, and evaluating the significance of the legal landmarks for the development of church law and its place in wider English society.

The Legal History of the Church of England

From the Reformation to the Present

Edited by
Norman Doe
and
Stephen Coleman

·HART·
OXFORD · LONDON · NEW YORK · NEW DELHI · SYDNEY

HART PUBLISHING

Bloomsbury Publishing Plc

Kemp House, Chawley Park, Cumnor Hill, Oxford, OX2 9PH, UK

1385 Broadway, New York, NY 10018, USA

29 Earlsfort Terrace, Dublin 2, Ireland

HART PUBLISHING, the Hart/Stag logo, BLOOMSBURY and the Diana logo are trademarks of Bloomsbury Publishing Plc

First published in Great Britain 2024

Copyright © The editors and contributors severally 2024

The editors and contributors have asserted their right under the Copyright, Designs and Patents Act 1988 to be identified as Authors of this work.

All rights reserved. No part of this publication may be reproduced or transmitted in any form or by any means, electronic or mechanical, including photocopying, recording, or any information storage or retrieval system, without prior permission in writing from the publishers.

While every care has been taken to ensure the accuracy of this work, no responsibility for loss or damage occasioned to any person acting or refraining from action as a result of any statement in it can be accepted by the authors, editors or publishers.

All UK Government legislation and other public sector information used in the work is Crown Copyright ©. All House of Lords and House of Commons information used in the work is Parliamentary Copyright ©. This information is reused under the terms of the Open Government Licence v3.0 (http://www.nationalarchives.gov.uk/doc/open-government-licence/version/3) except where otherwise stated.

All Eur-lex material used in the work is © European Union, http://eur-lex.europa.eu/, 1998–2024.

A catalogue record for this book is available from the British Library.

A catalogue record for this book is available from the Library of Congress.

Library of Congress Control Number: 2023947669

ISBN: HB: 978-1-50997-319-4
       ePDF: 978-1-50997-317-0
       ePub: 978-1-50997-318-7

Typeset by Compuscript Ltd, Shannon

To find out more about our authors and books visit www.hartpublishing.co.uk. Here you will find extracts, author information, details of forthcoming events and the option to sign up for our newsletters.

FOREWORD

DAVID IBBETSON[*]

It is something of a curiosity of English legal historiography that relatively little attention has been paid to the law of the Church of England. This despite the fact that, for more than four centuries after the Reformation, the Church played a major part in the life of most people in England. The essays comprising this volume, based on the inaugural meeting of a new Church Law History Consortium that took place in Cambridge in the spring of 2022, inevitably cannot be totally comprehensive, but they give a chronological overview of the law of this Anglican Church from its medieval prehistory to the present day.

Over this period, church law has mutated from something touching on the lives of everybody – primarily through its jurisdiction over marriage and divorce and over the transmission of moveable property on death, but also through such things as the collection of tithes and the capricious incidence of chancel repair liability – to something that is primarily of concern to the clergy and committed churchgoers. That said, however, the legal history of the Church of England has relevance to the wider Anglican Communion and cannot be set aside as nothing more than a niche interest. We may no longer be quite as concerned about liturgical niceties, vestments and the ringing of bells as were some of our forebears, but current concerns about, for example, monuments to those with (supposed) links to slavery raise questions of historical complexity, not only about the individuals concerned but also about the Church itself. Ignorance of history too easily leads to facile assumptions and misunderstandings.

The editors and contributors should be encouraged to see this volume as the bedrock on which further studies of the history of the law of the Church of England can be anchored. There is almost no end to the topics that could be covered, and the voices of different scholars will give greater relief to the history than the single voice of a monograph. We might also look to voices from outside England, given the varieties of Anglicanism in the world today. As well, given the centrality of the University of Cardiff's Centre for Law and Religion in the study of church law, consideration might be given to a comparison between the legal

---

[*] David Ibbetson is a Fellow of the British Academy (elected 2003) and served as Regius Professor of Civil Law, University of Cambridge (2000–22) and as President of Clare Hall, Cambridge (2013–20).

history of the Church of England with the legal history of the Church in Wales. As with any branch of law, it is historical and comparative studies that sharpen our perceptions of what is wholly contingent in contemporary thinking and what is at its core. Volumes like the present one have a central part to play in shaping our understanding of the contemporary church order.

PREFACE

The study of English legal history is seeing something of an academic renaissance. Whilst the Selden Society, founded by FW Maitland in 1887, is the standard bearer of the discipline, recent encouraging developments include the foundation of the Cambridge Centre for English Legal History in 2012. There is also clearly significant interest in the history of ecclesiastical law. The LLM in Canon Law in the School of Law and Politics at Cardiff University, now in its 32nd year, has a module focused on the historical development of ecclesiastical and canon law that is much appreciated by the students and has produced some remarkable studies, many of which have been published. Furthermore, the Ecclesiastical Law Society regularly hosts lectures devoted to historic legal topics, and the *Ecclesiastical Law Journal* publishes articles, comments and book reviews on this legal history in almost every issue.

Yet while the ecclesiastical law of England has been and continues to be hugely influential on the English legal system, and indeed the history of canon and ecclesiastical law has been a well-established focus of much scholarship, there is to our knowledge no society that exists to promote scholarship focused specifically on the legal history of the Church of England.

It was with this in mind that the Cardiff University Centre for Law and Religion founded a new network, the Church Law History Consortium, which held its inaugural meeting at Magdalene College, Cambridge, from Thursday, 31 March to Friday, 1 April 2022. Convened by the editors of this book, the Consortium consists of a small number of invited scholars, early-career and established, with the common interest of researching and discussing the history of canon and ecclesiastical law in the wider context of the theology of the Church of England.

For the first meeting, the Consortium received papers on the landmark ecclesiastical legal developments in the history of the Church of England 1533–2022, with an opening paper on the medieval antecedents. Each paper broadly covered a 50-year period and considered the landmark ecclesiastical legal developments of each period in terms of leading statutes, canons (and other instruments), cases, commentaries and controversies. A wide-ranging discussion followed each paper, and common themes began to emerge in terms of continuity and change in the law, the significance of legal commentaries and the legal profession, the relationship between Church and State, and the effect of that relationship on the development of the law.

We are very grateful to the Master and Fellows of Magdalene College, Cambridge, for hosting the event. The Consortium was honoured to be joined at dinner in the Parlour by Professor David Ibbetson, then Regius Professor of

Civil Law at the University of Cambridge, and Professor Sir John Baker, Downing Professor Emeritus of the Laws of England at the University of Cambridge. After dinner, Sir John generously offered some reflections on the study of English legal history at Cambridge during his career. A further major boost to the work of the Consortium came in October 2022 during a conference to mark the 30th anniversary of the LLM in Canon Law at Cardiff, when the distinguished American historian of canon law, Richard Helmholz (of Chicago) assessed the work and place of this new Consortium in the wider context of studies in ecclesiastical legal history.

The chapters of this book are the fruits of the Cambridge meeting. Covid-19 meant that not all of the authors were present at that meeting; some papers were therefore kindly presented by others. But out of a shared common interest, and considerable conviviality, comes this publication, which we hope opens the door to recognition of the significance, today and historically, of the ecclesiastical law in shaping the life, identity and mission of the Church of England. We are extremely grateful to Kate Whetter, Senior Commissioning Editor, and to all of her colleagues at Hart Publishing, for their confidence in this project, for their constant patience and support, and for their professionalism in the production of this volume, particularly Catherine Minahan for all her hard work and good cheer in the process of copy editing.

Norman Doe
Stephen Coleman
Cardiff
June 2023

CONTENTS

Foreword by David Ibbetson..v
Preface..vii
List of Contributors xi

Introduction 1
Norman Doe and Stephen Coleman

1. *The Medieval Antecedents: Pre-Reformation Canon Law* 5
   Sarah B White

2. *The Reformation and the King's Ecclesiastical Law: 1533–58*............27
   Michelle L Johnson and Will Adam

3. *The Elizabethan Settlement: 1558–1603*...49
   Paul Barber and Morag Ellis

4. *The Source and Limit of the King's Ecclesiastical Law: 1603–60* 69
   Ian Blaney

5. *The Restoration and Re-Establishment: 1660–1701*..........................95
   Russell Sandberg

6. *The Church in Danger – Legal Perspectives: 1701–60*.....................115
   Stephen Coleman

7. *The Ecclesiastical Law and Religious Pluralism: 1760–1837*...........135
   Norman Doe

8. *The Victorian Church: Revival, Reform, Ritualism: 1837–1901* 153
   Charlotte Smith

9. *The 'New World' of Ecclesiastical Law: 1901–47*.............................175
   Russell Dewhurst

10. *The Post-War Church – Revision and Stability: 1947–94*................193
    Neil Patterson

11. *Change and Decay – The Twilight Years of an Established Church: 1994–2023*..213
    Mark Hill

Conclusion 233
Norman Doe and Stephen Coleman

Bibliography..*241*
Index *257*

LIST OF CONTRIBUTORS

The Ven Dr Will Adam is the 99th Archdeacon of Canterbury and a Residentiary Canon of Canterbury Cathedral. He was formerly on the staff of Lambeth Palace, acting as ecumenical adviser to the Archbishop of Canterbury, and served as the Deputy Secretary General of the worldwide Anglican Communion. He holds the LLM in Canon Law and a PhD in Anglican Legal History from Cardiff University and is a Fellow of the Royal Historical Society.

Paul Barber MA (Cantab) MA (Canon Law) JCL FCCT is a barrister who has practised in the consistory courts and is an appeal court judge in the Catholic system. He studied canon law at Cardiff, Heythrop College London, and Leuven, where he also taught, and is a member of the Editorial Board of *Law and Justice*.

Ian Blaney is a partner in the firm of solicitors Lee Bolton Monier-Williams, Westminster. He is Registrar of the Dioceses of Derby and Lincoln, Deputy Registrar of the Diocese of Guildford and Deputy Registrar of the Faculty Office of the Archbishop of Canterbury, and holds the degree of LLM in Canon Law from Cardiff University.

The Revd Stephen Coleman is Priest in Charge of the Grosvenor Chapel in the Diocese of London. He is assistant director of the Centre for Law and Religion at Cardiff University, and deputy course director of the LLM in Canon Law. He is researching for a PhD on the legal history of the advowson, and he convenes the Church Law History Consortium and the Colloquium of Anglican and Roman Catholic Canon Lawyers. He is a trustee of the Ecclesiastical Law Society, an Honorary Research Fellow at St. Stephen's House, Oxford, and practises ecclesiastical law at Birketts LLP.

The Revd Russell Dewhurst is a doctoral student and fellow at the Centre for Law and Religion, School of Law and Politics, Cardiff University. He is also Communications Officer of the Ecclesiastical Law Society, book reviews editor of the *Ecclesiastical Law Journal*, research fellow at St Augustine's College of Theology, West Malling, and a priest in the Diocese of Chichester. He holds the degree of LLM in Canon Law from Cardiff University.

Norman Doe is a Professor of Law, School of Law and Politics, Cardiff University, and Director of its Centre for Law and Religion and LLM in Canon Law, Chancellor of the Diocese of Bangor, Church in Wales, a Master of the Bench of Inner Temple, London, a Life Member of Clare Hall, Cambridge, and a member of the Council of the Selden Society.

Morag Ellis KC is the Dean of the Arches and Auditor and Master of the Archbishop of Canterbury's Faculty Office, offices which she has held since June 2020. She is the KC Church Commissioner, a member of the Legal Advisory Commission of the General Synod, and on the editorial board of the *Ecclesiastical Law Journal*. She is currently studying for the Cardiff LLM in Canon Law. She practises as a barrister at Francis Taylor Building, Temple, specialising in planning and environmental law, and is a Master of the Bench at Gray's Inn.

Mark Hill KC is Chancellor of the Dioceses of Chichester, Leeds and Europe; Bencher of Inner Temple, London; Visiting Professor, Dickson Poon School of Law, King's College, London; and Visiting Professor and Distinguished Fellow at the University of Notre Dame London Law Programme. He holds the degree of LLM in Canon Law, Cardiff University.

Michelle Johnson is a Lecturer in Law at King's College London. Her research focuses on the intersection between law, religion, and politics in early modern England. Specifically, she explores the works of the common lawyer Christopher St German, the Henrician Reformation, and the authority of the nascent English Church.

The Revd Neil Patterson has served in Hereford Diocese since ordination in 2004, currently as Director of Vocations and Ordinands. He is a member of General Synod and a Trustee of the Ecclesiastical Law Society, and is the author of *Ecclesiastical Law, Clergy and Laity* (2019).

Russell Sandberg is a Professor of Law at the School of Law and Politics, Cardiff University and a Fellow of the Royal Historical Society. His research interrogates the interaction between Law and the Humanities with particular reference to Law and Religion and Legal History.

Dr Charlotte Smith holds the posts of Modern Legal Records Specialist at the National Archives of the United Kingdom, and Associate Professor in Law at the University of Reading. Having begun her academic life by completing a doctoral thesis on church-state theory and parliamentary efforts to reform clergy discipline in the nineteenth century, she has since worked predominantly in the fields of nineteenth-century ecclesiastical legal history, the legal and ecclesiastical history of the British Empire, and legal biography. She has also, on occasion, delved into more modern matters – including the Church of England's place in the British Constitution today and debates about same-sex marriage.

Dr Sarah B White is Assistant Professor in Law and Co-Director of the History of Law and Governance Centre at the Law School, Faculty of Social Sciences, University of Nottingham. Previously she has held the posts of Lecturer in Medieval History at Lancaster University, and Research Fellow at the University of St Andrews Institute of Legal and Constitutional Research, working on the European Research Council funded comparative legal history project entitled 'Civil Law, Common Law, Customary Law'.

Introduction

NORMAN DOE AND STEPHEN COLEMAN

This book provides for the first time in a single volume a comprehensive analysis of the principal legal landmarks in the evolution of the law of the established Church of England since the Reformation to the present day. This body of law, ecclesiastical law (part of the law of the land), has played a crucial role in the development of the Church of England over the centuries. The law has often been the site of major political and theological controversies, hot topics in their day shaping the very identity of the Church as a national Church today, with the monarch as its legal head, as well as the nature and scope of religious freedom in England.

The book does so by examining landmark statutes, canons, case law and other regulatory sources, as well as the many commentaries on these over the centuries, in relation to fields such as church governance and ministry, doctrine and liturgy, rites of passage (from baptism to burial) and church property. In respect of method, each chapter in the book studies a broadly 50-year period – it describes the laws in terms of continuity and change, explains these laws by reference, for example, to the politics and theology underlying them, and evaluates the significance of the legal landmarks for the development of law in the life of the Church, then and now, and its place in wider English society. A great number of primary sources have been consulted for the studies in each of the chapters. The book is original: no study exists to date that seeks to present this legal history in its entirety. The contributors are experts on English ecclesiastical law from historical, political and theological perspectives.

In 10 years' time, during 2033, the Church of England marks the five-hundredth anniversary of the creation of a series of Acts of Parliament that heralded its foundation as the national, established Church in England. Those statutes, alongside other regulatory instruments, and the works of jurists, have played a crucial role in the development of the Church of England. They have sought both to facilitate and to order the evolution of the national mission of the English Church over the centuries in all areas of its life. The law, and the legislative and judicial processes underlying it, has been the crucible for ecclesiastical development and vision to meet the changing needs and aims of the Church in wider society, as well as a battleground on which theological, political and other forces have struggled for supremacy.

This book is designed to prepare the way, and to stimulate new ways of thinking, for those who will mark that important anniversary in all the richness of the life of the English Church. By providing a long historical perspective of legal evolution, in the changes and chances of each passing age, it seeks to enable not only an understanding of, but also critical reflection on, the legal history of the Church of England from the Reformation to the present day. The book is also intended to feed and shape the growing interest in the legal history of the Church of England as evidenced, for example, in the Ecclesiastical Law Society and its *Ecclesiastical Law Journal*, the study of canon law at university level (such as the LLM in Canon Law at Cardiff University set up in 1991) and the work of the Church law History Consortium itself.

In addition, the book seeks to complement, build on, and develop the existing and growing secondary literature in the field of ecclesiastical law. To date, no book exists that sets out a comprehensive legal history of the Church of England covering each phase in its evolution since its foundation in the sixteenth century. Needless to say, there are of course excellent studies on the history of the Church – its political and social, its theological and missional, and its doctrinal and liturgical history. Some of these studies deal with aspects of English ecclesiastical law but in a piecemeal, topic-specific fashion; and unlike this book, they do not tell the whole connected story of the development of church law in its manifold manifestations.[1]

Similarly, there have also been many notable studies devoted to the medieval canon law of the Church of Rome, and to specific aspects of the legal evolution of the English Church at different stages of its history. The work of Gerald Bray is seminal in its long coverage of the textual evolution of the canons of the Church of England from the Reformation.[2] That of Richard Helmholz has contextualised the canon law and ecclesiastical jurisdiction of the Church in England in the light of the pre-Reformation Roman canon law.[3] Like John Baker and his work on famous English canonists,[4] Professor Helmholz has also introduced us to the profession of ecclesiastical lawyers and the work of the civilians.[5] Then there is Robert E Rodes'

---

[1] See, eg, the multi-volume *Oxford History of Anglicanism* (Oxford, Oxford University Press, 2017-19).

[2] G Bray (ed), *The Anglican Canons: 1529-1947* (London, The Boydell Press, 1998): this is an invaluable collection of texts of historic canons, with an excellent introduction, but does not look at statute law, case law and commentators.

[3] RH Helmholz, *The Canon Law and Ecclesiastical Jurisdiction from 597 to the 1640s* (Oxford, Oxford University Press, 2004); a monumental work, vol I in the series *The Oxford History of the Laws of England*, makes a major contribution to the field – it focuses on the domestic law of the Church on a subject-by-subject basis and takes to story to the Civil War, but, unlike this book, does not treat in detail the wider law. See also RH Helmholz, *Roman Canon Law in Reformation England* (Cambridge, Cambridge University Press, 1990), which takes the story to the 1640s.

[4] JH Baker, *Monuments of Endlesse Labours: English Canonists and Their Work 1300-1900* (London, The Hambledon Press, 1998).

[5] RH Helmholz, *The Profession of Ecclesiastical Lawyers: An Historical Introduction* (Cambridge, Cambridge University Press, 2019): this is invaluable on selected historic English commentators on church law, the first who died in 1179 and the last in 1865, and is drawn on in the pages of this book.

ambitious work on the history of establishment.[6] By far the most studied aspect of English ecclesiastical law, however, has been the work of the church courts – and studies by Michael Smith and Brian Outhwaite are obvious examples,[7] carrying on the long scholarly tradition of studies on the extensive business of the church courts in Reformation England.[8]

However, none of these excellent works described above provides in a single volume the principal legal landmarks of the Church's history. This is a distinct missing link in the rich resources of English ecclesiastical history. This volume, therefore, seeks to fill this gap and provide for the first time connected studies devoted to a long perspective on this legal story.

There are 11 chapters in the book. Chapter 1 sets the scene and deals with the medieval antecedents: the pre-Reformation Roman canon law as it applied to the Church in England. Chapter 2 examines the Reformation and the rise of king's ecclesiastical law in the turbulent years of ecclesial establishment, disestablishment and re-establishment, 1533–58. In chapter 3, the Elizabethan settlement is explored as it developed over the years 1558–1603/04. Next, in chapter 4, we examine the legal controversies that took place in 1603–60 over ecclesiastical authority, including during the Republic. Chapter 5 then studies the development of ecclesiastical law from the Restoration of the Monarchy in 1660 to the Act of Settlement 1701. There follows the period characterised by the war-cry of the 'Church in Danger', and chapter 6 provides the legal landmarks from 1701 to 1760. The story continues in chapter 7 with the gradual expansion of ecclesiastical law in the period 1760–1837 as it began to accommodate increasing religious pluralism. Next, in chapter 8, comes the Victorian Church, 1837–1901, and the legal aspects of revival, reform and ritualism. Chapter 9 deals with the 'new world' of ecclesiastical law: 1901–47. This is followed in chapter 10 by a study of legal revision and reform following the Second World War, taking us to 1994. The legal history of the Church of England is brought up to date in chapter 11, covering 1994 to 2023, and exploring the themes of the Church, secularism and globalism. The Conclusion summarises the legal landmarks around the themes of continuity and change in the evolution of ecclesiastical law.

This book is intended for a wide range of readers. There are the practitioners of the law of the Church of England. These include Diocesan Chancellors

---

[6] RE Rodes, *A Study of the Legal History of Establishment in England* (Notre Dame and London, Notre Dame Press, 1977, 1982, 1991); its three volumes are: *Law and Modernization in the Church of England: Charles II to the Welfare State* (1991); *Lay Authority and Reformation in the English Church: Edward I to the Civil War* (1982); and *Ecclesiastical Administration in Medieval England: The Anglo-Saxons to the Reformation* (1977).

[7] MG Smith, *The Church Courts, 1680–1840: From Canon to Ecclesiastical Law*, ed P Smith (Lampeter, The Edwin Mellen Press, 2006); and RB Outhwaite, *The Rise and Fall of the English Ecclesiastical Courts, 1500–1860* (Cambridge, Cambridge University Press, 2006).

[8] See, eg, RA Marchant, *The Church Under the Law: Justice Administration and Discipline in the Diocese of York, 1560–1640* (Cambridge, Cambridge University Press, 1969); and GIO Duncan, *The High Court of Delegates* (Cambridge, Cambridge University Press, 1971), which takes the story to 1832 when the court was abolished.

(who preside over the Consistory Court of each Diocese in the Church of England); Diocesan Registrars (who advise on legal matters); the staff at the Legal Services department of the Church of England (at Church House, Westminster); clergy responsible for ministering ecclesiastical law in the Church of England, including Bishops and Archdeacons; members of the General Synod of the Church of England – the law-makers of the Church for whom, often, debate includes consideration of historic antecedents to proposed legislative changes; and other officers at various diocesan and local levels involved in applying law, such as Churchwardens. Clergy and members of the Church of England with an interest in its history are also an obvious and large readership. All these constituencies have a professional or scholarly interest in the history of English ecclesiastical law, and many of them are also members of the Ecclesiastical Law Society.

Internationally, there are also equivalent practitioners of church law in the member churches of the global Anglican Communion. In 2022, the second iteration of *The Principles of Canon Law Common to the Churches of the Anglican Communion* was launched at the Lambeth Conference 2022. The working groups that revised the 2008 version of this document engaged in historical enquiry to explain the reasons for their laws, which, when compared, generated these common principles. Many of these churches have societies devoted to historic and modern church law – and church legal history forms part of the staple diet of the Anglican Communion Legal Advisers Network (among whose leaders are contributors to this book, which it is hoped will help stimulate similar studies across the Communion). It is also hoped that the book will be of interest to ecumenical partners of the Church of England and Anglican Churches, not least the Roman Catholic and the Eastern Orthodox Churches.

Finally, needless to say, the book is designed for scholars and students in the fields of law, church history and applied theology, in order to equip them to describe juridically, explain politically and theologically, and evaluate on the basis of continuity and change, the legal history of the Church of England from the Reformation to the present day, to understand better the Church of England and its law as that Church approaches its 500th anniversary.

1

The Medieval Antecedents: Pre-Reformation Canon Law

SARAH B WHITE

The termination of papal jurisdiction in England in the sixteenth century heralded a system of ecclesiastical law for the Church of England, established under the royal supremacy, many features of which are still with us today. However, the phenomenon of law within the life of the Church was not new. This chapter contextualises the later English ecclesiastical law by providing an overview of the development of pre-Reformation Roman canon law in the Late Middle Ages, with a particular focus on the period c 1100–1300 and the ecclesiastical courts. The twelfth and thirteenth centuries were when many of the landmark events in the history of church law took place: the creation of judicial institutions, the emergence of professional lawyers, the systematisation of legal authority, and the clarification of the relationship between temporal and spiritual powers.[1] There is much that could be said about the immense changes that took place in this period, but this introductory chapter concentrates on two themes. The first, briefly, is the development of classical canon law and legal science, much of which took place on the Continent. The second is the development of canon law in England, especially in the areas of court structure, the legal profession, and the relationship between secular and spiritual law. The two themes are, of course, connected, and the second is, in some ways, a result of the first. And, as with many histories of church law, we shall begin on the Continent, in 1140.

I. The Classical Canon Law

There were three main, intertwined forces in the creation of what we consider to be classical canon law: first, the systematic collection of previous sources of church

---

[1] For an excellent, up-to-date introduction to canon law in this period, see A Winroth and JC Wei (eds), *The Cambridge History of Medieval Canon Law* (Cambridge, Cambridge University Press, 2022). See also JA Brundage, *Medieval Canon Law* (London, Longman, 1995); RH Helmholz, *The Canon Law and Ecclesiastical Jurisdiction from 597 to the 1640s* (Oxford, Oxford University Press, 2004) chs 2–3.

law; second, the beginning of scientific legal study; third, the expansion of papal authority and legislation.[2]

A. Collections

One of the greatest achievements of this period was the collection we know as the *Corpus iuris canonici*, the authoritative texts of the law of the Church of Rome. This collection was accompanied by a vast number of commentaries and glosses. While there were several important collections in circulation prior to 1140, such as the *Decretum* of Burchard of Worms (d 1025),[3] the *Panormia* of Ivo of Chartres (d 1115),[4] and, for England, the *Collectio Lanfranci* of Archbishop Lanfranc (d 1089),[5] for the sake of brevity and debatable tradition, we start with Gratian in the year 1140.

Gratian, who, as tradition has it, was a monk who taught at Bologna, compiled a massive text called the *Concordia discordantium canonum*, commonly known as the *Decretum*, a collection generally heralded as a watershed moment in the history of church law. The work collected conciliar decrees, papal decretals, works of the Church Fathers, the Bible, and even some royal legislation, all taken from earlier collections. The innovativeness, date and indeed authorship of this text have all been subject to some debate in recent years.[6] Controversies about authorship aside, however, we can still single out the *Decretum* as a new type of text, in that Gratian actively sought to reconcile the laws and solve contradictions with

---

[2] For a discussion of whether 'classical canon law' is still a useful term of analysis, see M Bertram, 'The Late Middle Ages: Four Remarks Regarding the Present State of Research' in Winroth and Wei (eds) (n 1) 108–21.

[3] For a recent monograph on Burchard, see G Austin, *Shaping Church Law Around the Year 1000: The Decretum of Burchard of Worms* (Aldershot, Ashgate Publishing, Ltd., 2009). See also J Burden, 'Reading Burchard's Corrector: Penance and Canon Law' (2019) 46 *Journal of Medieval History* 77-97.

[4] For a recent monograph on Ivo, see C Rolker, *Canon Law and the Letters of Ivo of Chartres* (Cambridge, Cambridge University Press, 2010). Rolker's forthcoming volume in the *History of Medieval Canon Law* series will also be of great value: C Rolker, *Canon Law in the Age of Reforms (ca 1000 to ca 1150)* (Washington, DC, Catholic University of America Press, 2023).

[5] For Lanfranc, one of the best sources is still M Philpott, 'Archbishop Lanfranc and Canon Law' (DPhil Thesis, University of Oxford, 1993); more recently, see N Alvarez de las Asturias, *La 'Collectio Lanfranci': Origine e Influenza Di Una Collezione Della Chiesa Anglo-Normanna* (Milan, Giuffrè Editore, 2008); an excellent source for these and other early collections remains L Kéry, *Canonical Collections of the Early Middle Ages (ca 400–1140): A Bibliographical Guide to the Manuscripts and Literature* (Washington, DC, Catholic University of America Press, 1999) esp 136–48.

[6] A Winroth, 'III. The Two Recensions of Gratian's Decretum' (1997) 83 *Zeitschrift Der Savigny-Stiftung Für Rechtsgeschichte. Kanonistische Abteilung* 22–31 at https://doi.org/10.7767/zrgka.1997.83.1.22; A Winroth, *The Making of Gratian's Decretum* (Cambridge, Cambridge University Press, 2000); A Winroth, 'III. Where Gratian Slept: The Life and Death of the Father of Canon Law' (2013) 99 *Zeitschrift Der Savigny-Stiftung Für Rechtsgeschichte. Kanonistische Abteilung* 105-28; A Winroth, 'Gratian and His Book: How a Medieval Teacher Changed European Law and Religion' (2021) 10 *The Oxford Journal of Law and Religion* 1–15.

a kind of consistency that had not yet been attempted.[7] The texts Gratian was confronted with were diverse, to say the least, and his attempts to reconcile them vary in their levels of success. Even so, the *Decretum* demonstrates a concerted effort to produce intellectual standards for the laws of the Church – standards that were drawn not simply from the arrangement of the texts into themes but from Gratian's attempts to discern meaning and intent. It was very much a product of the emerging study of law and quickly became immensely popular. The *Decretum* was circulated widely throughout Europe, including in England, within a few years of its production. For example, we know that John of Salisbury had the text available to him in the 1150s, and a large part of the arguments in the famous Becket dispute drew heavily on Gratian's work.[8] The appearance of the *Decretum* was quickly followed by a plethora of commentaries on the text, written by the so-called decretists, and the spread of new types of legal literature. We see the appearance of *distinctiones* and *quaestiones*, mainly stemming from the schools, and *brocarda* and *ordines*, which were tied to legal practice.[9]

In England and Normandy specifically, in the late twelfth century through to the middle of the thirteenth century, there was an important school of Anglo-Norman canonists, with strong ties to Paris and Bologna. Members of this school included Gerard Pucelle,[10] Master Honorius[11] and Ricardus Anglicus,[12] and many of them had careers in both England and on the Continent. The group produced sophisticated commentaries on the *Decretum* and decretals (papal letters written in response to legal queries), as well as treatises on many aspects of canon law, *quaestiones* for the schools and *ordines* on procedure. The most famous and

---

[7] See WP Müller, 'The Reinvention of Canon Law in the High Middle Ages' in Winroth and Wei (eds) (n 1) 79–95.

[8] C Duggan, 'The Reception of Canon Law in England in the Later-Twelfth Century' in S Kuttner and JJ Ryan (eds), *Proceedings of the Second International Congress of Medieval Canon Law* (Città del Vaticano, Bibliotheca Apostolica Vaticana, 1965) 378–82.

[9] *Brocarda*: Romano-canonical texts containing arguments for specific cases, starting with a general legal concept and listing propositions that either supported or contradicted it. *Distinctiones*: differing definitions of a single word used to reconcile apparently contradictory texts; the form of jurisprudential writing based on this process. *Ordo, ordines*: Romano-canonical procedural treatises, concerning either procedure as a whole or a single element of procedure such as exceptions. *Quaestiones*: the written form of the disputations held at the law schools, based on the opposition of arguments pro and contra cases of problematic interpretation. For these and further definitions, see the Encyclopaedia of Legal Terms created by the research team on the ERC-funded project, 'Civil Law, Common Law, Customary Law: Consonance, Divergence and Transformation in Western Europe from the late eleventh to the thirteenth centuries', grant agreement number: 740611 CLCLCL at https://clicme.wp.st-andrews.ac.uk/encyc/ (accessed 12 January 2023).

[10] S Kuttner and E Rathbone, 'Anglo-Norman Canonists of the Twelfth Century: An Introductory Study' (1949) 7 *Traditio* 279–358; C Donahue, 'Gerard Pucelle as a Canon Lawyer: Life and the Battle Abbey Case' in RH Helmholz et al (eds), *Grundlagen Des Rechts: Festschrift Für Peter Landau Zum 65. Geburtstag* (Paderborn, Schöningh, 2000) 333–48.

[11] Kuttner and Rathbone (n 10) 296, 304–10, 344–47.

[12] RC Figueira, 'Ricardus de Mores at Common Law – The Second Career of an Anglo-Norman Canonist' in L Kolmer and P Segl (eds) *Regensburg, Bayern Und Europa. Festschrift Für Kurt Reindel Zu Seinem 70. Geburtstag*, (Regensburg, Universitätsverlag, 1995) 281–99; Kuttner and Rathbone (n 10).

far-reaching of the *ordines* were those of Tancred of Bologna (1215)[13] and William Durantis (*c* 1271),[14] which drew on the best texts of the Anglo-Norman tradition, but there were many others, of varying quality. William of Drogheda, an English bishop, wrote a treatise he called the *Summa aurea*, famously described by Maitland as 'none too honest' for its prolific and dubious advice on how best to delay cases in court.[15]

B. Legal Science

It is worth noting at this point that it is difficult, if not impossible, to look at the development of canon law without speaking about the development of Roman law. The study of Roman law, and Roman law itself, pre-dated canon law and was generally more sophisticated. The canonists could hardly ignore it. The rediscovery of the *Corpus iuris civilis* and the organised study of Roman law that emerged in the twelfth century were crucial to the development of canon law – the two laws were blended, and, in many instances, it is difficult to draw a line between them.[16]

For England, we know that the study of Roman law occurred well before the establishment of the ecclesiastical courts, even as early as the Anglo-Saxon period.[17] But the revival of Roman law in Bologna in the eleventh century was a turning point, and the development of legal science there, by amongst others Inerius (d 1125), Azo (d 1230) and Accursius (d 1263), set the standard for much of Europe. The treatises of the commentators are worth mentioning, as they emerged

---

[13] K Pennington, 'The Decretalists 1190-1234' in W Hartmann and K Pennington (eds), *The History of Medieval Canon Law in the Classical Period, 1140-1234 from Gratian to the Decretals of Pope Gregory IX* (Washington, DC, Catholic University of America Press, 2008) 211–45.

[14] K Pennington, 'The Jurisprudence of Procedure' in W Hartmann and K Pennington (eds), *The History of Courts and Procedure in Medieval Canon Law* (Washington, DC, Catholic University of America Press, 2016) 125–59.

[15] FW Maitland, 'William of Drogheda and the Universal Ordinary' in FW Maitland, *Roman Canon Law in the Church of England: Six Essays* (London, Methuen & Co, 1898) 110–31. See also RH Helmholz, 'William of Drogheda (c 1200-1245)' (2014) 16 *Ecclesiastical Law Journal* 66–71; JE Sayers, 'William of Drogheda and the English Canonists' in P Linehan (ed), *Proceedings of the Seventh International Congress of Medieval Canon Law, Cambridge, 23-27 July 1984* (Città del Vaticano, Biblioteca Apostolica Vaticana, 1988) 205–22.

[16] On the development and use of Roman and canon law, see M Bellomo, *The Common Legal Past of Europe, 1000-1800* (Washington, DC, Catholic University of America Press, 1995); P Stein, *Roman Law in European History* (Cambridge, Cambridge University Press, 1999).

[17] Master Vacarius is still hailed as one of the first to teach Roman law in England, and there are several good works on his writings and career. RW Southern, 'Master Vacarius and the Beginning of an English Academic Tradition' in JJG Alexander and MT Gibson (eds), *Medieval Learning and Literature: Essays Presented to Richard William Hunt* (Oxford, Clarendon Press, 1976) 257–86; P Stein, 'Vacarius and the Civil Law' in CNL Brooke et al (eds), *Church and Government in the Middle Ages: Essays Presented to CR Cheney on His 70th Birthday* (Cambridge, Cambridge University Press, 1976) 119–37; P Stein, 'The Vacarian School' (1992) 13 *The Journal of Legal History* 23–31; J Taliadoros, *Law and Theology in Twelfth-Century England: The Works of Master Vacarius (c 1115/20-c 1200)* (Turnhout, Brepols Publishers, 2006).

from the same environment that produced Gratian and the decretists; they were used in the same circles and courts. This did not mean that the civil and canon laws were always in agreement, but contradictions were the exception rather than the rule. Gratian himself advocated using Roman law to resolve conflicting canons, and a large number of Roman law texts were included in the *Decretum*.[18] Of course, canon law dealt with some subjects that Roman law did not, but for all else, the canonists were as comfortable turning to the *Digest* as they were to the decretals.[19]

C. Decretals

Another significant development was the substantial increase in papal decretals, which were collected and commented on in turn. Beginning in the twelfth century, the papacy began to take a more active role in the affairs of its far-flung churches. Despite being sent in response to specific legal queries, usually from bishops, the decretals were deemed universally applicable and became a form of case law. Referred to as the 'new law', decretals were the latest decisions on issues of law and served as precedent for future cases. The most famous decretal collection, commissioned by Pope Gregory IX in 1230, was the *Liber extra* or simply 'the Decretals'. This massive work was compiled by Raymond de Peñafort and completed by 1234. In the process of compilation, he removed doubts, contradictions and extraneous material, and divided the decretals into titles according to subject. The result was a text that was far more systematised and useable than Gratian's *Decretum* or any previous canonical collections. The *Liber extra* was also extensively glossed by Bernard of Parma, and, like the *Decretum* before it, the contents of the text inspired a new wave of commentaries and ancillary writings composed by the decretalists.[20]

D. The Years 1300–1500

In the two centuries following, very few changes occurred in the content of the *Corpus iuris canonici*. The first addition to the *Corpus iuris canonici* was a volume known as the *Liber sextus*, commissioned by Pope Boniface VIII and promulgated in 1298. The work did not introduce any new subjects to the corpus but expanded on the topics in the decretals, incorporating recent conciliar decrees. As ever, this text was quickly glossed, this time by the famous canonist Johannes Andreae (d 1348). Three other, smaller collections were also added

---

[18] See d.p. C. 15 q. 3 c. 4.
[19] See G Dolezalek, 'Roman Law: Symbiotic Companion and Servant of Canon Law' in Winroth and Wei (eds) (n 1) 230–61.
[20] See G Drossbach, 'Decretals and Lawmaking' in Winroth and Wei (eds) (n 1) 208–29.

to the corpus: a small decretal collection known as the *Clementines*, named after Pope Clement (1305–14) and promulgated by Pope John XXII in 1317, the *Extravagantes Johannis XXII* and the *Extravagantes communes*. These texts were edited at the end of the fifteenth century by Jean Chappuis, a Parisian canonist, to make them conform to the style of the *Liber extra*. These additional collections resolved some of the outstanding questions from the earlier works.[21]

Compared to the preceding period, there was relatively little innovation in the legal literature in England. Explanations for this vary, ranging from the predominance of the common law in England, the absence of Roman law in secular courts, or the lack of a professorial career path comparable to the situation at Bologna. It is also striking that so few noteworthy canonists and civilians came from the English universities. In general, the history of church law in England in the fifteenth century is dominated by William Lyndwood (d 1446). Lyndwood was the Dean of Arches and eventually bishop of St Davids and wrote the famous *Provinciale* (c 1436), a collection of constitutions from the province of Canterbury (from 1222 to his day), with a substantial gloss on their meaning. He arranged the constitutions more or less in the same order as the decretals, and since these constitutions continued to be relevant after the Reformation, Lyndwood's work endured. Much like Gratian several centuries earlier, Lyndwood tried to bring harmony to his collection of constitutions and show how they were not as at odds with canon law as it might initially seem. Lyndwood was by no means the only canonist writing in this period, but his work has certainly been the longest-lasting.[22] With this background in mind, let us now turn to the English Church specifically and draw out some of the developments as they appeared.

II. The English Church

The development of ecclesiastical law in England can, like many other things, be divided into three phases and themes. The first is the creation of regular courts. The second is the emergence of a legal profession. And the third is the recognition by secular powers of the autonomy of religious law and the ongoing jurisdictional disputes between secular and religious forums.

A. Regular Courts

The renewed study of Roman Law at Bologna, which focused upon the *Corpus iuris civilis* produced by, or at the command of, Justinian I (527–65 CE), reignited

---

[21] A Meyer, 'The Late Middle Ages: Sources' in Winroth and Wei (eds) (n 1) 122–41.
[22] Helmholz (n 1) 205–06; the most recent edition of Lyndwood is, I believe, JV Bullard and HC Bell (eds), *Lyndwood's Provinciale: The Text of the Canons Therein Contained, Reprinted from the Translation Made in 1543* (London, Faith Press, 1929).

the idea that law could be treated as a scientific, intellectual system. Roman law formed the basis of developments in ecclesiastical and secular law in various European territories and had a lasting impact on European jurisprudence. Canon law also underwent significant development during the period. Following the wave of legal reforms in the twelfth century, cases were becoming increasingly complex and appeals to the Roman *curia* more frequent. A more sophisticated system of justice than that provided by the twelfth-century synodal courts was needed, and the constant influx of papal decretals meant that the body of written law upon which litigants could draw was ever-increasing. By the end of the thirteenth century, the ecclesiastical courts were operating almost exclusively within an extensive framework of written law that was anchored in a growing body of commentaries and treatises. The courts changed from a somewhat informal system of bishops presiding over synods into the highly organised and well-recorded institution that appeared by the 1270s. By the end of the thirteenth century, the procedural elements involved in a case were clear and well-established.[23] The exactness with which procedure was adhered to in the case material demonstrates that the adoption of Romano-canonical judicial procedure was not just a theoretical development but a practical one too. This 'legal revolution' meant that the success or failure of litigants' cases became more and more dependent on establishing a clear relationship between legal argument and legal sources, either through oral arguments in the court or, occasionally, through written arguments presented during the proceedings.[24]

The procedure operating in the medieval ecclesiastical courts developed within the hierarchical structure of the Church, which rested on a distinction between inferior and superior courts and included appellate processes. The lowest court was that of the archdeacon, which had jurisdiction over all types of cases.[25] Superior to it was the diocesan court of the bishop, sometimes called his consistory. Both were courts of first instance, but the consistory was also the court of appeal from the court of the archdeacon. The metropolitan (or archbishop) of each province also maintained a court. In the south of England, this was the Court of Canterbury, and in the north of England, that of York. At the top of this hierarchy was the *curia* of the Apostolic See, which heard appeals from episcopal and archepiscopal courts, and from which there was no further appeal.[26] This clear

---

[23] See WP Müller, 'Procedures and Courts' in Winroth and Wei (eds) (n 1) 327–42.

[24] The survival of written arguments is, by and large, serendipitous. Far more common was the phrase *habita disputacio diutina*, generally taken to mean that the advocates took over, but that they always or even often submitted something in writing is not clear.

[25] Helmholz (n 1) 135–37. It is not clear by the end of the 13th century that all archdeacons' courts were courts of general jurisdiction. Mention is made here of rural deans along with the discussion of the courts of the archdeacons, but the focus remains on the latter. See also AH Thompson, *Diocesan Organization in the Middle Ages: Archdeacons and Rural Deans* (Oxford, Humphrey Milford, 1943); CNL Brooke, 'The Archdeacon and the Norman Conquest' in DE Greenway, CJ Holdsworth and JE Sayers (eds), *Tradition and Change: Essays in Honour of Marjorie Chibnall Presented by Her Friends on the Occasion of Her Seventieth Birthday* (Cambridge, Cambridge University Press, 1985) 1–19.

[26] FD Logan, *Excommunication and the Secular Arm in Medieval England: A Study in Legal Procedure from the Thirteenth to the Sixteenth Century* (Toronto, Pontifical Institute of Mediaeval Studies, 1968);

system of organisation was the ideal, but in practice it was more complicated. This is because there were many partially exempt jurisdictions, called 'peculiars', and various jurisdictional agreements made between bishops and archdeacons over time.[27]

Ecclesiastical jurisdiction heard both civil cases and criminal cases and was also cognisant of spiritual cases, which concerned matters of faith and the sacraments. The subject matter of cases may be divided into four main groups, concerning: (i) ecclesiastical offices or revenues, benefices, tithes, pensions, oblations and mortuaries; (ii) marriage, divorce or legitimacy; (iii) last wills and testaments; and (iv) miscellaneous matters, including violence against clerks, defamation and breaches of faith (such as breaking vows or oaths).[28] Cases entered an ecclesiastical court in one of three ways. In instance cases (brought at the instance of an individual), the plaintiff brought a complaint to the judge. In *ex officio* cases, the judge inquired into a matter (possibly based on a report or on *fama*) by virtue of his office. Lastly, in probate cases, the court became cognisant of a matter either when the executors of a testament sought to prove a will and receive administration, or when a dispute was initiated concerning a will.[29] The proper forum for a case was determined by the nature of the case, not the person of the litigant.[30]

Procedure in Roman law, and consequently canon law, differed slightly between civil and criminal cases. In Roman law, the primary difference between civil and criminal procedures was the nature of the sentence, but there was also some difference at the start of the trial – not everyone who could bring a civil case was eligible to bring a criminal case. Additionally, in criminal cases, the accuser was responsible for proving his case, and if he could not then he was to undergo the same punishment as the accused would have received.[31] Gratian did not distinguish between civil and criminal procedure, but later canonists attempted to distinguish the two, with civil cases following Roman procedure and criminal cases following procedure modified by the canons.[32] Tancred of Bologna, William Durantis and Aegidius de Fuscarariis all devoted titles to criminal procedure in their treatises, and William of Drogheda promised to do so in his treatise, but this title was one of the many he never managed to write.[33] Despite the devotion of titles to criminal procedure, however, there was actually very little difference in practice between civil and criminal procedure. As was noted, the

---

see also D Millon, 'Ecclesiastical Jurisdiction in Medieval England A Symposium in Legal History: Medieval and Early Modern Law: The Birth of Modern Jurisprudence' (1984) *University of Illinois Law Review* 621–38.

[27] C Donahue, *The Records of the Medieval Ecclesiastical Courts*, Part II: *England. Reports of the Working Group on Church Court Records* (Berlin, Duncker u Humblot, 1994) 23.

[28] Winroth and Wei (eds) (n 1). See the sections on 'Clerus', 'Conubium' and 'Crimen'.

[29] BL Woodcock, *Medieval Ecclesiastical Courts in the Diocese of Canterbury* (Oxford, Oxford University Press, 1952) 30.

[30] Helmholz (n 1) 144.

[31] L Fowler-Magerl, *Ordines Iudiciarii and Libelli de Ordine Iudiciorum* (Turnhout, Brepols, 1994) 50.

[32] ibid 52–53.

[33] ibid 53.

primary difference between the two was the outcome following sentencing. In the fourteenth and fifteenth centuries, criminal proceedings were usually handled *ex officio*, but in the thirteenth century, this was not the case, and matters such as defamation, which was considered a criminal proceeding, were brought in the same way as civil cases.

One might wonder, in the midst of this, whether the English church courts actually considered the decisions of the Roman court binding – a topic that was debated more than a century ago by Bishop William Stubbs and Frederic W Maitland. Stubbs declared that the 'canon law of Rome' was respected but was not binding in the English church courts.[34] Maitland, on the other hand, argued that large portions of this law – the decretals especially – were indeed binding throughout Christendom, of which England was a part.[35] He used the work of Lyndwood as a key example. The Stubbs–Maitland debate has given rise to a vast body of scholarship on the topic since then, but we can say with some certainty that Maitland was more correct. The idea attributed to Stubbs of England's independence from Roman jurisdiction can certainly no longer be accepted. That being said, Maitland tended to treat the *Corpus iuris canonici* rather like a modern code and neglected the importance of local custom in church law. Even so, he was correct that the English Church was subject to papal jurisdiction.[36] Since Maitland's time, there has been much work done on the records of the English ecclesiastical courts, shedding light on how this hierarchy of courts and sources functioned. A key point is that unlike in modern legal systems, medieval ecclesiastical appellate courts did not necessarily 'correct' local practices and customs through appeal – indeed, tolerance for local practice was remarkably high.[37]

B. The Legal Profession

This vast court structure and the plethora of issues under the Church's jurisdiction attracted – or perhaps even required – the presence of legal experts well versed in court practice and written law.[38] Legal experts appeared in two main roles: as advocates and, to a lesser extent, as proctors. No clearly defined boundaries divided the roles initially, and the same individual might act in the capacity of either role throughout his career. Advocates were at the top of the profession and advised litigants as well as judges on the law. The procedural treatise of Pseudo-Ulpian,

---

[34] *Ecclesiastical Courts Commission, Report of the Commissioners into the Constitution and Working of the Ecclesiastical Courts* (Gr Brit, 1883) xviii.
[35] See, in general, Maitland, *Roman Canon Law* (n 15).
[36] Helmholz (n 1) 161–62.
[37] ibid 164. See also C Donahue, 'Roman Canon Law in the Medieval English Church: Stubbs vs Maitland Re-Examined after 75 Years in the Light of Some Records from the Church Courts' (1974) 72 *Michigan Law Review* 647–716.
[38] See, in general, A Winroth, 'Law Schools and Legal Education' in Winroth and Wei (eds) (n 1) 262–84.

De edendo (1140–70), notes that advocates provided necessary assistance for the parties and that judges should provide advocates for those who had none (or, if necessary, better advocates).[39] Much of their role consisted of informing the court and parties on the law and presenting well-reasoned, eloquent arguments.[40] Mention should also be made of the *iuris periti* (legal counsellors, and often advocates as well), who aided the judge by providing opinions, analysing proofs, and possibly supplying articles and interrogatories – documents essential for interviewing witnesses.[41] Proctors were often less well-trained in law than advocates but more familiar with the practicalities of pursuing cases, and appeared in court on behalf of their clients.[42]

There was a steady shift from self-representation at court to the use of proctors and advocates for representation and counsel. At the start of the thirteenth century, many litigants would self-represent or hire someone from outside the court with some previous experience in legal proceedings; advocacy in the ecclesiastical courts was not, for the most part, conducted by professionals, and advocates' involvement in cases is seldom recorded. Proctors were much more prominent, and their names were usually listed in the *acta* (official records of the court). Unlike advocates, proctors were not subject to any explicit, formal requirements for legal training. Some are referred to as *magister*, which may indicate that at least some of them had university training, but this was also used as a general honorific. For the most part, it seems they were appointed as a matter of convenience rather than out of a desire for legal expertise. However, by the mid-thirteenth century, self-representation within the newly organised church courts did not bode well for the outcome of the lawsuit.[43] As the anonymous author of the *Summa* 'Elegantius in iure divino' said (c 1169), '[I]f someone is brash enough to presume to rely on his own devices even though he is inexperienced and does not wish to have an advocate, let him do so. Everyone is free to muck up his own case.'[44] For the courts to operate successfully and for litigants to be able to use

---

[39] B Brasington, *Order in the Court: Medieval Procedural Treatises in Translation* (Leiden, EJ Brill, 2016) 148–49.

[40] Thomas of Marlborough, in his *History of Evesham Abbey* (1218–29), distinguished between proctors, who informed the court on the facts, and advocates, who informed it on the law: JE Sayers and L Watkiss (eds), *Thomas of Marlborough, History of the Abbey of Evesham* (Oxford, Clarendon Press, 2003) 303.

[41] See generally N Adams and C Donahue (eds), *Select Cases from the Ecclesiastical Courts of the Province of Canterbury, c 1200–1301* (London, Selden Society, 1981).

[42] JA Brundage, 'The Practice of Canon Law' in W Hartmann and K Pennington (eds), *The History of Courts and Procedure in Medieval Canon Law* (Washington, DC, Catholic University of America Press, 2016) 55–56.

[43] It seems likely that litigants in the archdeacon's and rural dean's courts would start by self-representing or hiring a local proctor. In the provincial court material, however, it was common for litigants to hire legal counsel of some sort, either because they did not wish to make the journey to Canterbury themselves or because some of the appellants were wealthier and could afford to do so.

[44] *Summa* 'Elegantius' 6.65, 2:133: '[S]i quis de se presumens, etiam cum imperitus sit, aduocatum habere nolit, suo ingenio relinquatur. Liberum est cuique suam causam negligere.' Translation by Brundage in JA Brundage, *The Medieval Origins of the Legal Profession: Canonists, Civilians, and Courts* (Chicago, IL, University of Chicago Press, 2008) 152.

them, expert legal representation was needed. Sentences usually state that they were made 'with the counsel of the *jurisperitii*', which indicates the participation at least of counsellors for the court.[45]

James Brundage places the emergence of a professional identity of canon lawyers around the turn of the thirteenth century.[46] There is some evidence of the teaching of canon and civil law in England before *c* 1190, though not in the universities.[47] During the period of *c* 1190 through to 1274, the study of canon law became available at the new English universities, and paid canon law experts started to be treated as members of a profession.[48] By 1234, the faculty of canon law at Oxford was using the *Decretals* as well as Gratian as its essential texts, and the faculty of civil law had replaced the *Liber Pauperum* with the *Code* and *Digest*. Legal education became more accessible and better organised, and consequently there were more individuals with academic legal training. Procedural changes also meant that legal experts were becoming increasingly necessary for the ecclesiastical courts to function, from the perspectives of both the judges and litigants.

Advocates have been aptly referred to as 'shadowy figures'.[49] The names of these men, let alone any information about their careers, rarely appear in the court records, and they are challenging to track down even when we know their names. The increasing university records in England and elsewhere are central to such inquiries and, in some cases, can assist us in identifying advocates. Boyle has written extensively on the study of canon law at Oxford in the thirteenth century, and his work, along with Emden's student lists for Oxford and Cambridge, has been instrumental in tracing the careers of legal experts and for the study of legal education in general.[50] Likewise, Logan includes a list of advocates known to have practised in the Canterbury provincial court.[51] He also includes a list of proctors,

---

[45] The phrase is formulaic, but judges were likely interested in imposing legally sound sentences and would not necessarily have had the training to do so without advisors.
[46] Brundage (n 42) 53.
[47] P Brand, *The Origins of the English Legal Profession* (Oxford, Blackwell, 1992) 143.
[48] ibid 143.
[49] Adams and Donahue (eds) (n 41) 22–23.
[50] LE Boyle, 'The Beginnings of Legal Studies at Oxford' (1983) 14 *Viator* 107-32; LE Boyle, 'Canon Law before 1380' in JI Catto (ed), *History of the University of Oxford*, vol I: *The Early Oxford Schools* (Oxford, Oxford University Press, 1984) 1–36; AB Emden, *A Biographical Register of the University of Oxford to AD 1500* (Oxford, Clarendon Press, 1957); AB Emden, *A Biographical Register of the University of Cambridge to 1500* (Cambridge, Cambridge University Press, 1963). See also HG Richardson, 'The Schools of Northampton in the Twelfth Century' (1941) 56 *The English Historical Review* 595-605; HG Richardson, 'The Oxford Law School under John' (1941) 57 *Law Quarterly Review* 319-38; Kuttner and Rathbone (n 10); JE Sayers, 'Canterbury Proctors at the Court of "Audienta Litterarum Contradictum"' (1966) 22 *Traditio* 311-45; Southern (n 17); Stein, 'Vacarius and the Civil Law' (n 17); AB Cobban, 'Theology and Law in the Medieval Colleges of Oxford and Cambridge' (30 September 1982) 65 *Bulletin of the John Rylands Library* 57; P Stein, 'The Vacarian School' (1992) 13 *Journal of Legal History* 23-31; DM Owen, *The Medieval Canon Law: Teaching, Literature and Transmission* (Cambridge, Cambridge University Press, 1990).
[51] FD Logan, *The Medieval Court of Arches* (Woodbridge, Canterbury and York Society, 2005) 209.

with most names from the thirteenth century coming from bishops' registers.[52] Woodcock provides as comprehensive a list as can be found for proctors practising in all the courts of Canterbury, using the only two extant lists from the thirteenth century, the 'Boniface Roll' of 1259 and a list on the dorse of an *acta* from 1271. Woodcock addresses the ambiguity of the profession as well, suggesting that the rules for proctor's training in the provincial court were not applied in the inferior courts and that in these lower courts, the distinction between advocates and proctors was blurry, or perhaps even non-existent.[53] The provincial court, however, drew clear distinctions between the two in the second half of the thirteenth century through the implementation of professional standards.

The statutes of Archbishop Kilwardby (1273–78) provide the most precise picture of the requirements for advocates and proctors in the second half of the century.[54] Advocates and proctors were required to swear to work faithfully and honestly for their clients and not to knowingly undertake desperate or wicked causes (and if they discovered a cause was unjust, to give it up). They were also not to delay matters out of malice, not to disturb or wittingly infringe upon the liberties of the Church, and to be moderate in the fees they took from their clients. Advocates had to study civil and canon law for a minimum of four years in the schools of a university or town and must further attend court for a year. Priests were ineligible unless acting for themselves, their lord or the poor. Proctors were not to take up a cause without an advocate, and both proctors and advocates were to provide their services at no cost to poor clients.[55] These statutes also limited the number of advocates retained by the court to 16, and the number of proctors to 10, and stated that no party could have more than six advocates or two proctors.[56]

After *c* 1274, advocates were subjected to still further specific educational requirements. Some ecclesiastical courts imposed additional quotas on the number of those allowed to practise regularly. Further, all had to take an admission oath before practising law. However, these requirements did not mean all lawyers were particularly good at their jobs. At the Council of Lambeth in 1281,

---

[52] ibid 219.

[53] Canterbury Cathedral Archives, CCA-DCc-ChAnt/A7b; 1; Court of Canterbury Rolls – ESRoll/14, 15, 18, 20, 21, 22, 39, 208, 222; Woodcock (n 29) 11.

[54] See the *Ordo Bambergensis* on advocates and proctors, especially the guidelines for advocates arguing on behalf of clients. Anon., 'Ordo Bambergensis', tr Brasington in Brasington (n 39) 216–23; 224–27. See also VF Snow, 'The Evolution of Proctorial Representation in Medieval England' (1963) 7 *The American Journal of Legal History* 319–39; RH Helmholz, 'Ethical Standards for Advocates and Proctors in Theory and Practice' in *Proceedings of the Fourth International Congress of Medieval Canon Law* (Vatican City, Biblioteca Apostolica Vaticana, 1976) 283–99; JA Brundage, 'The Calumny Oath and Ethical Ideals of Canonical Advocates' in *Proceedings of the Ninth International Congress of Medieval Canon Law: Munich, 13–18 July 1992* (Vatican City, 1997) 793–805; C Donahue, 'Ethical Standards for Advocates and Proctors of the Court of Ely (1374–1382) Revisited' in TL Harris (ed), *Studies in Canon Law and Common Law in Honor of RH Helmholz* (Berkeley, CA, Robbins Collection, 2015) 41–60.

[55] Brand (n 47) 149; IJ Churchill, *Canterbury Administration: The Administrative Machinery of the Archbishopric of Canterbury Illustrated from Original Records*, 2 vols (London, SPCK for the Church Historical Society, 1933) vol 1, 450.

[56] Adams and Donahue (eds) (n 41) 22–23.

Archbishop Pecham (1279–92) complained about poorly trained advocates practising law and impeding the judicial process. Consequently, further training requirements were imposed.[57] The 1281 Canons from the Council of Lambeth established that one had to have attended lectures in canon and civil law for a minimum of three years before practising as an advocate (interestingly, a less stringent requirement than that of Archbishop Kilwardby). The 1295 statutes of Archbishop Winchelsey reiterated the requirements for advocates wishing to be admitted to practise in the Canterbury provincial Court of Arches. They must have attended lectures for a minimum of four years (preferably five) and to have attended that court for at least one year, presumably to become familiar with the practices specific to it.[58]

The increased use of advocates and proctors over the thirteenth century indicates that parties were not willing to risk their cases by self-representing. Judges, too, were turning to legal experts to assist them in deciding cases. Statutes regulating the practice of proctors and advocates, as well as the brief mentions of them in the case records, indicate that there was an increase in trained legal professionals in England. Still, their individual careers remain obscure. Although we have several letters of proxy (in which a party appoints a proctor to act on their behalf), these provide only the names of the parties, and frequently proctors and advocates, even when named, cannot be found in other records that might illuminate their careers.

It is also worth noting here that, certainly in the second half of the century, the officials and commissaries of the court were, on the whole, a very learned group of men.[59] For the provincial court, Master Henry de Stanton, commissary from 1270–72, was a professor of canon law who was trained at Oxford, where he was later chancellor.[60] Peter de Ickham, a monk of Canterbury and commissary in 1271, had an extensive library that included the *Digest*, *Code*, *Institutes* and *Decretals*, along with a number of other legal and theological texts.[61] Master Henry de Depham, another monk and commissary in 1271, had a similarly extensive collection, as well as books on astronomy, physics and surgery.[62] Richard de Clyve, commissary general of the consistory court and monk of Christ Church (prof 1286), had been a master of arts, possibly at Oxford, before his profession.[63] He was a student at Paris by 1288 and began his legal career in Canterbury when he was 'young and right out of law school'.[64] Given the books he bequeathed to

---

[57] Brundage (n 42) 56.
[58] Brand (n 47) 149.
[59] Adams and Donahue (eds) (n 49) 19.
[60] Emden, *A Biographical Register of the University of Oxford to AD 1500* (n 50) vol 3, 1768.
[61] MR James, *The Ancient Libraries of Canterbury and Dover* (Cambridge, Cambridge University Press, 1903) nos 1538–47, 128–29.
[62] ibid nos 1487–1522, 125–28.
[63] T Sullivan, *Benedictine Monks at the University of Paris, AD 1229–1500: A Biographical Register* (Leiden, EJ Brill, 1995) no 185.
[64] C Donahue, *Law, Marriage, and Society in the Later Middle Ages: Arguments about Marriage in Five Courts* (Cambridge, Cambridge University Press, 2007) 567.

the priory library in Canterbury, his interests were in canon law, not theology. Between 1292 and 1313, Richard was also regularly employed by the prior as proctor, and in 1298, he was proctor to the court of Rome.[65] A key point to take from this is that legal experts fulfilled many roles in the courts at various points in their careers, and their expertise was valued as much in advising and judging as it was in arguing cases.

The profession of ecclesiastical lawyers saw further opportunities for expansion in the fifteenth century, with the lesser equity courts and others that required an education in civil law. Most important, however, was the creation of Doctors' Commons, the College of Advocates in London, which provided a level of organisation and cohesion to the profession that rivalled the inns of court.[66]

III. The Secular and Religious Jurisdictions

Although there are many instances in which the relationship between secular and religious law had to be worked out for better or worse, we shall focus here on the Constitutions of Clarendon from 1164 and the events that followed. The intent in doing so is to highlight the types of issues that were raised in jurisdictional disputes. These Constitutions, presented by Henry II, had three main objectives.[67] The first was to delineate secular and ecclesiastical jurisdiction. Key issues under dispute were the right of advowson, the *ius patronatus*, reserved to the king's court; disputes involving land held in free alms (as a gift for spiritual services), which fell to the ecclesiastical courts after the status of the land had been decided in the secular courts; and pleas concerning debts, which were to be subject to the king, even when they involved breach of faith. Another key issue, and the most memorable, concerned the prosecution of criminous clerks. Disagreement emerged, and neither side was willing to surrender its claims. Criminous clerks were, of course, the main point of dispute between Henry II and Thomas Becket.[68] The second objective was to limit procedures in the ecclesiastical courts, restricting pledges demanded under a sentence of excommunication, requiring 'lawful accusers' to prosecute crimes in the spiritual forum and limiting appeals to the pope. The last of these was received especially poorly, as it was seen as denying the pope's status as the universal ordinary. The third objective was to protect royal prerogatives, especially feudal ones, which required bishops to have the king's permission before leaving the realm, that the king be able to review

---

[65] SVSB/1/170.

[66] See, in general, GD Squibb, *Doctors' Commons: A History of the College of Advocates and Doctors of Law* (Oxford, Clarendon Press, 1977).

[67] J Hudson, *The Oxford History of the Laws of England*, vol II: *817–1216* (Oxford, Oxford University Press, 2012) 513–14; 567–68; Helmholz (n 1) 114–18.

[68] For a relatively recent piece on this, see J Hudson, 'Constitutions of Clarendon, Clause 3, and Henry II's Reforms of Law and Administration' in C Whittick, S Jenks and J Rose (eds), *Laws, Lawyers and Texts: Studies in Medieval Legal History in Honour of Paul Brand* (Leiden, EJ Brill, 2012) 1–19.

any excommunications of those working in his administration and that the king maintain his rights in episcopal elections. The pope condemned all these out of hand – they clearly encroached on the freedom of the Church.

Some of the Constitutions listed at Clarendon were soon forgotten; others became points of strife between the secular and ecclesiastical jurisdictions for years to come. But the Constitutions were important more broadly for three reasons: first, they were the product of careful legal analysis on both sides of the argument; second, they were detailed and addressed immediate concerns, rather than merely stating general principles; and, third, their form and the debate that followed set a precedent for similar clashes in the future.[69] The Constitutions were not the end of the secular–ecclesiastical conflict, but disputes after this took on a 'properly legal form', consisting of ecclesiastical complaints or *gravamina* and royal responses.[70] The writ *Circumspecte agatis* of 1286[71] and the *Articuli clerici* of 1315–16[72] defined the sphere of ecclesiastical jurisdiction in a way that was acceptable to the Crown. And although this did not completely address the Church's complaints, it remained the basis for its jurisdictional claims. An important point to note in all of this is that, generally, the jurisdiction in English courts was demarcated according to subject matter rather than by persons – the appropriate forum was decided on the nature of the case, not the status of the litigant. This resulted in a certain amount of cooperation between the two jurisdictions – for example, the secular courts referred questions of legitimacy and marriage to the church courts, and the church courts invoked the secular arm against excommunicates who refused to appear.

A. Interaction and Influence

As already seen, with two monumental legal traditions functioning in the same space, the question of influence automatically arises. Much ink has been spilled on the subject, and it is not my intention to repeat all of it here. However, there are a few points that can be made, and several caveats. Regarding the caveats, Charles Donahue sums up the difficulties very succinctly:

> The standard word is 'influence', and the standard meaning of the word is direct borrowing of rules and sometimes of broader principles: 'reception', if you will, in one of the multifarious senses of the word. The word 'influence', however, need not have so narrow a meaning. It can be used to describe any relationship between people, institutions, or

---

[69] A good discussion of this is still 'Henry II and the Criminous Clerks' in Maitland, *Roman Canon Law* (n 15) 132–47.

[70] WR Jones, 'Bishops, Politics, and the Two Laws: The Gravamina of the English Clergy, 1237–1399' (1966) 41 *Speculum* 209–45; Helmholz (n 1) 118–19.

[71] EB Graves, 'Circumspecte Agatis' (1928) 43 *English Historical Review* 1–20; D Millon, 'Circumspecte Agatis Revisited' (1984) 2 *Law and History Review* 105–27.

[72] JH Denton, 'The Making of the Articuli Clerici of 1316' (1986) 101 *Ecclesiastical History Review* 564–89.

ideas where one can posit that a development in one person, institution, or idea would not or might not have taken place had it not been for the fact that another person, institution, or idea was present or known. When we speak of the influence of one legal system on another, I think it is well to speak broadly. ... Rather than speaking of conscious borrowings, one must speak instead of parallels, of similarities of language, of coincidences that seem too striking to be coincidental.[73]

In many of the supposed borrowings from the canon law of the Latin Church into the temporal common law of England, it turns out that there is an adequate explanation within the common law itself for the doctrine that the court adopts. The same is true in the case of apparent borrowings from the common law in the English church courts. There is normally a satisfactory explanation within the canonical *ius commune* itself for the judgments of the church court. The influence that we are looking for is not found at the level of specific borrowings of rules.[74]

Despite a number of these coincidences, there are a few general points that should be kept in mind when thinking of the interaction between common law and ecclesiastical law. From the common law side, it is important to note that training in the *ius commune* and ecclesiastical law was not required (although some were indeed familiar with it). Neither was Roman canon law a formal source of law in the royal courts. From the church law side, canon lawyers were likewise not required to study common law (though once again, some certainly understood it). Likewise, common law was not a source of law per se in the ecclesiastical courts. That said, there are, of course, similarities, especially as to practice, but even in these instances, it is best to take a broad approach.[75] In this context, three examples are given here – testaments, juries and witnesses, and writs of prohibition – all three of which concern practice and the working out of jurisdictions.[76]

i. Testaments

The canonical doctrine of the testament was made clear in the 60 years following the publication of the *Decretum*, and 'behind the canon law and its discussion, there was a competent knowledge of the testament in the strict sense of Roman law'.[77] Canonists viewed wills as ambulatory and revocable, in the same way as Roman testaments.[78] This is the form of testament we see appearing later in

---

[73] C Donahue, '*Ius Commune*, Canon Law and Common Law in England' (1992) 66 *Tulane Law Review* 1745–80, 1747–48.
[74] ibid 1775.
[75] See a recent project comparing the concept of dispossession, created by the CLCLCL team at the University of St Andrews, at https://clicme.wp.st-andrews.ac.uk/dispossession/.
[76] For other examples, see Donahue (n 73); RH Helmholz, 'The Early History of the Grand Jury and the Canon Law' (1983) 50 *The University of Chicago Law Review* 613–27.
[77] MM Sheehan, *The Will in Medieval England: From the Conversion of the Anglo-Saxons to the End of the Thirteenth Century* (Toronto, Pontifical Institute of Mediaeval Studies, 1963) 134.
[78] ibid 144–45.

Bracton, where the will is described almost exactly as the canonists describe it; perhaps unsurprising given the sources upon which *Bracton* depended. However, there is no mention of the Roman law requirement of naming an heir in the testament. *Bracton* discusses donations that are either *inter vivos* or *mortis causa*, the latter form seemingly derived directly from the same title in the *Digest*.[79] However, the issue of the heir was generally left in the background, since their primary interest was the legacies, especially those made for pious purposes. After the Conquest, there was a considerable use of Roman law phraseology, and especially that of 'making an heir'. This can be found in many examples from the time, even in royal agreements.[80] Yet this phrasing was somewhat problematic by the end of the twelfth century, since 'only God could make an heir'. Even so, we see Roman vocabulary being used in testamentary cases in which the Roman law on heirs is used with seemingly no contradiction.[81]

Yet the influence went both ways. One of the changes that allowed a specifically English testamentary practice to emerge was the shift in the stance of the royal courts towards the distribution of land. During the second half of the reign of Henry II (1154–89), the bequest of land was prohibited. Now, land was not a form of property that was usually involved in litigation over wills, which primarily concerned chattels. Sheehan notes that if bequests of land had continued to be made, then the common law would have exercised its usual enthusiastic involvement in land actions and the Church would not have retained its control over testaments to the same extent. But this did not happen, and testaments became almost solely under the jurisdiction of the Church. Sheehan neatly sums up this jurisdictional interaction:

> Whatever was done by the ecclesiastical courts was done with the knowledge of the king's courts. Whatever decisions were made as to the ability or inability of one legal system to provide for the control of the will were made with the knowledge that the other was quite able to supply. The crucial decision was one of division of labour between two jurisdictions made by men who were aware of the claims and resources of each.[82]

ii. Juries and Witnesses

The preference for witnesses in Romano-canonical procedure has often been contrasted with the secular juries to suggest fundamental differences between the two systems.[83] For example, *ex officio* procedure seems very similar to

---

[79] That is, in the treatise called *Bracton*, namely *De Legibus et Consuetudinibus Angliae*, which in some versions bears the name Henry Bracton (d 1268), D. 39.6.2.
[80] Sheehan (n 77) 139.
[81] Adams and Donahue (eds) (n 49) 633–87.
[82] Sheehan (n 77) 138.
[83] See primarily F Pollock and FW Maitland, *The History of English Law before the Time of Edward I*, vol 2 (Cambridge, Cambridge University Press, 1968) 603–04 and fn 1. For a discussion of whether or not secular juries were truly self-informing, see D Klerman, 'Was the Jury Ever Self-Informing?' (2003) 77 *Southern California Law Review* 123–49.

secular presentment procedure, to the extent that Richard Helmholz has suggested concrete connections between secular and canon law in the sphere of criminal procedure, due to parallels in the three procedural stages of both systems: public fame, use of inquests and purgation. However, there is one significant difference between the two: canonical inquests in *ex officio* proceedings required the questioning of individuals, and presentment relied on the self-informing secular jury.[84] Yet this distinction breaks down somewhat when we look at how juries and witnesses are used in their respective courts. In general, it is safe to say that the medieval church courts followed Roman witness procedure, but sometimes it was not always possible to follow this procedure to the letter, and in these cases, the courts took a more flexible approach. In Romano-canonical procedure, the ideal witness would have seen the events in question first-hand and have a reputation that was beyond reproach. In reality, however, these ideal witnesses would seldom be available. In cases where the judge was presented with an array of suspect witnesses and varying testimonies, public reputation was essential for corroborating accounts. Proof then depended on the uniformity of a group's testimony concerning public knowledge. In this way, witnesses could be treated more like a trial jury than like the eyewitnesses found in the Romano-canonical tradition, and the evidence in the English ecclesiastical material suggests that witnesses were indeed being used in this unconventional way.[85]

The use of witnesses almost as a secular jury could be attributed in part to the litigants themselves, who, lacking witnesses in whom they were confident, sought to present the judge with witnesses who instead could testify to opinion in the community. Regardless of the content of the case, litigants may have been hard pressed to produce unexceptionable witnesses; those ideal witnesses who had been present at a marriage or institution might be ill, absent or deceased when it came to the litigation. It seems that litigants were also, unsurprisingly, only concerned about the suitability of the other party's witnesses. Presenting as many witnesses as possible, then trying to discredit opposing witnesses until a conclusion was achieved through sheer numbers was a reasonable tactic to try. In cases like this, a version of events agreed upon by as many people as possible, regardless of the source of their information, must have seemed like a reasonable substitute, especially keeping in mind the self-informing jury of the secular courts or the oath-helpers of compurgation procedure. In the secular courts, jurors were required to come from the locality of the case so that they could hear the proceedings and judge the evidence presented on the basis of informed knowledge, even if they themselves had not been eyewitnesses to an event.[86] Even in cases where eyewitness testimony was requested, parties seem to have been unwilling to abandon the notion that the witness was to testify concerning not only what they themselves

---

[84] Helmholz (n 76) 616, 623, 625.
[85] See SB White, 'The Procedure and Practice of Witness Testimony in English Ecclesiastical Courts, c 1193–1300' (2020) 56 *Studies in Church History* 114–30.
[86] M MacNair, 'Vicinage and the Antecedents of the Jury' (1999) 17 *Law & History Review* 538.

had seen, but also what the community believed the truth to be.[87] This could have been due to litigants' reluctance to abandon older forms of proof dependent on local reputation, as MacNair suggests, or a familiarity with jury-like proceedings, as argued by Donahue.[88]

iii. Writs of Prohibition

The royal courts sometimes directly impacted how ecclesiastical jurisdiction should be exercised, for example, by requiring that copies of libels be delivered to the accused in ecclesiastical cases (something that was already in line with canon law, and therefore not particularly disruptive); this requirement was because Chancery mandated inspection of the libel in order to take action on writs of prohibition and consultation.[89] Although this solution was not generally available in the thirteenth century, it was possible that during an ecclesiastical suit, either of the parties could acquire a writ of prohibition from the royal chancery and directly challenge the jurisdiction of the court over the case.[90] This writ led to an action against both the opposing party and the judge, and no proof was needed on the part of the demandant to procure it. If it was successful, the ecclesiastical court would be prohibited from proceeding in the case on jurisdictional grounds. This approach usually resulted in the issuing of a writ of *certiorari* by the chancery, which required the court to send the libel from the case concerned to the chancery so that it could determine whether the case fell under the jurisdiction of the ecclesiastical court.[91] The chancery made its decision based on the court records supplied to it. Often only the libel was required, but in some cases it seems that the *processus* and other associated documents were necessary to determine whether the case fell under the jurisdiction of the court. If the chancery decided in favour of the court, it issued a consultation (ie a confirmation that the chancery had been consulted on the jurisdiction and come to a decision, which was usually endorsed on the libel), which allowed the church court to continue its action, and the protesting litigant was required to submit to the court's

---

[87] C Donahue, 'Proof by Witnesses in the Church Courts of Medieval England: An Imperfect Reception of the Learned Law' in MS Arnold et al (eds), *On the Laws and Customs of England: Essays in Honor of Samuel E Thorne* (Chapel Hill, NC, North Carolina University Press, 1981) 127–58.
[88] MacNair (n 86) 576–78; Donahue (n 87) 140, 150–51.
[89] Helmholz (n 1) 168–81; 232.
[90] See also N Adams, 'The Writ of Prohibition to Court Christian' (1936) 20 *Minnesota Law Review* 272–93; GB Flahiff, 'The Use of Prohibitions by Clerics against Ecclesiastical Courts in England' (1941) 3 *Mediaeval Studies* 101–16; GB Flahiff, 'The Writ of Prohibition to Court Christian in the Thirteenth Century' (1944) 6 *Mediaeval Studies* 261–313; GB Flahiff, 'The Writ of Prohibition to Court Christian in the Thirteenth Century. Part II' (1945) 7 *Mediaeval Studies* 229–90; RH Helmholz, 'Writs of Prohibition and Ecclesiastical Sanctions in the English Courts Christian' (1976) 60 *Minnesota Law Review* 1011–33; RH Helmholz, 'The Writ of Prohibition to Court Christian before 1500' (1981) 43 *Medieval Studies* 297–314; E De Haas and GDG Hall (eds), *Early Registers of Writs* (London, Selden Society, 1970) 384–86 (Index of Writs, V–1–E–i–vi).
[91] Similar to examples in De Haas and Hall (eds) (n 90) 380; 383 (Index of Writs, V–1–B–i).

jurisdiction and pay his opponent's expenses for the delay.[92] This practice led to the framing of libels in a way that was very broad and clearly within the jurisdiction of the church courts.

When the Tudors arrived on the scene, a new level of legislation affecting the ecclesiastical courts appeared. Some changes were required by the Reformation, for example those regulating images in churches and public worship, and these had an indirect effect in that they defined new offences falling under ecclesiastical jurisdiction. Others improved the functioning and personnel of the church courts and were reforms that had been a long time coming. More ambitious attempts on the part of Reformers to enact large-scale change were generally unsuccessful. This is partly because, as a reformation, the past could not be rejected wholesale – the declared intent was to correct current practices and end abuses. It is also partly because the civilians who controlled the English courts were by and large very conservative, trained in the *ius commune*, and resistant to large-scale change. Lastly, the Reformation, both in England and elsewhere, did not entail the rejection of the entirety of canon law but only the rejection of papal powers. As we shall see, there were very practical reasons to retain the majority of Romano-canonical law – there was no need to change matters such as the collection of tithes or the basics of marriage law.[93]

IV. Conclusion

This chapter highlights some of the main developments in the pre-Reformation Roman canon law, for which the period 1140–1300 was particularly important. With the creation of the *Decretum* and the *Liber extra* and the many resulting commentaries, the canonists had made three very important achievements in just a few years short of a century, and these achievements carried through until the end of the Middle Ages. The first was bringing order to the laws of the Church – laws that had previously been subject to local custom (although custom was not entirely eliminated). In England, this resulted in the establishment of a hierarchical system of courts with a clearly-defined procedure. This order was not entirely complete – for example, there were still some gaps in the law of wills and testaments – but the laws of the Church had become far more useable. The second achievement was the assertion of spiritual sovereignty and a change in the status of the clergy. The clergy were now afforded legal privileges (as well as some prohibitions), setting them outside of secular jurisdiction and almost exclusively under the jurisdiction of the Church. The Church was likewise not subject to secular powers, and, as Helmholz puts it, for the canonists, 'all that stood in

---

[92] P Brand, 'The Common Lawyers of the Reign of Edward I and the Canon Law' in Harris (ed) (n 54) 27–40; Logan (n 51) xlvii; De Haas and Hall (eds) (n 90) 143–44.
[93] Helmholz (n 1) 181–86.

the way of a real theocracy was the modesty which the founder of the Christian religion had enjoined upon his followers'.[94] The third achievement was the expansion of the scope of canon law – it was concerned with far more than the sacraments and heresy, and touched upon most legal aspects of life, civil, criminal and spiritual. Although there were points of conflict with the secular courts of the English common law, the church courts had a well-established and wide jurisdiction. In the centuries following, the sources of law changed very little, the legal profession was well-established and well-trained, and the courts still functioned much as they always had.

By the end of the fifteenth century, we begin to see a decline in the volume of litigation in the English ecclesiastical courts. There are several possible reasons for this. A popular one is that the decline in litigation mirrored a decline in the respect for the church courts, but it is more probable that this reflects the jurisdictional changes in the period. The ecclesiastical courts no longer held jurisdiction over breach of faith, testamentary debt and defamation via accusations of temporal crime – areas in which the church courts frequently heard cases – and the Reformation did away with appeals to the Roman see. To quote Helmholz once again, this decline was 'gradual, but final'.[95] Yet even as the Church's courts and jurisdiction declined, the canonists of the twelfth century might have found some comfort in the fact that the law of the Church had remained remarkably stable for over 300 years before the English Reformation.

[94] ibid 103.
[95] ibid 233.

2

The Reformation and the King's Ecclesiastical Law: 1533–58

MICHELLE L JOHNSON* AND WILL ADAM

The Henrician Reformation abruptly signalled the end in England of the Roman Church's authority, which had been so stably enjoyed throughout the medieval period.[1] The Act in Restraint of Appeals 1533 severed papal jurisdiction in England. This immense unseating of a Rome-centric ecclesiastical authority left a significant power gap and critical questions that demanded swift and definitive answers. These questions were inherently interlinked with the notion of royal versus Parliamentary authority and the development of the nascent national English Church. In particular focus was that Church's formulary of faith and the future of canon law within England as a defined and separate system of law, and ecclesiastical law more broadly.[2] Predominantly, this chapter will focus upon the most significant of these questions, which was, following the break with Rome, where the jurisdictional boundaries between the English common law and other

---

* Most of this chapter is adapted from a chapter in the principal author's doctoral thesis: ML Johnson, 'The Works of Christopher St German' (PhD thesis, University of Reading, 2019). The thesis is currently being prepared for publication as a monograph.

[1] Among the more well-known abundant studies on the Reformation under Henry VIII, see variously: A Dickens, *The English Reformation* (London, Batsford, 1964); SE Lehmberg, *The Reformation Parliament 1529-1536* (Cambridge, Cambridge University Press, 1970); GR Elton, *Policy and Police: The Enforcement of the Reformation in the Age of Thomas Cromwell* (Cambridge, Cambridge University Press, 1972); G Elton, *Reform and Renewal: Thomas Cromwell and the Common Weal* (Cambridge, Cambridge University Press, 1973); GW Child, *Church and State under the Tudors* (New York, Lennox Hill, 1974); GR Elton, *Reform and Reformation England 1509-1558* (London, Edward Arnold Ltd, 1977); JJ Scarisbrick, *The Reformation and the English People* (Oxford, Blackwell, 1984); A Fox and J Guy, *Reassessing the Henrician Age: Humanism, Politics and Reform 1500-1550* (Oxford, Blackwell, 1986); R Rex, *Henry VIII and the English Reformation* (Hong Kong, MacMillan, 1994); C Haigh (ed), *The English Reformation Revised* (Cambridge, Cambridge University Press, 2000); GW Bernard, *The King's Reformation: Henry VIII and the Remaking of the English Church* (New Haven, CT, Yale University Press, 2005); GW Bernard, *The Late Medieval English Church: Vitality and Vulnerability before the Break with Rome* (New Haven, CT, Yale University Press, 2012).

[2] See G Bray, *Canon Law and the Anglican Church* (Martlesham, Boydell & Brewer for The Church of England's Record Society, 2018) xvi: 'canon law is the law made by the Christian church(es) in order to deal with legal matters within their competence'; and 'ecclesiastical law' is 'a broader concept that includes secular legislation and unwritten laws relating to the church, as well as canon law'.

forms of authority, such as the canon law, should lie? And who should wield ultimate authority in spiritual matters? Of particular interest in exploring the answers to these questions is how the minds of independent scholars (such as common lawyer Christopher St German c 1460–1540/41) and the use of the press were harnessed during the 1530s to enforce and engender popular support for Henry VIII's divorce and remarriage. This was to be achieved through the conduit of a supremacy that was at once royal and parliamentary, and which was imposed through a focused legislative campaign, backed by the printed propaganda. This chapter will explore these themes.

Henry's death in 1547 catalysed a period of further change when he was succeeded by his third surviving legitimate child, Edward VI. Edward was a minor and under the protection of his uncle, the Duke of Somerset. Edward's short reign (1547–53) led to a marked evangelical shift in the direction of the Reformation. However, along with the increased Protestant character of the Church in this period, the idea of State (or royal) control of the Church was strengthened and the enforcement of uniformity increased. Many doctrinal matters that did not change under Henry VIII did change under Edward.

Upon Edward's death and after a brief succession crisis, when opponents of the accession of the Catholic Queen Mary I attempted to place Lady Jane Grey on the throne, Mary (the daughter of Henry VIII and Katherine of Aragon) succeeded her younger brother in 1553. She would reign until her death in 1558. As well as igniting serious religious divisions in the country, Mary also faced concerns about whether a Queen could reign in her own right. Once again, statute came to her aid. Mary's parliaments were systematic in the undoing of the reforms of her father and brother, but within limits.

Therefore, the chapter also (though necessarily more briefly) explores themes of continuity and change throughout Edward's and Mary's reigns, which ultimately influenced the religious, political, social and legal landscape inherited by Elizabeth I (1558–1603).

I. The Reign of Henry VIII (1509–47)

A. The 'Ideal' Prince

On his accession in 1509, the new king, Henry VIII, was 'hailed as an ideal prince'[3] by his subjects, and married his brother Arthur's widow, Katherine of Aragon. The only surviving child of Henry and Katherine was the later queen, Mary I (b 1516). Bernard notes that the lack of a male heir was a particular blow for Henry; it was a genuine concern evidenced, for example, when he vowed that

---

[3] G Walker, *Writing under Tyranny: English Literature and the Henrician Reformation* (Oxford, Oxford University Press, 2005) 1.

should a male heir be born, he would lead in person a crusade against the Turks.[4] However, at this point Henry was still a seemingly faithful son of the Catholic Church, defending papal supremacy and earning the title 'Defender of the Faith' from Pope Leo X in 1521 for his written attack on Martin Luther entitled *Assertio Septem Sacramentorum* (or *Defence of the Seven Sacraments*).[5] Yet Henry would go on to break definitively with Rome, and his previously won title would be revoked by Pope Paul III.[6]

Evangelical, or Protestant, thought simultaneously began to spread across Europe in earnest during the first quarter of the sixteenth century. The year 1517 saw the publication of Martin Luther's *95 Theses* in Wittenburg, Germany. These lambasted the Church for the selling of indulgences, and Luther would also go on to question the biblical support for Rome's approach to the sacraments and salvation. In December 1520, Luther would go as far as to burn the books on canon law, including 'Gratian's *Decretum* … and four books of later papal laws that formed the *Corpus iuris canonici*'.[7] Throughout the 1520s, effective networks of scholars around the universities of Europe enabled evangelical thought to spread rapidly, including to England. Closer to home, scholars such as William Tyndale 'would be converted to the new religion at Oxford'.[8] Tyndale would be exiled from England in 1524 and travelled to Worms. He translated the New Testament into English in 1526 (this would be banned – a new edition emerging in 1534) and published his *Obedience of a Christian Man* in 1528. In 1530 he issued his translation of the Pentateuch and *The Practice of Prelates*, which would particularly earn the ire of Henry VIII, as within it Tyndale opposed annulment of the king's marriage. Work had also begun on Tyndale's translation of the Old Testament. Ultimately, he would be seized in Antwerp in 1535 by authorities of the Holy Roman Empire, convicted of heresy, and strangled and burned at the stake for heresy in 1536. This was despite intercession by Thomas Cromwell on his behalf. Yet in 1537, Parliament would officially approve his bible, though under the

---

[4] Bernard, *The King's Reformation* (n 1) 3–4.

[5] How far Henry was involved in the writing of the document has been questioned, with arguments regarding Thomas More's significant involvement in its compilation. For example, this is considered in JJ Scarisbrick, *Henry VIII* (Berkeley, CA, University of California Press, 1968) 112. However, most recently, McNicoll has argued that the *Assertio* was Henry's own work and therefore that, as he was 'sufficiently well educated in theology and Latin' to write it, he would have been perfectly aware of the Levitical impediments concerning marriage to one's brother's widow. M McNicoll, 'Henry VIII: Conciliarist?' 5 *Journal of Early Modern Christianity* (2018) 109–49, 126.

[6] In 1544, Parliament would re-grant this title to Henry, and English monarchs as defenders of the faith in their position as Supreme Governor of the Church of England still use the title to this day.

[7] J Witte, *Law and Protestantism: The Legal Teachings of the Lutheran Reformation* (Cambridge, Cambridge University Press, 2004) 53.

[8] E Shahan, 'The Emergence of the Church of England 1520-1533' in A Milton (ed), *The Oxford History of Anticlericalism*, vol 1: *c 1520–1562* (Oxford, Oxford University Press, 2017) 28–44, 32. See also D Daniell, *William Tyndale: A Biography* (New Haven, CT, Yale University Press, 1994); D Daniell, *The Bible in English: its history and influence* (New Haven, CT, Yale University Press, 2003); and A Ryrie, *The Gospel and Henry VIII: Evangelicals in the Early English Reformation* (Cambridge, Cambridge University Press, 2003).

pseudonym of 'Thomas Matthew' as translator. This was probably a wise effort not to 'rub the king's nose in the fact that it was the heretic Tyndale's book' that had been approved.[9]

B. The King's 'Great Matter'

It was the king's 'Great Matter', the protracted attempt to set aside his marriage to Katherine of Aragon, that would catalyse England's 1533 break with Rome. Reformist ideology would ultimately and ironically provide Henry with his much-desired solution. The year 1527 was a key official turning point in Henry and Katherine's marriage – it was then that Henry started (according to official dated evidence) to assert that the marriage was invalid according to canon law.[10] In fact, the marriage had never been valid, Henry now claimed – it should never have been allowed, because Katherine had previously been married to Arthur; and according to Leviticus 20:21, 'if a man shall take his brother's wife, it is an unclean thing: he hath uncovered his brother's nakedness; they shall be childless'. On 17 May, Thomas Wolsey (Cardinal Archbishop of York[11]) established a secret ecclesiastical court at Westminster to discuss the legitimacy of the marriage. The court was short-lived and was abandoned on 31 May, so that further theological guidance might be sought before any more progress was made.[12]

At this point, Henry still wanted to explore all orthodox options open to him, and thus, in the same year, he sent William Knight (secretary to the king) to Rome to promote the case for annulment. Knight's aim was to obtain the desired annulment and to secure permission for the king's remarriage. Bernard confirms that Henry did this without first consulting Wolsey, who, at the same time, in a clearly orchestrated strategy in his position as cardinal and a papal legate, had announced his own concerns over the legitimacy of the marriage and proposed a series of arguments against it.[13] Pope Clement V refused the annulment. With the most obvious route to annulment now out of the question, the break with Rome became a closer reality and the need for alternatives to secure an official end to the marriage (such as via the conduit of royal rather than papal authority) was engendered. The use of legislation and the use of the press being two particularly effective methods of deploying the necessary materials to undermine the authority of the Pope whilst simultaneously promoting that of the King.

---

[9] Shahan (n 8) 37.
[10] Although it has been argued that Henry desired an official separation from Katherine as early as 1514. See B Behrens, 'A note on Henry VIII's divorce project of 1514' (1934) 11 *Bulletin of the Institute of Historical Research* 163–64.
[11] Wolsey took up his position as Archbishop of York in 1514 and a year later was made a cardinal by Pope Leo X. See P Gwyn, *The King's Cardinal: The Rise and Fall of Thomas Wolsey* (London, Barrie & Jenkins, 1990); and SJ Gunn and PG Lindley, *Cardinal Wolsey: Church, State and Art* (Cambridge, Cambridge University Press, 1991).
[12] Walker (n 3) 136.
[13] Bernard, *The King's Reformation* (n 1) 8–9.

C. The Reformation Parliament (1529–36)

In May 1529, a papal legatine court was established at Blackfriars to consider the divorce. It was headed by Cardinals Wolsey and Campeggio, and Henry anticipated a favourable decision within weeks. In July, Campeggio adjourned the court. It was never reconvened. The case was transferred to Rome.[14] Henry totally lost confidence in a papal remedy and turned to Parliament for a potential solution.[15] The first session of what was to become known as the Reformation Parliament was called in October 1529. It was the first meeting of Parliament for six years, which would continue to sit in multiple sessions until April 1536 to consider and finally decide on the 'Great Matter'.[16] The first session has been described as 'notoriously "anticlerical"', though disappointing in practice.[17] However, the Parliament was heavily criticised by contemporaries for so many different reasons that Lehmberg argues that '[n]early every sort of special interest has been alleged', from the ultimate sway held by the clergy to arguments that the king was packing Parliament with those partisan to his interests.[18]

Thomas More (the new Lord Chancellor) described the focus of the Parliament as

> how divers laws before this time were made now by long continuance of time and mutation of things, very insufficient, & [vnperfight], and also by the frail condition of man, divers new enormities were sprung amongst the people, for the which no law was yet made to reform the same, which was the very cause why at that time the king had summoned his high court of parliament.[19]

Edward Hall's account in his *Chronicle* highlights the obvious anticlericalism of the gathering, relaying how the Commons expressed their 'griefs wherewith the spirituality had before time grievously oppressed them, both contrary to the law

---

[14] SE Lehmberg, *The Reformation Parliament 1529–1536* (Cambridge, Cambridge University Press, 1970) 2.

[15] Lehmberg goes as far as to suggest that Henry's recourse to Parliament may have been not only to seek a solution to the divorce issue but also 'as a stage for his action against Wolsey', further noting that Chapuys comments that 'the whole purpose of Parliament was to take away the chancellor's seals from the cardinal' (though Wolsey was ultimately dealt with under a writ of *Praemunire*: ibid 3–4).

[16] ibid 1.

[17] Walker (n 3) 36. For an alternative perspective on whether the Reformation Parliament was indeed anticlerical in nature, and for a denunciation of the traditional assertion of the supposed widespread popular anticlericalism of the period, see C Haigh, 'Anticlericalism and the English Reformation' in Haigh (ed) (n 1) 56–74.

[18] Lehmberg (n 14) 8–9.

[19] E Hall, *Hall's Chronicle: containing the history of England, during the reign of Henry the Fourth, and the succeeding monarchs, to the end of the reign of Henry the Eighth, in which are particularly described the manners and customs of those periods* (London, printed for J Johnson et al, 1809) 764. The discussion of the Parliament is found in the 1548 edition. This was published a year after Hall's death. When Hall died, the work had been completed up to 1532. It was printer Richard Grafton who penned the work from this point up to Henry's death in 1547, but with the use of Hall's own notes. Hall used Vergil's and More's (1543 edition) *Histories* as the basis for his account.

of the realm, & contrary to all right, and in especial they were sore moved with six great causes'.[20]

The six causes dealt with were: (i) the fees due to the clergy for the probate of wills (with Wolsey and Warham, Archbishop of Canterbury, specifically named); (ii) how the mortuaries taken for the payment of burials had hit the poor so hard that they would die of starvation or have to turn to begging;[21] (iii) how priests took and used grazing land from the poor or charged them heavily to use it; (iv) how priests ran tan houses and traded in wool and cloth in direct competition with temporal tradesmen; (v) how clergy lived richly in the houses of lords at the expense of the poor who had nothing spent on them; and (vi) how priests were frequently non-resident, possibly having as many as 10 or 12 benefices.[22] Voicing how anticlerical sentiment was now acceptable, the Commons noted that before 'God has illumined the eyes of the king', such claims would have ended in accusations of heresy due to the holding by bishops of the chancellorship.[23] The chancellorship had usually been given to a cleric since the inception of the role in the eleventh century.[24] Chancellors were responsible for overseeing the king's scribes, who produced the writs necessary to start an action at common law.[25] However, now men had begun to 'desire a reformation'.[26] Therefore, Thomas Audley (barrister and judge, and future Lord Chancellor between 1533–44 following More's execution), their elected speaker, appointed a commission of men learned in the law to set about drawing up legislation to make the necessary amendments to correct these abuses.

With the repeated sittings of the Parliament throughout the 1530s, a statutory campaign was instituted for this 'reformation' and the legal, religious and political change necessary to settle the 'Great Matter'. Concomitantly, it would also significantly expand upon the competence of Parliament more generally. Thereafter, powers that had previously rested with the Church alone were brought within the ambit of Parliament's governance. Religious authority was transmitted to the

---

[20] *Hall's Chronicle* (n 19) 765. Though it is important to acknowledge that Hall himself may not have been a neutral witness, and he may himself have held strong anticlerical views. He was a close friend of Cromwell and may well have had sympathy for the Reformers. In 1545, for example, he witnessed the confession of Anne Askew, which resulted in her release. He was also charged as part of a commission with enforcing the *Six Articles*, 'perhaps because of his earlier enthusiasm for Henry VIII's role in prescribing religious belief': see PC Herman, 'Hall, Edward (1497–1547), lawyer and historian' in *Oxford Dictionary of National Biography* (2012) at www.oxforddnb.com.

[21] Fees paid to the Church for the preparation and burial of the dead. Helmholz notes how the 1529 statute (21 Hen 8 c 6) 'turned all mortuaries into money payments'. During the medieval period they had normally consisted of chattels: RH Helmholz, *The Ius Commune in England: Four Studies* (Oxford, Oxford University Press, 2001) 141.

[22] *Hall's Chronicle* (n 19) 765.

[23] ibid 766.

[24] Thomas More, appointed Chancellor in 1529, was the first lay chancellor in almost three-quarters of a century since Richard Neville, 5th Earl of Salisbury, held the title briefly between 1454 and 1455.

[25] For more on the role of the Tudor chancellor, see WJ Jones, *The Elizabethan Court of Chancery* (Oxford, Clarendon Press, 1967).

[26] *Hall's Chronicle* (n 19) 766.

monarch, and thus the Reformation Parliament confirmed the primacy of the king's supremacy, or more particularly the King-in-Parliament's supremacy.

The transformation of the role of Parliament during the 1530s is evidenced through the statutes enacted during the period to bring about the required change. Rex provides and effective summary of this legislation, with the fourth to seventh sessions of the Parliament between 1533 and 1536 proving the most successful in the legislative campaign to solidify the royal supremacy with the enactment of various key statutory measures, beginning in the fourth session of Parliament with the Act in Restraint of Appeals (1532 – but passed by both houses by April 1533).[27] Lehmberg provides the most thorough and chronologically complete account of the entire Reformation Parliament's activities.[28]

Lehmberg describes the Act in Restraint of Appeals as 'the most important single piece of legislation to be enacted by the Reformation Parliament: it forms a climax, with the earlier anti-clerical measures preparing its way and the subsequent ecclesiastical regulation flowing from it'.[29] The Act identified the English Crown as imperial, forbade appeals to Rome in any matter and made the king the supreme legal authority in the realm in ecclesiastical causes. It allocated the power of deciding finally on the 'Great Matter' to the English Church. The clerical Convocation, therefore, pronounced that it considered the marriage between Henry and Katherine invalid. Now what was needed was a formal trial wherein an official judgment could be announced. The trial began on 10 May and did not last even a fortnight. Queen Katherine did not appear and was pronounced contumacious by Archbishop Thomas Cranmer. Lehmberg notes that no witnesses were heard; instead the four-year-old depositions of testimony presented to Wolsey and Campeggio were relied upon.[30] On 23 May, Cranmer officially pronounced that the union between Henry and Katherine was invalid; and on 28 May, he pronounced Henry and Anne Boleyn's union lawful – as by this point, they had been 'married' since 25 January 1533. Despite the significant implications of the Act, it nevertheless faced little direct opposition in the Parliament. As Lehmberg summarises:

> A few great men could not reconcile their consciences to the break with Rome which the appeals act implied. Some lesser figures grumbled in taverns and gossiped with foreign envoys. But on balance there was surprisingly little evidence of serious opposition to the king's new marriage or to the steps which had been taken to validate it. Seldom has so momentous a change, affecting the religious life of a whole people, been initiated so easily.[31]

Chronologically, the next significant statute was the Act Concerning Ecclesiastical Appointments and Absolute Restraint of Annates 1533.[32] This represented a

---

[27] 24 Hen VIII c 12; Rex (n 1) 19–23.
[28] Though see also G Bray, *Documents of the English Reformation* (Cambridge, James Clarke & Co, 2019).
[29] Lehmberg (n 14) 175.
[30] ibid 179.
[31] ibid 181.
[32] 25 Hen VIII c 20.

partial victory for the clergy in respect to annates;[33] the aim had been to try to transfer their payment from the pope to the king, but this failed to meet the approval of the House of Lords and the idea of transfer was dropped in favour of an end to all annates. In relation to the appointment of bishops, the Act effectively sealed the monarch's authority to direct their election. The Ecclesiastical Licences Act 1533 followed,[34] making it illegal to pay 'Peter's Pence'[35] or other payments to Rome. It also granted previously held 'legatine' powers to the Archbishop of Canterbury for the granting of dispensations and licences where the tax due to Rome would have been less than £4. This Act is interesting as 'it is one of the earliest documents to speak of a papal usurpation', because it restates the theory that England has 'no superior under God, but only your king's grace', and because it argues that the authority of the king's 'imperial crown' is diminished by 'the unreasonable and uncharitable usurpations and exactions' of the Roman pontiff'.[36] This statute is still operative today.

The Act for the Submission of the Clergy 1534,[37] which had been endorsed in 1532 by the Convocation of Canterbury, was the next statute passed by the Reformation Parliament in 1534.[38] This Act empowered the king to establish a commission to revise the canon law and replaced appeals to Rome, from church courts in England, with an appeal to the Court of Delegates.[39] But section 7 of the Act allowed for the continued use of domestic provincial and legatine law, provided that law was not repugnant to the law of the realm and the royal prerogative. It is a matter of debate whether foreign papal law also continued to apply on the basis of that Act and/or on that of its reception – English lawyers, though, continued to use it.[40]

---

[33] Annual payments from the holder of an ecclesiastical benefice made to the Apostolic Camera (Papal Treasury). They were also known as 'first fruits'. JJ Scarisbrick, 'Clerical Taxation in England, 1485–1547' (1960) 11 *Journal of Ecclesiastical History* 44.

[34] 25 Hen VIII c 21.

[35] A contribution or donation to Rome that was collected more like a tax. As Lehmberg clarifies, Peter's Pence was 'originally an annual tribute to the Pope consisting of a penny from each householder owning land of a certain value, [which] had been collected in England since the time of King Alfred; in the twelfth century it had been fixed at two hundred pounds a year for the whole country': Lehmberg (n 14) 191.

[36] ibid 192.

[37] 25 Hen VIII c 19.

[38] 'By custom the Convocation of the English Church in the Province of Canterbury met concurrently with Parliament. ... The clerics once gathered together, could discuss ... matters affecting the welfare of the Church, and they were available for negotiations with the king and Parliament'; indeed, from 1529 to 1536, 'the interaction between Parliament and the Convocation was so close that it would be folly for the historian to separate out the two assemblies': Lehmberg (n 14) 64.

[39] Though the Act also established an appeal direct to a royal commission for certain monasteries and other religious houses, 'since these houses were by tradition exempt from archiepiscopal jurisdiction': ibid 193.

[40] N Doe, 'Pre-Reformation Roman Canon Law in Post-Reformation English Ecclesiastical Law' (2022) 24 *Ecclesiastical Law Journal* 273–94. Doe builds upon Helmholz's work here, so see also RH Helmholz, *The Canon Law and Ecclesiastical Jurisdiction from 597 to the 1640s* (Oxford, Oxford University Press, 2004); RH Helmholz, *Roman Canon Law in Reformation England* (Cambridge, Cambridge University Press, 1990) for the period up to 1625; and RH Helmholz, *The Profession of Ecclesiastical Lawyers: An Historical Introduction* (Cambridge, Cambridge University Press, 2019) for the period post-1640.

The Act of Succession[41] emerged during the spring of 1534 in response to the pope's formal judgment the previous July that Katherine and Henry's marriage should not be put aside and ordering Henry to return to her.[42] The Act of Succession (earlier known as the Act Respecting the Oath to the Succession) excluded Henry and Katherine's daughter Mary from the succession[43] and imposed on all male subjects an oath accepting a new dynastic settlement on Henry's future male heirs with Anne (or a subsequent wife) or, failing the birth of a male, on the new-born daughter of Henry and Anne, the Princess Elizabeth, and her descendants. Mary was not specifically bastardised by the Act as is sometimes said, as '[i]t might later prove desirable to give Mary a place in the succession, and theoreticians could argue, as Chapuys did on occasion, that she was lawfully born since her parents were unaware at the time of any impediment to their union'.[44] The Act confirmed that the Bishop of Rome and the Apostolic See had in times past tried to override the power of emperors, kings and princes, 'contrary to the great and inviolable grants or jurisdictions given by God immediately to' them, which both the spirituality and temporality in the realm 'do most abhor and detest'.[45]

Henry and Katherine's marriage was deemed unlawful, while Henry and Anne's marriage was deemed 'undoubtful true sincere and perfect'; and, as Henry wanted to reinforce the unquestionable legitimacy of the union, it was highlighted that it had been confirmed by the 'just judgement' of Cranmer as Archbishop of Canterbury, the whole clergy of the realm and by the Universities of 'Bologna Padua Paris Orleans Toulouse Anjou and divers others, And also by the private writings of many right excellent well learned men'.[46]

Thereafter, the next key statutory measure in severing the authority of the pope within the realm appeared with the Act of Supremacy, passed by the Reformation Parliament in November 1534. It built upon the Act in Restraint of Appeals and provided the first statutory recognition of Henry's (and his descendants') power (or responsibility, based upon the wording of the Act[47]) as 'Supreme Head' of the Church in England; and it required the clergy to swear an oath to that effect, as the Act of Succession had contained a defect and had not specified the precise wording to be used to swear obedience to the king. Parliamentary members had been sworn earlier in the spring and, as Lehmberg notes,

> the oath administered to them was intended as the oath which the act required, but it went beyond the act in several particulars, especially in its requirement that the persons sworn renounce the power of any 'foreign authority or potentiate' and repudiate any oath previously made to such a ruler.[48]

---

[41] 25 Hen VIII c 22.
[42] Walker, *Writing under Tyranny* (n 3) 225.
[43] Katherine had already been demoted by statute (25 Hen VIII c 28) to Princess Dowager, as the widow of Prince Arthur.
[44] Lehmberg (n 14) 198.
[45] *Statutes of the Realm*, 3:472.
[46] ibid.
[47] ibid 3:492.
[48] Lehmberg (n 14) 203.

The new Act clearly set out the wording of the oath. Those who would not swear were to be certified into the King's Bench. Fisher and More were imprisoned for not taking the oath and attainted for misprision of treason.[49] But the Act imposed no specific penalties for denying or opposing the King's status, thus laying the foundations for the next key statutory measure.[50]

The Act of Treasons 1534 prescribed the penalties for 'maliciously' denying the supremacy. It made malicious denial of the supremacy by 'wish, will, or desire by words or in writing' a capital offence.[51] Rex notes passionate debates in the Commons over the term 'maliciously' and confirms that this was due to a general feeling that the Act demonstrated a huge practical extension of the concept of treason as it now seemingly applied to merely verbal offences.[52] Notably, it was under this Act of Treasons that Bishop Fisher and More were put to death in June and July 1535 respectively, even though by this time Fisher was a cardinal. Following his beheading, Henry had Fisher's head placed upon London Bridge and morbidly joked that it was 'so that it might look in vain for his [Fisher's] Cardinal's hat coming from Rome'.[53]

By the opening of the final session of the Reformation Parliament, Lehmberg notes how Henry was already tiring of the woman he had seemingly broken with Rome to marry.[54] Cranmer would declare Anne and Henry's union void on the eve of her execution.[55] Cromwell, a lay-man, who according to Lehmberg had become 'a dominant figure during this second stage [of the Reformation Parliament], lasting from 1532 to 1534',[56] had been named as 'Vicegerent of Spirituals'[57] by Henry at some point following the Act of Supremacy, which, according to Lehmberg and MacCulloch, was likely to have been in early 1535.[58] He would begin his visitation of the monasteries, making some significant progress by the end of the year. The final session of the Reformation Parliament thus closed on 14 April 1536.

The following Parliament (sitting between 8 June and 18 July 1536) passed the Act against the Authority of Rome 1536.[59] This formally extinguished the

---

[49] ibid.
[50] Fisher and More were not the only ones to suffer for refusing to swear the oath. Monks at the London Charterhouse were also imprisoned in chains for their disobedience: Walker (n 3) 226.
[51] 26 Hen VIII c.13. The Act came into effect in February 1535.
[52] Rex (n 1) 15.
[53] ibid.
[54] Parliament did not meet in 1535 for various reasons, among them a severe outbreak of plague in London: Lehmberg (n 14) 217.
[55] Cranmer had previously served as the personal chaplain of Thomas Boleyn (Anne's father), and it is reputed that when Cranmer thanked the king for his elevation to the Archbishopric of Canterbury, the king is reported to have told him that it was Anne he had to thank: D MacCulloch, *Thomas Cranmer: A Life* (New Haven. CT, Yale University Press, 1996) 82.
[56] Lehmberg (n 14) 250.
[57] A Latin translation of 'exercising in the place of', which MacCulloch understands as meaning 'of King Henry's powers as Supreme Head of the Church': D MacCulloch, *Thomas Cromwell: A Life* (London, Allen Lane, 2018) 269.
[58] SE Lehmberg, 'Supremacy and Vicegerency: A Re-examination' (1960) 81 *English Historical Review* 225; MacCulloch (n 57) 269.
[59] 28 Hen VIII c 10.

authority of Rome and was the first to state explicitly that it was treason to refuse an oath of royal supremacy. It upheld the pre-existing notion of the 'prerogative royal' and reaffirmed Richard II's Statute of Praemunire 1392,[60] which had made it an offence to appeal to the pope against the will of the king, or indeed to act in any way that suggested the pope held authority over the King.[61] The First Henrician Injunctions of the same year referred to the observance by the clergy of domestic law that had been made with a view to 'abolishing … the bishop of Rome's pretensed and usurped power and jurisdiction' in England.[62] All in all, through the legislative campaign over the preceding seven years, the circle was complete – the power of the pope had been thoroughly repudiated and the royal supremacy aggressively and solidly established and enforced, and Parliament was one key conduit through which this was achieved.[63]

D. Independent Thinkers and the Use of the Press

Alongside the use of parliamentary legislation to effect the changes necessary to hasten the expansion of the king's supremacy, there was also a decided stream of propaganda emanating from the presses of England supporting the king's cause (particularly in the form of polemics). The ideas of independent writers, particularly those with a legal background, such as common lawyer Christopher St German, were harnessed to garner wider popular support for the legality of Henry's 'domestic solution'. St German (c 1460–1540/1), from Shilton in Warwickshire, a Middle Temple barrister,[64] likely came to the attention of the official party thanks to his most famous work, *Doctor and Student* of 1530, in the form of a dialogue between a doctor of divinity and a student of the common law.[65] During this period, the issue of the parameters of ecclesiastical jurisdiction, and its perceived encroachments into the rights of the common law, was hotly contested by lawyers on both

---

[60] 16 Ric II c 5. Indeed, Richard II's judges had attempted to provide a definition of the royal prerogative in 1387. See SB Chrimes, 'Richard II's Questions to the Judges, 1387' (1956) 73 *Law Quarterly Review* 365–90, for a discussion of this in the context of Richard II's meetings with the judges in 1387 to discuss the prerogative power of the Crown and the power of Parliament. With respect to the powers of the king, the judges 'ruled that the king could dissolve parliament whenever he wished, and further that the lords and commons had no right to put forward articles of their own and insist on their discussion before dealing with the king's business'. See also N Saul, *Richard II* (New Haven, CT, Yale University Press, 1999) 174: the judges would also confirm that Parliament could not impeach a minister without the consent of the Crown. For Saul, the answers of the judges comprise 'the most remarkable statement of the royal prerogative ever made in England in the middle ages': ibid.
[61] For a succinct summary of Cromwell's legislative campaign of the early 1530s see, Rex (n 1) 20–23.
[62] Bray (n 28) 153–54.
[63] Though it was of course not without opposition; see, eg, for the Pilgrimage of Grace 1536, G Moorhouse, *The Pilgrimage of Grace: The Rebellion that shook Henry VIII's throne* (London, Weidenfeld & Nicolson, 2002); and ML Bush, 'The Tudor Polity and the Pilgrimage of Grace' (2007) 80 *Bulletin of the Institute of Historical Research* 47–72.
[64] There are limited biographies of St German that are explored in Johnson's thesis, *The Works of Christopher St German* (n 1) ch 1.3.
[65] Authoritative modern edition, J Barton and T Plucknett (eds), *Christopher St German, Doctor and Student* (London, Selden Society, 1975).

sides. Much of St German's writing was focused on 'reconciling' these two sides (but with a sustained bias in favour of the common law). At the heart of *Doctor and Student*, a key legal issue concerns the 'ownership of conscience' and its connection with the equity jurisdiction. St German rejects the primacy of canon law over the equity jurisdiction by claiming ownership of the notion of conscience for the common law. His student of the common law espouses, for example, the notion (and it should be noted that St German argues this by bald assertion rather than evidenced proof) that

> for such a law of man has not only the strength of man's law but also of the law of reason or the law of god whereof it is derived for laws made by man which have received of gods power to make laws be made by god. And therefore conscience must be ordered by that human law.[66]

Here he re-enforced a domestic common law basis for what were now to be seen by common lawyers as pre-existing common law ideals. St German's treatise was, therefore, effectively to lever the perceived foreign jurisdiction of the Roman Church out of domestic English law and government by circumventing that Church's historic primacy and authority in areas relating to conscience, whilst re-enforcing the idea of equity as rightfully belonging to the common law. The attractiveness of such ideas to the members of the official party around Henry, who were desperately searching for alternative solutions to the king's 'Great Matter', are obvious.

In his writings, St German is keen to reinforce the demotion of the pope to the Bishop of Rome, and to attack his usurpation of kingly power. In his *Answer to a Letter*, of 1535,[67] he discusses how bishops of Rome had claimed authority over kings and princes, and how they had done so out of pretended power and brought the people to think that to doubt the power of the pope is to commit heresy.[68] However, as St German's writing progressed it became clear that he was also not prepared to argue that the king himself could or should wield authority over what should be considered to be 'spiritual matters'. But what was to be considered a spiritual matter was contentious. His *Power of the Clergy*, also 1535,[69] diverges in certain fundamental ways from other propaganda at the time. Certain matters were reserved for a clergy, sufficiently reformed,[70] to effectively serve people who made up St German's notion of the 'universal church'. For St German,

---

[66] *Doctor and Student* (n 65) 111.
[67] Short Title Catalogue [hereinafter STC] (2nd ed)/21558.5.
[68] *Answer to a Letter*, sig B1r.
[69] STC (2nd ed)/212588.
[70] For example, St German would have agreed with the Canons of 1529, and especially that requiring bishops to be present and celebrate mass on the principal feast days and for the Nativity, Easter, Pentecost and Holy Week. As he also noted in his *Parliamentary Draft*, a second article requiring curates to be present in their own parishes once a month, etc had already been discussed in chapter eight of the *New Additions*, which also appeared in 1531. The authoritative modern edition of *New Additions* is Christopher St German, 'A Little Treatise called the New Additions' in *Doctor and Student* (n 65) 316–40.

this followed a Marsilian-inspired notion of a collective of both the clergy and the people.[71] For example, the king had no power to minister the sacraments or to exercise other spiritual powers that Christ left to his disciples.[72] In his *New Additions*, St German again uses the dialogue format to enquire whether laymen have the power to enact laws that deal with mortuaries. The student is clear:

> There was a law made of mortuaries in the parliament held in the .xxi. year of our sovereign lord king Henry the .viii. by the assent of all the commons: and I hold it not best to reason or to make arguments whether they had authority to do that they did or not. For I suppose that no man would think, that they would do any thing, that they had not power to do.[73]

The student goes on to explain that Parliament may enact law on temporal matters, and these laws also bind the clergy. All goods, even those held by clerics, remain temporal. Therefore, referencing the citation to Jean Gerson,[74] in chapter three of the first dialogue of *Doctor and Student*, the king may judge these matters by his own laws due to his right in the Crown, and Parliament has the right to enact laws accordingly. The Church cannot make binding law in the realm without basis, as the Church has no temporal power.[75] Elsewhere power was settled within Fortescue-like notions of the King-in-Parliament, on the basis of the king's power as *regale et politicum*;[76] the king 'may make no law to bind his subjects without their assent'.[77]

Though St German maintained his independence and was not, as far as records show, an employed propagandist, his works were *used* as propaganda. And, more importantly (thanks to Rex's keen scholarship), we now know that St German was published by Berthelet (the king's printer) up to 1538. Not only was he encouraging support for Henry, but he was also actively drafting legislation. Though his *Parliamentary Draft*, of 1531/32,[78] was likely never laid before Parliament, Guy identifies it as 'a remarkably comprehensive, creative and original programme for the reform of church and commonwealth in the context

---

[71] 'To that it may be answered that by that word church is not to understand only the clergy ... It is to be understand thereby / that it shall be showed unto the[e] that by the law & custome there used have authority to correct the offence': *Power of the Clergy*, sigs D3v–D4v.

[72] ibid sigs G2r–G2v; and ibid sigs D4v–D5r, which demonstrate that spiritual offences should be presented to the Ordinary or his officers.

[73] *New Additions* (n 70) 317.

[74] Gerson (1363–1429) was a French conciliarist (ie supporting the notion that supreme authority in the Church lay with a general council) and key source for St German, who returned to the notion of the unity of Christianity and the authority of general councils more as his writing progressed, and most significantly in his *Treatise concerning General Councils, the Bishops of Rome and the Clergy* (1538): STC (2nd ed)/24237.

[75] *New Additions* (n 70) 318.

[76] For Fortescue (d c 1476), see N Doe, *Fundamental Authority in Late Medieval English Law* (Cambridge, Cambridge University Press, 1991) ch 1.

[77] See St German's comments to this effect in *Answer to a Letter* (n 67) sig G6r.

[78] Authoritative modern edition: Christopher St German, 'Parliamentary Draft' in J Guy (ed), *St German on Chancery and Statute* (London, Selden Society, 1985) 127–35.

of 1530–2'.[79] Indeed, Guy describes it as 'the most impressive reform manifesto conceived during the entire reign of Henry VIII'.[80] The first two-thirds of the draft deal with the key issue of the reform of Church and clergy, reiterating the now familiar difficulties of relations between Church and State, with the remaining third specifically covering social policy and poor relief.

Henry had a veritable army of scholars engaged in the 'Great Matter' throughout the later 1520s and early 1530s, to provide added support for the legitimacy of the domestic solution. This produced far more material that can be discussed here, but it is important to highlight some, as the initial investigation into the diverse opinions on the divorce would then develop throughout the 1530s into a broader consideration of the difference between royal and ecclesiastical power, resulting in replacement of papal supremacy with that of the monarch.

The first work to demote the pope to his ancient title of 'Bishop of Rome' was the *Articles devised by the whole consent of the king's most honourable council* (1533).[81] The *Articles* were intended to lay down what people should believe, as Elton puts it, 'in straight forward terms; the absence of argument, of learned authorities, of theological debate, produces a pervasive air of absolute conviction and calm assurance, a firm basis from which to attack the problem of dissent'.[82] Thereafter, *A Little Treatise against the Muttering of Some Papists in Corners* (1534)[83] was an appeal to the people directly. According to Elton, 'it repeats the usual arguments, the Petrine claim and the point from the *Articles* concerning appeals to General Councils'.[84] The work demonstrates that the Government was aware of what was being said around the country and aimed to discredit popular grumblings. Elton notes no author. However, Rex attributes it to Thomas Swinnerton (d 1554), an evangelical preacher and one of the first Englishmen to study at Wittenberg University, matriculating in 1526. Rex describes the *Muttering* as 'a dull, though genuinely brief, piece of anti-papal polemic'.[85] Rex considers his other work, published under the alias of John Roberts, the *Mustre of Schismatic Bishops of Rome* (1534),[86] as 'far superior'. Swinnerton was another who may have enjoyed Cromwell's patronage and dedicated his *Tropes and Figures of Scripture* to him.[87] This work 'used a basic application to scripture of certain elements of Renaissance rhetoric to advance an evangelical agenda on such subjects as faith, purgatory and

---

[79] ibid 26.
[80] ibid.
[81] STC (2nd ed)/9177.
[82] Elton, *Policy and Police* (n 1) 181.
[83] STC (2nd ed)/23551.5.
[84] Elton, *Policy and Police* (n 1) 183.
[85] R Rex, 'Swynnerton [Swinnerton], Thomas (d 1554), evangelical preacher' in *Oxford Dictionary of National Biography* (n 20).
[86] STC (2nd ed)/ 23552.
[87] The work remained unpublished at the time, but has since been edited and published: R Rex (ed), *A Reformation Rhetoric. Thomas Swynnerton's The Tropes and Figures of Scripture* (Cambridge, RTM Publications, 1999).

monastic vows'.⁸⁸ Ryrie thinks the work demonstrates Swinnerton's ambitions to 'provide a vernacular guide to its [Scripture's] interpretation; in particular, he was trying to establish clear and objective criteria governing when Scripture should be read literally and when figuratively'.⁸⁹ St German too wrote on the same subject in his *Power of the Clergy* in approximately 1535.⁹⁰

In his discussion of other propaganda of the period, Elton also deals with a proposal outlining points to be covered in a treatise, attacking the pope's claims to supremacy, which 'goes over some old ground such as the early councils and powers of General Councils nowadays, but also wants to remind the Church that the pope augmented his power at the expense of other bishops'.⁹¹ Elton notes the arguments only really get interesting towards the end of the work; one of these 'insists that Englishmen "are bounden in conscience to obey the Parliament" since its acts do not contravene the law of God, the issue over which More was to die'.⁹² He also notes a 1536 call for a text from leading clergy to prove that John 20:21 and Acts 20:28 did not prove the superiority of bishops over princes, but that this call also came to nought.⁹³

Another significant work, by Thomas Starkey,⁹⁴ was *An Exhortation to the People instructing them to Unity and Obedience* (1536).⁹⁵ Elton considers the title a misnomer. Rather, Starkey argued for a 'middle way in policy, justified by a theological system of things indifferent – *adiaphora* – which sensible men can agree are not doctrinally necessary and may therefore be varied from place to place and time to time without endangering the unity of Christendom'.⁹⁶

For Starkey, papal supremacy was a matter of *adiaphora*. In his unpublished work of 1537, *Things Necessary to Salvation*, St German too favours permissible

---

⁸⁸ ibid.
⁸⁹ See A Ryrie's book review of Rex's book (ibid) (2001) 52 *Journal of Ecclesiastical History* (2001) 745.
⁹⁰ STC (2nd ed)/212588.
⁹¹ Elton, *Policy and Police* (n 1) 185.
⁹² ibid. Elton notes that this is also referenced in J Gairdner et al (eds), *Letters and Papers, Foreign and Domestic, of the Reign of Henry VIII* [hereinafter *LP*] (London, Longman, 1862–1932) 8:295 (see www.british-history.ac.uk). However, there is a slight discrepancy in the number of arguments listed by Elton at 14, and the number recorded in the *LP* record at 15.
⁹³ Elton, *Policy and Police* (n 1) 185, citing *LP* (n 92) 11:83. On the authority of bishops, the following was stated: 'Things to be remembered before the breaking up of parliament. Many of the clergy take the two texts following to prove the authority of bishops to be above that of kings and princes. "It is expedient that the question be demanded of such of the clergy as be most like by their authority and learning to be disposed to declare the truth therein", and their declaration to be made so manifest that all who list may take exception to it, and not say afterwards that they would have spoken, but durst not. The texts are John xx. *Sicut misit me Pater, et ego mitto vos*, and Acts xx. *Attendite vobis et universo gregi in quo vos posuit Spiritus Sanctus episcopos regere Ecclesiam Dei quam acquisivit sanguine suo*. Explains how these are interpreted by some of the clergy.' This was an issue raised earlier in 1531 in *A Document of the year 1531* on the subject of the pope's supremacy.
⁹⁴ Starkey (c 1489–1538) was a humanist and political theorist. He served Reginald Pole, of all people, as Secretary after studying at Oxford and Padua. He also travelled on the Continent with Pole and studied civil law at Avignon. He subsequently caught Cromwell's attention and was used by Cromwell to manage Italian intelligence, and as a propagandist.
⁹⁵ STC (2nd ed)/23236.
⁹⁶ ibid.

variance on non-essential matters of faith, provided the overall unity of the Christian faith is not jeopardised.[97] He would also turn his attention in the same year to which sacraments should be followed.[98]

Starkey further argued that 'spiritual blindness' was caused by 'superstition and arrogance', including superstitions 'geared to the moment'.[99] In similar fashion, St German, in *Thinges Necessary to Salvation* (1537), took a critical look at pilgrimages and saints, having discussed images earlier in *The Division* (1532).[100] In his later work, *Constitutions Provincial*,[101] St German saw no reason why saints should be worshipped; Starkey was silent on the issue.

Importantly, in his *Constitutions Provincial*, St German reviews the domestic canon law as found in the medieval provincial archiepiscopal legislation and constitutions of the papal legates Otho (1237) and Othobon (1268).[102] He explores whether the domestic canon law was repugnant to the common law and royal prerogative. The chapters of *Constitutions Provincial* are largely replicated from his earlier *Power of the Clergy*, the second dialogue of *Doctor and Student*, and the *New Additions*. In it St German invokes once again divine law and human law; in chapter twenty-one, he writes:

> It is rested in a Constitution that is in [the] third boke in the title of churches liberties and begins thus: ... That lay men be forbidden as well by the laws of god as of man to order and dispose the church's good[s]: by the which term church's good[s], spiritual men understand as well lands and tenements as chattel personals. And I suppose that there is no law of god that does prohibit lay men to dispose and determine the right of lands and goods of the church: but that it most properly appertains to them and not to the clergy.[103]

Eppley neatly summarises the point: for St German, 'the civil authorities are authorised to order the temporal affairs of the Church by the will of Christ as expressed in scripture'.[104]

St German, thus, is important for the jurisprudence he proposes, justifying the authority of the King-in-Parliament and the law of the land over papal authority

---

[97] TNA, PRO, SP 6/8, fos 1–20.

[98] TNA, PRO, SP 6/2, fos 89–168. For an exploration of this published work, see ML Johnson, 'Christopher St German's "Discourse of the Sacramentes Howe Many There Are": a reflection on St German's ideas in the context of Law and the Reformation' (2018) 181 *Law and Justice* 189–206. And for a transliteration of the work from the manuscript see www.lawandjustice.org.uk/Discourse%20of%20the%20Sacraments.pdf.

[99] Johnson (n 98) 194.

[100] Authoritative modern edition: Christopher St German, 'A Treatise Concerning the division between the Spirituality and the Temporality' in J Trapp (ed), *The Complete Works of St Thomas More*, vol 9 (London, Yale University Press, 1979) 177–212.

[101] STC (2nd ed)/24236.

[102] Othobon became Pope Adrian V. Otto and Othobon were both cited by Reginald Pole in his Legatine Constitutions of 1556. G Bray (ed), *The Anglican Canons 1529–1947* (Woodbridge, Boydell Press, 1998) 73.

[103] St German, *Constitutions Provincial* (n 101) sigs E6r–E6v.

[104] D Eppley, *Defending Royal Supremacy and Discerning God's Will in Tudor England* (Aldershot, Ashgate, 2007) 89, fn 84.

and Roman canon law. In *New Additions* (1531), in what he styles the eighth of his additions to *Doctor and Student*, 'concerning the authority of the parliament and the spirituality', St German sums up:

> If there were a schism in the papacy, who were right wise pope the king in his parliament as the high sovereign over the people which has not only charge on the bodies, but also the souls of his subjects hath power for the quietness and surety of his realm to ordain and determine, who shall be in this realm held for right wise pope, and may command that no man spiritual nor temporal shall name any other to be pope, but him that is so authorised in the parliament.[105]

After all, for St German, this was axiomatic: at the outset of *New Additions* he understood 'that no man would think, that they would do anything, that they had not power to do'.[106] St German is also important for another reason. The reign of Henry VIII also saw the dissolution of the Faculties of Canon Law at Oxford and Cambridge – though the Faculties of Civil Law survived. St German was one of the first common lawyers to write on the emergent King's ecclesiastical law, as Hooker the theologian jurist was to do later in Elizabeth's reign. The monopoly of the canonist and civilian commentators was to be broken – though, as we shall see, later generations of English ecclesiastical lawyer continued to invoke the Roman canon law. Indeed, as Helmholz put it:

> The canon law continued to be studied by students of the civil law even after formal abandonment of a separate canon law faculty. The ecclesiastical courts weathered the storms of the early sixteenth century. During the second half of the century, they recovered their nerve, and indeed they flourished.[107]

II. The Reign of Edward VI (1547–53)

A. A New King

In 1547, Henry VIII died and his son Edward VI succeeded to begin his short but religiously impactful reign.[108] As a minor (b 1537), he needed a lord protector and governor of his person. This role was given to his uncle on his mother's (Jane Seymour's) side, the Duke of Hertford, Edward Seymour. Hertford became Duke of Somerset very shortly thereafter. Somerset would play a key role in the Edwardian reformation, which was distinctly evangelical in nature.

---

[105] *New Additions* (n 70) 327.
[106] ibid 317.
[107] RH Helmholz, 'University Education and English Ecclesiastical Lawyers 1400–1650' (2011) 13 *Ecclesiastical Law Journal* 132–45, 135.
[108] See D MacCulloch, *The Later Reformation in England, 1547–1603* (New York, St. Martin's, 1990); and D MacCulloch, *The Boy King: Edward VI and the Protestant Reformation* (Berkeley, CA, University of California Press, 2002).

Edward's coronation oath was a keen signal of the further religious changes under Archbishop Cranmer. By proclamation of 31 January 1547, Edward was

> by the grace of God King of England, France, and Ireland, defender of the faith and of the Church of England and also of Ireland in earth the supreme head … now invested and established in the crown imperial of this realm, and other his realms, dominions, and countries, with all regalities, pre-eminences, styles, names, titles, and dignities to the same belonging or in any wise appertaining.[109]

As Hoak puts it:

> Gone were the historic promises by which kings protected the clergy and upheld law and liberty; it was for the crown to decide what in future constituted law and liberty, and for church, parliament, and people to give their consent. The oath thus gave the evangelicals the legal opening they needed to launch their reformation.[110]

This began the same year, once again using legislation to effect significant changes for the English Church.

B. The 'Ideological' Reformation

The religious reformation under Edward was a distinctly more ideological affair than that under Henry VIII. Some changes ultimately survived the passage of time more successfully than others. Henry's insistence that receiving communion in both kinds (bread and wine) was not necessary was reversed by the Sacrament Act 1547.[111] Bray provides a fulsome analysis of the statute: receiving 'in both the kinds' was a 'universal custom of the early Church, and continued into the Middle Ages in the West, but it gradually died out, possibly because of the plague'.[112] Attempts to reintroduce it were then considered heretical. The 'blessed sacrament' was now to be 'ministered to all Christian people under both kinds', reflecting the practice of Christ and the early Church. The congregation should 'receive the same with the priest, than the priest should receive it alone'. The priest should cause the people to prepare themselves to receive the sacrament, lest they take the sacrament in an unworthy state, and to prevent this every man should examine his own conscience before receiving the sacrament. The statute gave a right to Holy Communion, and the priest had no right to deny the sacrament to any person who 'devoutly and humbly desire it', with the exception of where he might have 'lawful cause'. Lawful cause was not, however, further defined in the statute.[113] This Act (and particularly the saving phrase within it, 'except necessity

---

[109] PH Hughes and JL Larkin, *Tudor Royal Proclamations*, vol 1 (New Haven, CT, Yale University Press, 1964) 381.
[110] D Hoak, 'Edward VI' in *Oxford Dictionary of National Biography* (n 20).
[111] 1 Edw VI c 1.
[112] Bray (n 28) 227.
[113] ibid 230–231.

otherwise require', which should prevent the taking of communion in both kinds) came to prominence in 2020 with the restrictions on the use of the common cup through public health concerns during the Covid-19 pandemic.

A further statute of 1547 was the Election of Bishops Act.[114] The earlier Act of 1534 set out the process for 'election' of bishops, whereas the 1547 Act calls out the process as being 'in very deed no election' but simply amounting to 'shadows or pretences of elections'; and the pretence of such is 'derogatory and prejudicial to the King's prerogative royal'.[115] The king would now elect the individual expressly by his letters patent.[116] The scheme was thoroughly Erastian.[117] However, the Act was to be repealed by Mary I in 1553, and would not be reinstated by Elizabeth I, who preferred her father's statute for the appointment of bishops.

The year 1549 then saw the first Act of Uniformity.[118] This provided for the first Prayer Book of Edward VI, compiled by Archbishop Cranmer. The Prayer Book was designed to ensure uniformity in worship throughout the realm alongside the provision of a public liturgy. According to Bray, the Act would 'incidentally help congregations worship in their own language', and the Prayer Book cut out that which was 'untrue', 'uncertain' or 'vain or superstitious', allowing instead focus on the 'very pure Word of God'; but some evangelicals considered the Prayer Book to be insufficiently radical and Protestant.[119]

In addition, 1549 saw an attempt to reform the law on excommunication in a bill introduced by Archbishop Cranmer, 'touching Ecclesiastical jurisdiction'. As Spalding notes, this bill (passed by the Lords and sent to the Commons) 'would have given the bishops and their ordinaries the power to excommunicate and to imprison those who were in need of discipline in order to help tidy up what was regarded then to be an immoral and disorderly nation'.[120] The Commons read the bill on 21 January 1550. The bill was defeated the same day. Spalding theorises that this was due to the fact that the Commons 'were not about to extend the power of church officials until the ecclesiastical laws were such as they felt they could live with'.[121]

In turn, therefore, another bill was read to revive the Henrician plan to constitute a royal commission for wholesale reformation of ecclesiastical law. A commission was established and, led by Archbishop Cranmer, had members drawn from the temporality and spirituality: eight bishops, eight civilians, eight canonists and eight common lawyers. The *Reformatio Legum Ecclesiasticarum* (1551–52) was presented to Parliament in 1553. However, the Duke of Northumberland, John Dudley, blocked its progress and directed Cranmer to 'look to [his] own business', a reference to preachers preaching sedition against the

---

[114] 1 Edw VI c 2.
[115] Bray (n 28) 232.
[116] ibid 233.
[117] After Swiss theologian Thomas Erastus (1524–83).
[118] 2–3 Edw VI c 1.
[119] Bray (n 28) 242.
[120] J Spalding, 'The *Reformatio Legum Ecclesiasticarum* of 1552 and the Furthering of Discipline in England' (1970) 39 *Church History* 162–71, 162.
[121] ibid 163.

nobility.[122] Edward VI died soon after. The *Reformatio* was resurrected again in 1571 but Parliament rejected it.

Another example of Henry's conservative leanings was his opposition to married clergy. Canon 21 of the First Lateran Council (1123) outlawed clerical marriage and ordered existing clerical marriages dissolved (thus recognising such marriages as having been valid). Canon 6 of the Second Lateran Council (1139) prescribed deprivation of office for any who fell foul of canon law on this matter, and its Canon 7 required any clergy who had married to separate from their partner as the union was not regarded as matrimonial.[123] But in 1549, Parliament passed the Act to Take Away all Positive Laws against the Marriage of Priests.[124] Elizabeth I did not restore this statute after its repeal by Mary I. Whilst married clergy were found in the late sixteenth-century Church, the provisions of the 1549 Act were not restored until 1603.

The penultimate year of Edward's reign, 1552, saw a second Act of Uniformity.[125] This brought in a new and, as Haigh notes, 'decisively Protestant prayer book', with a Calvinist eucharistic doctrine; indeed, 'Most of the ceremonies which had been condemned by Protestants … were removed: baptism, confirmation, and burial services were rewritten; and in the communion service, the structure of the mass was abandoned and many of the prayers omitted.'[126] It is likely that the Prayer Book was drafted by Cranmer and Nicholas Ridley (Bishop of London), with the advice of (Italian reformer) Peter Martyr. The Act provided for enforcement, including imprisonment for failure to use the Prayer Book. As we see in later chapters, whilst suppressed under Mary I, the Prayer Book was modified in 1559 and 1662, but remains a normative liturgical text, as an historic formulary, in the Church of England today.

The promulgation of the Forty-Two Articles occurred on 19 June 1553 – a statement of the doctrine of the Church of England, Protestant in nature and even Calvinist in tone.[127] Once the Articles were promulgated, the clergy were meant to be required to subscribe to them. However, the sudden death of Edward VI less than a month later, on 6 July 1553, meant that this never happened. Yet the king's minutes of his last will contained instructions to his executors that they were not to

> suffer any piece of religion to be altered, And they shall diligently travail to cause godly ecclesiastical laws to be made and set forth; such as may be agreeable with the reformation of religion now viewed within the realm and that done to cause the canon law to be abolished.[128]

This did not happen.

---

[122] ibid 167.
[123] See https://sourcebooks.fordham.edu/basis/lateran2.asp.
[124] 2–3 Edw VI c 21.
[125] 5–6 Edw VI c 1.
[126] C Haigh, *English Reformations: Religion, Politics, and Society under the Tudors* (Oxford: OUP, 1993) 168, 179–80.
[127] Bray (n 28) 253, 259.
[128] *Literary Remains of King Edward the Sixth* (London, JB Nichols & Sons, 1857) 574.

III. The Reign of Mary I (1533–58)

Edward VI's will named Lady Jane Grey, the Protestant great-granddaughter of Henry VII's younger daughter Mary, as his successor. Jane's reign began on 10 July 1553, but support for the Roman Catholic Mary, daughter of Henry VIII and Katherine of Aragon, grew, to the extent that she was proclaimed Queen on 19 July 1553. Jane was executed in February 1554.

Mary sought to return the English Church to the position it had occupied in 1529. This would be completed in several stages. England was reconciled with Rome on 29 November 1554. Like her father and brother before her, Mary used parliamentary statute to accomplish her religious vision. Her first Parliament sat in autumn 1553 and produced the First Statute of Repeal 1553.[129] The statute sought to undo the reforms made by Edward VI and took the religious landscape back to where it was at the death of Henry VIII in 1547. It was also through this statute that the Queen's authority as Queen regnant was confirmed. This is an interesting early example of parliamentary assent to and confirmation of the authority of the monarch.

The Marian injunctions of 1554 expunged any reference to royal supremacy in ecclesiastical matters.[130] Mary married King Philip II of Spain and welcomed Cardinal Reginald Pole back from Rome[131] as Archbishop of Canterbury, and began to unpick more Reformation changes. The Second Statute of Repeal came in 1555.[132] It undid the Henrician statutes back to 1529.

However, with respect to the ecclesiastical jurisdiction, as Helmholz writes, '[t]he brief reign of the Catholic monarchs, Philip and Mary, had done nothing to breathe new life into the [spiritual] courts'.[133] This was despite Cardinal Pole's Legatine Constitutions of 1556, which would, in the second decree, reinstitute the public teaching of canon law.[134] Mary's reign would end after just five years on 17 November 1558 during an epidemic of influenza, which would also claim the life of Pole later the same day. Her death opened the way for the Elizabethan settlement and the re-establishment of the Church of England and its law.

IV. Conclusion

The period 1530–58 was a time of immense change and upheaval affecting the religious, constitutional and legal life of England. The changes shaped profoundly

---

[129] 1 Mar st 2, c 2.
[130] Bray (n 28) 281, 282.
[131] Reginald Pole had earned the ire of Mary's father by not supporting his separation from Katherine of Aragon. He entered a period of self-imposed exile in France in 1532 and broke formally from King Henry in 1536: see J Edwards, *Mary I: England's Catholic Queen* (New Haven, CT, Yale University Press, 2011).
[132] 1 & 2 Ph & M c 8.
[133] Helmholz, *The Canon Law and Ecclesiastical Jurisdiction* (n 30) 234.
[134] Bray (n 102) 76–77.

the legal history of the Church of England. Much Tudor legislation, repealed by Mary and brought back by Elizabeth, remains in force and provides the bedrock of much of the life of the Church of England to this day. The period saw the effective use by Henry VIII of parliamentary statute as the preferred means of effecting the break from Rome and the consequent changes needed to sustain the new institutional Church of England established by law. The ecclesiastical law reflected a view of the English Church as nationalised and independent of foreign jurisdiction – but dependent on the royal supremacy. Papal powers were transferred by statute to the Crown and to the royal officials – to appoint bishops, to receive church revenues, to hear appeals in ecclesiastical causes, and to issue dispensations and licences. The canon law faculties at Oxford and Cambridge were dissolved. The Roman canon law was domesticated: it continued to apply to the English Church, provided it was not repugnant to the laws of the realm and royal prerogative. Key legal landmarks under Edward VI were the introduction by statute of a Prayer Book, the Sacrament Act 1547 and the doomed *Reformatio Legum Ecclesiasticarum*. But the provisionality of the ecclesiastical law also came to the fore – because the period ended with the disestablishment of the Church of England and a return to Rome under Mary Tudor.

3

The Elizabethan Settlement: 1558–1603

PAUL BARBER AND MORAG ELLIS

The task for Elizabeth I and her government was to reverse the return to Rome under Mary and to revive the Henrician revolution and convert it into a settlement. This meant steering a course between two extremes: the radical puritans and the recusant Catholics, both of whom were a threat to the endeavour. However, the puritans were, at least until the latter part of the period, 'the enemy within' the Church, whereas the Catholics were an external threat.[1] For that reason, we shall see the developments of the ecclesiastical law being more focused on the former threat than the latter. In true Tudor style, as we have seen in chapter 2, this revolution was, in so far as possible, fully clothed in constitutional propriety, giving every appearance of lawfulness. Every tool in the legal armoury was used to give whatever 'authority' the State was using the maximum possible credibility. It was a tactic that, with hindsight, ultimately proved successful, but at the time that was far from certain. Alongside this ideological warfare, there was also the simple jockeying for position, as in any new settlement, by parliament, bishops, clergy, laity and others.[2] The settlement has, broadly, endured, although in heavily modified form, as later chapters of this book demonstrate.

Throughout the reign of Queen Elizabeth, we can detect her hand behind the reforms, but her prudence and caution, particularly early in her reign, meant acting through others, principally her Archbishop of Canterbury. Neatly, three Archbishops cover her reign almost exactly, and the personalities of each therefore defined many of the possibilities and limits for reform during each tenure (and such limits are demonstrated starkly with Archbishop Grindal). Accordingly, this chapter approaches the material broadly chronologically, dividing the reign into four periods: the immediate period before the appointment of Matthew Parker, and then the tenures of each Archbishop in turn.

---

[1] This threat was largely dealt with by the various penal statutes and the criminal law, which are beyond the scope of this chapter.
[2] See generally J Hurstfield, *Elizabeth I and the Unity of England* (West Drayton, Harmondsworth, 1960).

I. The Preliminary Period: Between Archbishops – Royal Supremacy

We begin with a U-turn. Parliament was in session when Queen Mary died on 17 November 1558. Despite the Succession to the Crown Act 1536,[3] declaring her 'preclosed, excluded and barred' from the succession, the Archbishop of York (and Lord Chancellor) immediately proclaimed Elizabeth queen in this newly dissolved Parliament. The death of Cardinal Pole on the same day also left one fewer obstacle to the accession, and with it the inevitable consequence that England would, again, sever its bonds of communion with the See of Rome.

Writs for a new Parliament were sent out on 5 December, which was to meet on 23 January. On Christmas Day the queen ordered the Bishop of Carlisle not to elevate the blessed Sacrament after the consecration at the Mass he was about to sing in her presence, a command he declined to obey, with the result that the queen left after the Gospel so as not to witness the elevation.[4] Two days later, a more general proclamation was issued, ordering the epistle and the gospel of the Mass, and the litany before Mass to be conducted in English, and forbidding reformed clergy deprived under Mary to resume 'their former offices in preaching and ministering'.[5] The Coronation Mass took place on 15 January 1559. At first all the bishops refused to crown her, but at the last moment the Bishop of Carlisle gave way. Nevertheless, the Mass was sung, and the sermon preached, by reformed clergy. Evidently, controversy and compromise also characterised the ceremony. While accounts contradict each other about the queen's exact behaviour, commentators appear to agree that, whatever she did, she was making a statement about the nature of the settlement, 'with something to confuse and offend everyone'. It anticipated the inconsistencies of her early religious settlement, which was less often a *via media* than an erratic 'mingle-mangle': the elevation of the host continued to be omitted, but the use of communion wafers, 'eucharistic vestments, and kneeling during communion was prescribed despite strenuous Protestant opposition'.[6]

The Parliament originally had a bit of a false start. Bills were introduced on 9 and 15 February 1559, but these were subsequently abandoned, to be followed by what appears to have been a composite Bill providing both for royal supremacy and liturgical reform. Passing through its Commons stages in four days, the Bill arrived in the Lords for first reading on 28 February, but there was then a delay of a fortnight. This may have been caused by the meeting that same day of the Lower

---

[3] 28 Hen VIII c 7. See also Succession to the Crown Act 1543 (35 Hen VIII c 1).

[4] F Proctor and WH Frere, *A New History of the Book of Common Prayer* (London, Macmillan, 1910) 97.

[5] H Gee and WJ Hardy, *Documents illustrative of English Church History*, 4th edn (London, MacMillan and Co, 1921) 416–17.

[6] R McCoy, '"The Wonderfull Spectacle": the Civic Progress of Elizabeth I and the Troublesome Coronation in Coronation Studies, Past, Present and Future' in JM Bak (ed), *Coronations: Medieval and Early Modern Monarchic Ritual* (Berkeley, CA, University of California Press, 1989) 217–25.

House of Convocation, which voted a strong protest and a public profession of faith in five points in opposition to the proposals.

When the Bill was again produced on 15 March, the bishops fought it and succeeded in reducing it to dealing with the supremacy only. It completed its final stages, and by the Wednesday in Holy Week awaited the royal assent. The royal assent never came, and on Good Friday Parliament was adjourned to the Monday of Low Week. If assent had been given, Elizabeth would have become 'Supreme Head on Earth of the Church of Christ in England' against the wishes of the lords spiritual and, it would seem, the queen herself.

After Easter, two separate Bills were introduced – one on the supremacy and one on uniformity of worship. These were passed on 29 April, with all the lords spiritual present voting against them.[7] The Act of Uniformity had a margin of three votes on its final reading. The Act of Supremacy 1558[8] repealed the 1554 Act of Philip and Mary,[9] which had in turn repealed the earlier anti-papal statutes, and revived 11 of those Acts. Ten of these were from Henry VIII (two as modified by Edward VI, and the others in full) and one of Edward VI. These were the Ecclesiastical Jurisdiction Act 1531,[10] Annates Act 1532,[11] Ecclesiastical Appeals Act 1532,[12] Submission of the Clergy Act 1533, Appointment of Bishops Act 1533, Ecclesiastical Licences Act 1533,[13] Suffragan Bishops Act 1534,[14] Ecclesiastical Licences Act 1536,[15] part of the Marriage Act 1540, part of the Ecclesiastical Jurisdiction Act 1546,[16] and the Sacrament Act 1547.[17] The Act of Supremacy explicitly forbade the exercise of jurisdiction by any foreign prelate and it annexed all such jurisdiction to the Crown. This jurisdiction could be exercised by Ecclesiastical Commissioners in the name of the Crown. The Act imposed an oath, to be taken by a wide range of ecclesiastics, office holders and others, and this is where the new title 'Supreme Governor' is to be found.[18]

---

[7] E Gibson, *Codex Juris Ecclesiastici Anglicani* (1713) I, 48.

[8] 1 Eliz c 1. The statutory date of 1558 is calculated from the first day of the parliamentary session (in old-style dating).

[9] An Act repealing all Articles and Provisions made against the See Apostolick ... etc 1 & 2 Ph & M c 8. This was Mary's second Act of repeal, which restored the status quo of 1529. The first such Act (1 Mar Sess 2 c 2) had restored the status quo of 1547: see ch 2 of this volume.

[10] 23 Hen VIII c.9.

[11] 23 Hen VIII c 20: An Act concerning restraint of payments of Annates to the See of Rome. This is described in the Act of Supremacy 1558 as being made in the *25th* year of Henry's reign, probably because, in accordance with the provisions of the Act, it did not come into force until it was ratified by means of letters patent of 9 July of that year (1534). The text thereof is printed in the footnote to the 1532 Act in Halsbury's *Statutes of England*, 1st edn (London, Butterworths, 1929) vol VI, 950.

[12] 24 Hen VIII c 12.

[13] 25 Hen VIII cc 19, 20 and 21 respectively.

[14] 25 Hen VIII c 14.

[15] 28 Hen VIII c 16.

[16] 32 Hen VIII c 38 and 37 Hen VIII c 17 respectively: in both these cases, only those parts of the Act that had not been repealed during the reign of Edward VI were revived.

[17] 1 Edw VI c 1.

[18] On a very rough count, there are over fifty Elizabethan Acts of Parliament which deal with religious and church-related matters. However, there is no space in this chapter to look at them all in any detail.

The Act of Uniformity 1558[19] revived the Act of Uniformity 1551[20] and the 1552 Prayer Book as amended by the new Act in what we now know as the Book of Common Prayer 1559. There were small but significant changes to some wording relating to the Eucharist.

The Prayer Book, like the liturgical books it succeeded, contained 'Rubricks': 'direction[s] for the conduct of divine service', and so called because they were normally written or printed in red, to accompany the (black) text of the rite. Bullard and Bell tell us that a rubric 'presupposes a knowledge of the principles upon which the liturgy is constructed, and some knowledge of the Canon Law which lies behind it. The relation of a rubric to a canon is very much that of a bye-law to an Act of Parliament.'[21] Liturgical law largely grew from local customs, these being subsequently compiled into liturgical books, and moderated by diocesan bishops and local synods.[22] In that sense, the sixteenth century in general, and the Book of Common Prayer in particular, began to depart from that tradition by introducing a new level of uniformity, but the rubrics in the new books seem to have been afforded a similar legal status to those they replaced. Edmund Gibson (in his *Codex*, 1713) cites the rubrics extensively, and they are listed as sources of canon law in the preface, where he notes the statutory authority they enjoy by virtue of the Acts of Uniformity.[23]

On 23 May 1559, 18 lay privy councillors were appointed as commissioners under the Great Seal to administer the oath to those already in office. The commissioners began with the bishops. With 10 sees vacant, that left 16, who were all summoned between May and November. All refused to take the oath and were deprived of their sees.[24] In June, work began on a general ecclesiastical visitation of the country, with six commissions being issued to a mixture of peers, gentry and clergy (one covering the Province of York, and the rest covering the dioceses of Canterbury). Their work was underpinned by the Royal Injunctions of 24 June 1559, and was completed by about November of that year.

These injunctions contained material from the injunctions issued by Thomas Cromwell in 1536 (eg, royal supremacy, clergy conduct) and 1538[25] (eg, Bible and prayers in English, the keeping of parish registers) and those of Edward VI, issued by Thomas Cranmer in 1547 (eg, prohibition of processions and destruction of shrines). These were supplemented by a number of new Articles, such as the

---

[19] 1 Eliz c 2.
[20] 5 & 6 Edw VI c 1, which itself had modified and enforced the provisions of the first Act of Uniformity of 1549: 2 & 3 Edw VI c 1.
[21] JV Bullard and HC Bell, *Lyndwood's Provinciale* (London, Faith Press, 1929) xlvii.
[22] See, eg, the evolution of the Uses of Sarum, York, Hereford and Bangor, and the eventual eclipse of most of them by Sarum: Proctor and Frere (n 4) ch 1. See more generally JM Huels, *Liturgy and Law* (Ottawa, Wilson & Lafleur, 2006) 29–34; and also RH Bursell, *Liturgy, Order and the Law* (Oxford, Clarendon Press, 1996).
[23] Gibson (n 7) preface, x–xi; eg Title XIII: I, 362–70.
[24] Apart from Kitchen of Llandaff, who appears to have been granted a deferral: R Dixon, *History of the Church of England*, vol V: *1558–1563* (Oxford, Clarendon Press, 1902) 122.
[25] G Bray, *Documents of the English Reformation* (Cambridge, Clarke, 1994) 175 and 179.

requirements for the approval of clergy wives, the forbidding of religious images in private houses, and the licensing of teachers and books.[26]

The revival of the Henrician requirements under the Appointment of Bishops Act 1533 for the confirmation and consecration of new diocesan bishops caused some difficulty – as William Cecil (Secretary of State) remarked at the time, 'there is no Archbishop nor four bishops now to be had'.[27] The chosen solution was a royal commission with a widely drawn *supplentes* clause, supplying by royal authority any form or capacity that was lacking, but the efficacy of this was challenged only a few years later. The former Bishop of London, Dr Bonner, was charged in 1564 with refusing the oath of allegiance. His defence was that the oath had to be administered by the diocesan bishop, and Dr Horne, who had brought the charges, was not the Bishop of Winchester, as he had not been elected or consecrated as the law required. This argument evidently troubled Sir James Dyer, Chief Justice of the Common Pleas, but the point was never resolved judicially, as the case was ultimately not brought to trial, but a sanating Act of Parliament was passed shortly thereafter.[28]

II. Period One: Archbishop Parker (1559–75)

The appointment of Matthew Parker as Archbishop of Canterbury in July 1559 increased the range of possibilities for continuing to lay out the foundations of the settlement, piece by piece. Parker was charged with doing the queen's bidding, but perhaps with less backing from her than he might have liked, and therefore proceeded pragmatically with a variety of instruments.

At this juncture, it is appropriate to touch briefly upon the various forms of legal and quasi-legal documents we are about to encounter, their forms and the significance (or otherwise) of their titles. Parliamentary statutes and canons are both reasonably precise categories of legal instrument, their authority clearly given to them by the process through which they are made and put into force.[29] The same may be said of liturgical rubrics, but perhaps to a slightly lesser degree (see section I). There is, however, more ambiguity in the other forms we are about to see deployed by successive archbishops, and other terminology was often used quite loosely.

The most widely used term encountered is that of 'Articles', which, far from being a technical term, is a generic one, used extensively in ecclesiastical affairs,

---

[26] G Bray, *The Anglican Canons 1529-1947* (Woodbridge, Boydell Press, 1998) xlvii. For the text, see Bray (n 25) 335–48.

[27] Note in Cecil's hand, PRO State Papers, Domestic, V, no 25, July 1559.

[28] Bishops Act 1566, 8 Eliz c 1; JH Baker (ed), *Reports from the Lost Notebooks of Sir James Dyer*, vol I (London, Selden Society 1994) lxviii, 103, 105–07. See also AS Barnes, *Bishop Barlow and Anglican Orders* (London, Longmans, 1922) 90–91.

[29] Although contemporary usage also allowed the terms 'constitutions' and, more loosely, 'injunctions' to describe canons.

such as court proceedings and visitations. An 'Article' is simply a section of a document, and sometimes (though not always) the term 'Articles' is given to the whole document. It is therefore necessary to look at each document to see if it falls within a particular type of 'Articles' to understand its place in the ecclesiastical firmament. Articles of various types rarely stand on their own; rather, they are part of a process, and their effect relies on other parts of that process. One form is 'Articles of Religion': a series of doctrinal statements to which adherence was usually required by means of another legal instrument, such as a statute. Another species can be found in 'visitation articles': a list of questions issued by the visiting Ordinary (archdeacon, bishop, Crown, etc), enforced by means of the visitation itself; they were frequently accompanied by a 'charge' exhorting particular behaviour, and this could be both retrospective and prospective – these exhortations were also termed 'advertisements'.

The term 'injunctions' was also used loosely to cover any set of orders issued by ecclesiastical authority, whether national or covering a particular diocese or church. Injunctions were often closely associated with visitations, as they afforded an opportunity to distribute them and make them known, or they could be drawn up as a result of presentments made during a visitation. These are also sometimes termed 'orders' or 'directions'.[30]

A. The Eleven Articles 1559/60

The Eleven Articles were issued by Parker during his first year as Archbishop of Canterbury, for subscription of the clergy twice a year. These Articles were principally aimed at securing the royal supremacy.[31] They were superseded by the Thirty-Eight Articles of 1563,[32] which were a revised version of Cranmer's Forty-Two Articles of 1553. These, in turn, were revised in 1571 as the Thirty-Nine Articles. These 'Articles' are after the type of Articles 'of Religion' issued by the queen's father and brother.[33]

Whatever status the Articles possessed before 1571, by section 2 of the statute 13 Eliz c12 it was provided that ecclesiastical persons who 'advisedly maintain or affirm any doctrine directly contrary or repugnant to any of the' Thirty-Nine Articles, and not revoking them after their errors were pointed out through due process, would be deprived of their livings. Decisions of the Court of Arches and

---

[30] K Fincham (ed), *Visitation Articles and Injunctions of the Early Stuart Church*, vol 1 (Woodbridge, Boydell Press, 1994) xiii–xxv. For a collection from this period, see WH Frere (ed), *Visitation Articles and Injunctions of the Period of the Reformation*, vol 3 (London, Longmans Green & Co, 1910) 1559–75. In his Introduction (ibid vol 1, 93–117), Frere sets out in some detail, with examples, the different types of documents associated with visitation.

[31] Bray (n 25) 349–51.

[32] Thirty-nine were passed by Convocations, but Art XXIX was suppressed by the Queen as offensive to Lutherans: G Bray (ed), *Records of Convocation* (Woodbridge, Boydell Press, 2006) 420–30.

[33] See ch 2 of this volume.

Privy Council throughout the succeeding centuries laid down the principles to be applied to this provision. In *The King's Proctor v Stone*,[34] the Dean of the Arches, Lord Stowell, described the Articles as having been framed in Convocation and 'adopted' by the legislature. This understanding reflects the approaches of both Edmund Gibson and Richard Burn. The latter states in the preface to his *Ecclesiastical Law* (1763) that both the Thirty-Nine Articles and the Rubric of the Book of Common Prayer, being 'established by Act of Parliament, are to be esteemed as part of the statute law'.[35]

Subscription to the Articles became mandatory in 1571 for all ordination candidates and those presented to benefices.[36] As a generality, the laity have never been required by the Church to subscribe to the Articles of Religion; they are primarily 'tests for teachers'.[37] The form of subscription was settled in the Canons of 1603/04; the law on subscription underwent numerous changes and in 1975 it was replaced by a declaration of assent to church doctrine.[38]

B. The Latin and Welsh Prayer Books

The combined provisions of the Acts of Uniformity provided for the prescribed Book of Common Prayer of 1559, approved by Parliament, with a concession in the first Act of Uniformity 1549 allowing the universities to use the same in Greek, Latin or Hebrew (but excluding the Holy Communion). Notwithstanding this, a Latin version of the Book of Common Prayer was produced in 1560 that, although ostensibly a translation of the 1559 book, differed from it, with some of the text coming from the 1549 Prayer Book or the Roman Missal instead.[39] This publication was issued with the authority of Letters Patent of 6 April 1560, for use in the colleges of Oxford, Cambridge, Winchester and Eton, but, in the absence of a text in Irish, also for those parts of Ireland where the clergy and laity spoke no English.[40] The wording of the Letters Patent – *statuto illo praedicto de ritu publicarum ... anno primo regni nostri promulgato in contrarium*

---

[34] *The King's Proctor v Stone* 1 Consist 424.
[35] Gibson (n 7) I, xi; R Burn, *Ecclesiastical Law* (1763) vol I, preface, xviii.
[36] Ordination of Ministers Act 1571 (13 Eliz c 12).
[37] EJ Bicknell, *A Theological Introduction to the Thirty-Nine Articles of the Church of England*, 3rd edn (London, Longmans, 1955) 19. Today, Readers and Lay Workers are required to make a similar Declaration of Assent: see Canons E6 and E8 and *Common Worship, The Admission and Licensing of Readers*. There is no statutory requirement for ecclesiastical judges, but Canons G2–G4 require judges and registrars to make a Declaration of Assent, along with the statutory oaths of Allegiance and the Judicial Oath, in the following terms: 'I, A B, declare my belief in the faith which is revealed in the Holy Scriptures and set forth in the catholic creeds and to which the historic formularies of the Church of England bear witness.'
[38] See, eg, the Clerical Subscription Act 1856 (an affirmation of assent, including to the Thirty-Nine Articles); and *Duffield, St Alkmund* [2013] Fam 158 [24]: the Court of Archies stated that the Thirty-Nine Articles are 'no longer a definitive formulation of Anglican doctrine, even though they bear witness to that faith'.
[39] Proctor and Frere (n 4) 112.
[40] An Irish Act of Uniformity (2 Eliz c 2 Ireland) was passed in 1560.

non obstante – seems to indicate an intention to dispense from the requirements of an Act of Parliament by extending the scope of the original exemption. Notwithstanding subsequent political and legal developments, in the context of the time this is perhaps not as striking as it might appear to modern eyes, and perhaps built upon the existing precedent of the French Prayer Book (for Calais and the Channel Islands), which had been in existence since the first Act of Uniformity of 1549 and was simply modified following each subsequent Act.[41]

In contrast to both of these, the translation into Welsh of the Prayer Book (and the Bible) was explicitly provided for by an Act of Parliament of 1563.[42] The statute required 'the Bible and Divine Service' to be translated into the 'British or Welsh tongue', so that the people, inter alia, 'to rule and guide their lives according to the commandments of God, might much better learn to love and fear God, to serve and obey their prince, and to know their duties to their neighbours', in the 'Country of Wales'. It also required the translations to be printed, and to be distributed to churches in areas where Welsh was commonly spoken, provided that versions in English were available for those who understood English. The Bible and Prayer Book were so translated in 1567.[43] The sixteenth- and seventeenth-century Acts of Uniformity constituted the first statutory recognition of the official use of the Welsh language.[44] Elizabeth Tudor's Act of 1563 required a Welsh translation of the Prayer Book to be placed in all churches in Wales, alongside the English version, modifying her brother Edward VI's decree in the 1549 Act, which required all public worship to be conducted in English (except as stated above).

C. Parker's Admonition and Table of Impediments to Marriage 1560/63

The revived Marriage Act once again swept away dispensation for the impediments of consanguinity and affinity, permitting all marriages that were not forbidden by divine law. The trouble was that theologians disagreed on which marriages were forbidden by God's law. Furthermore, the exact delineation of

---

[41] For a discussion of what falls within or without the scope of the Acts of Uniformity, see RH Bursell, 'Consecration, *Ius Liturgicum*, and the Canons' in N Doe, M Hill and R Ombres (eds), *English Canon Law: Essays in Honour of Bishop Eric Kemp* (Cardiff, University of Wales Press, 1998) 71–81, esp 73–75.
[42] 5 Eliz c 28.
[43] See, eg, RL Brown, 'The Age of the Saints to the Victorian Church' in N Doe (ed), *A New History of the Church in Wales: Governance and Ministry, Theology and Society* (Cambridge, Cambridge University Press, 2020) 9–26, 12–13. The (then) four Welsh dioceses were part of the Province of Canterbury.
[44] After the suppression of its use for official secular purposes by the Laws in Wales Acts of Henry VIII. Soon after the Act of Supremacy 1558, Elizabeth I ordered that Irish language print be made 'solely to present the doctrines of the reformed church to the minds of the Irish people', but the first translation of the Book of Common Prayer into Irish was not made until 1608.

these prohibitions was a political 'hot potato' – on which depended the legitimacy of the queen and her succession to the throne. A Table listing these impediments was first published in 1560,[45] under the title 'An Admonition [for the Necessity of the present Time till a further Consultation] to all as such intend hereafter to enter the State of Matrimony godly and agreeable to Law'. The Archbishop of Canterbury re-published it 'by authority' in 1563, omitting the wording in square brackets above.[46] A number of unconvincing explanations as to the exact nature of that authority have been put forward,[47] but authority was retrospectively supplied in increments by the Advertisements of 1566,[48] the Canons of 1571[49] and the Canons of 1603.[50] John Strype (1643–1737) also notes that, in the first printed edition of the Table, a completely unrelated order (forbidding those under the degree of Master of Arts from preaching or expounding the Scripture) was printed after the text of the Table. Strype presumes this was simply because the order thus subjoined would thereby be set up in every church along with the Admonition printed above it.[51]

D. The Articles for Ecclesiastical Government 1563

Attempts by Convocation to legislate for the Elizabethan Church began slowly.[52] Some papers, written in preparation for discussions at the Convocation of 1563 and annotated by Parker and others, survive, and these led to the formulation of 56 'Articles for Ecclesiastical Government', which were passed by the lower house but were not subsequently approved.[53] These Articles were wide-ranging in scope, and drew on preparatory papers that were drawn up by a secretary of Archbishop Parker, and amended by him and others. They are not set out in

---

[45] Strype has Parker as the principal drafter, whereas the Archbishop's Commission has him publishing it: J Strype, *Annals of the Reformation and Establishment of Religion: and other various occurrences in the Church of England, during Queen Elizabeth's happy reign*, vol 1 (Oxford, Clarendon Press 1824) pt 1, 332–33; and J Strype, *The Life and Acts of Matthew Parker*, vol 1 (Oxford, Clarendon Press, 1821) bk II, 174–76; *Kindred and Affinity as Impediments to Marriage: being the Report of a Commission appointed by His Grace the Archbishop of Canterbury* (London, SPCK, 1940) 41.
[46] The Table is fully reproduced in Gibson (n 7) I, 500; in R Burn, *Ecclesiastical Law* (1763) vol II, 7–9; and in E Cardwell, *Documentary Annals of the Reformed Church of England*, vol I (London, 1844) 316–20 (the three differ slightly in the order of the material and the quotations from Scripture, but all substantive provisions are the same). See also R Helmholz, *Roman Canon Law in Reformation England* (Cambridge, Cambridge University Press, 1990) 75–76.
[47] The full Table, complete with its explanatory notes, was never published in the Book of Common Prayer – only the lists. It is clear from note 4 that the list was never drafted as a taxative one: it provides for the consultation of 'men learned in the laws' in contracting 'betwixt persons doubtful, which be not expressed in this table'.
[48] Art 4, para 8.
[49] Canon 10, para 6.
[50] Canon 99.
[51] Strype, *Annals* (n 45) 176.
[52] Judging from the contents of Bray (ed) (n 32), the volume of business in Convocations during this period does not seem to be markedly different from that in former times.
[53] Bray, *The Anglican Canons* (n 26) lxxxviii–lxxxix, 724–61.

any logical order, but topics include ecclesiastical jurisdiction and procedure (including the abolition of peculiar jurisdictions), ecclesiastical discipline (including behaviour of clergy and laity), tithes, advowsons and chancel repairs, examination of the clergy, preaching and pluralities, fasting and the keeping of holy days, and matrimonial discipline. They also ranged from restatement of the existing law (eg, the role of deans and archdeacons) to new provisions, such as those relating to the communion table, communion and chalices, and the provisions against the sayers and hearers of Mass.[54]

E. The Advertisements for Due Order 1566

Frustrated by lack of more radical reform, some of the puritan clergy agitated against the wearing of ecclesiastical vestments. This displeased the queen, who commanded Archbishop Parker to draw up guidelines for behaviour in church. Parker having drafted the document, the queen refused to sign it on two occasions.[55] Thereupon Parker published the guidelines 'by virtue of the queen's letters' and they were 'agreed on and subscribed by' himself and five of his suffragans as 'Commissioners in causes ecclesiastical'. The exact legal status of the Advertisements is unclear, but in a similar way to the Table before them, they were subsequently to be treated as authoritative in the 1571 Canons (see section II.G) and were to become one of the sources for the 1603 Canons.[56] The Advertisements consisted of a preface, four sections on doctrine and preaching, administration of prayer and sacraments, orders in ecclesiastical polity, and ecclesiastical apparel, and a form of 'protestation' to be taken in the future by all ecclesiastical officeholders. The Advertisements were mainly concerned with holding back puritanism, which was, at the time, seen as the more pressing, internal threat. Bray concludes that the Advertisements were 'not much in themselves, but they were the humble beginning of much bigger things, and survived the test of time in a way of which Archbishop Parker would scarcely have dreamed'.

F. The *Reformatio Legum Ecclesiasticarum*

The *Reformatio* never had any legal standing, but it was an influential text with a complex history that formed part of the background to the Elizabethan settlement. Its origin had been in the Submission of the Clergy Act 1533, which provided for most of the existing canon law to continue in force until such time as it was reviewed by a commission of 32 persons.[57] No commission was appointed

---

[54] ibid.
[55] 3 March 1565 and 12 March 1566.
[56] Bray, *The Anglican Canons* (n 26) xlvii–xlviii, 163–71.
[57] 25 Henry VIII c 19.

under this or a subsequent Act in 1544,[58] and it was only eventually constituted in 1551, following a third Statute, passed in 1550.[59] The commission's first draft was rejected by Parliament in 1553.[60] The full text of the *Reformatio* of 1552 was published by John Foxe in April 1571, with an introduction encouraging its adoption by Parliament alongside the reformed Articles of Religion and liturgy. The text was introduced in Parliament that same month, but the only immediate result was to cause the bishops to promise to deal with canon law reform in Convocation. The subject matter of the *Reformatio* was intended to replace the existing canon law wholesale. Gerald Bray analyses the content thematically under: doctrine, sacraments, benefices, worship, ministry, discipline, courts and their procedure, crimes, the rules of law.[61]

Edmund Gibson, in his influential *Codex*, quoted from the *Reformatio* extensively. His technique was to use the *Reformatio* as an authoritative statement, by learned men, of the existing laws in force in the mid-sixteenth century. Recognising that certain passages that clearly advocated a change in the existing law (such as those on divorce) could not be treated in that way, this approach was successful, and we later find the *Reformatio* being used in this way in the courts (indeed, Gibson claimed that it had already been so used in the case of *Haynes v Jescott*).[62] In 1792, Sir William Scott, giving judgment in the consistory court of London, justified his interpretation of certain canons (as to the lawfulness of chanting in parish churches) by quoting from the *Reformatio*; it was 'a work of great authority in determining the practice of those times, whatever may be its correctness in matters of law'.[63]

G. The Canons of 1571

The failed Revolt of the Northern Earls in 1569, and the papal Bull *Regnans in excelsis* of 1570, solidified the direction of travel for the Church in England. The Articles of Religion were re-affirmed in their current form (Article 29, which offended Lutherans, having been reinstated). An attempt to have the draft *Reformatio Legum Ecclesiasticarum* adopted was introduced in Parliament by

---

[58] 35 Henry VIII c 16.
[59] 3 & 4 Edw VI c 11, which extended to 'the Ecclesiastical Laws of long time here used'. For an analysis of the precise scope of these Acts, see N Doe, 'Pre-Reformation Roman Canon Law in Post-Reformation English Ecclesiastical Law' (2022) 24 *Ecclesiastical Law Journal* 273–94, 288–92, esp 291–92.
[60] JC Spalding, *The Reformation of the Ecclesiastical Laws of England, 1552* (Kirksville, MO, Sixteenth Century Journal Publishers, 1992) 41.
[61] See also the monumental study, G Bray (ed), *Tudor Church Reform: The Henrician Canons of 1535 and the Reformatio Legum Ecclesiasticarum* (Woodbridge, Boydell Press, 2000) xli–clv; and, for the text of the *Reformatio*, ibid 145–743.
[62] *Haynes v Jescott* 5 Mod Rep 168–70.
[63] *Hutchins v Denziloe* 1 Hag Con 179, 161 ER 518; quoting s 19.6 of the *Reformatio*. See Bray (n 61) cvi–cxiii, an expanded version of G Bray, 'The Strange Afterlife of the *Reformatio Legum Ecclesiasticarum*' in Doe, Hill and Ombres (eds) (n 41) 36–47.

Thomas Morton on 5 April 1571. This proposal did not find favour with the queen or the bishops, and the latter countered by promising to draw up a new set of canons in Convocation.[64] A draft was ready before the Convocation dissolved on 30 May, and was sent to the queen by Archbishop Parker on 4 June.[65] The final version, which was in Latin, was signed by the bishops of both provinces, and had been printed by August.[66]

The Canons were a mixture of old and new. Standard topics, such as the requirements for ordination (Canon 1.6), archdeacons' examination of clergy (Canon 3.3) and the licensing of preachers (Canon 6.1), were firmly rooted in the tradition of the *Corpus juris canonici*, with the last of these being more clearly defined at the Council of Oxford in 1407 as an anti-Lollard measure. The preponderance of these canons, however, demonstrated a more protestant ecclesiology. The rediscovery of the bishop as the chief evangelist (Canon 1.1) in the diocese was based on ancient precedent, but the category of 'preachers' (clerical or lay) alongside clergy who were not licensed to preach was typical of this approach, as was the requirement for less educated clergy to memorise parts of the New Testament and recite them at the diocesan synod.[67]

The 1571 Canons also began the process of giving (or strengthening) the legal authority of some previous provisions, such as the Royal Injunctions of 1559 (Canons 2.5 and 5.11); the Advertisements of 1566 (Canons 5.5, 5.11, 6.3 and 9.2); and Archbishop Parker's Table of 1563 (Canon 10.5).

How was the legal effect of these canons understood at this time? Relying on subsequent legal developments, particularly those in the common law courts, will not give the correct answer, as Richard Helmholz has demonstrated.[68] The most striking example of this is the decision in *Middleton v Crofts* (1736),[69] that the 1603 Canons (and, presumably, on the same basis, the Elizabethan canons) did not, *proprio vigore*, bind the laity. The legal understanding of the canons in the sixteenth century did not recognise such a distinction or limit its binding effect (although it recognised other restrictions in the tradition of the Roman *ius commune*).[70]

III. Period Two: Archbishop Grindal (1575–83)

Archbishop Edmund Grindal was more of a puritan sympathiser than his predecessor. His support for puritan 'prophesyings' led to him earning the displeasure

---

[64] Spalding (n 60) 51.
[65] Bray (ed) (n 32) VII 468–484.
[66] Bray, *The Anglican Canons* (n 26) xlviii. Spalding suggests that the queen refused to authorise these canons specifically, being of the view that any act of Convocation was authorised by her, leading, once again, to legal ambiguity about the exact status of the legislation: Spalding (n 60) 52.
[67] Bray, *The Anglican Canons* (n 26) xlviii–l.
[68] RH Helmholz, 'The Canons of 1603: The Contemporary Understanding' in Doe, Hill and Ombres (eds) (n 41) 23–35.
[69] *Middleton v Crofts* (1736) 2 Atk 650.
[70] Helmholz (n 68) 28–30.

of the Queen and being sequestered at her command: in May 1577 the Privy Council deprived him of all ecclesiastical jurisdiction and imposed a kind of house arrest.[71] Despite a number of attempts, including an address from Convocations in 1581, the sequestration was never lifted. This left the newly appointed Bishop of London, John Aylmer, as Dean of the Southern Province, exercising metropolitical jurisdiction during the suspension and indeed until Grindal's death in 1583.[72]

The principal legal landmark in this period was the promulgation of the Canons of 1575.[73] Grindal was not able to go back on the 1566 Advertisements or the 1571 Canons, but in the short window of 100 days between his consecration and his sequestration, he was able to steer through Convocations a short set of canons addressing one of the concerns of the puritans: unlearned clergy.[74] Fifteen canons were agreed, largely on the education, training and appointment of the parish clergy.[75] These became 13 canons after the queen refused to approve two of them – one forbidding the administration of baptism by lay persons, and the other permitting the public solemnisation of marriage all year round.[76]

IV. Period Three: Archbishop Whitgift (1583–1603)

After the impasse of Grindal's primacy, the appointment of John Whitgift as Archbishop of Canterbury initiated another period of reform. Whitgift, like Parker, was unsympathetic to puritans and had the queen's confidence. Partly due to the foundations established in Parker's time, he was able to take a stronger line against the puritans. His legal reforms were more of a consolidation of what had been laid down before, and he was able to make detailed improvements in church administration by Articles, canons and archiepiscopal legislation.

A. Articles for the Clergy

Archbishop John Whitgift's first task was to continue the fight against puritanism, and within a month of his appointment he had issued 12 Articles for the

---

[71] The exact terms of the sequestration are uncertain as no text of the order (if there ever was a text) has survived: P Collinson, *Archbishop Grindal 1519–1583: The Struggle for a Reformed Church* (London, Jonathan Cape 1979) 248; P Collinson, 'The Prophesyings and the Downfall and Sequestration of Archbishop Edmund Grindal 1576–1583' in M Barber, S Taylor and G Sewell (eds), *From the Reformation to the Permissive Society* (Woodbridge, Boydell Press, 2010) 1–41.
[72] P Collinson, J Craig and B Usher (eds), *Conferences and Combination Lectures in the Elizabethan Church, 1582–1590* (Woodbridge, Boydell Press, 2003) xxvii, xxxiv–xxxix.
[73] 1576 in modern dating.
[74] Collinson, *Archbishop Grindal 1519–1583* (n 71) 219–32.
[75] Bray (ed) (n 32) VII, 493–498.
[76] Bray, *The Anglican Canons* (n 26) li, 211–15. They were published on 17 March: Bray (ed) (n 32) XIX, 162. See also J Strype, *The History of the Life and Acts of The Most Reverend Father in God Edmund Grindal* (Oxford, Clarendon Press 1821) 287–92.

Clergy. Although they had no legal force, 10 of them became the source of 12 of the Canons of 1603.[77] These provisions include uniformity of worship, regulation of preaching and apparel of ministers, qualifications for holy orders and appointment to benefices, and regulation of matrimony. Only the Articles about the authorised translation of the Bible and the commutation of penance failed to make the cut, although the latter did make it into the Canons of 1584.

B. The Canons of 1584

The House of Commons petitioned Convocation in December of 1584.[78] The Archbishops of York and Canterbury replied in February, but it also spurred Convocation on to enact six new canons the following month.[79] The canons dealt with admission to ministry and benefices, commutation of penance, restricting marriage by licence, regulation of excommunication, restriction of pluralities, ecclesiastical fees and inquiries to be undertaken by bishops.

C. Further Archiepiscopal Legislation

Archbishop Whitgift continued a programme of legislation using instruments of various types. In this period, highlights include 'statutes' for the ecclesiastical courts (1587), additional 'articles' concerning the ecclesiastical laws (1591), and the 'orders' of 1593. All of these were to become material sources for some of the Canons Ecclesiastical of 1603.[80]

The statutes for the ecclesiastical courts are self-explanatory: detailed provisions for the internal procedures of the courts, replacing but improving similar previous documents, but the other two documents are more unusual. The Articles of 1591 are short: five Articles in total, two of which contain an acknowledgement of the supremacy of the Crown in ecclesiastical jurisdiction, and two of which assert that episcopal governance of the Church is lawful and allowable by the word of God: any other form of government is unlawful and dangerous. The fifth Article asserts that the Church of England is a true member of the true Church of Christ, whose sacraments are godly and rightly ministered. The Orders of 1593 also deal briefly with a range of procedural matters: enquiries to be made before the admission of ministers and records to be kept; requirements for the form of marriage licences and the consent of parents; procedures relating to citations; the warnings to be given during excommunication; tables of fees to be produced; requirements of conformity before ordination or admission

---

[77] Bray, *The Anglican Canons* (n 26) lii, 770–72.
[78] 1585 in modern dating.
[79] Bray, *The Anglican Canons* (n 26) li–lii; 216–31; Bray (ed) (n 32) VII 510–17.
[80] Bray, *The Anglican Canons* (n 26) lxxxix–xc, 782–816.

to benefices; and provision for the absolution of the poor from excommunication without paying fees.

D. The Canons of 1597

Whitgift's (and Elizabeth's) last canons were the 12 canons passed by Convocation in 1597,[81] once more prompted by agitation from the House of Commons. They were largely a reissue of the 1584 Canons, but went further in preventing certain abuses – they introduced the fixed table of fees and a standard form of marriage licence. For much of the Elizabethan period, there was a considerable opinion that divorce for adultery was *a vinculo matrimonii*. Canon 6 of these canons clarified the illegality of a further marriage after a judicial separation, which was confirmed the following year with the Star Chamber case of *Rye v Foljambe*.[82] For the first time, the queen approved these canons under the Great Seal of England, and ordered that they be observed in the province of York as well as Canterbury.[83]

V. The Ecclesiastical Courts and Lawyers

During Elizabeth's reign, the volume of litigation in the courts increased, and the standard of record keeping also saw a marked improvement.[84] The courts' wide jurisdiction was largely unchanged. For example, the provincial Chancery Court of York, under its original jurisdiction, over the years 1570–74, entertained 134 instance and office cases, including: 21 on institution to a benefice; seven on sexual immorality; four on administration of wills; three on clerical non-residence; two on marriage; and one on tithes. In 1594–95, there were 98 causes, with a similar breakdown.[85] After 1559, appeals form 'a small but integral part' of the York diocesan Consistory Court and its provincial Chancery Court – most instance suits to the Consistory with office suits to Chancery; both dealt with wills. For instance, over the years 1570–74 there was only one appeal each year; over 1579–84, there were seven, two each from Chester, Carlisle, and York, and one from Sodor and Man; none from Durham.[86]

---

[81] 1598 in modern dating.
[82] *Rye v Foljambe* (1598) 72 ER 838. L Stone, *Road to Divorce* (Oxford, Oxford University Press, 1990) 302–07. See also JH Baker, 'Some Elizabethan Marriage Cases' in TL Harris (ed), *Studies in Canon Law and Common Law in Honor of RH Helmholz* (Berkeley, CA, The Robbins Collection, 2015) 181–211.
[83] Bray, *The Anglican Canons* (n 26) liii–liv; 232–257; Bray (ed) (n 32) VII 590–601.
[84] Helmholz (n 46) 42–43.
[85] CIA Ritchie, *The Ecclesiastical Courts of York* (Arbroath, The Herald Press, 1956) 29–31.
[86] WJ Sheils, *Ecclesiastical Cause Papers at York: Files Transmitted on Appeal 1500–1883* (York, University of York, Borthwick Institute of Historical Research, 1983) iv–vi; Ritchie (n 85) 33; RA Marchant, *The Church under the Law: Justice, Administration and Discipline in the Diocese of York 1560–1640* (Cambridge, Cambridge University Press, 1969) 64, 66, 68.

As well as new courts for the newly erected dioceses, the Court of Delegates was re-established by the revival of the statutes forbidding appeals to Rome (after their repeal under Mary); but rather than ad hoc commissions, as had been the case in former times, in the Elizabethan period it became a true standing court, with regular sittings and permanent officials.[87] The new Court of High Commission (Commissioners for Causes Ecclesiastical) was created to enforce the new settlement.[88] The basis of the Court's jurisdiction, originally rooted in the royal prerogative, was now section 8 of the Act of Supremacy 1559, which annexed to the Crown all ecclesiastical jurisdiction previously exercised for the visitation, order or correction of the ecclesiastical state and persons.[89] The actual jurisdiction of the Commission was set out in each of the letters patent appointing commissioners. Eight of these general commissions were issued in Elizabeth's reign for the southern province, beginning in 1559.[90] The Court could hear any ecclesiastical cause at first instance or on appeal, alongside the jurisdiction of the regular courts. Unlike the church courts, however, it could imprison and fine to enforce its orders. Although it would routinely decline merely ecclesiastical cases (such as routine matrimonial cases), it would become involved to enforce the orders of the church courts or to punish clergy who had flouted the ecclesiastical law.

The proliferation of litigation also saw a flourishing of legal and civilian scholarship in England. Ironically, references to Roman canon law texts began to appear in consistory court records for the first time. As the Elizabethan settlement became more stable, the civilians became bolder in defending the ecclesiastical jurisdiction. Against this optimism, there were also threats. This included the encroachment of the common law through statute and the use of prohibition, and a widespread lingering suspicion towards the Roman canon law.[91]

This period also marks the beginnings of a distinctly Anglican jurisprudence, though even some reformers still valued the Roman canon law to the extent it continued to apply in England; Ralph Lever, for instance offers one of the earliest Elizabethan statements that Roman canon law was by statute a 'wholesome part' of English law.[92] The two big names of this period were probably born within

---

[87] GIO Duncan, *The High Court of Delegates* (Cambridge, Cambridge University Press, 1971); GR Elton, *The Tudor Constitution* (Cambridge, Cambridge University Press, 1968) ch 7.

[88] RG Usher, *The Rise and Fall of the High Commission* (Oxford, Clarendon Press, 1913).

[89] 1 Eliz c 1 s 8.

[90] Seven of these are now extant: LH Carlson, 'The Court of High Commission: A Newly Discovered Elizabethan Letters Patent, 20 June 1589' (1982) 45 *Huntingdon Library Quarterly* 295–315, 295–96. A separate Commission was appointed for the northern Province, starting in 1561: EJ Carlson, 'Marriage Reform and the Elizabethan High Commission' (1990) 21 *The Sixteenth Century Journal* 437–52, 443–44, citing P Tyler, *The Ecclesiastical Commission for the Province of York* (DPhil Thesis, University of Oxford, 1965).

[91] Helmholz (n 46) 41–54. RB Outhwaite, *The Rise and Fall of the English Ecclesiastical Courts, 1500–1860* (Cambridge, Cambridge University Press, 2006).

[92] See, eg, N Doe, 'Rediscovering Anglican-Priest-Jurists: V – Ralph Lever (c 1530–1585)' (2023) 25 *Ecclesiastical Law Journal* 66–80.

a year or so of each other: Richard Hooker (1554–1600) and Henry Swinburne (c 1555–1624). The influence of both of these Elizabethans was largely to be felt after the queen's reign, but both published some of their important work during it.

As Master of the Temple in the 1580s, Hooker was engaged in the so-called 'Battle of the Pulpit' with his Calvinist Reader, Walter Travers, who had been passed over as Master by Hooker's appointment.[93] This exchange, almost certainly observed by a young Edward Coke, won Hooker the esteem of Archbishop John Whitgift, who encouraged him to write a book supporting Whitgift's campaign against the puritans.[94] This resulted in an eight-volume work, *The Laws of Ecclesiastical Polity*, in which Hooker set out extensively a basis for what would become known as 'Anglicanism', following a very similar pragmatic *via media*, which appeared to have been favoured by the queen herself.[95] Paul Avis defines '*Ecclesiastical Polity*' as 'a form of applied ecclesiology, underpinned by canon law'.[96] Although not a lawyer by training or profession, the evidence demonstrates that Hooker not only had extensive knowledge of the pre-Reformation canonical sources, but was also adept at handling them; and Norman Doe considers *The Laws* to be 'first and foremost a law book'.[97]

In articulating a coherent legal and theological basis for the Settlement, Hooker drew on a wide range of earlier sources, not simply Scripture, thus marking out a different and more complex path from those of the 'puritans', who are his unseen protagonists. In particular, he referred to the 'authorities of Councils',[98] and did so on many aspects of Christian life and discipline.[99] He referred to the canon law of the Roman Church on many issues, citing Gratian widely, commended the study of civil law, and regarded custom and tradition as authoritative.[100] The first part of the *Laws* appeared in print in 1593, but when Hooker died in 1600 (aged 46), three of the books remained unpublished, and it would be over 60 years before they were all in print.[101]

---

[93] D Little, 'God v Caesar: Sir Edward Coke and the Struggles of His Time' (2016) 18 *Ecclesiastical Law Journal* 292.
[94] D MacCulloch, 'Richard Hooker: Invention and Reinvention' (2009) 21 *Ecclesiastical Law Journal* 137–52, 138. See also J Strype, *The Life and Acts of John Whitgift DD*, vol II (Oxford, Clarendon Press, 1822) 199–202 and 393–95.
[95] MacCulloch (n 94) 139.
[96] P Avis, 'Polity and Polemics: The Function of Ecclesiastical Polity in Theology and Practice' (2016) 18 *Ecclesiastical Law Journal* 2–13, 2.
[97] RH Helmholz, 'Richard Hooker and the European *Ius Commune*' (2001) 6 *Ecclesiastical Law Journal* 4–11, 5–6; N Doe, 'Richard Hooker, Priest and Jurist' in M Hill and RH Helmholz (eds), *Great Christian Jurists in English History* (Cambridge, Cambridge University Press, 2017) 115–38.
[98] Book VI, 6.10.
[99] Doe, in 'Richard Hooker' (n 97), gives the following examples: excommunication, Nicaea, Canons 11–13 (VI.5.8); reading Scripture, Laodicea, Canon 59 (V.20.1); keeping Sunday, Apostolic Canons, Canon 55 (V.72.10); and barring bishops from uninvited ministry outside their diocese, Antioch, Canon 9 and First Council of Constantinople, Canon 2 (VII.8.3).
[100] Doe (n 97) 122–23.
[101] Books I–IV were published in 1593, and it took 11 years to sell the 1,200 or so copies that were printed. Book V (which was more than the size of the first four put together) followed in 1597, but books VI and VIII did not appear until 1648 and book VII not until 1662: N Sagovsky, 'Hooker, Warburton

They would turn out to have a continuing and lasting influence in successive centuries.[102]

Swinburne, on the other hand, was an advocate and judge in the ecclesiastical courts in York. His three years studying for the degree of Bachelor of Civil Law at Oxford would have overlapped with Hooker's time there. His principal work, *A Briefe Treatise of Testaments and Last Wills*, was first published in 1590.[103] This landmark tome was not only the first on the canon law to be written in English, but arguably also the first modern textbook on English law. It was organised systematically, with full references to the extensive sources, and remained in print under successive editors for over 200 years.[104] At this later juncture in Elizabeth's reign, Swinburne was part of a consolidation exercise: he recognises in his preface that the codification foreseen earlier in the century was unlikely to materialise in the near future. The longer title of his work includes the words 'Compiled of such laws Ecclesiastical and Civill, as be not repugnant to the lawes, customs, or statutes of this Realme nor derogatory to the Prerogative Royall'. This clearly acknowledges that the basis of the canon law in England for the foreseeable future was to be that set out in the statute of 1534.[105] Swinburne's other major work, *Treatise of Spousals, or Matrimonial Contracts*, remained unfinished on his death in 1623, and was not published until 1686. Though original, however, Swinburne arguably also represented 'one of the last major English legal writers in the *ius commune* tradition'.[106]

Less well known, but possibly at least as influential as Hooker and Swinburne during Queen Elizabeth's reign itself, is Sir Daniel Dun, of Welsh forebears. Dun graduated as a Doctor of Civil Law at Oxford in 1580, entered Doctors' Commons in 1582 and was an ecclesiastical judge by 1585; and he had risen to become Dean of the Arches by 1598.[107] Helmholz sets out the evidence that Dun was a leader among lawyers who kept the learning of the traditional *ius commune* alive and successfully defended the existing law against the 'silent critic' of the *Reformatio*.[108] Whilst doing this, he also encouraged improvements in the way in which the ecclesiastical courts worked, and defended their independence from the encroachments of the common lawyers.

---

and Coleridge and the "Quadruple Lock": State and Church in the Twenty-first Century' (2014) 16 *Ecclesiastical Law Journal* 140–46, 141; P Hughes, *The Reformation in England*, vol III (London, Hollis and Carter, 1954) 226–27.

[102] See MacCulloch (n 94) and Sagovsky (n 101), and also R Williams, 'Richard Hooker: The Laws of Ecclesiastical Polity Revisited' (2006) 8 *Ecclesiastical Law Journal* 382–91.

[103] JH Baker, *Monuments of Endlesse Labours: English Canonists and their Work 1300–1900* (London, Hambledon Press, 1998) 60.

[104] The 7th (and final) English edition was published in three volumes in 1803: ibid 66 (there had also been two printings of what became known as the 4th edition, as well as an Irish 7th edition).

[105] Submission of the Clergy Act 1533, 25 Hen VIII c 19.

[106] Baker (n 103) 69.

[107] GD Squibb, *Doctors' Commons* (Oxford, Clarendon Press, 1977) 116.

[108] RH Helmholz, 'Notable Ecclesiastical Lawyers: V – Sir Daniel Dun (c 1545–1617)' (2014) 16 *Ecclesiastical Law Journal* 205–10.

VI. Church-Related Social Legislation

Two other interlinked 'spin-offs' from the Reformation's impact on ecclesiastical law were the beginnings, in Elizabeth's reign, of modern charity law, and of the poor law that lasted until the twentieth century. Both of these have their origins in the suppression and appropriation of the monasteries and chantries, and the impact these had on the social and legal infrastructure.

A. Statutes of Charitable Uses 1597 and 1601

Before the Reformation, bequests to pious causes, charitable bequests, were largely a matter for canon law.[109] However, the involvement of the Chancellor in feoffments to uses from the fifteenth century onwards provided a channel that was to allow the transition to the secular jurisdiction. Once the Edwardian legislation had introduced the concept of the 'superstitious use', 'piety and charity could no longer be to all Englishmen synonymous conceptions'.[110] This secularisation of objects led to a shift from the church courts to that of the Chancellor, and to procedural reform in the shape of the Statute of Charitable Uses 1601. This set the scene for the development of the law for the next 400 years, and its preamble set the framework for the substantive jurisprudence on the scope of charity until the early twenty-first century.[111]

B. The Poor Law

The dissolution of the monasteries had removed a major support infrastructure for the poor, and had at the same time increased the importance of the parish as the primary unit of local administration.[112] The Poor Relief Acts 1597 and 1601,[113] built on earlier foundations,[114] put in place a parish-based welfare system that was to last until the twentieth century. The Elizabethan Poor Law was superseded by the modern (national) welfare state of Beveridge in the 1940s, foreshadowed by Lloyd George four decades earlier, but the last provisions of the 1601 Act were not finally repealed until 1967.[115] Churchwardens, alongside

---

[109] RH Helmholz, *The Canon Law and Ecclesiastical Jurisdiction from 597 to the 1640s* (Oxford, Oxford University Press, 2004) 417–23.
[110] G Jones, *History of the Law of Charity 1532–1827* (Cambridge, Cambridge University Press, 1969) 3–15, esp 15.
[111] ibid 16–58.
[112] N Orme, *Going to Church in Medieval England* (Newhaven. CT, Yale University Press, 2021) 390.
[113] 39 Eliz c 3 and 43 Eliz c 2.
[114] Obligations to contribute to the 'poor man's box' date at least from 27 Hen VII c 25, and were enforced in the Elizabethan ecclesiastical courts: Helmholz (n 109) 468–70.
[115] General Rate Act 1967, sch 14.

their religious duties, were also given responsibilities for certain matters now assigned to secular local government.[116]

VII. Conclusion

By the end of Elizabeth's long reign, the settlement was far stronger than at the beginning, when some elements were quite precarious. By the clever use of ambiguous authority, a path had been negotiated that did not put the queen (and her authority) in more danger than necessary but had created at least a quasi-legal order, which was able to be consolidated as the settlement became stronger. In theological terms, the settlement was a *via media* compared to religious reform in other countries; but in legal terms, the Church of England ended up as the least reformed Church in Europe. This continuity, too, had played its part in bolstering the authority of the canon and ecclesiastical law. With hindsight, we know that many of the important legal instruments discussed in this chapter turned out to be authoritative, but that is not to say that such would have been obvious to those dealing with them at the time.

The laws of the new polity were to be found in many different instruments: parliamentary statutes, Orders in Council, rubrics in the Book of Common Prayer, the Articles of Religion, Canons of Convocation and decisions of the courts. There was continuity in practical terms, in spite of the major religious and constitutional changes, with many areas of law now regarded as secular remaining within the ecclesiastical jurisdiction for 200 or 300 years.[117] Although diminished in their normative doctrinal significance, the Thirty-Nine Articles continue to feature in contemporary ecclesiastical regulation and case law. Similarly, the Canons, admittedly in amended form, continue to be a primary source of law for Church of England clergy and judges, featuring in both the faculty and disciplinary jurisdictions.[118] The evolution of the Elizabethan settlement in the constitutional and religious life of the United Kingdom will be traced in later chapters, but we can note here its foundational significance and enduring influence for the ordering and worship of the Church of England.

---

[116] William Lambarde, *The Duties of Constables* (1601) lists among the functions of churchwardens the annual election of overseers of highways (deriving from a 1555 statute of Mary I but extended by Elizabeth I in 1562) and *The Distributors of the prouision for the destruction of noisome foule and vermine*, an early system of public health regulation.

[117] See *Halsbury's Laws of England*, 5th edn, vol 34 (LexisNexis, 2011) 865–66, paras 1022, 1024.

[118] See, eg, *Re Holy Trinity Wandsworth* [2012], a faculty judgment in which Petchey Ch conducted an extensive historical survey on the law relating to the position and number of fonts, starting with Canon F7, available at www.ecclesiasticallawassociation.org.uk/index.php/judgements/repairs/search-result?filter_category_id=12&filter_search=fonts&layout=columns&show_category=0 (accessed 27 December 2022); and *Chedzey v Evans* [2022], a disciplinary tribunal decision in which an issue that arose as to emergency baptism was discussed by reference to Canon B22, available at www.churchofengland.org/sites/default/files/2022-03/Tribunal%20decision%20on%20facts%20and%20conduct%2009.12.21%20FINAL.pdf (accessed 27 December 2022).

4

The Source and Limit of the King's Ecclesiastical Law: 1603–60

IAN BLANEY

It is difficult to provide an adequate account of the history of the ecclesiastical law in the period commencing with the ascension of James I of England and ending with the restoration of the monarchy in 1660. It was a busy and tumultuous period in the law, particularly because of intervention by Act of Parliament and because of legislative efforts to reconstruct the Church after the execution of Charles I. Due to the many political and religious events, the period is a rich seam to explore the source and limits of the ecclesiastical jurisdiction in matters legal. While academic texts abound on the constitutional, political, theological and social reverberations of the period, it is important not to lose track of the actual legal developments that underlie these.

After the neglect and disempowerment of the Church under Elizabeth I, James I and Charles I strengthened the institutions of the Church by supporting the episcopacy and giving the Church more financial independence. On accession, James I convened the Hampton Court Conference (January 1604) to consider calls for church reform in the Millenary Petition 1603. The king sided with the bishops, and the administration of Archbishop of Canterbury Richard Bancroft (1604–10) saw a confident reassertion of canon law, church courts and clergy discipline. In 1603, new canons received the royal assent, and in 1611 a new vernacular Bible – the King James Bible – was approved, with a view to producing consistency in biblical interpretation. Under Charles I, William Laud was made Archbishop of Canterbury (1633–45) and promoted the 'beauty of holiness' – that church buildings, vestments and liturgy should edify and uplift the people. The backlash against the prerogatives of the Church and the 'Laudian' reforms was given energy, however, on the weakening of the king and the episcopacy after 1640, which led to the suppression of the instruments of Laudianism, the abolition of the episcopacy, the king's execution, the establishment of a presbyterian national Church and unsettled religious toleration.[1]

---

[1] See further A Milton (ed), *The Oxford History of Anglicanism*, vol I: *Reformation and Identity c 1520-1662* (Oxford, Oxford University Press, 2017); JP Kenyon (ed), *The Stuart Constitution*

The main theme of this chapter is the constitutional attachment of ecclesiastical lawyers to the king, the jurisdictional clash between the church courts and the common lawyers, and the impact this had on the substantive ecclesiastical law. In a nutshell, it explores the claimed source of the authority of the church courts and the limits to that authority. In the reign of James I (1603–25) the authority of the church courts was theoretically strong, but subject to attack from the common lawyers and by some in Parliament. This chapter will show the alliance between royal and church authority and how that gave strength to the ecclesiastical law. In the reign of Charles I (1625–49) that theme continues, but with the weakening of the king and his eventual execution – and the church courts are first shorn of their coercive authority and then swept away altogether. The first main legislative measures to diminish the church courts are in 1641. The period following 1641 and ending in 1660 involves various phases of government, and varying levels of religious radicalism, first the setting up of an established Presbyterian Church in 1646, and then substantial legal religious toleration from around 1653, before a return to a more conservative approach in 1657. The years 1643 to 1660, as this chapter will set out to show, were without ecclesiastical law as we would define it – because the Church of England as an episcopal Church was legally suspended. However, this was a fertile period for new state law of religion, which provides a comparison with the periods that precede and follow it. The Church of England and the church courts were then restored in 1660.

I. Legal Landmarks in the Jacobean and Caroline Church

A. The Canons of 1603

Our period opens with the making of the Canons of 1603. They were comprehensive, and to a large extent codified church teaching, practice and rules. They were also long-lasting; they were revised (in a limited fashion) in 1865 and survived until 1969. Of the 141 Canons, 44 were new and related to procedure in church courts, the others were based largely on the old canon law. The Canons covered the constitutional and doctrinal foundations of the Church of England; divine service and the sacraments; ministers, their ordination, function and charge; schoolmasters; the fabric and furnishings of churches; churchwardens and sidesmen; parish clerks; the ecclesiastical courts and their officers; and synods. Gerald Bray provides an excellent synopsis:

1603–1688: Documents and Commentary (Cambridge, Cambridge University Press, 1986, repr 1993) 111–17, 'The Jacobean Church' and the documents that follow, including 'The Millenary Petition 1603' (document 39), 'A Proclamation enjoining conformity etc' 1604 (document 40), 'Commons petition on religion 1610 (document 43), 'The Laudian Revolution' (130–36); 'A proclamation [on] the Church of England' 1626 (document 46); 165–71, 'The Catholic Problem'.

The canons of 1603 (1604) were the most serious attempt the post-reformation church ever made to reduce its canon law to order. The 141 canons were collected by Bishop Bancroft (as he then still was) out of the articles, injunctions and synodical acts published in the reigns of Edward VI and Elizabeth I. The canons were passed by the convocation of Canterbury in the 1604 session, and were confirmed by letters patent under the great seal. The king wished to impose them unilaterally on the province of York, but objections to this led to a separate ratification by the northern convocation in 1606. However, their authority as law was severely contested by parliament, which maintained that the clergy had no power to create offences that might be subject to civil punishments. The bishops did their best to override parliamentary objections, but an early dissolution made it impossible for either side to carry the day. In the end, the decision was made by the judges of Westminster Hall, who declared that the canons of 1603 (1604) bind the clergy who framed them, but not the laity …[2]

The finessing and confirmation of this statement, that the canons bind the clergy only, was not reached until the decision of the Court of Chancery in the case of *Middleton v Crofts* (1736), in which it was held that the Canons of 1603, not having been confirmed by Parliament, do not *proprio vigore* (of their own force) bind the laity.[3]

B. The Source of Ecclesiastical Authority

With the benefit of hindsight, we now view the 1603 Canons as legislation made by and for the Church with limited authority over the laity – but this was not something that was settled in 1603. It is also the case that the Canons were applied by the church courts in matters involving the laity, and such matters could lead to sanctions being imposed against the laity. However, the arguments around the authority and effect of the 1603 Canons is something of a fundamental question for this period, namely: what is the source of ecclesiastical authority, which has one of its expressions in ecclesiastical law, and what are the limits of that authority? Conflict between the courts of the common law and the church courts was hardly new by this time, but in this period it was particularly rife. In 1605, Archbishop Bancroft of Canterbury presented a formal protest to the king about the use of writs of prohibition. In this, the archbishop argued that as all legal jurisdiction, both temporal and spiritual, flowed from the Crown, it was for the king to determine where the boundaries between the two jurisdictions lay, and that the common law judges were overreaching themselves.

---

[2] G Bray (ed), *The Anglican Canons 1529–1947* (Woodbridge, Boydell Press, 1998) 258. See further G Bray, 'Canon Law and the Church of England' in Milton (ed) (n 1) 168–85.
[3] *Middleton v Croft* (1736) 95 ER 211. The *Case of Proclamations* (1611) confirmed that the king could make no law without the consent of Parliament. For earlier cases on the issue, see RH Helmholz, 'The Canons of 1603: The Contemporary Understanding' in N Doe, M Hill and R Ombres (eds), *English Canon Law* (Cardiff, University of Wales Press, 1998) 23–36.

The answer of the judges was prepared by Chief Justice Coke, who, while careful not to impugn the king's ecclesiastical authority, argued that the practice of prohibitions was lawfully established and could only be altered by Act of Parliament.[4] Thus, the royal authority under which the archbishop asserted the Church's rights was limited, in that the Crown's law-making power could only be exercised through Parliament. This was a period when the extent of the royal prerogative itself was debatable, and in the extra-judicial opinion known as the *Case of Proclamations* (1611), the two chief justices held that the king may not create new offences by proclamation alone, and the king had no prerogative but that which the law of the land allows him, and could only use proclamations to admonish subjects in relation to existing laws. The judges said 'the law of England is divided into three parts, common law, statute law, and custom, but the King's proclamation is none of them'.[5]

The disputations between Coke and King James were emblematic of differing constitutional and legal opinions on the role of the Crown in the governance of the kingdom. Coke stood for the independence of the judiciary and the free application of the common law and statute law by the judges. The king held that all justice, in both the temporal and the spiritual courts, derives from the supremacy of the Crown, and that the king had a freestanding ability to make interventions. In response, Coke argued that any change in the law or intervention had to be justified by legal precedent or authorised by Act of Parliament. While in former ages, bishops may have sought to dispute the supremacy of the Crown in matters spiritual, in this age they were more likely to cling to the royal supremacy as an ecclesial fundamental.

The consequence of this is that the bishops and the place of ecclesiastical law were at the same time in a strong and a weak position. While the king commanded wide powers, there were voices in Parliament and in the judiciary that sought to check that power by requiring legislation to exist solely in Acts of Parliament. Thus, when the Convocations passed new canons in 1603 that obtained royal assent, that was sufficient for them to have legal force but, as mentioned, their enforceability against the laity was said to be limited because Parliament had not approved them.

There was also a specific disputation between Coke and Lord Chancellor Ellesmere on whether the ecclesiastical law was an autonomous branch of the law of the land, or whether the ecclesiastical law rested in the Crown by the authority of the common law. Their disputation has been analysed by Conrad Russell who sets out the opposing positions of Coke on the one hand, and the king and bishops on the other; Russell concludes 'Up to the end of James's reign,

---

[4] 'Certain Articles of Abuses which are desired to be reformed in granting of Prohibitions, and the Answers thereunto' in JR Tanner, *Constitutional Documents of James I* (Cambridge, Cambridge University Press, 1930) 177–86.

[5] The Reports of Sir Edward Coke (1572–1617), *Twelfth Report* (1777 edn); 'Proclamations, 1610' in Tanner (n 4) 187–88.

the legislative and jurisdictional independence of the clergy appeared fairly safe. It was securely defended by the King, and it was as strong as the King was.'[6] However, while the royal supremacy of Henry VIII over the Church had subjugated its institutions and prerogatives to the Crown, the royal supremacy itself had been authorised by a series of Acts of Parliament. This meant that, unless the king had sufficient persuasive or coercive authority in Parliament, the Church was liable to be stranded in a political logjam or, worse, on the losing side of a wider jurisdictional conflict between king and Parliament.

Due to royal supremacy over the Church from the time of Henry VIII, the powerful law-making ability of the Sovereign-in-Parliament, concepts about the divine right of kings, and customary privileges long-claimed and revived as part of the Crown's supervisory role, this period contains many examples of legislation enacted by Parliament for the Church. This legislation had the effect of modifying or making new ecclesiastical law.

For example, an Act of 1603 had as its stated aim the prevention of the diminution of the possessions of the archbishops and bishops and avoiding dilapidations of the same. It restricted the disposal of episcopal lands and justified its intervention in the Crown's founding of new bishoprics, with the king as their rightful patron.[7] Much of the religious legislation of James I was concentrated on rooting out Roman Catholic recusants and defending orthodoxy – and it used the officers of the Church to report and prosecute offenders.[8] This went hand-in-hand with the Church's own longstanding method of investigating irregularity: the visitations of bishops and archdeacons in the parishes under their jurisdiction. In the reigns of James I and Charles I there was generally a close compact between Church and State, and this created an amalgam of statute law, canon law, custom and practice that we may quite conveniently call the ecclesiastical law. While Parliament intervened in church affairs, there were also boundaries. For example, the occasional Acts of General Pardon from a whole catalogue of crimes tended to except specifically ecclesiastical offences from its application.[9] Those were spiritual offences in which it would not be right for Crown or Parliament to meddle, and where the sanctions of penance and excommunication derived from a spiritual realm rather than an earthly dominion.

C. Church Court Business before 1640

In the period 1603 until 1640, there was a general growth in the business of the church courts. In the consistory court of York, the number of tithe cases was at

---

[6] C Russell, 'Whose Supremacy? King, Parliament and the Church 1530–1640' (1997) 4 *Ecclesiastical Law Journal* 700–08, 707.
[7] 1 Jac I c 3.
[8] eg 1 Jac I c 4, 'An Act for the due Execution of the Statutes against Jesuits, Seminary Priests, Recusants, etc'.
[9] See, eg, 7 Jac I c 24 and 21 Jac I c 35.

least seven times greater in 1611–12 than in the year 1541–42.[10] Testamentary matters increased, as did the making of wills.[11] Many more slander causes were brought, such as in the London Consistory Court, where numbers rose by 129 per cent between 1572 and 1633.[12] Marriage litigation 'fell to insignificant levels by the 1630s', but marriage licences 'expanded considerably at the same time'.[13] The activity of the church courts in disciplinary matters, arising from visitations and churchwardens' presentments, was high; Outhwaite states that '[c]ertainly in many jurisdictions the volume of corrective activity seems to have increased between 1530 and 1640, perhaps reaching its apogee in the later 1630s, when the see of Canterbury was occupied by William Laud'.[14]

Reasons that have been given to explain the increase in the business of the courts (and decline in some areas) include population growth, inflation, changes in the economy, social mobility, and changes in the customs and manners of the people.[15] In terms of the range and number of cases, church courts remained active and important during the period up to 1640. This despite an increase in the use of writs issuing out of the temporal courts to prohibit ecclesiastical courts from hearing cases that, it was argued, fell within the temporal not spiritual jurisdiction,[16] and the passing of legislation that restricted the ability of the church courts to deal with certain matters. The seeds of later decline in the ecclesiastical jurisdiction were being sown in our period but had not yet fully taken root. Outhwaite expressed this thus:

> [A] few of these statutes effectively removed jurisdiction from the spiritual to the temporal courts, examples of this being the more serious forms of witchcraft, usury, buggery and bigamy. However, none of these, with the possible exception of witchcraft, ever accounted for large numbers of cases coming into the church courts … Other statutes effectively gave the temporal courts concurrent jurisdiction … examples here include aspects of tithe business, and probate where legacies were involved.[17]

Outhwaite continues:

> These measures undoubtedly increased the opportunities for the temporal courts to interfere in the workings of the ecclesiastical courts through the issue of prohibitions. But change was slow and it must not be forgotten that it was in such areas that church

---

[10] WJ Sheils, '"The right of the Church": the clergy, tithe and the courts at York, 1540–1640' in WJ Sheils and D Wood (eds), *The Church and Wealth* (Woodbridge, Boydell & Brewer, 1987) 231–55, 234–36, as cited in RB Outhwaite, *The Rise and Fall of the Ecclesiastical Courts, 1500–1860* (Cambridge, Cambridge University Press, 2006) 26.

[11] Outhwaite (n 10) 33–39.

[12] ibid 41 and the authorities mentioned there.

[13] ibid 49, 50, 54.

[14] ibid 58.

[15] See generally ibid. The population doubled between the early 16th century and the middle of the 17th century.

[16] These were usually about tithes – 75% of all prohibitions issued against proceedings in the church courts involved tithe causes: B Levack, *The Civil Lawyers in England, 1603–41: A Political Study* (Oxford, Oxford University Press, 1973) 76, cited in Outhwaite (n 10) 69.

[17] Outhwaite (n 10) 69.

court business actually expanded during these years ... Perhaps the more serious consequence was that these statutes gave the temporal courts a greater foothold, one that they were subsequently able to enlarge through the continual citing of legal precedents.[18]

Particularly controversial was the *ex officio* oath employed in some courts. This was a religious oath, requiring the swearer to answer all forms of question truthfully, and thus leading to self-incrimination. If the person being asked to swear the oath did not speak truthfully, they would have committed perjury, and if they answered truthfully, they might incriminate themselves. Silence could lead to contempt of court. The oath was abolished in 1641.[19] While not used in the mainstream church courts, it was used by the Court of High Commission, and by the feared Star Chamber. There had been special commissions in ecclesiastical affairs since the time of Henry VIII, but the 'Court' of High Commission was given statutory authority in the Act of Supremacy of 1559. Kenyon describes the High Commission as a 'manifestation of the king's powers as Supreme Governor of the Church of England', which

> had mutated from a visitorial commission dealing only with the clergy into a full-blown court with jurisdiction over almost any crime which could be brought within the purview of Christian morality and able to award almost any punishment short of mutilation or death – not just the ecclesiastical sanctions of deprivation, excommunication and penance.[20]

The Commission, as with the other church courts, was assailed by prohibitive writs from the common law judges during the reign of James I. Due to judicial scepticism regarding the powers of the Commission, James I expressly provided the power to imprison and to use the *ex officio* oath in his commission of 1611.[21]

D. The Use of Royal and Archiepiscopal Instructions

As we saw in chapter 3, Elizabeth's reign saw the use of a range of legal instruments, as such 'Articles', 'orders' and 'injunctions'. Likewise, the relationship between the first two Stuart kings and the bishops was a close one and gave rise to several normative instruments – 'instructions' – with a hybrid character, quasi legislative-executive, and combining and sometimes blurring the powers of the Crown and those of the Church. They include instructions to the Archbishop of Canterbury issued by James I in 1622 regarding preachers, and those of Charles I in 1629 'concerning certain orders to be observed and put in execution by the several Bishops in his province'. The latter required, inter alia, that: the bishops

---

[18] ibid 69–70.
[19] See further J Gray, 'Conscience and the Word of God: Religious Arguments against the *Ex Officio* Oath' (2003) 64 *The Journal of Ecclesiastical History* 494–512.
[20] Kenyon (ed) (n 1) 158. For the High Commission generally, see R Usher, *The Rise and Fall of the High Commission* (Oxford, Clarendon Press, 1913).
[21] Kenyon (ed) (n 1) 159.

keep residence in their dioceses, except when necessary to attend at court; ordinations be of solemn and not unworthy persons; and the clergy not to minister as private chaplains in the houses of persons, except nobles or others qualified by the law to have such. Further and expanded instructions were issued by the king to the archbishop in 1635. No particular legal authority is given by the Crown to issue these instructions in the instructions themselves, but we must see their issuing as one further example of the exercise of the royal supremacy in ecclesiastical matters. However, the 1629 instructions had in fact been devised by the Archbishop of York and Bishop Laud of London in consultation with the king, again reflecting the closeness of royal and episcopal authority during this period. The instructions inter alia required an account to be made annually by the archbishop on prescribed matters. In turn the archbishop served on all of his diocesan bishops annually a list of questions the answers to which were returned on the basis of data provided by their archdeacons.[22] During the years of Charles I's personal rule (1629–40), with the support of prominent bishops the king had a powerful role in directing the Church without reference to Parliament.[23]

Another example of the compact between Church and Crown was the clerical subsidy. It was a custom of the realm that the King-in-Parliament did not tax the clergy. Instead, the clergy were taxed by resolutions of the Convocations of Canterbury and York. For example, an Act of 1605 confirmed the subsidies granted through the Convocation of Canterbury.[24] The Act provided that the bishops would collect the tax from their clergy and that an incumbent would forfeit his benefice on non-payment.[25] There were several such statutes during the reign of James I. An interesting feature of them is that they rely upon the meeting of the Convocation of Canterbury during the session of Parliament; but the statutes apply equally to the Province of York. The clergy continued to be taxed by their convocation (although enforced by Act of Parliament) until the Illegality of Benevolences Act 1661, when the clerical subsidy was replaced by a land and poll tax. According to Burn, a private agreement of 1664 between Archbishop Sheldon and Lord Chancellor Clarendon and other ministers concluded that the clergy should silently waive their privilege of taxing their own body and permit themselves to be included in money bills prepared by the Commons. This made Convocations unnecessary to the Crown and an inconvenience to themselves.[26]

---

[22] The instructions of 1629 and 1635 are reprinted in K Fincham, 'Annual Accounts of the Church of England, 1632–1639' in M Barber and S Taylor with G Sewell (eds), *From the Reformation to the Permissive Society: A miscellany in celebration of the 400th anniversary of Lambeth Palace Library* (Woodbridge, Boydell Press, 2010) 79–81.
[23] See more generally, J Davies, *The Caroline Captivity of the Church* (Oxford, Oxford University Press, 1992) 27–31, 126–71.
[24] 3 Jac I c 25.
[25] This had also been a sanction of 26 Henry VIII c 3 and 2 and 3 Edward VI c 20 in relation to the non-payment of clerical tithes to the Crown.
[26] R Burn, *Ecclesiastical Law*, 3rd edn (1775) vol II, 27.

II. The Civil War and the Laws of the Long Parliament

For such a significant period in ecclesiastical history as the Civil War, it is notable that canonists of later periods had so little to say about it. There is very little mention in the long commentaries of Richard Burn and Robert Phillimore, for example, of the period and its impact.[27] This gives the impression that the Civil War period was something of a blip, momentous at the time but completely reversed at the Restoration, and hardly of any continuing importance to the state and history of ecclesiastical law.[28] However, it is submitted, an investigation of this period suggests otherwise.

During 1640–48, the Long Parliament operated, increasingly in concert with the Scots, and steps were taken to bring the Church into uniformity with the Church of Scotland, which was of course presbyterian. In 1643, Parliament ratified the Solemn League and Covenant with Scotland, which pledged the introduction of a Presbyterian Church in England. It was not until 1646, however, that such a Presbyterian Church was established, and by then a degree of religious liberty and sectarianism was being practised.[29] Presbyterians soon fell from favour, especially during the Second Civil War when the Scots sided with Charles I. Factions from the independent churches become dominant. When in 1650, the Rump Parliament repealed the Act of Uniformity 1558 and other statutes with criminal sanctions attached to non-conformity in religion, it removed the provision that had required all residents of England to worship in the established Church.[30] Oliver Cromwell in particular was keen to allow for religious toleration of all peaceable Protestant independent churches, and provided for toleration under his Instrument of Government of 1653, which, inter alia, established him as Protector and changed the Parliament into a unicameral body.[31]

---

[27] For example, Phillimore's only reference to Oliver Cromwell was in mentioning that Jamaica had been a colony of Great Britain since Cromwell had acquired it: R Phillimore, *The Ecclesiastical Law of the Church of England*, 2nd edn (London, Sweet & Maxwell, 1895) vol II, 1790. He makes no reference to the interregnum period that I can find.

[28] From the restoration of the monarchy in 1660, the legislative acts of the republic were disregarded as having been a nullity. This is because an Act of Parliament can only be made if approved by both the House of Commons and the House of Lords and given Royal Assent by the monarch. This is implicit in the Acts passed during the early reign of Charles II, which were enacted as if the republic had not happened.

[29] There was no single legal instrument that established the Presbyterian Church in England. The key act was first to abolish the bishops, and then the reconstruction of the existing Church was carried out in stages – largely ad hoc – with which we will deal at greater length in section III.

[30] September 1650: Act for the Repeal of several Clauses in Statutes imposing Penalties for not coming to Church. Aside from the Act of Uniformity 1558, the legislation that was repealed was the Religion Acts of 1580 and 1592.

[31] Art XXXVII: 'That such as profess faith in God by Jesus Christ (though differing in judgment from the doctrine, worship or discipline publicly held forth) shall not be restrained from, but shall be protected in, the profession of the faith and exercise of their religion; so as they abuse not this liberty to the civil injury of others and to the actual disturbance of the public peace on their parts: provided this liberty be not extended to Popery or Prelacy, nor to such as, under the profession of Christ, hold forth and practice licentiousness.'

When the Instrument was replaced by the Humble Petition and Advice 1657, there was a move to greater conservatism, and official sanction for independent congregations and sects became less liberal. The Sabbath Act 1657 re-introduced compulsory church attendance on Sundays, but this need not be in the established Presbyterian Church.[32] This trend continued in earnest – and following the death of Cromwell, a disintegration in the Government paved the way for the restoration of the monarchy, shortly followed by the re-establishment of the Church of England.[33]

In 1640, 17 new Canons were made and given royal assent. They upheld the divine right of kings, attacked popery, puritan sectaries and Socinianism, regulated the situating of communion tables and other matters of ceremonial and ritual, and prescribed a new oath of conformity that clerics and those holding named public offices must take in the presence of a public notary. While some of the content can be interpreted as a buttress to Laudian 'high church' reforms, seven of the 17 expressly concerned the work of the church courts and dealt with such matters as the appointment of chancellors, the respective roles of lay ecclesiastical judges and clergy, marriage licences and vexatious litigation. One objective appeared to be to limit the role of lay ecclesiastical judges so that, for example, no suspension of a member of the clergy or any more serious penalty was to be imposed unless the proceedings had been heard by the bishop in person, or with the assistance of his chancellor or commissary; and if the bishop could not be present, by the chancellor or commissary and two 'grave dignified, or beneficed Ministers of the Diocese to be assigned by the Bishop'.[34] The Canons were made, however, after the dissolution of Parliament and, with the impending fall of the bishops, they had a limited effect and are now something of a historical footnote.[35] In 1640, the Clerical Disabilities Act was passed (commencing 1642), prohibiting the clergy from exercising temporal authority and excluding the bishops from the House of Lords and the Privy Council.[36] In 1641 the *ex officio* oath was abolished, the High Commission abolished, and the church courts were stripped of their corrective powers.[37] In 1643, episcopacy was abolished. Archbishop Laud was executed in 1645 and the episcopal estates put up for sale in October of 1646. The king was executed in 1649, the monarchy and House of Lords were abolished, and the constitution took the form of a commonwealth or republic (1649–60).

---

[32] June 1657: 'An Act for the better observation of the Lords Day'.

[33] See, eg, C Cross, 'The Church in England 1646–1660' in GE Aylmer (ed), *The Interregnum: The Quest for Settlement 1646–1660* (London, Macmillan, 1972) 99–120.

[34] Canon XII of 1640.

[35] See, eg, Bray (ed) (n 2) lxxiii–lxxviii and, for the text of the Canons, ibid 553–78.

[36] 6 Car I c 27, 'An Act for disabling all persons in Holy Orders to exercise any temporal jurisdiction or authority'.

[37] 17 Car I c 11, 'An Act for the repeal of a branch of a Statute primo Elizabeth, concerning Commissioners for causes ecclesiastical'.

The period saw legislation made in the form of 'ordinances'.[38] In May 1643, an ordinance was enacted against William Laud, Archbishop of Canterbury, preventing him from exercising his patronage rights without leave of Parliament and forbidding all archdeacons, registrars and other officers, ministers and persons to make any admission, institution, collation or induction to any ecclesiastical preferment, other than to such person nominated and appointed by Parliament. Vacant preferments belonging to the archbishop had to be notified to the Lord Speaker.[39] An ordinance of June 1643 suspended until trial the archbishop *ab officio & beneficio & omni & omnimoda jurisdictione Archiepiscopali* and sequestered all of the temporalities of his office. All preferments were to be instituted and inducted by the archbishop's vicar general or his surrogate, upon the nomination and recommendation of Parliament; it provided that 'the Jurisdiction of the said Archbishop shall be executed and exercised by his Vicar General, and other his inferior Judges and Officers, as formerly the same hath been'.[40] In January 1645, an ordinance attainted the archbishop for high treason, and provided that his lands and goods were forfeit, but protected all 'singular Persons, and Bodies Politic and Corporate, their Heirs and Successors (other than the said Archbishop and His Heirs ...), all such Right, Title, and Interest, of, in and to, all and singular such of the Lands, Tenements, and Hereditaments, as he or any of them had'; the ordinance was personal to Laud and did not apply to his office or the bishops generally. The same month another ordinance was made ordering Laud's execution: 'the Head of the said Archbishop shall be cut off, at the Tower Hill'.[41]

While this legislation was surgically focused on the person of Laud, other more radical legislation sought to reconstruct the Church of England into a 'reformed' and Presbyterian Church. An ordinance of June 1643 summoned an assembly of divines to replace 'the present Church-Government by Archbishops, Bishops, their Chancellors, Commissaries, Deans, Deans and Chapters, Archdeacons, and other Ecclesiastical Officers depending upon the Hierarchy'. The ordinance

---

[38] In this section I refer to 'legislation', 'acts' and 'ordinances'. The strict legal position, in terms of post-Restoration perspectives, is that all Acts of Parliament from 1642 until 1660, with the restoration of the monarchy, were not proper Acts as they did not receive royal assent. Between 1642 and 1649, Parliament referred to its own legislation as ordinances. The Rump Parliament then started to revert to using the term 'acts' in 1649. Between December 1653 and September 1654, ordinances made by the Protector and his Council were said to be not binding until confirmed by Parliament, many of which were so confirmed in 1657. For the purpose of this chapter, all these legislative initiatives are treated as laws, whatever their ultimate binding effect or the composition of the legislature at the time. See further, I Roots, 'Cromwell's Ordinances: the early legislation of the Protectorate' in Aylmer (ed) (n 32) 143–64. For the text of the ordinances, see CH Firth and RS Rait (eds), *Acts and Ordinances of the Interregnum, 1642–1660* (London, HMSO, 1911), British History Online at www.british-history.ac.uk/no-series/acts-ordinances-interregnum (accessed 8 January 2023).

[39] May 1643: 'An Ordinance concerning the Arch-Bishop of Canterbury, who by reason of many great and weighty businesses, cannot as yet be brought to his Trial'.

[40] June 1643: 'An Ordinance that all the Temporal Livings, Dignities and Ecclesiastical promotions belonging unto William Laud Archbishop of Canterbury, be forthwith Sequestered by and unto the Parliament'.

[41] January 1645: 'Ordinance for beheading the Archbishop of Canterbury'.

described the latter system as 'evil, and justly offensive and burdensome to the Kingdom, a great impediment to Reformation and growth of Religion'. The aim was that 'such a Government shall be settled in the Church, as may be most agreeable to Gods Holy Word, and most apt to procure and preserve the Peace of the Church at home, and nearer Agreement with the Church of Scotland, and other Reformed Churches abroad'. This was not a summons for a synod of bishops or a convocation of the Church but a gathering of divines appointed by Parliament. Each member is named in the ordinance. Their purpose was to review 'the Liturgy, Discipline and Government of the Church of England, or the vindicating and clearing of the Doctrine of the same from all false aspersions and misconstructions as shall be proposed unto them by both or either of the said Houses of Parliament'. However, the ordinance contained the proviso that it did 'not give unto the Persons aforesaid, or any of them, nor shall in this Assembly assume to exercise any Jurisdiction, Power or Authority Ecclesiastical whatsoever, or any other Power then is herein particularly expressed'.[42] Ultimate legislative power over the Church vested in Parliament; the assembly of divines was simply to report to it.

There followed ordinances of August 1643 and May 1644 to demolish what they described as monuments of idolatry and superstition: they sought 'the better to accomplish the blessed Reformation so happily begun, and to remove all offences and things illegal in the worship of God'. Stone altars were to be demolished and communion tables removed from each church. Representations of the Trinity and any angel or saint in any place of worship were to be 'taken away, defaced, and utterly demolished'; raised chancels were to be levelled, and such items and ornaments as 'Copes, Surplisses, superstitious Vestments, Roods, or Roodlons, or Holy-water Fonts' prohibited; organs and organ cases 'utterly defaced'; and representations on communion plate discontinued.[43] Specific provision was made for enforcement and fines were to be imposed for want of performance. In the case of parish churches, the duty to implement these rules fell on churchwardens and overseers of the poor.[44]

While the objects of reverence were to be wrecked by parliamentary ordinance, the attack on the church courts was more indirect if not more sudden. Episcopacy was not itself abolished until an ordinance of October 1646 (effective retroactively from 5 September that year). It was this ordinance that abolished the church courts by taking away all the archiepiscopal and episcopal jurisdiction

---

[42] June 1643: 'An Ordinance for the calling of an Assembly of Learned and Godly Divines, to be consulted with by the Parliament, for the settling of the Government of the Church'.

[43] August 1643: 'An Ordinance for the utter demolishing, removing and taking away of all Monuments of Superstition or Idolatry'; May 1644: 'An Ordinance for the further demolishing of Monuments of Idolatry and Superstition'.

[44] As to the mixed implementation of these laws, see J Spraggon, *Puritan Iconoclasm During the English Civil War* (Martlesham, Boydell & Brewer, 2012); and J Walter, '"Abolishing Superstition with Sedition"? The Politics of Popular Iconoclasm in England 1640–1642' (2004) 183 *Past & Present* 79–123.

on which the courts were based: as Outhwaite puts it, '[t]he church courts essentially fell with the bishops'.[45] No law was passed to abolish canon law. But without the church courts to enforce the canons, they became voluntary. Two key provisions in the ordinance replaced the church courts with a secular scheme:

> The Sheriff of every County and Place, who is to attend the respective Courts where any Felony is to be tried and determined, shall provide and present to the Judge or Judges of such Courts, some able and fit person to do such things as by the Office of the Ordinary have been used to be done: which person and persons shall have Authority, and are hereby enjoined to perform their services in such manner as the respective Ordinaries heretofore have used to do …

and 'all issues triable by the Ordinary or Bishop, shall be tried by Jury in usual course'.[46]

However, the ordinance only treated those causes that related to felonies, and not the non-contentious business of the church courts, nor matters matrimonial or those relating to tithes and slander.[47] Moreover, the only specific provision that Parliament made to continue the non-contentious business of the church courts, only part of which was truly 'ecclesiastical', was in the area of wills and probate. In November 1644, the Keeper of the Prerogative Court of Canterbury, Dr Merrick, was removed by Parliament from office (having already abandoned it) and Sir Nathaniel Brent appointed instead.[48] This key probate court in England and Wales, which had a particular role in granting probate for wealthy persons who owned property in multiple dioceses, was sufficiently important for Parliament to keep it operational. In 1653, on the death of Brent, a centralised probate court was established in London for the whole of England and Wales.[49] This replaced the former ecclesiastical jurisdiction with a civil one. In the same year, an ordinance established a legal preliminary for marriage in place of banns or licences, and provided for a new ceremony of civil marriage: it stated 'And no other Marriage whatsoever within the Commonwealth of England, after the 29th of September, in the year One thousand six hundred fifty three, shall be held or accompted a Marriage according to the Laws of England'.[50]

---

[45] Outhwaite (n 10) 78.

[46] October 1646: 'An Ordinance for the abolishing of Archbishops and Bishops within the Kingdom of England, and Dominion of Wales, and for settling of their Lands and Possessions upon Trustees, for the use of the Commonwealth'.

[47] 'For nearly twenty years, until the Restoration, English men and women went unpoliced by the ecclesiastical courts, and for over a decade they had to find other ways of resolving their tithe, testamentary, matrimonial and slander conflicts': Outhwaite (n 10) 79. Most tithes were recovered in the equity side of the exchequer: WH Bryson, *The Equity Side of the Exchequer* (Cambridge, Cambridge University Press, 1975) 11–12, 19, 31, 163, 200.

[48] November 1644: 'Ordinance for the speedy constituting of Sir Nathaniel Brent Judge of the Prerogative Court of Canterbury, for the Probate of Wills and granting of Letters of Administration'.

[49] April 1653: 'Act for the Probate of Wills and granting administration'; December 1653: 'An Ordinance for the reviving of an Act of Parliament of 8 April 1653, entitled An Act for Probate of Wills and Granting Administrations'.

[50] August 1653: 'Act touching Marriages and the registering thereof, and also touching Birth and Burials'.

III. The Commonwealth: Republican Church Law

A new body of church law emerged during the Commonwealth. What follows sets out landmark laws in the context of earlier laws from the Long Parliament. As we shall see, Parliament legislated in 1646 to establish a national Presbyterian Church and enjoin uniformity in religion. However, the legislation also protected the independent churches favoured in the military, by Cromwell and by many in government. The Instrument of Government (1653), the written constitution of the Commonwealth of England, Scotland and Ireland, provided expressly for toleration of churches (other than Rome). According to Matthews, '[t]he protectorate's religious settlement was founded on the principle that the civil state assume two responsibilities: first, to provide financial support to preachers who would propagate the gospel; and second, to protect Christian liberty by guaranteeing liberty of conscience'.[51] Crucially, the Instrument of Government stated that 'all laws, statutes and ordinances, and clauses in any law, statute or ordinance to the contrary of the aforesaid liberty, shall be esteemed as null and void'.[52] This was the fundamental new rule of recognition, replacing the king's ecclesiastical law.

When the episcopacy was abolished in 1646, the property of the bishops was vested by Parliament in named trustees, with surveyors to be appointed.[53] The trustees held the lands on a trust for sale, with a view to liquidating the assets quickly. Parliament made several ordinances over the following years, to streamline, facilitate and speed up the process of selling the episcopal lands.[54] By an ordinance of April 1649 (with effect from 29 March), cathedral deans and chapters (Christ Church Oxford excepted) and other cathedral office-holders were abolished in name and in function, and all the property of the same was vested in named trustees for the purpose of sale.[55] Under the Instrument of Government (1653), all titles and profits of the remaining royal and ecclesiastical lands were vested in the Protector and his successors.[56]

However, the patronage rights of these office-holders were not abolished in the ordinance for cathedral lands of April 1649, but they were exercisable by

---

[51] NL Matthews, *William Sheppard, Cromwell's Law Reformer* (Cambridge, Cambridge University Press, 1984) 180: four Articles in the Instrument (XXXV–XXXVIII) and three ordinances issued by the Protector and Council were 'the authorities upon which this settlement rested'. Those ordinances are those of March 1654: 'Ordinance for appointing Commissioners for a Probation of Public Preachers'; June 1654: 'An Ordinance for giving further time for Approbation of Public Preachers'; and June 1654: 'An Ordinance for ejecting Scandalous, Ignorant and insufficient Ministers and Schoolmasters'.

[52] Instrument, Art XXXVIII.

[53] October 1646: 'Ordinance for the abolishing of Archbishops and Bishops in England and Wales and for settling their lands and possessions upon Trustees for the use of the Commonwealth'.

[54] Ordinances of 30 November 1646, 5 March 1647, 24 September 1647, 16 October 1650.

[55] April 1649: 'An Act for abolishing of Deans, Deans and Chapters, Canons, Prebends and other offices and titles of or belonging to any Cathedral or Collegiate Church or Chapel within England and Wales'.

[56] Instrument, Art XXXI.

purchasers of those lands. The same provision was made in the April 1649 ordinance, somewhat late and haphazardly, for those who had purchased episcopal lands since 3 November 1640, 'until the Parliament shall take further order'. While the ordinance abolished the ecclesiastical hierarchy and seised its property, it did not dismantle the whole of the former Church of England. In addition to rights of patronage, incumbents of benefices and parish churches were left alone.[57] A proviso in an ordinance of October 1650 (seizing manors, rectories and glebe lands latterly belonging to the episcopacy and deans and chapters) stated that it 'shall not extend to the sale of any Church or Public Chapel, or to any Church-yard or Ground used for a common Burial-place'.[58]

The parsonages and glebe of incumbents not part of the hierarchy were also left untouched, and as were tithes due to incumbents. In fact, Parliament enforced the payment of tithes in ordinances of 1644, 1647 (three that year), 1648 and 1660.[59] It was easier to abolish the episcopacy, to sell its land and to bring down the system of church courts, than to reconstruct the Church root and branch. Tithes were a case in point. While its intention was remove reliance on tithes, the Government still needed the money to fund support for ministry. Members of the independent churches were often opposed to tithes, but members of successive parliaments prevented laws from passing because of the threat it posed to tithes received by lay landowners and the absence of some other adequate stream of funding. As Cromwell's law reformer, William Sheppard, wrote, 'I wish they were taken away, so that first of all a more convenient way of maintenance instead thereof be provided for the minister; but this I suppose will ask time'.[60]

As the Henrician dissolution of the monasteries resulted in the transfer of a large degree of their wealth to the Crown and private landowners, so in our period the wealth of the bishops and cathedrals was put to public purposes. Much of it paid for Parliament's war, and that came from the sale of episcopal and capitular land.[61] But the tithes and income of the hierarchy were redistributed in ways

---

[57] That is, the office of incumbent, although many holding that office came to be ejected.

[58] October 1650: 'An Act for Sale of the Manors of Rectories and Glebe-Lands, late belonging to Archbishops, Bishops, Deans, Deans and Chapters'.

[59] November 1644: 'Ordinance for the due payment of Tithes and other such Duties according to the Laws and Customs of this Realm'; August 1647: 'An Ordinance for the true payment of Tythes and other Duties'; August 1647: 'Ordinance amending that of 8th November, 1644, for the true payment of tithes to continue till 1st November, 1648'; August 1647: 'An Ordinance for keeping in Godly Ministers, placed in Livings by authority of Parliament; April 1648: Ordinance for the payment of Tithes in London, amending those of 8th November, 1644, and 9th August, 1647'; March 1660: 'Act for ministers and Payment of Tithes'.

[60] Matthews (n 51) 107.

[61] In an Act of 16 October 1650, Parliament ordered the Council of State to take care that £120,000 be borrowed on the basis of that Act, concerning the sale of manors, rectories and glebe lands of the episcopacy and cathedrals: £50,000 for the use of the army, £50,000 for the navy, 'proportionably as the same comes in'; and the £20,000 residue, as they think fit, with regard to the payment to the surveyors of what is ordered to be paid to them: 'House of Commons Journal Volume 6: 16 October 1650' in *Journal of the House of Commons*, vol 6: *1648–1651* (London, HMSO, 1802) 484, British History Online at www.british-history.ac.uk/commons-jrnl/vol6/p484 (accessed 29 December 2022).

that showed the priorities of the religious reformers to promote preaching. Even before the seizure of the cathedral lands, an ordinance of March 1646 provided for the payment of six cathedral preachers in the City of Hereford to preach at times and places designated by the law.[62] They were to be maintained by stipends paid out of the possessions of the Dean and Chapter, and were to be provided cathedral housing rent-free. Those preachers appointed to preach and officiate in the parish churches of the City of Hereford were to have the houses and yearly profits belonging to the ministers of the several parishes.

Not only did the law benefit preaching, it also benefited teaching. An ordinance of June 1649 appropriated all the tithes, rents, revenues, offerings and other emoluments of the late hierarchy of bishops, archdeacons, deans and so forth, and vested them in trustees to pay salaries and augmentations to schoolmasters and masters of colleges in the universities, as well as to preaching ministers appointed by Parliament.[63] Also, the first fruits that church dignities and livings had to pay to the Crown, and the tenths of all revenues, rents and tithes that had to be paid, under legislation dating back to Henry VIII, were not abolished but vested in the trustees established by the ordinance. Where the revenue of benefices was low, the trustees were empowered to make up the income of the incumbent of a benefice out of the funds at their disposal. Thus, the ordinance aimed not only to increase the number of preaching ministers and teachers but also to equalise the value of benefices, something that was not to be repeated until the establishment of Queen Anne's Bounty in the early eighteenth century, which also augmented benefices out of the first fruits and tenths. Gentiles and Sheils write:

> The confiscation and sale of the episcopal estates was never intended as part of a long term policy designed to bring about a fundamental re-distribution of church lands they for the most part intended to remain within the church and use the wealth of the hierarchy to improve the income of the parochial clergy.[64]

Provision had been made for new presbyterian forms of worship during the Civil War. By an ordinance of January 1645, the Book of Common Prayer was abolished and the Directory for the Public Worship of God was instituted to be 'used, pursued, and observed ... in all Exercises of the public Worship of God, in every Congregation, Church, Chapel, and place of public Worship within this Kingdom of England, and Dominion of Wales'. The Directory provided 'Uniformity in Divine Worship, which we have promised in our Solemn League and Covenant' (see section II). The ordinance set out the preface to the Directory with key doctrinal statements on matters such as Scripture, baptism, the sacrament of the Lord's

---

[62] March 1646: 'Ordinance for the maintenance of preaching ministers in the City and County of Hereford'.

[63] June 1649: 'An Act for Maintenance for Preaching Ministers, and other Pious Uses'.

[64] IJ Gentiles and WJ Sheils, *Confiscation and Restoration: the Archbishopric Estates and the Civil War* (York, University of York, 1981) Borthwick Paper no 59, 33–34.

supper, marriage, the burial of the dead and like matters previously treated by the Thirty-Nine Articles. The ordinance also required each parish to provide at their own expense a register book of vellum, to be kept by the minister and other officers to record baptisms, marriages and burials.[65]

The law was further strengthened by an ordinance of August 1645 that created punishments for the use of the Book of Common Prayer and for neglect in using the Directory. Copies of the Book of Common Prayer were to be seized and disposed of.[66]

Special provision was made to keep the Lord's Day holy. An ordinance of June 1647 abolished all festivals and holy days – instead, the second Tuesday of every month was to be taken for rest, 'any Law, Statute, Custom, Constitution, or Canon to the contrary in any wise notwithstanding'.[67] Ordinances of 1644 and 1650 created punishments for various types of work done in 'profanation' of the Lord's Day.[68]

In addition to liturgical reformation, new church structures were instituted in place of the former synodical system. Incumbents, curates and churchwardens were to remain, but ruling elders for each parish and congregation were to be elected by the ministers and members of their congregations. An ordinance of August 1645 set out the qualifications and procedure for election as an elder; for instance, the candidate had to have taken the National Covenant. Congregations were to sit within the lowest level of a new governance system, namely congregational assemblies; then came classical, provincial and national assemblies.[69] A key difference from the former convocation system was the level of lay involvement. But there was continuity as well as change: the national assembly was to meet when summoned by Parliament, and to sit and continue to sit as the Parliament ordered and not otherwise. Thus, Parliament retained its pre-eminence in church matters, as it had with the convocations before.[70]

In 1646, an ordinance was passed to allow ordination of ministers by the presbytery of ministers and established the qualifications and procedures to be admitted to the class of presbyter.[71] With the protectorate, ordinances (in 1654) established commissions of triers and ejectors: the former a committee of laymen and ministers from various churches to vet appointments to spiritual preferments; and the latter, commissions to eject ministers from their preferments if

---

[65] January 1645: 'An Ordinance for taking away the Book of Common Prayer, and for establishing and putting in execution of the Directory for the public worship of God'.
[66] August 1645: 'An Ordinance for the more effectual putting in Execution the Directory for Public Worship, in all Parish-Churches and Chapels within the Kingdom of England and Wales'.
[67] June 1647: 'An Ordinance for Abolishing of Festivals'.
[68] April 1644: 'An Ordinance for the better observation of the Lords-Day'; April 1650: 'Act for the better observation of the Lord's Day, Days of Public Humiliation and Thanksgiving'.
[69] August 1645: 'Ordinance regulating the Election of Elders'.
[70] In practice, however, the new provincial system was only properly implemented in London and Lancashire.
[71] August 1646: 'An Ordinance for the Ordination of Ministers by the Classical Presbyteries, Within their respective Bounds for the several Congregations in the Kingdom of England'.

they were shown to be inefficient, the cause of scandal, or ignorant.[72] In the same year, an ordinance established trustees to consider pastoral reorganisation, with such powers as to unite and divide parishes for the better provision of ministry.[73] In 1657, Parliament confirmed these ordinances.[74]

All this is of interest in showing the anatomy of a church-law revolution. Various legal and extra-legal means were used by Parliament and by Cromwell as Protector to reconstruct the Church and exercise control over it. Such legislative creativity brings to mind the legal devices and justifications of the Reformation under Henry VIII. What the period also shows is that Parliament did not expressly disestablish the Church of England.[75] Far from it. Parliament sought to reconstruct it – without the royal supremacy and episcopacy – while maintaining the system of patronage, tithes, benefices, churches and churchyards. It replaced the Book of Common Prayer with its own Directory and enjoined uniformity of public worship. It sought to replace the convocations with its own assembles, and the dioceses with a new governance system.

To this extent, Parliament sought to defend an established Church, and by necessity it created new ecclesiastical law or, to put it a better way, a state law of religion. Of course, it was no longer an episcopal church, and the whole bedrock of the making of canon law, episcopal and ordinary jurisdiction, and the role of the church courts, was taken away. The status and nature of the republican Church was the subject of debate at the time and since. John Stoughton, writing in the 1860s, argued somewhat polemically that it did not deserve the status of a Church at all, as it

> did not include or recognize any internal organization whatever of an ecclesiastical kind; it had no Church courts, no Church assemblies, no Church laws, no Church ordinances. It repudiated Prelacy without enforcing Presbyterianism or recognizing Congregationalism. While denying the aid of the civil power for carrying out one method of discipline, it gave no direct sanction to any other. It said nothing about rites and ceremonies … The particular society so organized really stood outside the Establishment. Hence it follows that the Protectorate Establishment was nothing more

---

[72] March 1654: 'Ordinance for appointing Commissioners for a Probation of Public Preachers' (commissioners for triers); June 1654: 'An Ordinance for ejecting Scandalous, Ignorant and insufficient Ministers and Schoolmasters' (commissioners for ejectors).

[73] September 1654: 'An Ordinance for the better maintenance and encouragement of Preaching Ministers, and for uniting of Parishes'.

[74] June 1657: 'An Act touching several Acts and Ordinances made since the twentieth of April, 1653. and before the third of September, 1654, and other Acts'. On the commissions of triers and ejectors, see further NF Collins, *Oliver Cromwell's Protectorate Church Settlement: The Commission for the Approbation of Public Preachers: The Triers and the Commission for the Ejecting of Scandalous, Ignorant and Insufficient Ministers and Schoolmasters: The Ejectors* (unpublished dissertation, 1970) (Order No 7113539) available from ProQuest Dissertations & Theses Global (302557157) retrieved from www-proquest-com.ezproxy.is.ed.ac.uk/dissertations-theses/oliver-cromwells-protectorate-church-settlement/docview/302557157/se-2; and JR Collins, 'The Church Settlement of Oliver Cromwell' (2002) 87 *History* 18–40.

[75] By 'establish' and 'disestablish' is meant the creation and removal by means of civil legislative action of a Church that has constitutional links with the State.

than an institution for *preaching and teaching*. The ministers were acknowledged by the State only in the capacity of instructors.[76]

Christopher Haigh has investigated brilliantly what people at the time had thought had happened to the Church of England – was it the same Church, although deformed, had it ceased to exist, or did it only exist in hiding? Most pre-Commonwealth clergy continued to serve in the Church and considered it to be the Church of England.[77] Between 1646 and 1660, perhaps as many as 2,500 men were ordained by bishops, even though that had ceased to be a requirement in 1646 and bishops had no official status as such.[78] In the view of Aylmer, the republican Church was 'a modified, Erastian Presbyterianism'.[79] Andrew Milton, in a far-reaching survey of 'the Cromwellian Church', has said that 'Presbyterians in the 1650s remained committed to the notion of a national church and never ceased to refer to the existence of the national Church of England, however temporarily deficient it might be in some of its features'; further, 'many aspects of the Church settlement were conceptualized and organized at a national level', even though the parliamentary ordinances themselves avoided the terminology of a national Church.[80] Our view is that the combination of surviving remnants of the pre-Commonwealth church (parish churches, tithes, etc), together with a state law of religion that sought to supervise the way in which those structures were conducted, amounted to an established republican Church, although not one with a confessional monopoly over the citizens of the Commonwealth. Alongside the republican Church, the State legislated in matters of morality and religion (eg, concerning adultery and blasphemy) to enforce certain norms of Christian behaviour.

It is the case, however, following the Instrument of Government (1653), that the coercive instruments of uniformity that the presbyterian national Church had were nullified, and toleration for independent churches was legislated for. The period was typified, according to Cross, as 'the failure of the plan to create a system of rigid Protestant uniformity in England, and then the temporary successful evolution of a very broad Protestant Church with toleration in practice for all peaceable Christians who could not accommodate themselves within it'.[81] Much of what Parliament and Cromwell did was reversed on the restoration of the monarchy, most particularly though an Act of 1660, but also by reverting to former practices (such as using Latin in the records of the church courts as opposed to English), as we shall see in chapter 5.

---

[76] J Stoughton, *Ecclesiastical History of England*, vol II (London, Walford and Hodder, 1867) 93–94.
[77] C Haigh, 'Where was the Church of England, 1646–1660' (2019) 62 *The Historical Journal* 127–47.
[78] K Fincham and S Taylor, 'Vital statistics: episcopal ordination and ordinands in England, 1646–1660' (2011) 126 *English Historical Review* 319–44.
[79] GE Aylmer, 'Introduction: the Quest for Settlement 1646–1660', in Aylmer (ed) (n 33) 1–28, 10.
[80] A Milton, 'The Cromwellian Church' in A Milton (ed), *England's Second Reformation: The Battle for the Church of England 1625–1662* (Cambridge, Cambridge University Press, 2021) 335–78.
[81] C Cross, 'The Church in England 1646–1660' in Aylmer (ed) (n 33) 99–120.

However, some of the experiments of the Long Parliament and Commonwealth were taken up in later years, such as the end of the right of clergy to tax their own kind, the levelling up of benefice endowments, and the appropriation of episcopal and cathedral lands by national authorities. Indeed, modern legislation is in some ways more radical than some of that of the Long Parliament and Commonwealth, such as that on: the diocesan appropriation of glebe in the 1970s; diocesan appropriation of parsonages by various legal means; the advent of common tenure; a permissive regime for public worship; and the use of suspension of benefices. Additionally, fewer and fewer cases are submitted to the consistory courts of the bishops, so that the consistory court now only tends to deal with faculty cases, and more church law and business comes to national committees and tribunals. It would be as well for us to ask ourselves the question where authority and jurisdiction lies in our own Church, and how much the present Church should rely upon canon made by synod, or measure confirmed by Parliament, and what it believes is the source and justification for legislating.

IV. The Jurists: From Royal to Republican

Of the significant ecclesiastical law jurists of the period, we must mention Edward Coke and William Sheppard, neither of them canonists but common lawyers. Edward Coke (1552–1634) had a profound influence on the common law through his law reports and the four-volume *Institutes of the Laws of England*. In the *Institutes*, Coke opined on ecclesiastical law, and his writing continues to be cited. This is despite his several detractors, who claim that his account of the ecclesiastical law was often misfounded. Indeed, Coke married Lady Elizabeth secretly, against the canons that forbade marriages in private houses or without a licence or publication of banns. Archbishop Whitgift moved to excommunicate Coke, Lady Elizabeth and the rector who married them. Coke petitioned for a dispensation, which was granted on account of Coke's 'ignorance of the ecclesiastical law'.[82] At least one modern author has impugned his interpretation of aspects of ecclesiastical law in his account of the consecration of churches.[83] Certainly, he was no friend to many civilian ecclesiastical lawyers of the day, who rightly saw him as a standard bearer for an assertive profession of common lawyers seeking to check the authority of the church courts and set up common law jurisprudence, in opposition to what was alleged to be authoritarian strains in those writers who supported strong monarchical and church prerogatives. Coke's significance is partly due to the quantity of case law and other authority he bequeathed to practitioners and legal historians – and to the attachment of

---

[82] S Sheppard (ed), *The Selected Writings and Speeches of Sir Edward Coke*, vol I (Indianapolis, IN, Liberty Fund, 2003) xli.

[83] K Homfray, 'Sir Edward Coke Gets It Wrong? A Brief History of Consecration' (2009) 11 *Ecclesiastical Law Journal* 36–50.

his writings with his personal role in various constitutional and legal wranglings of the day, the *Case of Proclamations* among them. Further, in the development of the common law, he provides an excellent prototype, and can be seen to be on the 'right side of history' in the rise of the common law as the dominant jurisprudence with considerable constitutional clout. Unfortunately, he also adds to a narrative that has diminished the importance and value of the ecclesiastical, canon and civil lawyers, who in 'Whig history' are seen to have been inevitably declining and, somewhat unfairly, to be attached to archaic and absolute forms of government, when in fact the systematic and humanistic credentials of these jurists provide much to celebrate.[84]

William Sheppard is not now well known, but Nancy Matthews has done much to put that right. Sheppard (d 1674) was a prolific writer of guides to the law in such various areas as justices of the peace, tithes and corporations. Matthews credits Sheppard with pioneering the genre of the legal encyclopaedia, including an ambitious *Epitome of all the common and statute laws of this nation now in force* (1656).[85] He wrote in English and was influential in propagating the law in the vernacular language.[86] While he wrote on ecclesiastical law, his importance to us is in his work to reform the law during the interregnum. Under the patronage of Cromwell, he developed proposals to reform the law as a whole, and as part of this to replace the ecclesiastical law with a new state law of religion and to administer those parts of the law that had formerly been under the jurisdiction of the church courts. Of particular relevance is his *A view of all the laws and statutes of this nation concerning the service of God or religion* (1655), which listed nullified laws, recently enacted ordinances and guidance on how the present laws could be enforced. In this work, Sheppard sought to show how the punitive laws enforcing religious uniformity (such as the Blasphemy and Heresy Acts of 1648 and 1650) were intended to punish popery and its practices that offended Scripture and not non-conformism to the established Presbyterian Church. In relation to the enforcement of the Directory under the ordinance of 1645, he concluded that this seemed to have been overridden by the toleration provisions of the Instrument of Government (1653). As to the repeal of the Act of Uniformity, dismantling of church courts, repeal of the Thirty-Nine Articles and abolition of the Book of Common Prayer, he gave a reasoned explanation for the legal toleration of independent churches that existed outside the established Presbyterian Church. He also advised on how certain cases formerly heard in the church courts might now be heard in the courts of the land.[87] Sheppard was retained by Cromwell between

---

[84] For an overview, see DC Smith, *Sir Edward Coke and the Reformation of the Laws: Religion, Politics and Jurisprudence, 1578-1616* (Cambridge, Cambridge University Press, 2014); for Coke on ecclesiastical law, see ibid 135–37, 177, 181–83, 188, 192–96, 205, 209.
[85] Matthews (n 51) 101.
[86] ibid 88-9.
[87] ibid 115–17.

1653 and 1657 to develop proposals for law and court reform, and the fullest articulation of his designs was given in *England's Balme* (1656). In this, the influence of the legal system in Massachusetts (itself drawn in part from Holland) can be traced.[88] While much of his portfolio of law reform was destined to remain a blueprint only, the abundance and thoroughness of his thinking provide us a useful counterpoint to the civilian jurists.

Amongst the pre-eminent civilians and canonists of the period is Richard Zouche (1590–1661), sometime Regius Professor of Civil Law at Oxford and Judge of the High Court of Admiralty. In Zouche we have the best of that pan-European tradition of civil and canon law scholarship, who wrote in the region of 15 books on various aspects of the civil law, several translated and read on the Continent of Europe.[89] His contemporary John Cowell (1554–1611) shares many of the same plaudits. Cowell was Regius Professor of Civil Law at Cambridge (1594–1611), sometime Vicar-General to Archbishop Bancroft of Canterbury (from 1608) and Master of Trinity Hall (from 1598), that nursery of the civil lawyers. Coquillette credits Cowell with inventing 'two vehicles that no English civilian had yet employed': namely, his *Institutes* of English law, following the headings of *Justinian's Institutes*; and his law dictionary, perhaps the most famous in English legal history, *The Interpreter*.[90] Cowell followed in the English Bartolist tradition,[91] and entered into dialogue with the common lawyers. The *Institutes* sought to 'restate the entire common law in a logical outline based on civilian forms'.[92] He prepared, at Bancroft's request, the complaints of the clergy against common law prohibitions.[93] In his attack on prohibitions, Cowell relied in *The Interpreter* on his understanding of the royal supremacy to argue that common law courts' interventions were unfounded: while formerly the church courts derived their authority from the papacy, following the royal supremacy in ecclesiastical matters, they now derived it from the king:

> For they [prohibition and praemunire] were helpers to the King's inheritance and Crown, when the two swords were in two divers hands. Whereas now both the Jurisdiction being settled in the King, there is small reason of either, except it be to weary the subject by many quirks and delays, from obtaining his right.[94]

Unfortunately for Cowell, his views on the common law and royal prerogative in *The Interpreter* stirred such uproar that the James I issued a proclamation in 1610 condemning them: Cowell was seriously affected by this and he died soon after.[95]

---

[88] ibid 172–73.
[89] RH Helmholz, 'Richard Zouche (1590–1661)' (2013) 15 *Ecclesiastical Law Journal* 204–07. For a substantial account of the civilian lawyers of this period, see Levack (n 16).
[90] DR Coquillette, 'Legal Ideology and Incorporation I: The English Civilian Writers, 1523–1607' (1981) 61 *Boston University Law Review* 71.
[91] After Bartolus de Saxoferrato, a 14th-century Italian civilian jurist. He also influenced Zouche.
[92] Coquillette (n 90) 88.
[93] ibid 77.
[94] J Cowell, *The Interpreter* (1607), note 155, entry on Prohibition, quoted in Coquillette (n 89) 79.
[95] For the proclamation, see Kenyon (ed) (n 1) 126 (document 42).

Coquillette credits another civilian, Thomas Ridley (1548–1629) as leading a new generation of civilians who abandoned the path of Cowell and the earlier Bartolist jurists in trying to collaborate with the common lawyers. This new generation

> adopted an entirely different approach to achieving a modus vivendi with the common lawyers. Abandoning the essential ends of Bartolism, most particularly the desire to achieve a constructive influence of civil law principles on the English common law, they focused instead on the existing strongholds of Doctors' Commons – the ecclesiastical courts, the universities and, most critically, the Admiralty Court. Instead of seeking a synthesis of civilian principles and methodology with the common law, they argued for a strict separation of English civil law and common law courts and for the utility of a separate legal élite that served the specialized needs of these civil law courts, particularly in those areas of English law that related to the outside world.[96]

Ridley was an advocate at Doctors' Commons, and, inter alia, Chancellor of the Diocese of Winchester from 1596, Vicar-General to the Archbishop of Canterbury from 1611 (succeeding Cowell) and a member of the Court of High Commission. When the church courts came under attack, it was to Ridley, Cowell and Sir Edward Stanhope that Archbishop Bancroft turned, to compile the Canons of 1603.[97] This showed the preoccupation in rationalising and improving the church courts to weather the criticisms levelled by the common lawyers and others. Ridley's principal contribution was entitled *A View of the Civil and Ecclesiastical Law* (1607), dedicated to James I.[98] In it, Ridley traces the antiquity of the civil and ecclesiastical law and their importance to England. It is a manifesto in defence of that law, assailed as it was by Coke and the common lawyers, as neatly put in the following passage:

> So then to deny a free course to the Civil and Ecclesiastical Law in this Land, in such things as appertain to their profession, or to abridge the maintenance thereof, is to spoil his Majesty of a part of his honour (whose glory it is to be furnished with all sorts of professions necessary for his state, and beneficial for his subjects) to weaken the State public, and bereave it of grave and sage men, to advise the State in matters of doubt and controversy between foreign Nations and themselves, to disarm the Church of her faithful friends and followers, and so to cut the sinews (as much as in them lies) of Ecclesiastical discipline, and to expose her to the teeth of those, who for these many years have sought to devour her up; and so now would do it, if the merciful providence of God, and the gracious eye of the Prince did not watch over her.[99]

---

[96] Coquillette (n 90) 83.
[97] See generally PW Hasler (ed), *The History of Parliament: the House of Commons 1558–1603* (Martlesham, Boydell & Brewer, 1981).
[98] ibid.
[99] T Ridley, *A view of the civile and ecclesiasticall law and wherein the practice of them is streitned, and may be releeved within this land. Written by Sr Thomas Ridley Knight, and Doctor of the Civile Law* (1607) 276.

V. Restoration

With the death of Oliver Cromwell in 1658, the establishment of Richard Cromwell's protectorate, that administration's speedy decline and the restoration of monarchy, one might expect a series of legislative measures to reinstitute the Church of England and the system of church courts. There were some legislative measures, the most important being the Ecclesiastical Jurisdiction Act 1661,[100] which expressly undid the Abolition of High Commission Court Act 1640,[101] the Act that had abolished the High Commission, removed the coercive powers of the church courts and abolished the *ex officio* oath. While the 1661 Act expressly restored the power and authority of coercive ecclesiastical jurisdiction, the provision in the earlier Act abolishing the High Commission was excepted, and it was expressly provided that those exercising spiritual or ecclesiastical jurisdiction might not tender self-incriminatory oaths (namely, the *ex officio* oath). An important caveat to this restorative legislation was that it was not to add to the powers or authority of those exercising spiritual or ecclesiastical jurisdiction that existed before 1639, 'nor to abridge the King's Majesties Supremacy in Ecclesiastical matters and affairs nor to confirm the Canons made in [1640] nor any of them nor any other Ecclesiastical Lawes or Canons not formerly confirmed or allowed or enacted by Parliament or by the established Lawes of the Land as they stood in [1639]'. While it turned back the clock to before 1640, it asserted the authority of Parliament to condone new canons and the king's supremacy in ecclesiastical matters. So, while restoring the coercive powers of the church courts (and being a legislative or statutory basis for that), the Act of 1661 also hedged around the ecclesiastical jurisdiction with a great many caveats.

The 1661 Act was not in fact repealed until the Ecclesiastical Jurisdiction Measure 1963, which left its section 4 (banning *ex officio* oaths) in place until that section was repealed by the Statute Law (Repeals) Act 1969. Although the ecclesiastical jurisdiction received regular emendation through legislation, the 1661 Act had a continuing relevance. While most of its provisions were negative, in delimiting the coercive powers of the ecclesiastical courts, it had in some sense revived them by restoring their coercive powers through legislation, a pre-1641 coercive power that was revived and remained until 1963, when the whole system of the church courts was simplified and the criminal jurisdiction over the laity was expressly abolished.

The other measures were, first, the Act for the confirming and restoration of ministers 1660. Long and detailed, it had to deal with the restoration of improperly dispossessed ministers and the ejection of usurping ones, and all the consequential complications around patronage and property rights. The second instrument,

---

[100] 13 Car II c 12.
[101] 17 Car I c 11.

the Act for confirmation of marriages 1660, confirmed the validity of marriages that had been solemnised before a justice of the peace since 1642 as if they had been solemnised in the established Church. There was no need, however, to pass legislation to recreate the episcopacy, their official principals, chancellors, and all of the bodies and structures swept away in 1646. The legal position was that the legislation by that time was of no effect, as it had not satisfied the legal requirements of an Act of Parliament with royal assent. It was the case, therefore, that the church courts could restart as if there had been no legal challenge to their authority. Helmholz gives a nice example of William Somner, Registrar of the Diocese of Canterbury, whose episcopal act book restarts in 1660 after a gap since 1643, using identical language as before the interregnum.[102] Parliament during the interregnum had not in fact legislated to abolish the canon and ecclesiastical laws. It did not need to, as the church courts went with the bishops.

VI. Conclusion

With the restoration of the church courts, the canon and ecclesiastical laws were revived without the need for legislative intervention. In that sense, when Richard Burn and Robert Phillimore ignored the interregnum period, they were justified in doing so, as the continuity of the ecclesiastical law had been paused but had not legally been destroyed or amended. Nonetheless, studying the period should cause canonists within the Church of England today to consider a host of questions: What might happen if the United Kingdom became a republic again; if the Church were disestablished; if the system of church courts in were to be reorganised so that they were not bishops' courts but national courts; and similar counter-factuals? There is also the question of where the authority in the Church comes from? While ultimately from God, how much coercive authority flows from the Crown, from the King-in-Parliament, from synods and convocations, from diocesan bishops and the apostolic succession? And how much from tradition and custom, from the canons, or from new national bodies created by measures under the Synodical Government Measure 1969? How much of the authority is local, at the level of individual parishes where the incumbent has cure of souls? Is such authority administrative and organisational, or does it have an intrinsic importance, so that if it were not present, the Church would have no legal sanction to minister as it does? In the earlier part of the period covered by this chapter, the authority of the Church and the Crown were conjoined, and the eminent canonists of the day helped provide legal arguments to defend church courts and the Crown from supervision by Parliament and by the common law. In the interregnum period, the church courts and the ecclesiastical jurisdiction

---

[102] RH Helmholz, 'Notable Ecclesiastical Lawyers: XIV: William Somner (c 1598–1669)' (2017) 19 *Ecclesiastical Law Journal* 224–29.

fell with the bishops. The extra-constitutional parliaments and protectorates that governed and legislated during this period reformed the Church of England into a new national Presbyterian established Church. The analysis of this period might provide some answers to the question of where authority lies in the church law and in the Church generally.

5

The Restoration and Re-Establishment: 1660–1701

RUSSELL SANDBERG

The year 1660 is often regarded as a turning-point in the history of English law.[1] The Restoration of the monarchy is often depicted as a return to the ancient constitution of the realm. Gone were most of the prerogative courts set up by the Tudors; gone was the absolute monarchy of the early Stuarts; gone was the republican personal rule of the Commonwealth.[2] Yet these periods had all left their mark. Moreover, the Restoration of the monarchy was actually the introduction of something new: a modified and long-lasting complex and largely unwritten constitutional compromise, whereby the royal prerogatives remained but within the context of what would eventually become a parliamentary democracy. However, it is important not to get ahead of ourselves. These developments took centuries to be achieved, and at times, after several steps one way, a couple were taken in another – or backwards. Institutions from the past did not fade but often slowly mutated to suit the new context. For instance, the Court of Chancery remained but became more legalistic, and a court of the people rather than one of royal whim, and eventually found itself in the common law system.[3]

---

[1] See, eg, FW Maitland and FC Montague, *A Sketch of English Legal History* (New York, GP Putman's Sons, 1915) 131.

[2] For discussion, see, eg, R Sandberg, *A Historical Introduction to English Law: Genesis of the Common Law* (Cambridge, Cambridge University Press, 2023) chs 9 and 10.

[3] The Court of Chancery developed from the role of the chancellor, the figure who was effectively the king's secretary of state for all departments, keeping the king's seal and supervising all of the writing done under the king's name. The chancellor was a member of the King's Council and usually a bishop. The chancellor and thereupon the Chancery began to give justice to those whose claims did not fit within a common law writ. The Court of Chancery developed its own separate and considerable jurisdiction; it followed canonical procedures. In particular, it borrowed the procedure used by the ecclesiastical courts to suppress heresy: the accused was examined upon oath and the chancellor decided questions of fact as well as questions of law. By the late 16th century, the rules that the chancellor administered became known as 'the rules of equity and good conscience': FW Maitland, *Equity: A Course of Lectures* (Cambridge, Cambridge University Press, 1969 [1936]) 7–8. As the centuries unfolded, the courts of equity had developed into a separate system of law, providing rights where the common law did not, with its own courts and separate lawyers. However, limits to their powers were not set out and, even by the 17th century, it was said that the protection of equity varied

Indeed, talk of 'the Restoration' risks over-simplifying this period, especially in relation to the position of the Church of England. As might be expected given the constitutional, legal and political upheavals of the periods leading up to and during the Civil War and the Commonwealth, turning back the clock was easier said than done. Moreover, the religious posture of the State was itself still rather new, being imposed only in the Tudor period and undergoing significant shifts during that and the age of the early Stuarts. The country did not simply time-travel back to the time before Charles I's execution. Legal fictions suggested that this was so. As we saw in chapter 4, laws passed during the Commonwealth were simply deemed void since they had not received royal assent. As Maitland noted, after the Restoration, 'no lawyer would have appealed to them as law, and no lawyer would do so at the present day: they have no place in our statute book'.[4] Charles II's reign was considered to begin *de jure* in 1649, as denoted in relation to statutes by the regnal years continuing numerically from before the Commonwealth without interruption. However, this was a mere legalistic fiction. As a matter of fact, there had been a disruption, and the upheaval was far from over. Indeed, as Richard Helmholz observes, following the Civil War it had 'all come crashing down', and what happened after the Restoration remains, relatively,[5] understudied:

> The courts, the English civilians and the bishops got their comeuppance. They all suffered twenty years of isolation and deprivation. What would happen to their fortunes in the years immediately following the restoration of episcopacy in the 1660s remains to be investigated in detail.[6]

This chapter contends that the period 1660 to 1701 is less of a restoration and more of a commotion, with differing ideas, about how England was to be

---

with 'the length of the chancellor's foot'. This meant that litigants went from court to court, and often to both courts of equity and courts of common law, to secure their rights. In the middle of the 19th century, this led to various piecemeal changes, allowing common law courts to grant some equitable remedies and the Court of Chancery to award common law remedies such as damages. However, real reform came shortly afterwards. The Supreme Court of Judicature Acts 1873 and 1875 (the 'Judicature Acts') consolidated and unified the courts into two parts: the High Court (which by 1880 had three divisions: King's Bench, Chancery and Probate, Divorce and Admiralty) and the Court of Appeal. Appeals would go from the High Court to the Court of Appeal and then to the Judicial Committee of the House of Lords (which over a century later would become known as the Supreme Court). All of these courts now administered the rights, reliefs and defences found in both the common law and in equity. Common law and equity remained separate bodies of rules but were now enforced in the same courts: see, eg, Sandberg (n 2) 201–05, 263.

[4] FW Maitland, *The Constitutional History of England* (Cambridge, Cambridge University Press, 1941 [1908]) 282.

[5] Some of the main works include J Spurr, *The Restoration Church of England 1646–1689* (New Haven, CT, Yale University Press, 1991); A Thomson, *Church Courts and the People in Seventeenth Century England* (London, UCL Press, 2022); MG Smith, *Pastoral Discipline and the Church Court: The Hexham Court, 1680–1730* (York, Saint Anthony, 1982); MG Smith, *The Church Courts, 1680–1840: From Canon to Ecclesiastical Law*, ed P Smith (Lampeter, Edwin Mellen, 2006); and B Till, *The Church Courts, 1660–1720: Revival of Procedure* (York, Borthwick Institute, 2006).

[6] RH Helmholz, *The Profession of Ecclesiastical Lawyers: An Historical Introduction* (Cambridge, Cambridge University Press, 2019) 90.

governed and the role of the Church, competing with one another. It explores some of the main developments by distinguishing two distinct phases within this period: the first roughly corresponding to the reigns of Charles II (1660–85) and James III (1685–88); and the second following the Glorious Revolution and covering the reigns of William and Mary (1689–94) and William III (1694–1702). This division underscores the turbulence of the period as a whole and undermines any neat but superficial narrative that sees this epoch as simply restoring what had come before. The Restoration actually brought about two new and distinct chapters in Church–State relations in this period, where the position of the Church of England and the question of whether and if so how to accommodate dissenters proved to be contested, changeable and controversial. This chapter explores these two phases, examining the changing legal position of the Church of England within the wider context of the main constitutional and legal changes of each phase.

I. An Insecure and Exclusionary 'Restoration': 1660–88

As the name implies, the Restoration led to the rejection of almost all of the reforms made under the Commonwealth. However, talk of 'restoration' is somewhat misleading, in that it is not always clear what is being restored and whether what occurred was the restoration of a pre-existing approach or the creation of something new. It was not just the Commonwealth legislation that was repealed. The Act for the Abolition of the Court of High Commission 1641 had removed the power of ecclesiastical judges and other personnel to punish any wrongdoing. The Ecclesiastical Jurisdiction Act 1661 repealed all provisions of the 1641 statute, with the temporary exception of those concerning the Court of High Commission. It provided that such ecclesiastical persons did not extend to include their 'power or authority to exercise, execute, inflict of determine any ecclesiastical jurisdiction or censure which they might not by law have done' before 1639, and the new statute did not extend to anything that was 'to abridge or diminish the King's Majesty's supremacy in ecclesiastical matters and affairs'. Most notably it explicitly stated that the 1640 Canons and 'any other ecclesiastical laws or canons not formerly confirmed allowed or enacted by the established laws of the land as they stood' in 1639 were not restored.[7] This was no simple return to Charles I's days.[8]

Jens Aklundh has argued that 'Parliament's decision not to revive the two most coercive features of the pre-Civil War jurisdiction, the *ex officio* oaths and the

---

[7] See *R v Tristram* [1902] 1 KB 816, 836, per Mathew LJ.
[8] Compare the Confirmation of Marriages Act 1660, which recognised marriages that had been conducted since 1 May 1642, and gave them 'force and effect as if such marriages had been had and solemnised according to the Rites and Ceremony established or used in the Church or kingdom of England'.

High Commission courts, seriously weakened the Church's discipline, especially in a religious landscape that witnessed the continued proliferation of heterodox groups such as the Quakers and Baptists, who willingly dissociated themselves from the restored episcopal Church'.[9] According to Claire Cross, the 'courts, which did come back, had no laws to administer adapted to deal with the conditions of the later seventeenth century or penalties to inflict which any longer raised real apprehension'.[10] The only effective remedy left was excommunication, and the church courts shifted to religious rather than moral or sexual breaches of ecclesiastical law.[11]

As Grant Tapsell graphically put it, 'the re-established Church of England developed within a Petri dish of festering political affairs' and reflected the 'chronic instability that was at the heart of the Restoration'.[12] Although the seeds of many long-lasting notions were sown in the post-Restoration years, it is important not to overplay the health and strength of the plants that slowly began to grow. During the reign of Charles II (1660–85) there remained tensions between king and Parliament, and, as usual, much of this concerned religion. At first, it appeared that the Restoration would usher in an era of religious tolerance. Ann Lyon notes that,

> if only for political reasons, Charles was keen to bring the less extreme Protestant groupings and the Anglicans ... under the umbrella of a single national Church. Once again, the issue lay between the different Protestant groupings, particularly those who favoured restoration of the episcopacy and the Presbyterians. Intensive negotiations culminated in the issue by the king of the Worcester House Declaration, proposing a church settlement that attempted to satisfy both persuasions. In the event, nothing concrete was achieved and the religious issue was left to fester.[13]

The Worcester House Declaration resulted from a conference between Anglicans and Presbyterians in 1660. Its spirit was reflected in the so-called Convention Parliament, which approved the Declaration of Breda. This promised the pardoning of all crimes during the Civil War and interregnum, provided the offender recognised Charles as king. The Declaration also promised religious tolerance in areas that did not disturb the peace of the kingdom. However, this came to be interpreted as allowing non-Anglicans to hold public office, which proved to be too much for Parliament. Subsequently, the second Parliament of Charles' reign introduced what became known as the Clarendon Code: a raft of legislation

---

[9] J Aklundh, 'The Church Courts in Restoration England, 1660–c 1689' (PhD Thesis, University of Cambridge, 2008) 8.

[10] C Cross, *Church and People, 1450–1660: The Triumph of the Laity in the English Church* (London, Wiley and Sons, 1976) 227–28.

[11] RB Outhwaite, *The Rise and Fall of the English Ecclesiastical Courts* (Cambridge, Cambridge University Press, 2007) ch 9.

[12] G Tapsell, 'The Church of England, 1662–1714' in J Gregory (ed), *The Oxford History of Anglicanism*, vol II: *Establishment and Empire, 1662–1829* (Oxford, Oxford University Press, 2007) 25–48, 28.

[13] A Lyon, *Constitutional History of the United Kingdom*, 2nd edn (Abingdon, Routledge, 2016) para 15.1.2.

that moved in the opposite direction.[14] Now, Parliament passed laws to penalise those who did not conform to the restored Church of England. As Lyon noted, 'religious toleration was severely restricted, at a time of reaction against extremist sects and their association with anti-monarchism'.[15]

There came to exist a 'narrow and exclusive "settlement"' that was based upon 'a narrow religious establishment, not an integrative institution dedicated to the wider goals of "healing and sharing"'.[16] As Tapsell noted, 'persecution became a key part of Restoration society'.[17]

Maitland commented that there were five significant Acts.[18] The Corporation Act 1661 required all holders of offices in municipal corporations to receive the sacrament under the rites of the Church of England. The Conventicle Act 1664 made it a crime punishable by three months' imprisonment for a first offence to attend any meeting for alterative religious worship where five persons were present in addition to the household. The Five Mile Act 1665 made it unlawful for a non-conformist minister to come within that distance of a corporate town, or to teach in any public or private school. The Test Act 1673 required all those who held on office of trust to meet the sacramental test. The Parliamentary Test Act 1678 imposed the declaration against transubstantiation upon members of both Houses, 'and thus for the first time excluded Roman Catholic peers from the House of Lords'. This raft of legislation excluded non-conformists from civil and military office and from being awarded university degrees.[19] As Tapsell comments:

> Although the repressive religious legislation of the age was never wholly successful in crushing the resolve of those outside the national Church, it sustained a chimerical vision that somehow, sometime, the Church of England would include all of the king's subjects. In other words, it underpinned a mindset that abhorred any notion of pluralistic toleration, or even qualified relief from the scrupulous.[20]

The position in relation to Catholics was particularly muddy. Maitland noted that while these laws were passed against the Protestant non-conformists, 'the terrible code against the Catholics remains unrepealed, though under Charles II and James II breaches of it are connived at by the king and sanctioned by virtue of the dispensing power'.[21] Indeed, the king had attempted to extend toleration

---

[14] The term is used to describe the legislation between 1660 and 1665 and was named after Lord Clarendon, despite the fact that he was not the architect of the measures and even spoke out against them.
[15] Lyon (n 13) para 15.1.2.
[16] Tapsell (n 12) 25, 27, 28.
[17] ibid 28.
[18] Maitland (n 4) 515. Other commentators group the Acts differently: they see the Clarendon Code as comprising four statutes – the Corporation Act 1661, the Act of Uniformity 1662, the Conventicle Act 1664 and the Five-Mile Act 1665.
[19] See also the Quaker Act 1662, which made it illegal for Quakers to worship together.
[20] Tapsell (n 12) 25, 28.
[21] Maitland (n 4) 515.

towards Protestant non-conformists and Catholics through Declarations of Indulgence issued in 1662 and 1672, suspending some of the penal laws against dissenters. However, parliamentary protest meant that these were abandoned. In February 1673, Parliament voted unanimously that 'penal statutes in matters ecclesiastical cannot be suspended but by an Act of Parliament'.[22] There were some exceptions to the rule – most notably the power to burn heretics was abolished in 1677[23] – but there was a 'general hardening of attitudes'.[24] The Test Act 1673 and the Parliamentary Test Act 1678 were aimed at Catholics in particular. As Lyon notes, 'no longer was the principal religious division between different Protestant groups, it was again between Protestant and Catholic'.[25] This was because of a shift in what Tapsell refers to as the 'anxious national debate' from the lingering hangover from the civil wars concerning fears about puritans' political disobedience to 'the renewal of the Stuart nightmare prospect of … popery and arbitrary government'.[26]

Missing from the five Acts listed by Maitland is one Act that imposed liturgical uniformity not on dissenters outside the Church of England but upon those within the Church: the Act of Uniformity 1662. In Tapsell's words, this Act 'provided the legislative coping-stone for the later Stuart Church as a national institution'.[27] It sought to protect 'the Reformed Religion of the Church of England' by reinstating the Book of Common Prayer, a single liturgical use for public worship in all churches throughout the realm. Moreover, clergy who failed to subscribe to the (Elizabethan) Thirty-Nine Articles of Religion were deprived of their livings by August 1661. All clergy were also required to renounce the Solemn League and Covenant of 1643 and be ordained by a bishop. Other legislation also impacted the Church. In addition to numerous Private Acts of Parliament that affected a range of ecclesiastical matters,[28] the Clergy Act 1661 disabled those in Holy Orders from exercising 'any temporal jurisdiction or authority', the Augmentation of Benefices Act 1665 facilitated the uniting of churches in cities and towns corporate, the Benefit of Clergy Act 1670 curtailed the use of benefit of clergy and the Sunday Observation Act 1677 mandated better observation of the Lord's Day.

The Act of Uniformity 1662 and the repressive treatment of dissenters were key to developing, as Tapsell puts it, 'a narrow religious establishment'.[29] For Tapsell, the first decades following the Restoration were characterised by a 'pursuit of "uniformity"', which 'would prove to be one of the most divisive issues

---

[22] Lyon (n 13) para 15.1.4. Compare *Thomas v Sorrell* (1673) 124 ER 1098, which held that the king had the power where certain conditions were met to dispense with penal statutes.
[23] Maitland (n 4) 516.
[24] Lyon (n 13) para.15.1.4.
[25] ibid.
[26] Tapsell (n 12) 25, 34-35.
[27] ibid 28.
[28] See, eg the Act enabling the Bishop of London to lease out tenements built on the site of his palace in 1662.
[29] Tapsell (n 12) 28.

of the age'; so, using the term Restoration is misleading, since it was a new and fragile settlement that was created. Tapsell continues:

> Recreating a legally privileged national Church was not viewed complacently by churchmen as a secure and permanent achievement. This was especially the case because it was recognized that the civil wars and Interregnum had entrenched passionate religious divisions to an unprecedented degree and a long and great separation from the Church made it difficult to win loyalties back. God's mercy to the realm of England was felt to be qualified, limited and something that needed regularly to be earned anew.[30]

This gradual working out of the new constitutional settlement was present not only in relation to church matters. A number of other significant constitutional steps were taken during the reign of Charles II. The independence of jurors was secured in *Bushell's Case*,[31] which protected the right of jurors to return a verdict against the weight of the evidence and the direction of the court.[32] The most important development was, however, the Habeas Corpus Act 1679.[33] This Act guaranteed that, with the exception of persons charged with treason, those who had been charged but not convicted could demand a writ of Habeas Corpus from the judge so that the prisoner would be presented in court and where 'the true cause of the commitment' would be certified. It further provided for the timely delivery of justice and that no person could be recommitted for the same offence or sent out of the country to be imprisoned.[34] As Montague has argued, although the Act 'merely improved the procedure for enforcing a single common-law right' that had been asserted in general terms by clause 39 of Magna Carta, the Habeas Corpus Act 1679 placed great significance upon the right to personal freedom and the notion that England was governed by the rule of law.[35]

However, despite these developments, echoes from the past dominated the end of this first phase. Concerns about Catholicism escalated during the brief reign of James II (1685–88), in which reign there was a move towards absolute rule. On his death-bed, Charles had converted to Catholicism, and James's own Catholic faith was of concern to Parliament. These fears were well-founded. In *Godden v Hales*,[36] the court upheld the king's power to dispense with laws requiring a colonel to take Church of England oaths. In 1686, the Court of Commissioners for Ecclesiastical Causes was established by James II under the royal prerogative to control the government of the Church. And in 1687 and 1688, James issued two Declarations of Indulgence, royal proclamations read in all churches that

---

[30] ibid 25–26.
[31] *Bushell's Case* (1670) 124 ER 1006.
[32] Maitland and Montague (n 1) 132–33.
[33] For detailed discussion of the law before and after the Act, see RJ Sharpe, *The Law of Habeas Corpus* (Oxford, Clarendon Press, 1976).
[34] It stated that the accused must be indicted in the first term after his commitment and tried in the following term.
[35] Maitland and Montague (n 1) 141.
[36] *Godden v Hales* (1686) 11 St Tr 1166.

suspended the laws against Roman Catholics. In *The Seven Bishops' Case*,[37] the Archbishop of Canterbury and six bishops were acquitted by a jury on a charge of seditious libel for having signed a petition claiming that reading the declaration was illegal and against their conscience.[38] The birth of a male and Catholic heir proved to be the final straw. In July 1688, James dissolved Parliament, and the resulting uprising led to his exile and to the replacement of James by Parliament.

II. A Compromise with a Revolutionary Legacy: 1688–1701

In November 1688, William of Orange (who had a legitimate claim to the throne through his grandfather Charles I) landed with an army. William was a renowned Protestant, famed as a champion of the faith due in part to his participation in wars against Catholic rulers such as Louis XIV of France. As nobles and officers defected to William, James II eventually fled abroad, leaving William free to take the Crown.[39] William assembled the Parliament that had sat during Charles II's reign, and they advised the summoning of a 'Convention' of the estates of the realm. In January 1689 this 'Convention Parliament' met, and the Commons declared that James had broken the contract between people and king and had therefore abdicated the government.[40] By the next month, the Lords had agreed, and William and his wife Mary (James II's daughter) were formally proclaimed king and queen.[41] The so-called 'Glorious Revolution' had taken place. As Maitland argued, although 'those who conducted the revolution sought, and we may well say were wise in seeking, to make the revolution look as small as possible, to make it as like a legal proceeding', nevertheless, it would be difficult to 'regard the Convention Parliament as a lawfully constituted assembly'.[42] What occurred was 'a revolution' and, as such, 'we cannot work it into our constitutional law'.[43]

---

[37] *The Seven Bishops' Case* (1688) 3 Mod Rep 212.
[38] See W Gibson, *James II and the Trial of the Seven Bishops* (London, Palgrave Macmillan, 2009).
[39] See, generally GM Trevelyan, *The English Revolution, 1688–1689* (Oxford, Oxford University Press, 1963); M Ashley, *The Glorious Revolution of 1688* (London, Hodder & Stoughton, 1966); and SE Prall, *The Bloodless Revolution: England 1688* (Madison, WI, University of Wisconsin Press, 1985).
[40] Maitland (n 4) 283–84.
[41] Many had felt that William and Mary should be termed 'regents', rather than monarchs in their own right, because the former king was still alive. William was not prepared to accept this, and on 6 February 1689 the House of Lords at last conceded the point.
[42] Maitland (n 4) 284.
[43] ibid 285. Indeed, it was not a completely bloodless matter. In March 1689, James had landed in Ireland with a French army, soon taking over most of Ireland; and in July 1689, conflicts broke out in Scotland between Protestants and Catholics. Peace was eventually restored in Ireland following the Battle of the Boyne in July 1690, after which James retreated, earning himself the Irish nickname 'Séamus á Chaca' (James the Shit). In Scotland, the Glencoe Massacre of 1692 terrorised the Jacobite clans into submission.

Like the term 'the Restoration', references to the 'Glorious Revolution' risk simplifying the complexity of what occurred by reducing it to an overnight change. Indeed, in respect of the Church of England, there is a further risk of regarding the 'Glorious Revolution' as a constitutional change that had little effect upon the religious posture of the realm other than to preserve 'what 1660 was supposed to have re-established': 'the Revolution only secured the hegemony of the largely Anglican aristocracy and gentry in the face of the threat apparently posed by a Roman Catholic monarchical bureaucracy'.[44] Yet this underplays the importance of the Glorious Revolution and the way in which it was the beginning of new forms of governance and thinking that would take centuries to work out. As Kenneth Hylson-Smith argues, 'these years did in fact see such significant political, constitutional, economic, social and religious changes that the ancient regime at the very least underwent major modification; and to a great extent the changes began with the blood-less Revolution'.[45]

The constitutional changes were undoubtedly significant. The conditions upon which William and Mary took the throne were articulated in a Declaration of Rights, which was later incorporated into the Bill of Rights 1688 and confirmed by Act of Parliament.[46] The Bill of Rights underlined how the king was now 'distinctly below statute'.[47] It declared illegal the levying of money, the raising of a standing army and 'the pretended power' of suspending or dispensing laws without the consent of Parliament.[48] It confirmed that all subjects had the right to petition the king and that 'excessive bail' or 'cruel and unusual punishments' must not be inflicted. Members of Parliament should be freely elected and have freedom of speech in parliamentary proceedings. The Bill of Rights also secured the succession of the Crown and proclaimed that it was 'inconsistent with the safety and welfare of this Protestant Kingdom to be governed by a Popish Prince'. However, Maitland argued that there was a plausible case for regarding this 'Glorious Revolution' as 'a restoration of the ancient constitution as it stood in the days of the Lancastrian kings', in that it was clear that it was 'no honorary president of a republic that the nation wanted, but a real working, governing king'.[49] All the old royal prerogatives existed, save in so far as they had been expressly abolished by statute, and so the monarch retained the prerogative of making war and peace, powers of patronage, such as choosing his or her own ministers, appointing bishops and other ecclesiastical persons, and summoning, discontinuing and dissolving Parliament. Yet the Coronation Oath Act 1688 highlighted that there had been some change. Now, in place of recognition that laws were the grant of the monarch, the monarch swore to rule according to the law agreed

---

[44] K Hylson-Smith, *The Churches in England from Elizabeth I to Elizabeth II*, vol II: *1689–1833* (London, SCM Press, 1997) 3.
[45] ibid, but see n 43.
[46] Crown and Parliament Recognition Act 1689.
[47] Maitland (n 4) 388.
[48] The Court of Commissioners for Ecclesiastical Causes was also declared to be illegal.
[49] Maitland (n 4) 388.

in Parliament. And the pledge to 'protect and defend the Bishops and Churches under [my] Government' was reformulated as an explicit oath to maintain 'the true Profession of the Gospel and the Protestant Reformed Religion Established by Law'.

A raft of further important constitutional documents followed throughout the reigns of William and Mary (1689–94) and William III (1694–1702), who became sole monarch on his wife's death. The Second Treason Act 1696 stated that those accused of a crime were to have the aid of counsel, two witnesses were required, and a copy of the indictment and jury list were to be given to an accused before the trial. The Act of Settlement 1701 made further arrangements for the succession, requiring the heir to the throne to be a 'protestant' and that the monarch 'shall join in communion with the Church of England as by law established'.[50] It stated that the 'laws of England are the birthright of the people' and monarchs 'ought to administer the government … according to the said laws and all their officers and ministers ought to serve them respectively according to the same'.[51] The authority of Parliament over the monarchy had been underlined again.

The most significant piece of legislation, however, was that which provided the answer to what was probably the 'most delicate question in 1689', namely, 'the degree of toleration to be allowed to Dissenters'.[52] The Act of Toleration 1689 allowed Trinitarian Protestants their own places of worship, provided they met with unlocked doors and with notice to the local Church of England bishop. With the benefit of hindsight, we can see the Toleration Act as constituting 'a sea change [that] pointed toward to ever-increasing pluralism'.[53] However, the Act was not as novel as it might first appear to be. The persecution and lack of toleration found in the statutes passed as part of the so-called Restoration did not represent a settled position. As Grant Tapsell notes:

> Reciting the list of statutes that together created a 'confessional state' in late Stuart England should not obscure the extent to which this was a partisan achievement by one faction triumphing over others. It was a matter of contingency, not of inevitability, that hard-line advocates of religious intolerance regularly imposed their views and this tended to reflect successful exploitation of divisions both within the royal courts and Parliament.[54]

As we have already noted, Charles I and James II had both attempted to achieve much wider toleration, and indeed 'between 1662 and 1689 there were numerous unsuccessful attempts to draft and pass legislation that might reshape the Church in ways that could comprehend a significant number of Nonconformists, primarily Presbyterians'.[55] Compared with such efforts, the Act of Toleration

---

[50] Act of Settlement 1701, s 3.
[51] ibid s 4.
[52] Hylson-Smith (n 44) 6.
[53] ibid 7.
[54] Tapsell (n 12) 25, 29–30.
[55] ibid 30.

appeared to be 'a disappointing and limited affair'. It was, in the words of Hylson-Smith, 'a strangely unsatisfactory solution'.[56] One reason for this was that it was not what had been intended. The Earl of Nottingham had introduced two Bills into the House of Lords, 'which were designed to go together':

> One was for comprehension, and laid down generous terms by which Dissenters might be admitted to the Church of England. The other was for toleration, and carefully specified limited terms for the toleration of the anticipated relatively small number who would not agree to participate in such comprehension.[57]

The Comprehension Bill, however, fell in the House of Lords as a result of the anger caused by the king's proposal to repeal the Test and Corporation Acts. As a result, the Toleration Act alone became law. The effect was that 'the new Act, which had been designed to deal with a small number of intransigent nonconformists, had to apply to nearly half a million sober and respectable citizens'.[58] Moreover, at the time, this led to a great deal of confusion as to what the Act meant: 'It was interpreted in different ways by the clergy, the government and by the great majority of ordinary lay-people.'[59] Some maintained that the Act had simply restored the settlement that had existed prior to James II's Declaration of Indulgence. However, as time went on, it became clear that the effects of the Toleration Act were 'enormous'.[60] As Grant Tapsell notes, on 'a personal level, individuals felt that a distinct era of persecution was over: a Presbyterian clergyman, Roger Morrice, recorded in February 1689 that after the passage of the Toleration Act he could walk through Westminster Hall, at the very centre of public affairs, without fear for the first time since 1662'.[61]

The effect upon the Church of England was earth-shattering. As Tapsell puts it, 'the Church of England remained the Established church but lost its full claims to be the national church'.[62] The Church took this demotion badly and two fundamental pillars of England's Church–State posture had been changed dramatically. First, even the limited toleration now afforded compromised the 'Restoration ideal of a single, all-inclusive national Church' and the 'ecclesiological consensus of the Restoration Church – her sense of being both Reformed and Catholic and her refusal to follow through the implications of her own episcopalism'.[63]

Second, as Hylson-Smith observes, the 'previous cherished principle of a divinely-ordained authority in the State' had been undermined by the involvement of Anglicans in the rebellion against James II; and this 'broke down that special relationship of the Church of England with the monarchy, and *via* the monarchy

---

[56] Hylson-Smith (n 44) 6.
[57] ibid.
[58] ibid.
[59] ibid 7.
[60] Tapsell (n 12) 25, 30.
[61] ibid.
[62] ibid.
[63] J Rule, *Albion's People: English Society 1714–1815* (Abingdon, Routledge, 1992) xiii.

with the whole apparatus of state'.[64] Ironically, schisms within the Church of England further underlined how the Toleration Act was the first step in the parting of the ways between Church and State (a process, of course, that remains incomplete,[65] as we shall see in later chapters). The 'non-jurors' represented the main such schism: those who refused to swear allegiance to William and Mary on the basis that they had already sworn inviolable oaths of allegiance to James.[66] These figures included a number of bishops and hundreds of members of the clergy, who were suspended and therefore broke away from the Church. The 'non-jurors' were a heterogeneous group, with non-jurors varying in terms of how outspoken and critical they became. Yet their 'departure undoubtedly inflicted damage on the Church' and non-jurors 'were important in their generation, and their successors continued to exercise a considerable influence'.[67]

The turbulence of the time was reflected in other important legal developments aside from the constitutional reforms. These included the further growth of statute law, bolstered by the end of long intervals between parliaments. In addition to a steady stream of Private Acts, Public Acts dealt with a wide variety of topics, ranging from numerous taxation statutes to the very particular Rebuilding of Saint Paul's and Westminster Abbey Act 1696. A number of statutes were passed on matters that touched ecclesiastical matters. The Simony Act 1688 dealt with situations where there had been a historic buying and selling of an ecclesiastical privilege. The Presentation of Benefices Act 1688 vested in the two universities of Oxford and Cambridge the benefices that had belonged to papists. The Benefit of Clergy etc Act 1691 further modified and limited reliance on claiming benefit of clergy. The Repairs of Churches Act 1692 provided that where two churches were united and one of them demolished, then parishioners of that latter church would then pay toward the repairs of the other. The Duties on Marriages etc Act 1694 dealt with rates and duties concerning births, marriages and burials in order to help fund the war against France.[68] Under the Profane Swearing Act 1694, any person who profanely swore in the presence of a justice of the peace or town mayor, and either confessed to this or was convicted on the oath of one witness, was fined, with the fine being doubled and then trebled for repeat offences.[69] The Act was to be read four times a year in all parish churches and public chapels, with the cleric liable for a fine if this was not performed. The Quakers Act 1695 permitted Quakers to make an affirmation in some contexts where the law required an oath,[70] but also gave powers to enforce payment where 'by Reason of a pretended scruple of Conscience, Quakers do refuse to pay Tithes

---

[64] Hylson-Smith (n 44) 8.
[65] See discussion in R Sandberg, *Law and Religion* (Cambridge, Cambridge University Press, 2011).
[66] Hylson-Smith (n 44) 8.
[67] ibid.
[68] See also the Marriage Duty Act 1695 and the Duties on Marriage etc Act 1697.
[69] Those who did not pay the fine were set in the stocks or, if they were under 16, were whipped.
[70] See also the Affirmation by Quakers Act 1701.

and Church Rates'.[71] The Arbitration Act 1697 represented the first recognition of the arbitration of disputes, a process that had existed in practice for several years. The Blasphemy Act 1697 made it an offence for those educated in or professing the Christian religion to deny the Holy Trinity, claim that there was more than one God, deny the truth of Christianity or deny the Bible as divine authority.[72] And the Popery Act 1698 strengthened existing anti-Catholic laws, providing that a Roman priest who celebrated mass would be liable to 'perpetual imprisonment' at the discretion of the king.

These examples underline how one consequence of the Glorious Revolution was 'restored unity and energy to the legislature'.[73] That said, most of the important changes were still made by other means.[74] Although the prerogative courts were no more, the monarch's prerogative powers remained significant. The role of the King's Council evolved at this time to form the Privy Council largely as it exists today. Two noticeable developments began at this time. The first was that the practice emerged of the king's consulting only a few of the Council's members. This became known as the Cabal, reflecting the initial letters of the names of its members: Clifford, Ashley, Buckingham, Arlington and Lauderdale.[75] In time, this would become known as the cabinet council, the forerunner of the modern-day cabinet, though this would be slowly developed over a number of centuries. This development was resisted by Parliament, and the Act of Settlement 1700 included provision that 'matters and things relating to the well-governing of this kingdom' should be transacted by the Privy Council as a whole; however, this clause never came into force, and during Queen Anne's reign the existence of a cabinet became more familiar.[76] The second development was that, despite the abolition of the prerogative courts, some limited judicial powers continued to rest in the Privy Council. It remained as a court of last resort in admiralty matters, and in all matters civil and criminal arising in the king's lands beyond the sea. Through conquest and colonisation, the reach of this court grew significantly, and today it still retains an important jurisdiction.[77]

There were also notable judicial developments during this period. Central to this was the securing of the independence of the judiciary. It became established that the judges no longer held office 'during the king's good pleasure' but rather 'during good behaviour'.[78] Their salaries became fixed, and judges were

---

[71] See also the Recovery of Small Tithes Act 1695 and the Recovery of Tithes Act 1698.
[72] The Act was ineffective and resulted in 'few if any prosecutions': Law Commission, 'Offences Against Religion and Public Worship' Working Paper no 79 (April 1981) para 2.24.
[73] Maitland and Montague (n 1) 147.
[74] ibid 148.
[75] Maitland (n 4) 389.
[76] ibid 390.
[77] Under the Judicial Committee Act 1833. It was confirmed in *Willers v Joyce* [2016] UKSC 44 that judgments concerning English law can state that decisions of the Supreme Court and Court of Appeal are wrong and can expressly direct that domestic courts should treat the Privy Council decision as representing the law of England and Wales.
[78] Maitland (n 4) 312–13.

only removable following a conviction for some offence or an address of both Houses of Parliament. This was also the age in which the Court of Chancery began to reach maturity. Maitland noted that Lord Nottingham, who became Chancellor in 1675, has been called 'the father of English Equity'.[79] Under his Chancellorship, the importance of precedents was stressed, and moves were made towards the systemisation of equitable principles. The Chancery jurisdiction now became 'a supplementary system of case law, giving additional remedies and enforcing additional duties – but a system of case law with precedents reported and respected'.[80] The House of Lords now heard appeals from the Court of Chancery. However, despite these changes, which slowly emerged, this was not generally a time of innovation. Montague has suggested that 'men were glad to return to the institutions of their forefathers. Satisfied to be rid forever of the Court of Star Chamber, and the Court of High Commission, they regarded little the barbarity of the criminal law, or the vexatious expense and delay of proceedings in Chancery.'[81]

There were, of course, a number of cases during this period that touched upon religious matters in both the church and temporal courts. However, as Spurr notes, 'although shafts of scholarly light have illuminated the workings of some courts in a few dioceses, most of the church courts of Restoration England remain unstudied, and consequently all generalisations about them remain fragile'.[82] Outhwaite commented that although 'few studies directly compare Restoration experience with pre-1640 realities', given 'the large number of courts in existence, it would not be surprising to find a wide variety of experiences'; for instance, business in the consistory courts of the Province of Canterbury 'revived after 1660, but at levels below those characteristic of the 1620s and 1630s'.[83] Some cases regulated the clergy, such as *Brown v Spence* on the requirement of clergy to subscribe on institution to the Thirty-Nine Articles.[84] *Ball v Cross* established that the rector of the parish was responsible for the repair of the whole church building under canon law,[85] but *Pense v Prouse*[86] clarified that according to the Roman canon law, the parson must repair the whole of the church building; by the custom of England, however, the parson must repair the chancel and the parishioners the nave of the church.[87] Other cases dealt with the laity. For example, *Rich v Gerard and Loder*[88] and *Dargavell v Langdon*[89] established that

---

[79] ibid 312.
[80] ibid.
[81] Maitland and Montague (n 1) 132.
[82] Spurr (n 5) 209. See, however, WH Bryson (ed), *Miscellaneous Reports of Cases in the Court of Delegates: From 1670 to 1750* (Richmond, VA, Centre for Law Reporting, 2016).
[83] Outhwaite (n 11) 80.
[84] *Brown v Spence* (1663) 1 Keb 590.
[85] *Ball v Cross* (1688) 1 Salk 164.
[86] *Pense v Prouse* (1695) 1 Ld Raym 59.
[87] *Halsbury's Laws of England*, 5th edn, vol 34: *Ecclesiastical Law* (London, LexisNexis, 2011) para 864.
[88] *Rich v Gerard and Loder* (1690) 1 Hag Ecc App B7.
[89] *Dargavell v Langdon* (1678) Rothery's Precedents Mo 68, 31.

'incontinence' (that is, 'sexual immorality') included 'indecent exposure, keeping company with women of ill repute and solicitations of chastity, as well as incest, adultery and sexual intercourse outside the bound of holy matrimony' – and that such was an ecclesiastical offence. And *Gwyn v Watkins*[90] confirmed that frequenting alehouses and tippling was also an offence.[91] However, generally 'sexual delinquents were often outnumbered by other categories of offender' and the 'focus of prosecutions shifted strongly to breaches of the religious code'.[92] Therefore,

> [s]ome men and women were presented for attending conventicles, failing to receive the sacrament, and neglecting baptism and other religious rites, but the overwhelming majority were cited for their failure to attend church at all. Almost a half of those cited to appear at the Peterborough court from 1662 to 1664, for example, were presented for religious offences.[93]

Outhwaite noted that the numbers prosecuted for religious offences 'rose and fell' during this period, with the prosecutions for nonconformity virtually ceasing after the Toleration Act 1689. Both clergy and laity were also increasingly refusing to appear before the church courts.[94] Towards the end of this period, 'some of the lesser courts found their office business shrinking to negligible proportions'.[95] Sexual delinquency again dominated prosecutions, but the number of those cited was noticeably lower than it had been. Litigation also involved charitable gifts and endowments. Gareth Jones found that although earlier cases were not cited, the principles that had previously been applied to gifts and endowments made to beneficiaries who were now outside the law continued to be applied.[96] *Attorney-General v Baxter*[97] underscored that such gifts were subject to a prerogative cy-près scheme whereby, since the mode of performance was illegal and void, the gift was forfeited to the Crown which could then apply it as of grace. As Jones stated:

> The courts would not uphold any trust for the support of any religion or any religious organisation which was not tolerated by the State. Public policy demanded that their funds be used to maintain the only good and lawful religious purpose, the Established Church.[98]

There were several influential jurists in this period. Matthew Hale (1609–76), a puritan who held high judicial office after the Restoration, is famed for his treatise on *The History of the Common Law of England*. His work as a whole often

---

[90] *Gwyn v Watkins* (1700) Rothery's Precedents Mo 106, 51.
[91] *Halsbury's Ecclesiastical Law* (n 87) para 1133.
[92] Outhwaite (n 11) 81.
[93] ibid.
[94] ibid 82.
[95] ibid 83.
[96] G Jones, *History of the Law of Charity 1532–1827* (Cambridge, Cambridge University Press, 1969) 81.
[97] *Attorney-General v Baxter* (1684) I Vern 248.
[98] Jones (n 96) 87.

addresses religious questions and showed a shift to liberal Protestantism.[99] For Hale, the duty to obey law is based on 'the law of God' and conscience.[100] He applied the principle of reception to the field of ecclesiastical law, stating that 'the strength that … the papal … laws have obtained in this kingdom is only because they have been perceived and admitted either by the consent of parliament, and so are part of the statute laws; or else by immemorial usage and custom in some particular cases and courts, and not otherwise'.[101] Thomas Hobbes (1588–1679), the philosopher best known for his formulation of social contract theory in *Leviathan*, also wrote on jurisprudence; for him, it was the 'will of the civil sovereign that obliges subjects to obey any law – and peace depends on a civil power absolute in its authority over both state and church'.[102] Hobbes also maintained that 'there ought to be no power over the consciences of men, but of the Word [of God] itself';[103] and he maintained that 'all lawful power is of God, immediately in the [civil] supreme governor' and so, consequentially, he saw 'Ecclesiastical law as part of Civil Law … proceeding from the power of ecclesiastical government, given to our saviour to all Christian sovereigns'.[104]

There were other jurists who focused in detail on ecclesiastical laws. John Godolphin (1617–78), judge of the High Court of Admiralty, became one of the king's advisors after the Restoration. He wrote a number of books on law and divinity, including *The Holy Limbec* and *The Holy Arbor*. Godolphin also wrote on the admiralty jurisdiction and a three-part book on wills, executors and legacies. His *Repertorium Canonicum, or an Abridgment of the Ecclesiastical Laws of this Realm Consistent with the Temporal* (1678) was a 400-page treatise, which remains in print, providing 'an abridgment of ecclesiastical law' that begun with 'the regal supremacy, a point that cannot be touched with too much tenderness'.

William Watson (1637–89), a cleric who had been educated with a view to being a practitioner in the church courts and who had taken the degree of doctor of laws, authored *The Clergy-Man's Law: or the Compleat Incumbent*, two volumes of 59 chapters, collated from primary material intended for church patrons, clergy, students and practitioners. William Cave (1637–1713), another cleric, wrote on the history of the early Church, including *A Dissertation Concerning the Government of the Ancient Church by Bishops, Metropolitans and Patriarchs*. William Beveridge (1637–1708), another cleric, similarly published on law of the early Church and in his works 'articulated within the High Church tradition the

---

[99] See A Cromartie, *Sir Matthew Hale 1609–1676: Law, Religion and Natural Philosophy* (Cambridge, Cambridge University Press, 1995).
[100] N Doe, 'Rediscovering Anglican Priest-Jurists IV: Robert Sanderson (1587–1663)' (2022) 24 *Ecclesiastical Law Journal* 68–86, 83.
[101] Quoted ibid 84.
[102] ibid.
[103] T Hobbes, *Leviathan* (London, Penguin Classics, repr 1986) 311.
[104] ibid 594, 725; T Hobbes, *The Elements of Law* (1650) II, 107–08.

early Christian foundations of what he saw as the proper relationship between Church and State'.[105]

It is tempting to see the Restoration era as a whole as building the foundations of what would become the modern state. Although it would only be in the heat of the Industrial Revolution that the court system would be thoroughly modernised, it can still be claimed that in several respects, the reigns of the later Stuart monarchs saw the main building blocks of the constitution put into place. England was a country subject increasingly to the rule of law, as shown by the Habeas Corpus Act 1679 and the demise of Star Chamber. The supremacy of Parliament was underlined by the fact that it was parliamentary statute that resolved the issue of succession, and royal assent to legislation had begun to be a formality. There was even some evidence of the separation of powers, the 'divide and rule' constitutional principle that ensures that no one part of government is all-powerful, and the legislature, executive and judiciary all discharge checks on one another. However, too much should not be attributed to the Glorious Revolution and its aftermath. The plethora of constitutional documents of this age did not come close to generating a written constitution. As Maitland stated, the powers of the monarch as outlined by law have remained largely the same since the start of the Tudor period: 'as a matter of fact our present kingship is radically different from the kingship of the fifteenth century; but law has done little to take away powers from the king'.[106] The extent of the royal prerogative was 'vague', because since the revolution, monarchs 'have seldom gone near to breaking the law in serious matters'.[107] Moreover, although the Glorious Revolution had an important political impact, it had little effect upon social change. England remained an agricultural nation. It was only in subsequent centuries that this changed. The move from an economy based on land would have far-reaching and often unintended effects, including the erosion of the link between land ownership and membership of the House of Commons.[108]

However, this focus on the law of the Glorious Revolution underplays its politics. As Kenneth Hylson-Smith observes, 'politically perhaps the most dramatic transformation resulting from the events of 1688 and 1689 was the redisposition of England within the European scene'.[109] The fact that the person who sat on the English throne was not just a Dutchman but one who had 'a suitably impressive pedigree to qualify him to be a Protestant protagonist' meant that the European

---

[105] N Doe and D Nikiforos, 'Rediscovering Anglican-Priest Jurists III: William Beveridge (1637–1708)' (2021) 23 *Ecclesiastical Law Journal* 82–99, 83–84.
[106] Maitland (n 4) 342.
[107] ibid 342–43.
[108] In *Ashby v White* (1702-4) 2 Ld Raym 938, the Commons considered that they had sole right to determine 'all matters relating to the right of election of their own members'. The Lords said 'who has a right to sit in the House of Commons may be properly cognisable there but who has a right to choose is a matter originally established even before there is a parliament. A man has a right to his freehold by the common law and the law having annexed the right to voting to his freehold, it is of the nature of his freehold and must depend on it.'
[109] Hylson-Smith (n 44) 3–4.

dimension came to the fore.[110] This 'inflamed long-standing debates about the relationship of the Church of England to foreign Protestant churches'.[111] As Grant Tapsell notes:

> Many Dissenters, and some within the Established Church, looked beyond England for theological and ecclesiological inspiration. Others viewed such a vision as tantamount to undermining the royal supremacy and Episcopal hierarchy of the Church. ... Both William's ecclesiastical patronage and the prospect of the Hanoverian succession helped to fuel an aggressive discourse of the 'Church in danger'. This rhetoric was at the heart of post-revolutionary Church politics and with developing use of 'High' and 'Low' church as pejorative labels. The former connoted those hostile to non-conformity and passionately committed to the ceremonies of the Church re-established in 1662; the latter those who were more interested in pragmatic dialogue with Dissenters, and who stressed 'reasonable' religion rather than minute concern with liturgical and ecclesiological norms.[112]

These two perspectives had to some extent animated the whole debate following the Restoration as to the constitutional position and protection of religion, and would come increasingly important as the centuries went on. There was no longer one true view on the place of religion. The entanglement of Church and State was beginning to be questioned if not undone. The distinction between 'High' and 'Low' positions would increase in importance. It would become a frequent general dividing line between political parties. As Hylson-Smith noted, 'the Tories were associated with the High-Anglican tradition and the Whigs were generally composed of the more moderate churchmen'.[113] This was yet another respect in which the toleration legislation was the beginning of what was to come.

III. Conclusion

Periodisation tends to emphasise change over continuity.[114] The labels we give to major shifts in constitutional and ecclesiastical law exacerbate this. In part this is because the labels we use, though superficially appealing and apt, simplify and reduce complex and nuanced changes that are worked out over time. In the same way that talk of the Reformation disguises the extent to which the Henrician legislation was prompted by political matters rather than any theological zeal to reform the faith of the land, so talk of the Restoration and Glorious Revolution similarly has the capacity to mislead. This chapter has suggested that the two need to be considered as two separate periods in the evolving English ecclesiastical law.

---

[110] ibid 4.
[111] Tapsell (n 12) 25, 35.
[112] ibid.
[113] Hylson-Smith (n 43) 5.
[114] See R Sandberg, *Subversive Legal History: A Manifesto for the Future of Legal Education* (Abingdon, Routledge, 2021) ch 5.

Tensions between different perspectives both within and outside the Church of England, and manifest in the actions of monarch and parliamentarians, meant that 1660–1701 was a period of flux. Constitutional matters were hotly contested and unstable, including the place and role of the Church of England. Despite talk of the Restoration and the legal fictions employed to suggest that the Commonwealth had been nothing but a dream, 1660 did not see the clocks turn back to the position in which the constitution and the Church of England had been before the decapitation of Charles I. Rather, it led to an era of legal persecution and intolerance due to the successful rebuff of kingly attempts to introduce the indulgence of religious tolerance.

Yet these victories were erected on shallow foundations and proved to be short-lived. The resurgence of kingly absolutism and Catholicism led to a so-called Glorious Revolution, which, rather than reinstating the Restoration settlement, led somewhat accidentally to a seemingly restrictive Toleration Act, which in time opened the flood gates and transformed not only the position of dissenters but also the status and role of the Church of England. The Established Church was, from now on, one amongst others; and although it was pre-eminent in many ways, as the centuries unfolded its burdens would come to outweigh its privileges.

Such changes would take centuries and are still on-going. But an argument can be made that the Toleration Act was the beginning of what would follow. The Restoration statutes, by contrast, were but a false dawn; not wiped from the statute book, as Commonwealth ordinances were, but nevertheless not shaping what was to follow except in so far as the restrictive toleration legislation following the Glorious Revolution was a response to the narrow establishment developed in the 1660s – and the piecemeal nature of toleration over the centuries that followed was a result of the comprehensive but complicated institutional system of intolerances that had been developed. The period 1660–1701 as a whole may therefore be seen as a turning point: it was the beginning of a new relationship between the State and religions, including the Established Church, where differences of political and religious beliefs were no longer completely dismissed. Church and State were never to be so synonymous ever again. And the ecclesiastical law had been a key site in all these battles.

6

The Church in Danger – Legal Perspectives: 1701–60

STEPHEN COLEMAN

The period 1701 to 1760 brings an end to the Stuart dynasty and sees the birth of the Hanoverian: it covers the end of the reigns of William III (d 1702) and the last Stuart, Anne (1702–14), and the first two Hanoverians, George I (1714–27) and George II (1727–60). For the Church of England, the beginning of the period is marked by controversy: there were fears about doctrinal laxity and 'latitudinarianism', and claims of 'the church in danger', the Tory and high-church propaganda slogan against occasional conformity, religious dissent and atheism, which they thought threatened the influence and liberties of the Church; there were attempts associated with the Whigs to reunite dissenters within the established Church, or at least to provide a broad scheme of 'comprehension'; and as we move toward the end of the period, the rise of Methodism as a movement, first within and later separate from the Church.[1]

For England, this period was pivotal in terms of succession to the Crown. Under the Bill of Rights 1689, with William III childless, Anne (the daughter of James II) was the only person remaining in the line of succession. Yet Anne's series of still births and the death of her only son William, Duke of Gloucester, in July 1700, resulted in the Act of Settlement 1701. Only 'protestants' could succeed, and those who 'are or shall be reconciled to or hold communion with the see or church of Rome or shall profess the popish religion or shall marry a papist shall be excluded and forever incapable' of succession; and the successor 'shall join in communion with the Church of England as by law established'.[2] The statute also provided that, failing the issue of William III and Anne by any future marriage, the Crown of England and Ireland would pass to Sophia, Electress of Hanover, and her Protestant descendants: Sophia was the granddaughter of James I through his

---

[1] G Tapsell, 'The Church of England, 1662–1714' in J Gregory (ed), *The Oxford History of Anglicanism*, vol II: *Establishment and Empire, 1662–1829* (Oxford, Oxford University Press, 2017) 25–48; and RG Ingram, 'The Church of England, 1714–1783' ibid 49–67. Also J Walsh, C Haydon and S Taylor (eds), *The Church of England c 1689–c 1833* (Cambridge, Cambridge University Press, 1993).
[2] Act of Settlement 1701, ss 1, 2, 3.

daughter Elizabeth, who was the sister of Anne's grandfather, Charles I. Religion was at the heart of this matter; the Catholicism of James II and the resulting Glorious Revolution of 1688 were recent memories in the mind of Parliament, and it was deemed essential to ensure a Protestant line of succession. Therefore, under the Act of Settlement 1701, over 50 Catholics with stronger claims were excluded from the line of succession. The Electress Sophia died on 28 May 1714, two months before Anne, meaning that Sophia's son, the Elector of Hanover, acceded to the throne as George I.[3]

This forms the backdrop to the life of the Church of England in this period. The relationship between England and Scotland, between the Crown and Parliament, and religious toleration were the key issues of the day stimulating landmark legal developments. The Act of Settlement 1701, passed by the English Parliament, applied in the kingdoms of England and Ireland but not Scotland, where a strong minority wished to preserve the Stuart dynasty and its right of succession. Following negotiations over a number of years, articles of union were presented to Anne on 23 July 1706 and ratified by the Scottish and English Parliaments on 16 January and 6 March 1707, respectively. Under the Acts of Union, England and Scotland were united into a single kingdom – Great Britain – with one Parliament, on 1 May 1707.

The Union with Scotland Act 1706 dealt, of course, with the Church of England; it provided that 'it is reasonable and necessary that the true *Protestant Religion* protected and established *by Law in* the Church of England, and the doctrine, worship, discipline and government thereof should be effectually and unalterably secured'.[4] This was merely one of over 65 Acts of Parliament enacted in the years 1701–60 that touched expressly upon ecclesiastical law.[5] They include, at the beginning of our period, several statutes limiting religious freedom.[6] For instance, the Toleration Act 1711 restricted occasional conformity as a means to enable individuals to hold public office – it was repealed in 1719.[7] The Schism Act 1714 required those (including dissenters) who sought to manage a school, or act as a tutor, to obtain a licence from the local Church of England bishop – the Act never came into force: the day it was due to do so was the day Queen Anne died; it was repealed in 1718.[8] Fourteen 'Papists Acts' (1715–57) were passed following Jacobite rebellions in 1715, 1719 and 1745. The 1715 Act inter alia

---

[3] E Gibson, *Codex Iuris Ecclesiastici Anglicani* (1713) [hereinafter '*Codex*'] I, 689–91.

[4] ibid I, 24–25, on 6 Ann c 5 (emphasis added).

[5] See, eg, Cathedral Statutes Act 1707, 6 Ann. c 75; Advowsons Act 1708, 7 Ann c 18; New Churches in London and Westminster Act 1711, 10 Ann c 20; Tithes and Church Rates Recovery Act 1714, 1 Geo I c 6; St Giles in the Fields Rebuilding Act 1717, 4 Geo 1 c 5; St James Westminster Improvement Act 1746, 20 Geo II c 29; Islington Church Act 1750 24 Geo II c 15; Church of St John Wapping Act 1756, 29 Geo II c 89.

[6] See, eg, the Foreign Protestant Naturalisation Act 1714, 1 Geo 1 c 6; Quakers Act 1721, 8 Geo 1 c 6; Naturalisation of Jews Act 1754, 27 Geo II c 1. See also, eg, CF Mullett, 'The Legal Position of English Protestant Dissenters, 1689–1767' (1937) 23 *Virginia Law Review* 389–418.

[7] 10 Ann c 6: a Tory measure, with bills having been debated in 1702 and 1704.

[8] 13 Ann c 7; it was repealed by the Religious Worship Act 1718.

classified Roman Catholics as 'enemies to His Majesty and to the present happy Establishment', and provided for all confirmed and suspected Roman Catholics to take the oaths of supremacy, allegiance and abjuration: any who had not taken the oaths by the prescribed deadline were required to sign a register that included information about their estates, which was designed to enable the imposition of a tax on Catholics because, the Act stated, they should pay any 'large share to all such Extraordinary Expenses as are and shall be brought upon this Kingdom by their Treachery and Instigation'; if they failed to do so, they risked forfeiture of their estates to the Crown; the legislation also relieved Protestants of the same duty to register property.[9] The later Papists Acts repeated these norms and extended deadlines for the oath-taking and registration.[10] The Witchcraft Act 1735 abolished the offence of witchcraft and made it a crime to claim a person had magical powers.[11] All this heralds the widening conception of 'ecclesiastical law' as State law on religion generally.[12]

I. The Boom in Works on Ecclesiastical Law

An assessment of the landmark ecclesiastical legal developments in the period 1701–60 would not be complete without a discussion of the contribution made by the ecclesiastical lawyers of the period, both through their practice and through their writings. As we have seen, the sixteenth-century Reformation brought with it the suppression of the faculties of Canon Law at Oxford and Cambridge, with the result that the advocates of the ecclesiastical courts no longer held a degree in canon law, so they became Doctors of Civil Law. A significant development from this was that Doctors' Commons came to be the key place where knowledge of canon law was gained through practice in the courts. It was effectively a society of individuals centred on their common professional interests, rather than a body whose teaching role was based upon any formal curriculum.[13]

Furthermore, the cessation of formal instruction in canon law at the time of the Reformation, and the consequent slow decline in general familiarity with the older Latin sources, brought a corresponding need for English ecclesiastical law to be systematised in a form that could be understood by members of the clergy and others, including common lawyers, whose professions brought them into contact with it. Whilst there was never really an attempt to fully systemise the English

---

[9] 2 Geo I c 55 (1715).
[10] 3 Geo I c 18 (1716); 9 Geo I c 24 (1722); 10 Geo I c 4 (1723); 6 Geo II c 5 (1732); 8 Geo II c 25 (1734); 11 Geo II c 11 (1737); 12 Geo II c 14 (1738); 14 Geo II c 21 (1740); 6 Geo II c 32; 19 Geo II c 16 (1745); 26 Geo II c 24 (1753); 28 Geo II c 10 (1755); 31 Geo II c 21 (1757); 33 Geo II c 13 (1759).
[11] 9 Geo II c 5.
[12] See ch 7 of this volume.
[13] See generally GD Squibb, *Doctors' Commons: A History of the College of Advocates and Doctors of Law* (Oxford, Clarendon Press, 1977).

ecclesiastical law, some progress was made. Indeed, the ecclesiastical lawyers made a major contribution through their writings, which have been called the abridgement phase of English canon law. This produced a set of writings that effectively set out the English ecclesiastical law in abridged format.[14]

Those who wrote commentaries on ecclesiastical law may be categorised into three groups: the civilians, who had studied for degrees in civil law and who practised out of Doctors' Commons in the ecclesiastical, admiralty and university courts; the common lawyers, who may have studied at the universities and/or the Inns of Court and who practised ecclesiastical law in the temporal courts; and the clerical jurists, clerics who were not qualified as lawyers, nor generally practised in the church courts, but whose collections of laws and their commentaries on them made an enduring contribution to ecclesiastical law in and beyond this period.[15]

Among the common lawyers are, for example, William Nelson, Middle Temple barrister, whose *The Rights of the Clergy of Great Britain, as established by the Canons, the Common Law, and the Statutes of the Realm* (1709) treats subjects in alphabetical order and is 'a methodical collection under proper titles, of all things relating to the clergy, which lie dispersed in the volumes of those laws', including 'cases concerning the rights, duties, powers, and privileges of the clergy'. The book also has a contemporary polemic aim; we read in the preface that Nelson offers it as 'a means to remove that contempt and scorn which some profligate men have raised against [the clergy], so it may be an effectual method to preserve the Church from Danger'.[16] The most celebrated common lawyer, however, is William Blackstone (1723–80) whose *Commentaries on the Laws of England* contain much on ecclesiastical law and began life as lectures on English law he delivered at Oxford 1753–58.[17]

Three civilians are of great note. John Ayliffe (1676–1732), who read law, took his doctorate in civil law in 1710, and became a fellow of New College, Oxford. Rather than at Doctors' Commons, he based himself in Oxford and worked as a proctor in the university court. His *Parergon Juris Canonici Anglicani: or a Commentary, by Way of Supplement to the Canons and Constitutions of the Church of England* was printed in 1726 (and reprinted in 1734). It discusses materials 'not only from the books of the canon and civil law but likewise from the statute and common law of [the] realm'. Like Nelson, Ayliffe treats the subjects alphabetically. With a lengthy historical introduction, the authorities used are wide-ranging – from Gratian and classical authors down to recent court decisions. It is written

---

[14] See JH Baker, *Monuments of Endlesse Labours: English Canonists and their Work 1300–1900* (London, Hambledon Press, 1998) 78, 80, 85–86, 122, 156.

[15] It would be interesting to work on the lists of subscribers in, eg, Gibson and Ayliffe.

[16] It has 551 pages, with a 2nd edn in 1715. He also wrote books on justices of the peace and hunting law.

[17] See, eg, Blackstone, *Commentaries* (1765–1769) Introduction, sections 2 and 3. See also JH Baker, *English Legal History*, 5th edn (Oxford, Oxford University Press, 2019) 181–83.

in an ornate style, which makes it, at times, difficult to read, and there is little analysis. It sits firmly in the school of Godolphin (though arranged differently) and much of the material is taken from Godolphin.[18] A rather different civilian is Thomas Oughton (d c 1740), who was a deputy registrar of the Court of Delegates until around 1720 and a proctor until his death. His *Ordo Judiciorum* (1728), two volumes in Latin, treats the method of proceedings in the ecclesiastical courts.[19] Two similar but shorter works were: Philip Floyer (proctor), *The Proctor's Practice in the Ecclesiastical Courts* (1744; 2nd edn, 1746); and William Cockburn (a cleric), *The Clerk's Assistant in the Practice of the Ecclesiastical Courts* (1753; 4th edn, 1792).[20]

Among the clerical jurists, Edmund Gibson (1669–1748) is pre-eminent. Born at Bampton, Westmorland, he went to the Queen's College Oxford in 1686 and became a fellow in 1696. Originally a historian, he was admitted to Middle Temple in 1694 but soon returned to Oxford to prepare for ordination. He became librarian at Lambeth Palace following his ordination as priest in 1697, and was one of the archbishop's chaplains. He had various ecclesiastical preferments, including benefices, canonries and the archdeaconry of Surrey, before becoming Bishop of Lincoln in 1716 and Bishop of London in 1723. He wrote widely, but his *magnum opus* was the *Codex Juris Ecclesiastici Anglicani or the Statutes, Constitutions, Canons, Rubricks and Articles of the Church of England*, which was published in 1713. The headings in the *Codex* are arranged according to the methods laid down by Pope Gregory IX for the ordering of the decretals, and at the end of each text there is gloss in smaller type. The *Codex* included the text of relevant Acts of Parliament, Canons, and pre-Reformation provincial and legatine constitutions, and according to the preface it was intended for the 'service of the clergy, and in support of the rights and privileges of the church'. Interestingly, Gibson had no intention of encroaching on the lawyers who (he said) had their proper place in the conduct of litigation and in advising on difficult points, but much of the law could be readily understood if only they had access to it. Controversially, he makes claims for the independence of the ecclesiastical courts – which he saw as equals to the temporal courts, even for interpreting Acts of Parliament – and for the independence of clerical authorities from lay encroachments, including legislative measures emanating from Parliament itself. The work is an assembly of texts, including those repealed or obsolete in order to show the law as it had stood – a monumental collection of sources alongside commentary. It has been criticised for shredding single texts and sifting them into headings, so removing them from their original context. Gibson also assumed that all of the readers understood

---

[18] There is a list of subscribers, ii–iv. His published criticisms of Oxford University and the Clarendon Press for misappropriating funds, and of his own college, led to his being deprived of his degrees and driven out of his fellowship. See Baker (n 14) 87–88.
[19] The first book was translated, with footnotes added, by James Thomas Law (Chancellor of Lichfield and Coventry) in *Forms of Ecclesiastical Law* (London, Saunders and Benning, Law Booksellers, 1831).
[20] For Oughton, Floyer and Cockburn, see Baker (n 14) 89–94.

Latin, and therefore the pre-Reformation constitutions are often produced without translation. But the impact of the work is significant, and it led later writers, including John Johnson (1662–1725) and Richard Grey (1694–1771) to compile what were commentaries based on the *Codex*.[21]

II. The Juridical Conception of the Church and its Law

Throughout the legal history of the Church of England, connections have been made between the law and ecclesiology, understandings of the nature of the Church.[22] The defence of the 'Church in Danger' often surfaces in these understandings. The ecclesiastical lawyers saw the very definition of the Church in the Thirty-Nine Articles of Religion as 'properly a part of the Statute Law', which obliged clergy to subscribe to those Articles.[23] As a Church 'by law established' and 'a True and Apostolical Church' (Canons 1603/4, Canon 3), they therefore saw the Church as a legal entity: William Nelson (in 1709), common lawyer, developed his exposition of the law on the basis of 'The Church being reduced to a public polity', that is, 'as established by the Canons, the Common Law, and the Statutes of the Realm'.[24] In turn, for cleric jurist Richard Grey (1730), ecclesiastical law pertains to 'the Nature and Constitution of the Church of England, its Government and Discipline, and the Rights, Privileges, and Duties of its Ministers'.[25] However, the Church of England is not 'a mere creature of the State' but 'has a divine right to the exercise of spiritual discipline', but not such as to make 'the Church independent of the State'; rather, 'the external administration of that discipline, and of all ecclesiastical matters, in established Courts, and established forms, is by authority from the Crown' and so 'in subordination to the Royal Supremacy'.[26]

As a legal entity, the Church needs law to carry out its purposes: law is a necessary element in the Church's nature and its mission. For example, according to Gibson (1713):

> In these [ecclesiastical] laws are contained, the securities which the church has for her ancient privileges, the rules of order and discipline by which she is to be governed

---

[21] Gibson, *Codex* (n 3) I, title page and preface, viii; see Baker (n 14) 95. A rejoinder was written by the Erastian common lawyer Sir Michael Foster, of Middle Temple: *An Examination of the Scheme of Church Power Laid Down in the Codex* (1735).

[22] This section draws on N Doe, 'Juridifying Ecclesiology and Moralizing Law in Enlightenment Anglicanism: The Ecclesiastical Lawyers' in *History of European Ideas*, forthcoming.

[23] Gibson, *Codex* (n 3) I, preface, xi.

[24] W Nelson, *The Rights of the Clergy of Great Britain, as established by the Canons, the Common Law, and the Statutes of the Realm* (1709) preface.

[25] R Grey, *A System of English Ecclesiastical Law* (1730), preface; Grey models his book on Gibson's *Codex*.

[26] ibid 3–4.

and administered, the duties incumbent upon ecclesiastical persons in their several stations, and the provisions that have been made ... for the knowing, preserving, and recovering of their just rights ...

and 'all laws [are] intended for the instruction of mankind in their several duties and rights'.[27]

By way of contrast, civilian John Ayliffe (1726) mixes the mundane and moral aspects of law when he discusses Roman canon law as a source of ecclesiastical law in the context of church courts: 'if you take away this [Canon] Law, we have no *just* method and form of proceedings in judicial causes of an ecclesiastical cognisance'; it is valuable because elements of canon law are 'taken from the Laws of Nature and of Nations'; and 'interpreters of the Civil Law [are] reckoned but mean lawyers without a due and proper understanding of the Canon Law'.[28] Ayliffe also integrates his definition of 'canon law' into his ecclesiology: 'Now the Canon Law is so called from the Greek word *kanon*, which in English signifies a Rule, because the Canon Law is as a Rule of Life unto all Christians in matters relating to Church Discipline ...'[29]

Richard Grey (1730) too offers a practical and a moral understanding of the purposes of the ecclesiastical law – for example, in the form of parliamentary statutes, it exists 'for the assistance of the Church', 'for the quiet and security of the clergy', 'for the suppression of vice and *immorality*, for the better ordering of the possessions of the Church, [for] the augmentation of her revenues, and [for] the more easy recovery of her *just* rights'.[30]

At the same time, these eighteenth-century authors saw ecclesiastical law as based on the general consent of the people. For Nelson (1709),

> as the Common Law by which our civil rights are determined, is made up of such Customs which by the general consent of the People, have time out of mind obtained the force of Laws, so the Ecclesiastical Law is made up of such Canons and Constitutions which have been received and approved by the People, and which by immemorial practice have been used in our National Church.[31]

Oughton (1728) combines these: if a judge 'introduces a style of court [ie a practice or custom] contrary to law, it is not valid, unless the same be founded on the knowledge and consent of the people ... or else is supported with the approbation of the prince, and respects the order and method of judicial proceedings'.[32]

In the field of ecclesiastical persons, the Church of England is seen as a community in which rights and duties are defined by law. For instance, Nelson

---

[27] Gibson, *Codex* (n 3) I, preface, i.
[28] J Ayliffe, *Parergon Juris Canonici Anglicani* (1726), Historical Introduction, xxxvi.
[29] ibid iv.
[30] Grey (n 25) 12.
[31] Nelson (n 24) 167.
[32] T Oughton, *Ordo Judiciorum* (1728), ed JT Law, *Forms of Ecclesiastical Law* (London, Saunders and Benning, 1831) Title II, 5–6.

(1709) writes of 'the rights of the clergy ... as established by the Canons, the Common Law, and the Statutes of the Realm'.[33] As to episcopal rights and duties, Ayliffe (1726) states that '[a] bishop, in his own Diocese, ought to be obeyed by all persons whatever under the Royal Dignity, how great soever they may be, in point of dignity or estate, provided they be of that Diocese that the matter of obedience does concern and relate to his episcopal office'; but 'a bishop cannot appoint anything that is contrary to the general Canons of the Church'; and 'a Bishop that is unprofitable to his Diocese, ought to be deposed, and no co-adjutors assigned him, nor shall he be restored again thereto'.[34] In similar vein, the law distributes various rights among different classes of parishioner; for example, for Joseph Shaw (1755), '[a] parishioner who is entitled to vote at a Vestry ... is any male inhabitant who pays to the Church and Poor'; and as to limits on their authority, 'the Spiritual Court, may ... compel the parish to repair the church; but they cannot appoint what sums are to be paid for that purpose, because the churchwardens by the consent of the parish, are to settle that'; moreover, 'if there be public notice given to the parishioners, and they will not come, the churchwardens may make a rate without them'.[35] It is to clergy as ecclesiastical persons in the law of the Church of England that we now turn.

III. The State and Maintenance of the Clergy: Queen Anne's Bounty

The first landmark development in the law of the Church of England in this period relates to the state of the clergy. As Best notes, 'the church's main material defect' at the end of the seventeenth century 'was the poverty that brought contempt upon so many of its clergy and inefficiency into so much of its work'.[36] He notes that whilst it is difficult to say which classes of clergymen were the worst off at this time, it is the case that generally rectors were unlikely to be destitute but, depending on the value of the tithes, the income of vicars varied greatly; and curates were often in the worst position, with perpetual curates not only lacking tithe rights but also probably lacking glebe (land vested in rectors and generating income). Dilapidations as regards the parsonage house, and the payment of fees, added to this hardship and affected all classes of clergy. Each incumbent, who had a duty to maintain his clergy house, had a right to claim from his predecessor (or predecessor's executors) the sum estimated to bring the house into a sufficient state of repair. Often the parties could not agree, and it was commonly felt that 'the system

---

[33] Nelson (n 24) preface.
[34] Ayliffe (n 28) 123–24.
[35] J Shaw, *Parish Law* (1755, 9th edn) 108, 224.
[36] GFA Best, *Temporal Pillars: Queen Anne's Bounty, the Ecclesiastical Commissioners, and the Church of England* (Cambridge, Cambridge University Press, 1964) 13.

of dilapidations was never anything but an aggravation and a blight, that lowered the church's vitality and, at the very best, imposed charges of an unpredictable amount upon its ministers, or on their widows or executors'.[37]

But as Best notes, the heaviest burden of all in the late seventeenth century, a burden from which the laity were entirely free, was that the clergy had to pay first fruits (annates) and tenths – royal taxes on ecclesiastical dignitaries and benefices. First fruits were the sum of money paid on entry into the benefice or other dignity, and tenths were a recurring annual charge of a smaller amount.[38] The Appointment of Bishops Act 1533 had diverted the amount raised from first fruits and tenths to the Crown.[39] Yet Best claims that the Exchequer's gains from the poorer clergy in this regard were negligible, and by the latter half of the seventeenth century it was recognised that the work and inconvenience in collecting these taxes far outweighed their value. So, as early as the reign of James II, a group of poor ministers in Lincoln Diocese petitioned the king for relief from their burden of arrears in tenths – 'accrued chiefly though the fault of their predecessors' – and relief was granted once it had been ascertained by reference to the Exchequer and to their bishop that their livings were small.[40] Such relief work continued in the reign of William and Mary, but it really took off on a grander scale under Queen Anne with a series of statutes known as the 'Queen Anne Bounty Acts'.[41]

Under the Queen Anne Bounty Act 1703,[42] in 1704 a corporation was established by royal letters patent called 'The Governors of the Bounty of Queen Anne for the Maintenance of the Poor Clergy'. To this corporation Anne granted all of her revenue of first fruits and tenths, which were collected by the treasurer of the Governors. The primary object of the bounty was the augmentation of the maintenance of parsons, vicars, curates and ministers officiating in any church or chapel in England and Wales where the liturgy and rites of the Church of England were used and observed.[43] Under the letters patent, the Governors were authorised to propose rules for the receiving, managing and distributing of the bounty and any other gifts that might be given or bequeathed for the same purpose. So, a committee of governors, initially including Archbishops Tenison and Sharp, was set up to draft rules and orders; a set was eventually accepted and added to a new charter for the corporation in 1714. A further statute, enacted in the first Parliament of the reign of the first Hanoverian George I, the Queen Anne's Bounty Act 1714, provided that the bounty must operate under the following principles: (i) augmentation by capital grant rather than pensions; (ii) the investment of the grants to

---

[37] ibid 18–19. See Grey (n 25) 186–89 (glebe) and 246–49 (remedies for dilapidations).
[38] Best (n 36) 21.
[39] 25 Hen VIII c 20. See also 34 Hen VIII c 17: new Bishops paid their Tenths to the Court of the First-fruits.
[40] Best (n 36) 27.
[41] For a legal history of first fruits and tenths, see Gibson, *Codex* (n 3) II, 870–920.
[42] 2 & 3 Ann c 20.
[43] 2 & 3 Ann c 20, s 1.

be in land; (iii) the division of poor benefices into: (a) a superior class, to which private benefactions were invited, and (b) the lowest class, the income augmented irrespective of private benefaction; and (iv) the choosing by lot of the benefices in the latter class.[44]

This was clearly a radical shift in the provision for clergy throughout the Church of England; subsequent Acts further amended the means by which the bounty was distributed.[45] The trend continued in the eighteenth century and beyond: for example, provision was made to make loans (from 1777) and disbursements (from 1803) to build and repair parsonage houses. The Governors continued until 1947, when the functions and assets of Queen Anne's Bounty were merged with the Ecclesiastical Commissioners to form the Church Commissioners.[46]

IV. The Reform of the Law of Patronage

Closely related to the augmentation of benefices and the provision for clergy from Queen Anne's Bounty was the continued development of the law surrounding parochial patronage. At its heart was (like today) the property law right of the advowson, which enables a patron to present a clerk to the bishop to be instituted and inducted into an ecclesiastical benefice. The law that developed in this area during this period demonstrates three particular concerns: the limits of religious toleration; the sale of advowsons; and 'next presentations'.

First, religious toleration. Following the sixteenth-century Reformation, patronage became a powerful tool for religious change: presenting a clerk who was sympathetic to either Roman Catholic or 'Puritan' Christianity could radically change the churchmanship and theology of a parish church; and under the law of the time, the bishop's ability to refuse a patron's candidate was greatly limited, and the parishioners had little or no say in the appointment.[47]

Attempts by Parliament had been made in the seventeenth century to address this,[48] all cemented with the Presentation of Benefices Act 1713.[49] Under it, where an advowson or right of patronage of a benefice was held by or in trust for a Roman Catholic, that right could not be exercised by the person(s) possessing it. However, the statute also provided that the University of Oxford could make the presentation if the vacant benefice was in the city of London or certain counties

---

[44] 1 Geo I stat 2 c 10.
[45] Acts were passed in 1706 (6 Ann c 24), 1707 (6 Ann c 54), 1714 (1 Geo I stat 2 c 10), and 1716 (3 Geo I c 10) plus others into the 19th century, known collectively as 'the Queen Anne Bounty Acts 1706–1870'.
[46] See ch 10 of this volume for the Church Commissioners Measure 1947.
[47] See, eg, DR Hirschberg, 'The Government and Church Patronage in England, 1660–1760' (1980–81) 20 *Journal of British Studies* 109–39.
[48] See the Presentation of Benefices Act 1605 (3 Jac I c 5) and the Presentation of Benefices Act 1688 (1 Will & Mary c 26).
[49] 13 Ann c 13.

in the Province of Canterbury; and the University of Cambridge had the right if the benefice was in the remaining counties in the Province of Canterbury or in the Province of York. The 1713 Act also set out various mechanisms if such a presentation was suspected. The Church Patronage Act 1737 made further provision: every grant of any ecclesiastical living, etc by any papist was void unless made for a valuable consideration to a protestant purchaser.[50] So we see being played out in patronage law in this period the battle to control recusancy, with further tightening of that law to ensure that Roman Catholics did not present to livings and, thus, exercise any patronage rights: the law of advowsons and parochial patronage was used as a tool to restrict religious toleration in the period, as recusancy was further reined in by restricting Roman Catholics' ability to present to livings.

The second area of concern was the sale of advowsons. The law of simony forbade the sale or purchase of spiritual benefits. The year 1703 saw the seventh edition of a treatise by Simon Degge (1612–1704), a barrister and bencher of Inner Temple, who writes that 'the very intention to buy spiritual gifts or preferments, carries with it the guilt of simony, as well as the act itself'; it was a 'sin', a *malum in se*, and a 'corrupt' contract, 'till the parliament of England took it into their care' with a statute of 1588, which enacted that if any person for any sum, directly or indirectly or by reason of any promise or agreement, present or collate any person to a benefice with cure of souls, etc, 'then every such presentation', etc is void and 'any person who gives or takes such sum or that take or make any such promise, etc, shall forfeit and lose the double value of one year's profit of every such benefice'.[51] However, in our period, there was a booming trade in the sale of advowsons – there were recognised places where dealers in advowsons could gather, such as Garraway's Coffee House in London, where hundreds of advowsons would have been on offer at any one time; and there were trade journals, such as *The General Register of Church Preferments for Exchange*.[52] There were few landmark developments in the law around the sale and exchange of advowsons in this period; but there were increasing attempts to reform the law around resignation bonds, which obliged a cleric to pay the patron if they did not resign at the patron's request. The resignation bond was a sealed instrument, which the patron required a cleric to execute upon presentation to the benefice, and which enabled a patron to have the living 'held' until a relative was ready to be presented.[53] On the face of it, resignation bonds appear to be simony, as they were something of value

---

[50] 11 Geo II c 17, s 5.
[51] S Degge, *The Parson's Counsellor with The Law of Tithes or Tithing* (1676; 7th edn 1703) 43–46; the statute is 31 Eliz I c 6. For the scriptural notion of simony as a sin, see the Acts of the Apostles 8.18–8.24.
[52] See B Palmer, *Serving Two Masters: Parish Patronage in the Church of England since 1714* (Lewes, The Book Guild Ltd, 2003) 37–38.
[53] Best (n 34) 53–59; RE Rodes, *Law and Modernization in the Church of England: Charles II to the Welfare State* (Notre Dame, IN, University of Notre Dame Press, 1991) 34–37.

to the patron, but attempts to abolish them in the courts on this basis failed,[54] and the law was not reformed until the case of *Bishop of London v Ffytche* (1783).[55]

A third problematic area was 'next presentations'. A separate right from an advowson, this was a one-off right to nominate a person (including the purchaser of the right) to the benefice when the current incumbent resigned or died. Canon law had always prohibited this but, having no statutory force, had been flouted freely. This was remedied by the Simony Act 1713: it forbade a cleric from buying the right of next presentation for himself, but he could still buy the whole advowson and do so.[56] This was a significant point in the reform of the law around the sale of advowsons, and indeed of patronage law, which culminated eventually in the Benefices Act 1898 and, finally, in the Patronage (Benefices) Measure 1986.

V. The Law of Marriage

The law relating to marriage also developed significantly in this period. The principal development concerned clandestine marriages, which were becoming more frequent. What for the parties were their advantages were for the State serious mischiefs: being conducted in secret, they could be entered quickly, they avoided parental control and they often concealed an illegitimate birth. Initially the courts sought to discourage them, using the idea that an informal marriage was not 'complete' and did not generate for the parties rights of dower or rights of succession to chattels. Parliament stepped in: under a statute of 1695, it became a criminal offence to marry without banns or a licence, though the Act's stated purpose was not to publicise the marriage but to facilitate the taxation of marriage certificates and licences.[57] In 1714, new Canons were drafted (though never approved) to regulate marriage licences for 'the more effectual preventing of clandestine marriages' and for the better enforcement of the Canons of 1603/04 to ensure that marriages were solemnised 'publicly' in the parish church.[58]

From the Restoration to the mid-eighteenth century, several proposals were put to Parliament to outlaw clandestine marriages. On the one hand, it was argued that such marriages, entered into hastily and without proper documentation,

---

[54] Anon (1701) 12 Mod 505, 88 ER 1479; *Hilliard v Stapleton* (1701) 1 Eq Ca Abr 87, 21 ER 898 (Cg); *Peele v Com' Carliol* (1719) 1 Str 227, 93 ER 487; *Grey v Hesketh* (1755) Amb 268, 27 ER 178 (Ch).

[55] *Bishop of London v Ffytche* (1783) 2 Brown 211, 1 ER 892 (HL).

[56] 13 Ann c 11. It should be noted that the patron's rights were also, separately, strengthened in this period. The Advowsons Act 1708 (7 Ann c 18) responded to the reality that the patron's remedy to recover their right of presentation was time-consuming and costly, and therefore this statute provided that usurpation upon the avoidance of a benefice would not displace the estate or interest of any person entitled to the advowson.

[57] Baker (n 17) 520; the statute of 1690 is 7 & 8 Will & Mar c 35, s 4.

[58] They open with the words 'We do straitly charge and enjoin all persons concerned to see that the 62, 63, 70, 99, 100, 101, 102, 103 and 104th canons be duly observed'. For the text of the draft Canons 1714, see G Bray (ed), *The Anglican Canons 1529–1947* (Woodbridge, Boydell Press, 1998) 836–37.

especially by young people, were more likely to fail and lead to property disputes. On the other hand, it was argued that formal marriages were too expensive, and that outlawing informal marriages would encourage people to live in sin. At the same time, a major concern was that such marriages could be obtained in places outside episcopal control but in ecclesiastical form and with the certification of a priest, such as the so-called 'Fleet marriage' at the Fleet Prison in London, which was an ecclesiastical liberty – here, alongside its tennis courts and coffee shops, at its so-called marriage shops, Church of England clerics could conduct hurried marriages for a small fee. Baker suggests that hundreds of thousands of couples took advantage of this in the eighteenth century.[59]

Fleet marriages were also the subject of litigation. For example in a case of 1717, before the Court of Delegates, the marriage of the plaintiff came in question after her husband's death upon granting administration of his estate: 'And it appeared they were married under feigned names at the Fleet'. The widow produced an affidavit of the intestate husband, made by him before a surrogate of Doctors' Commons, that he was married to her. In turn, '[t]he court allowed it to be read in confirmation of other evidence' and 'the marriage [was] confirmed'.[60]

Lord Hardwicke CJ was a strong opponent of such ecclesiastical liberties as the Fleet, and in 1753 his Clandestine Marriages Act was passed. The Act (commonly known as Lord Hardwicke's Marriage Act) prohibited secret marriages; abolished liberties such as the Fleet; and required the publication of banns or the obtaining of a licence (which required parental consent in the case of an infant under the age of 21), the solemnisation of the marriage in the parish church (subject to exemptions for the royal family, Jews and Quakers), the presence of at least two witnesses and the recording of the marriage in a public register.[61]

The wider significance of Lord Hardwicke's Marriage Act cannot be overstated: it marked a key moment in the development of the regulation of marriage by parliamentary statute, rather than by canon law, which came to a head in the following century (see chapter 8). At the same time, however, recent scholarship suggests: (i) that the 1753 Act was narrow in its scope – in seeking to prevent Fleet marriages – and that it was successful in doing so; (ii) that before it, the incidence of informal marriages effected simply by the exchange of parties' consents were not as widespread as hitherto thought – it demonstrates that such exchanges were merely contracts to marry and that marriage in church was almost universal outside London; and (iii) that before it, very few non-Anglicans married outside the church according to their own rites.[62] In any event, 1753 marks the first step on

---

[59] Baker (n 17) 521.
[60] *Sacheverell v Sacheverell* (1717) 93 ER 368 (Del).
[61] 26 Geo III c 33. See, eg, R Burn, *Ecclesiastical Law*, vol II (1763; 3rd edn 1775; 6th edn 1797) 418–27.
[62] R Probert, *Marriage Law and Practice in the Long Eighteenth Century: A Reassessment* (Cambridge, Cambridge University Press 2009).

the road to the transfer of the jurisdiction around marriage from Church to State. The question of jurisdiction continues, of course, to this day.

Another area of contention was the parishioner's right to marry, and the corresponding duty on the minister to solemnise the marriage, which derives from the common law. This was developed during this period, with the judgment of the Dean of the Arches, Sir George Lee, in the case of *Argar v Holdsworth* (1758).[63] According to this decision (still cited today), a minister who without just cause refuses to marry persons entitled to be married in their parish church, commits an ecclesiastical offence, for which clerical disciplinary process in the church courts may follow. This case was the first in a series of common law authorities on this issue, though it has been claimed that the right and duty constitute a legal fiction.[64] However, the duty was affirmed in an opinion of the Legal Advisory Commission of the General Synod of the Church of England.[65]

VI. The Legislative Power of the Convocations

There was in this period a very significant development, one at common law, that questioned the effect of the exercise of legislative power by the Canterbury and York Convocations. As we have already seen, under Tudor legislation from the sixteenth century, the Convocations had authority to legislate by Canon. The Act of Submission 1533 provided that Convocation could assemble, and confer on, conclude and execute canons – but each of these only with the consent of the Crown and subject to 'four limitations', namely, that canons were not against the royal prerogative, common law, statute law and the custom of the realm.[66] The Canons of 1603/04 upheld this statutory authority: they required excommunication for anyone who affirmed that Convocation was 'not the true Church of England by representation'; that no-one was 'subject to [its] decrees'; that it conspired 'against godly and religious professors of the Gospel'; and that those present in the 'making of canons ... by the king's authority ... ought to be despised and contemned'.[67] In turn, in 1689, Convocation was commissioned by the Crown 'to treat of alterations, and form canons and constitutions' on rites, ceremonies and church courts – it met in November but produced no canons, and so in January 1690, William III dissolved it. In similar vein, in 1717, under Queen Anne, to prevent the (clerical) Lower House of Convocation censuring Hoadley, Bishop of Bangor, Convocation was prorogued. Under the four Georges and

---

[63] *Argar v Holdsworth* (1758) 2 Lee 515.
[64] See N Doe, *The Legal Framework of the Church of England* (Oxford, Clarendon Press, 1996) 357ff.
[65] *Legal Opinions Concerning the Church of England*, 9th edn (London, Church House Publishing, 2020) pt 16, 'Marriage: right of parishioner to marry in parish church', para 5.
[66] R Phillimore, *The Ecclesiastical Law of the Church of England*, vol II (1873; 2nd edn 1895) 1535, citing *The Case of Convocations* (1611) 12 Co Rep 72.
[67] Canons 139–41.

William IV (except in 1741-42), as Phillimore put it, Convocation 'was never allowed to transact business'.[68] These political manoeuvres raised further questions about the legislative power of the Convocations.

They were answered at common law in the case *Middleton v Crofts* (1736).[69] For this we return to the subject of clandestine marriages and Lord Hardwicke, some years before his Marriage Act. The facts of the case were as follows: two inhabitants of the parish of Dove, John Middleton and Anne Ellis, were articled in the Consistory Court of Hereford for being clandestinely married by a priest, Thomas Allen, in his own dwelling house, out of canonical hours and without banns or licence. As such they were also exposed to the canonical penalties of cohabiting not as husband and wife. The couple subsequently applied to the Court of the King's Bench for a writ of prohibition on the basis that the 1695 statute (see section V) imposed penalties recoverable in a temporal court on both the cleric and the parties to the marriage. The judgment of Lord Hardwicke was that the couple had secured a prohibition on one point only, that of marriage at uncanonical hours, on the basis of the rule in Canon 62 of the Canons of 1603, which Canons had been passed by the Convocations with royal licence but without parliamentary approval, and therefore did not bind the laity. Lord Hardwicke stated:

> We are all of the opinion, that the Canons of 1603, not having been confirmed by Parliament, do not proprio vigore bind the laity; I say proprio vigore, by their own force and authority; for there are many provisions contained in these canons, which are declaratory of ancient usage and law of the church of England, received and allowed here which, in that respect, and by virtue of such ancient allowances, will bind the laity, but that is an obligation antecedent to, and not arising from, the body of canons.[70]

This was radical – not least as Convocation's power to make canons with royal assent had been approved by Parliament in the 1533 statute.[71] Indeed, the judgment was not without its critics, but in 1753 it was endorsed by the Dean of Arches in *Lloyd v Owen*[72] and affirmed by the House of Lords in *Bishop of Exeter v Marshall*.[73] Halsbury (1910) rests the non-binding effect of the Canons on statute,[74]

---

[68] Phillimore (1895) (n 66) 1541-42. See also WH Cripps, *A Practical Treatise of the Law Relating to the Church and Clergy* (1845; 7th edn 1921) 27 for the House of Laymen in the Canterbury province, 1885, and for that in the York, 1892.

[69] *Middleton v Crofts* (1736) 2 Atkyns 650.

[70] ibid 653.

[71] For earlier cases, see RH Helmholz, 'The Canons of 1603: The Contemporary Understanding' in N Doe, M Hill and R Ombres (eds), *English Canon Law* (Cardiff; University of Wales Press, 1998) 23-35.

[72] *Lloyd v Owen* (1753) 1 Lee 434, 437.

[73] *Bishop of Exeter v Marshall* (1868) LR 3 HL 17.

[74] Halsbury, *The Laws of England*, 1st edn. (London, Butterworth & Co, 1910) vol XI, para 717: 13 Car II, stat 1, c 12 'restored' ecclesiastical law; by s 5, nothing in the Act confirms 'the canons of 1640, nor any other ecclesiastical laws or canons not formerly confirmed, allowed or enacted by Parliament, or by established laws of the land as they stood in 1639; *R v Tristram* [1902] 1 KB 816.

and for the *Report of the Archbishops' Commission on Canon Law* 1947, 'it would be profitless now to attempt to call this judgment into question'.[75]

VII. The Courts: Roman Canon Law, Precedent and Morality

The business of the ecclesiastical courts did not change greatly in our period. For example, Troy Harris has compared the numbers of appeals in the York Chancery Court with those in the Canterbury Arches Court over 1725–45. The Arches Court heard 601: 211 in 1725–31; 242 in 1732–38; and 148 in 1739–45. The Chancery Court heard 130 – like Canterbury, they declined: 67 appeals in 1725–31, 44 in 1732–38, and 19 in 1739–45. Canterbury province was larger and more populated than York, and appeals from the diocesan Consistory Court of York went directly to the Court of Delegates;[76] but there were only 16 such appeals in this period; and, for instance, Durham consistory court dealt with over 1,400 causes over these years but only 18 went on appeal to the Chancery. In these years, of the 130 appeals to the Chancery Court, 85 (over half) were from Chester – 57 from the Chester diocesan court and 28 from Richmond archdeaconry court. Wills and disciplinary matters dominated the appeals – however, faculty and pew appeals were higher in the Chancery Court (19 out of 130) than in the Arches Court (41 out of 601).[77] By mid-century, almost all appeals to the Chancery Court of York concerned faculties issued by diocesan courts.[78] However, its original jurisdiction did not. Over 1750–60, suits included: pews, 7; probate, 3; defamation, 3; tuition of a child, 2; correction, 2; and 1 each for: removal of a tombstone from Barnard Castle chapel; disputed churchwardens' accounts; failure to exhibit accounts; unlawful preaching; unlawful marriage; failure to attend a visitation; false visitation presentment; refusal to serve as churchwarden; assault on a churchwarden; breach of promise to marry; and the administration of a will.[79]

---

[75] *The Report of the Archbishops' Commission on Canon Law* (London, SPCK, 1947) 77. For a further analysis, see G Bush, 'Dr Codex Silenced: *Middleton v Crofts* Revisited' (2003) 24 *The Journal of Legal History* 23–58.

[76] Because an appeal could not lie from the archbishop's Consistory to himself in Chancery.

[77] TL Harris, 'The Work of the English Ecclesiastical Courts, 1725–1745' in TL Harris (ed), *Studies in Canon Law and Common Law in Honor of RH Helmholz* (Berkeley, CA, The Robbins Collection, 2015) 251–79, 259 and 269; ibid at 252 he criticises BD Till, 'The Administrative System of the Ecclesiastical Courts in the Diocese and Province of York: Part III: 1660–1883: A Study in Decline' (University of York, Borthwick Institute of Historical Research, 1963, photocopy) 250 – Harris sees no 'clear "decline"'.

[78] WJ Sheils, *Ecclesiastical Cause Papers at York: Files Transmitted on Appeal 1500–1883* (York, University of York, Borthwick Institute of Historical Research, 1983) v, citing Till (n 77) table at 250.

[79] Sheils (n 78) 72–76.

First, it was commonplace for English ecclesiastical lawyers to include pre-Reformation Roman canon law in their expositions of the law applicable to the Church of England. These lawyers were familiar with its sources, purposes and history – and they distinguished foreign canon law, including papal law, and domestic canon law, composed of provincial laws of archbishops and constitutions of the papal legates in England. They used several ideas to explain its status in pre-Reformation England – chiefly that it had been received in England by king and people and so became part of the king's ecclesiastical law. They usually held that both the foreign and domestic canon law continued in force after the Reformation on the basis of section 7 of the Submission of the Clergy Act 1533 until reviewed by a royal commission (which never materialised) and if it was not repugnant to laws of the realm – and, they added, if it had been received in England before 1533. However, Doe suggests that it is difficult to find clear evidence from this Act and other relevant statutes that *both* domestic provincial and legatine *and* foreign canon law continued in force (subject to reception and the statutory non-repugnancy conditions). Doe argues that the 1533 Act continued only domestic provincial law, and perhaps legatine law, but not foreign papal law. Yet a 1543 Act (also providing for a commission) continued provincial law and 'other ecclesiastical laws' hitherto used in England, which may or may not have included legatine and foreign law. Another Act of 1549 has no continuance proviso, but the commission it proposed was to review 'ecclesiastical laws used here' hitherto – which also may or may not include legatine and papal law. A 1553 Act repealed these earlier statutes. A 1558 Act repealed that of 1553 but revived only the 1533 Act, not those of 1543 or 1549. Yet English church lawyers still used foreign canon law. This suggests that only domestic provincial law, and perhaps legatine law, continued on the basis of statute, and not foreign canon law: foreign law might have applied on a statutory basis from 1543 to 1553, but not after 1558, as only the 1533 Act continuing solely domestic law was revived. Post-Reformation lawyers differ, or else are inconclusive, as to whether the focus of the commission that produced the *Reformatio Legum Ecclesiasticarum* was pre-1533 domestic or foreign canon law, or both. By the nineteenth century, they see custom, not statute, as the basis for the continuance of the application of pre-Reformation Roman canon law to the English Church.[80]

Second, the courts continued to develop the principles of ecclesiastical law. Many cases from our period are still cited today in works on ecclesiastical law, and establish certain principles such as: the right to nominate a beneficiary belongs primarily to the settlor;[81] a parish is created not for the benefit of the cleric but for the people within it;[82] a parishioner cannot insist that a body be buried as near

---

[80] See N Doe, 'Pre-Reformation Roman Canon Law in Post-Reformation English Ecclesiastical Law' (2022) 24 *Ecclesiastical Law Journal* 273–94; the Statute Law (Repeals) Act 1969, sch, pt II repealed 'the whole act [25 Hen VIII c 19] except, so far as unrepealed, sections 1 and 3' – s 7 is thus repealed.
[81] *Attorney-General v Leigh* (1721) 3 P Wins 145.
[82] *Britton v Standish* (1704) Holt KB 141.

as possible to ancestors in a particular part of a burial ground;[83] the canons bind the clergy *proprio vigore*;[84] and a person seeking marriage is under a canonical duty to satisfy the statutory requirements as to capacity: this is binding in so far as the requirements are duplicated in civil law.[85] Furthermore, in a case *c* 1735, the 'archbishop's chancellor' at York held that a bishop could 'only oblige' his chancellor to exhibit at the 'archbishop's court at York' an account of money received for commutations, but the bishop could not seek inhibition of the chancellor by the archbishop's chancellor; in 'obedience' the diocesan chancellor exhibited an account and then the archbishop's chancellor 'dismissed the chancellor without costs'.[86] It is said that the first faculty issued at York, in the modern sense, was in 1736.[87] And in 1753, the Court of Arches required church courts to apply common law rules to determine whether an ecclesiastical custom exists.[88]

Third, the period was important for the doctrine of precedent. Burn cites a 1702 case in which, 'upon consideration of the precedents, his lordship said he was bound up by them'; and a 1748 case in which Lord Hardwicke chose one course, 'nor did he care to make a precedent to the contrary'.[89] Indeed, the reports of the Court of Delegates abound with the use of precedents.[90] Sir George Lee (d 1758) also developed the doctrine of precedent; as Dean of Arches he had the accidental honour of being the earliest English civilian whose reports of decided cases appeared in print, thanks to Joseph Phillimore, who had them published in 1853.[91] For Richard Helmholz, we see in George Lee a shift in emphasis (rather than a sea change) towards the use of judicial precedent, both spiritual and temporal, for authority.[92]

Fourth, however, as Doe argues, the ecclesiastical lawyers were also moralists. Part of their understanding of the Church as a juridical entity was that one material source of its law was morality. They developed a moral ecclesiastical jurisprudence. As such, in these enterprises, they juridified ecclesiology – by conceiving of the Church in legal terms; and they moralised ecclesiastical law – by

---

[83] *Fryer v Johnson* (1755) 2 Wils 28.
[84] *Matthew v Burdett* (1703) 2 Salkeld 412.
[85] *More v More* (1741) 2 Atk. 157.
[86] Phillimore (1895) (n 64) 1069, 'About the year 1735, Dr Burn says …'.
[87] RA Marchant, *The Church under the Law: Justice, Administration and Discipline in the Diocese of York 1560–1640* (Cambridge, Cambridge University Press, 1969) 75, citing P Winckworth, *A Verification of the Faculty Jurisdiction* (London, SPCK, 1953) 74.
[88] *Patten v Castleman* (1753) 1 Lee 387, 161 ER 143.
[89] Burn (n 61) (1797) IV, 250 and 345.
[90] *Thwaites v Smith* (1696) 24 ER 274 (Del).
[91] See R Helmholz, *The Profession of English Ecclesiastical Lawyers* (Cambridge, Cambridge University Press, 2019) 174ff.
[92] ibid 179. *Hughes v Herbert* (1756) 2 Lee 287, 161 ER 343 (Court of Arches); *Robins v Wolseley* (1757) 2 Lee 421, 443, 161 ER 391, 398 (Court of Arches); *Keeling v M'Egan* (1754) 1 Lee 607, 612, 161 ER 222, 224 (Prerogative Court of Canterbury).

deploying categories, such as divine and natural law, justice and equity, conscience and reason, into their practice, legal thinking and expositions of the law.[93]

On the other hand, our jurists recognise that human law was inferior to divine law and moral law. But it seems they did not apply this to parliamentary statute; they did not consider a parliamentary statute invalid if contrary to divine or moral law. In is rare to find a statement, such as that in Nelson (1709) that '[a]n Act of Parliament may abrogate any Canon, unless it consists in enjoining some Moral Duty'. That they did not habitually say that parliamentary statute was inferior to or void if in conflict with divine law or moral law might be surprising because they said 'human law' was. For instance, according to Ayliffe (1726), 'no Human Law can be made, which is contrary to the Divine Law (and it is only binding in those things which are permitted by the Divine Law)'.[94] For Gibson (1713), in taking power from the clergy, the Court of Delegates was against 'natural reason' and 'the general tenor of our Constitution'.[95]

Other large moral ideas were also invoked in, for instance, the commentaries. One example. Oughton (1728) explains: (i) 'a judge ought always to have *a supreme equity* before his eyes', but must not 'depart from written laws on the account of *unwritten equity* ... [u]nless it be through the authority of him to whom this alone belongs, in order to limit and restrain a severe written law'; (ii) 'though a judge may not extend a punishment beyond *the letter of the law*, yet he may mitigate the same according to the equity of the case; and if he cannot ... he is to report the same to the prince for his mercy'; (iii) '[e]very judge in pronouncing sentence ought to have a principal regard to *truth and equity*, always adhering thereunto, and despising the quirks and subtilties of the law'; and (iv) '[i]n cases not expressly specified by law, a judge ought always in ... punishments, to be inclined to the more humane and *equitable* part'.[96]

Doe suggests, therefore, that the search for Anglican ecclesiology in this period should not be confined to a study of theology but should also embrace church law; and the study of church law should not be confined to examination of bare rules but should also recognise the place of morality in ecclesial jurisprudence. Ecclesiology was not the sole preserve of theologians – it was also the domain of lawyers; and law was not only the site of positivism – it was also the site of moral reasoning associated directly with the nature of the Church and its norms. The categories juristic ecclesiology and moralistic jurisprudence, then, emerge as two fundamentals of Enlightenment Anglicanism worthy of investigation by scholars today.[97]

---

[93] See Doe (n 22); and N Doe, '"Legalists and Moralists" in the Historic Portrayal of the Constitution of the Church of England' (2023) 25 *Ecclesiastical Law Journal* 1–25.
[94] Nelson (n 24) 131; Ayliffe (n 28) Historical Introduction, xxxiv: ie under the statute 25 Hen 8 c 19.
[95] Gibson, *Codex* (n 3) I, Discourse, xxi–xxii.
[96] Oughton (n 32) Title VI.VII, 14–15, citing Ayliffe (emphasis added).
[97] See Doe (n 22).

VIII. Conclusion

The period 1701–60 was a seismic one in the legal history of the Church of England. Against the backdrop of auspicious political events during the twilight of the Stuart dynasty and the birth pangs of the Hanoverian, the life of the Church of England was centre stage. The law of marriage, the law of patronage and the maintenance of the clergy saw the beginnings of significant reform. But what was most significant was the increasing prominence of the status and work of the ecclesiastical lawyers in this period, through their establishment of new principles in ecclesiastical law and the growing use of precedent in their courts, the boom in their writings, and the development of their juridical concept of the Church and its law. For in all this, the ecclesiastical lawyers juridify ecclesiology. They present ecclesiology as a set of legal propositions and find ecclesiology in law. Ecclesiastical law itself provides an understanding of the nature and purposes of the Church of England, for the law constitutes, facilitates and orders or regulates the Church in both mundane and spiritual ways. And so the Church is seen fundamentally as a legal entity. In this sense, the juridical ecclesiology of the time is also experiential: ecclesiastical law is applied ecclesiology – theology is animated in action through norms of conduct. This does not displace but supplements a theology of the Church, an idea that would become increasingly important in the legal and theological trials and tribulations of the centuries to come.

7

The Ecclesiastical Law and Religious Pluralism: 1760–1837

NORMAN DOE

The period 1760 to 1837 covers the reigns of the Hanoverian kings George III (1760–1820), George IV (d 1830), and William IV (d 1837). It begins 100 years after the Church of England was re-established at the Restoration, with episcopal government and liturgical uniformity, and ends just after repeal of the Test and Corporation Acts and Roman Catholic emancipation 1828–29, and just before the Pluralities Act 1838. The period also sees great population growth, urban and industrial development, and the rise of a market economy and an empire, all of which impact on religion. But there were constants: the threat of death and divine judgment; hostile foreign powers, particularly Roman Catholic, Revolutionary and Napoleonic France; and the memory of the disorder of the civil wars. These too shaped religious, political, intellectual and social life in our period: 'A concern to be right with God was central to most people's lives, public and private. Satirists might lampoon gluttonous clergymen, canting priests and over-enthusiastic Dissenters, but never faith itself'; and 'The Church of England met the religious aspirations of most English people across the social spectrum, and most of them engaged with its spiritual, moral, and pastoral disciplines.'[1]

I. The Established Church and the Rise of Religious Freedom

The national Church of England continued throughout this period to be the established Church in England and Wales. However, at just about the half-way point, the Union with Ireland Act 1800 effected the constitutional union

---

[1] WM Jacob, 'England' in J Gregory (ed), *The Oxford History of Anglicanism*, vol II: *Establishment and Empire, 1662–1829* (Oxford, Oxford University Press, 2017) 90–120, 90–92. Also J Walsh, C Haydon and S Taylor (eds), *The Church of England c 1689–c 1833* (Cambridge, Cambridge University Press, 1993).

of the Church of England with the Church of Ireland as the United Church of England and Ireland, 'united into one Protestant Episcopal Church'.[2] Towards our period's end, though, the Government's plan to unite 10 Irish dioceses in 1833 prompted John Keble's famous sermon on National Apostasy and the rise of Tractarianism – and many within the Oxford Movement called for the separation of the Church from the State. By 1844, the Liberation Society was formed to disestablish the Church of England.

In the meantime, one key feature of the church establishment was that Parliament continued to legislate on ecclesiastical matters. As to the numbers of statutes enacted in our period, Archibald John Stephens, in his seminal work on ecclesiastical law of 1848, lists about 299 statutes relevant to his exposition of ecclesiastical law – namely: 128 statutes in the reign of George III; 66 in the reign of George IV; and 105 in that of William IV. That is, about four ecclesiastical statutes were made each year over 77 years. Those Stephens lists may not, of course, include statutes both enacted and repealed in our period, and so were not relevant to his work.[3] Four of them are still cited today by Mark Hill in the 2018 edition of his *Ecclesiastical Law*.[4]

The volume and complexity of legislation was reflected in an increase in commentaries on ecclesiastical law, many of which were designed to help clergy and lay people understand the law applicable to them. The profession of ecclesiastical lawyers was previously confined in the main to Doctors' Commons; in 1768 it was incorporated by royal charter as the College of Doctors of Law exercent in the Ecclesiastical and Admiralty Courts – the Dean of Arches was its president and doctors of civil law of Oxford and Cambridge admitted as advocates by the Archbishop of Canterbury could be elected as 'fellows'. Notable civil lawyers who wrote on ecclesiastical law included Samuel Hallifax (d 1790), Thomas Bever (d 1791) and Arthur Browne (d 1805).[5] The greatest common lawyer on ecclesiastical law was William Blackstone (d 1780).[6] Then there were the clergy who also wrote on or practised law – the most celebrated was Richard Burn (1709–85), parish priest and chancellor of Carlisle: the first edition of his *Ecclesiastical Law* appeared in 1763, and the ninth and last in 1842 (edited by Robert Phillimore).[7] Like so many of his generation, Burn used an alphabetical approach to the subjects

---

[2] Union with Ireland Act 1800, Art V. The union was dissolved under the Irish Church Act 1869.

[3] AJ Stephens, *A Practical Treatise of the Laws Relating to the Clergy* (1848) Statutes Cited, xviii–xxxv.

[4] M Hill, *Ecclesiastical Law*, 4th edn (Oxford, Oxford University, 2018) Table of Statutes and Measures, xxxvii–lv: House of Commons (Clergy Disqualification) Act 1801; Clergy Ordination Act 1804; Ecclesiastical Commissioners Act 1836; and, just outside the period, Pluralities Act 1838.

[5] On Doctors' Commons, see RH Helmholz, *The Profession of Ecclesiastical Lawyers* (Cambridge, Cambridge University Press, 2019) 49, 60, 140, 175, 178, 182, 201–03; for Bever, see ibid 181–87; and for Browne, ibid 194–201. See also N Doe, 'Rediscovering Anglican Priest-Jurists: II – Samuel Hallifax (1735–90)' (2020) 22 *Ecclesiastical Law Journal* 48–66. See also, eg, by 'A Gentleman of Doctors Commons', *The Clerk's Instructor in the Ecclesiastical Courts* (Dublin, 1766).

[6] Also, eg, 'Barrister', *The Ecclesiastical Legal Guide* (1839); H Clavering, *The New and Complete Parish Officer ... A Complete Library of Parish Law* (1808); and T Cunningham, *The Law of Simony* (1784).

[7] The last edition in our period (the 8th) was that of 1824 by Robert Tyrwhitt (1798–1836).

he treated.⁸ Other clerics included David Williams, author of *Laws Relating to the Clergy* (1813). Books were also written on the ecclesiastical law in Ireland, both before and after the union of the Churches of England and Ireland in 1800, such as those by William Cockburn (1st edn 1753), Edward Bullingbroke (1770) and Richard Ryan (1825).⁹

As well as treating ecclesiastical statutes, these books also relied on the growing number of reports of ecclesiastical cases that appeared in our period. In the eighteenth century, for example, the 'Common Place Book' of Sir William Burrell (d 1796) carried 'reports of proceedings in Ecclesiastical Courts' (Arches, Prerogative, London Consistory) 1765-69; he practised at Doctors' Commons from 1760 and was chancellor of Worcester and Rochester. By the nineteenth century, judgments of the Court of Arches, for example, were collected and published, for example, by Jesse Adams (1822-26) and by John Haggard (1827-33); and 'digests of cases' – effectively case summaries – were produced by, for instance, Edwin Maddy in 1835. It is also worth noting the Public Notaries Act 1801, under which the Court of Faculties of the Archbishop of Canterbury had jurisdiction over the appointment and removal of notaries.¹⁰

However, all this statute and case law did not simply seek to preserve the established Church of England. Much of English ecclesiastical law in our period was addressed to Dissenters, and so stimulated the rise of religious freedom in the form of the emancipation of Roman Catholics and integration of Nonconformists. For example, in the context of the temporal courts, Lord Mansfield (1705-93) issued a series of important judgments on religious freedom: a Dissenter is entitled to serve as a town clerk without taking the sacrament of the established Church (1760); a Presbyterian congregation had a right to elect its own minister (1762); 'Methodists have a right to the protection of [the] Court, if interrupted in their decent and quiet devotion' (1765); and a Quaker who refused to swear an oath in court proceedings was entitled instead to give evidence on the basis on an affirmation (1775).¹¹

Similarly, in the context of Parliament and statute, the Papists Act 1778 was the first to allow Roman Catholics, if they took an oath of allegiance to the Crown, to, for example, join the army, purchase lands freely and not be penalised for running schools.¹² An Act of 1791 made provision for Roman Catholics to

---

⁸ For the common law 'alphabetical treatise' in our period, and its antecedents, see M Lobban, *The Common Law and English Jurisprudence 1760-1850* (Oxford, Clarendon Press, 1991) 10ff. Further work is needed on the role of subscribers in the production of books on church law; they are listed, eg, in E Gibson, *Codex Juris Ecclesiastici Anglicani* (1713).

⁹ (Revd) W Cockburn, LLB, *The Clerk's Assistant in the Practice of the Ecclesiastical Courts* (Dublin, 2nd edn, 1756; 4th edn, 1792); E Bullingbroke, *Ecclesiastical Law* (Dublin, 1770); (Revd) R Ryan, *The Irish Incumbent's Guide or Digest of the Ecclesiastical Law of Ireland* (Dublin, 1825).

¹⁰ *Halsbury's Laws of England*, 4th edn, vol 14: *Ecclesiastical Law* (London, Butterworths, 1975) para 1273.

¹¹ *Crawford v Powell* (1760) 97 ER 681; *R v Baker* (1762) 97 ER 823; *R v Wroughton* (1765) 97 ER 1045; *Atcheson v Everitt* (1775) 98 ER 1142: NS Poser, *Lord Mansfield: Justice in the Age of Reason* (Montreal & Kingston, McGill-Queen's University Press, 2013) 349-59, 355.

¹² 18 Geo III c 60. Discord over the Act prompted the anti-Catholic Gordon Riots in 1780.

practise law, and for registration of their schools and places of worship; but the statute prohibited assemblies behind locked doors, church steeples and bells, priests wearing vestments, the holding of services in the open air, the admission of children of Protestants to Roman Catholic schools, monastic orders and the endowment of schools.[13] At the end of our period we see the enactment of the Roman Catholic Relief Act 1829, which sought to complete Catholic emancipation, and the Roman Catholic Charities Act 1832.[14]

Dissenters (about 6.2 per cent of the population) generally paid their tithes and church rates, rented pews in church and became churchwardens, whilst also attending their own meeting-houses. But some High Churchmen thought they attended church only to qualify for civic office from which to undermine the Church. The board of Protestant Dissenting Deputies (which first met in 1736) was politically organised, respected and active, notably in repeal of the Test and Corporation Acts in 1828.[15] Also, the Board of Deputies of British Jews was founded in 1760, when Sephardic and Ashkenazi congregations each appointed a committee to pay homage to George III; they then agreed that both committees should hold joint meetings.

The law reflected these religious, social and political developments. The Nonconformist Relief Act 1779 allowed Dissenters to preach and teach if they declared they were Christian and Protestant, took the oaths of allegiance and supremacy, and used the Scriptures as their rule of faith and practice.[16] The Places of Religious Worship Act 1812 revised the Toleration Act 1689 on registering places of worship used by Dissenters (but not Quakers); it repealed the Five Mile Act and Conventicle Act; and it allowed dissenting ministers to preach and teach in these registered places of worship if they made the 1779 Act declaration before a justice of the peace; no one was required to travel more than five miles to make the declaration, but it was an offence to preach, etc without making it.[17] In turn, the Doctrine of the Trinity Act 1813 (or Unitarian Relief Act) relieved Unitarians from various disabilities under the Toleration Act 1689 and Blasphemy Act 1697; it was repealed in 1873.[18] An Act of 1833 allowed Quakers and Moravians, or those who had been such, to make an affirmation instead of the prescribed oath in legal proceedings.[19] All these statutes on religious freedom helped develop a concept of ecclesiastical law as State law applicable to religion in general.[20]

---

[13] 31 Geo III c 32.

[14] 10 Geo IV c 7.

[15] Also known as the Deputies of the Three Denominations of Dissenters, Presbyterians, Independents and Baptists): see MR Watts, *The Dissenters: From the Reformation to the French Revolution* (Oxford, Oxford University Press, 1978).

[16] 19 Geo III c 44.

[17] 52 Geo III c 155.

[18] 53 Geo III c 160. The Dissenters (Ireland) Act 1817 (57 Geo III c 70) extended the 1813 Act to Ireland.

[19] Halsbury, *Ecclesiastical Law* (n 10) para 1419; see also Quaker and Moravian Act 1838.

[20] After all, the books on 'ecclesiastical law' also included these laws applicable to Dissenters.

Alongside these developments in religious freedom for Dissenters, the period also witnesses a revival in Anglicanism itself, most notably with Methodism and the Evangelical party within the Church of England. What became Methodism emerges from the 1730s and 1740s. But till the 1790s, most Church of England clergy did not regard Wesley's followers as Dissenters – they frequently attended the parish church even into the 1820s; separation dates from the 1830s. Also, by the end of the eighteenth century Anglican Evangelicals were common in the universities and armed forces, and influenced politics, including abolition of the slave trade and providing for missionary work in India; and under Charles Simeon, from the 1820s they established a patronage trust to provide livings for Evangelical clergy and ensure a continuing Evangelical tradition in those parishes. Some scholars suggest that this, and the annual Evangelical clergy conferences, contributed to the success of Dissent and to the establishment of Evangelicalism as the first coherent 'party' in the Church of England.[21]

From the 1780s to the 1790s, then, alongside the growth of Dissent, Methodism and Evangelicalism, other factors shook the Church of England's confidence, namely: the north American war (1775–83); the French Revolution and Napoleonic Wars; and urban, industrial and population growth. In turn, this stimulated reform and renewal. In 1783, Richard Watson, Bishop of Llandaff, writes to the Archbishop of Canterbury to equalise episcopal incomes and adjust those of deans and chapters to favour poor clergy. William Wilberforce and Bishop Porteus of London persuade George III to issue in 1787 a Proclamation for the Discouragement of Vice, to be read four times a year in churches and commanding prosecution of listed crimes. In 1802, Wilberforce sets up the Society for the Suppression of Vice. The Acts described above giving relief for Dissenters also fuel further anxieties in the Church that England as a 'confessional state' was disappearing: the Commons was no longer an Anglican assembly; church statutes were influenced by Dissenters; and Parliament could no longer be relied on to assist the Church. The High Church cry of 'the Church in danger' was heard once more.[22] All this anxiety, all this spirit of reform, all this zest for renewal, impacted on church law.

II. The Clergy – Appointment, Functions and Discipline

The Church continued with the threefold ministry of bishops, priests and deacons. Our period saw the creation of a colonial episcopate and the first episcopal church beyond the jurisdiction of the Crown, in the United States. At home, bishops were

---

[21] Jacob (n 1) 113–14.
[22] ibid 112–19. See also J Walsh, C Haydon and S Taylor (eds), *The Church of England c 1689–c 1833* (Cambridge, Cambridge University Press, 1993) 19–20.

generally diligent.[23] But they had latitude in key areas; for example, by case law: there was no duty on a bishop to give reasons for refusing a licence or permission to minister (1811); a bishop had 'absolute' discretion as to whom he ordained (1833); and a bishop could impose the censure of monition without recourse to church courts (1811).[24] Yet episcopal authority was limited in other areas: no bishop could allow a cleric to be elected to the Commons – the House of Commons (Clergy Disqualification) Act 1801 prohibited this; a cleric if elected was liable to forfeit a fixed sum for every day he presumed to sit or vote in the Commons.[25] And the Residence Act 1802 required bishops to make annual returns to the Privy Council on clergy residence.

An important statute was the Clergy Ordination Act 1804. It declared the ages for ordination as bishop (30), priest (24, but for a 23-year-old an Archbishop of Canterbury faculty could authorise ordination) and deacons (23, unless with a faculty). The Act sought to 'to enforce the observance of the canons and rubric' – in Ireland rules on the ages for ordination had 'been sometimes disregarded and rendered of no effect, to the great scandal and detriment of the Church, and to the prejudice of religion'; the Act was 'for the better prevention' of this, 'in order that one certain and undoubted rule and course of practice may hereafter prevail and be observed in this respect in England and Ireland'.[26] After a decline in ordinations from the 1790s, bishops take a greater interest in clergy training: in 1817, St Bees Theological College for non-graduates is set up in Cumberland;[27] and St David's College, Lampeter, founded in 1822, opens in 1827 as a degree-awarding body, part of a wider drive for more Welsh-speaking clergy.[28]

There were also developments in patronage law and practice. Most patrons were laypeople: individuals; the Crown; borough corporations; or inhabitants or rate-payers who elected their incumbent; but episcopal patronage increased from the early nineteenth century.[29] Patronage trusts also evolved; and it was decided judicially that an advowson could be held by trustees in perpetuity whether or not the beneficiaries under it were named.[30] The duty of a cleric to reside in the parish was the subject of occasional legislation, such as in a statute of 1817 (which also made provision for the maintenance of stipendiary curates).[31] Plurality too is a constant concern across our period; by the end of it, the Pluralities Act 1838 limited the

---

[23] Jacob (n 1) 103. But bishops were sometimes pluralist, holding livings *in commendam*, etc.

[24] *R v Bishop of London* (1811) 13 East 419; *R v Archbishop of Dublin* (1833) Alc & N 244; *Cox v Godday* (1811) 2 Hag Con 138, 142. For archdeacons as corporations, see *Tufnell v Constable* (1838) 7 Ad & El 798.

[25] The Act sought to remove 'doubt' about the whole matter. This disability was removed in 2001.

[26] Section 1 of the Act is still in force today: Hill (n 4) para 4.04.

[27] Jacob (n 1) 104.

[28] RL Brown, 'Pastoral Problems and Legal Solutions' in N Doe (ed), *Essays in Canon Law: A Study of the Law of the Church in Wales* (Cardiff, University of Wales Press, 1992) 9–12.

[29] Jacob (n 1) 94–100. See also, eg WM Jacob, *The Clerical Profession in the Long Eighteenth Century 1680–1840* (Oxford, Oxford University Press, 2006) 80–86.

[30] *Attorney-General v Bishop of Lichfield* (1801) 5 Ves 825.

[31] 57 Geo III c 99.

livings a cleric could hold to two, and the statute required clerics to reside on one of these. By the second half of the eighteenth century, parish clergy also served in large numbers as local magistrates; this lasted till after the Napoleonic Wars and the advent of stipendiary justices.[32]

In terms of clerical functions, generally, on the basis of a fair return for their tithes, the laity expected much of clergy in terms of prayer, preaching, pastoral care and practising charity, and complained about them if their expectations were not met;[33] but there was little anti-clericalism (beyond the normal round of irritation, animosity and criticism) or sustained intellectual attacks on Christianity in general or the Church and its clergy in particular.[34] Episcopal visitations developed as a less formal means of addressing complaints against clergy: for example, in 1790, Bishop Porteus of London refined practices (introduced by Bishop William Wake of Lincoln in 1707) and other bishops followed over time; they issued questionnaires well before the visitation, asking clergy to return them in advance, to be able to speak knowledgeably in their visitation charges and to respond to and discuss local and other issues meaningfully.[35] Archidiaconal visitations were also much revived in the 1820s.[36]

However, bishops took formal disciplinary action against clergy relatively rarely, and usually tried to resolve matters informally, because they were reluctant to risk scandal in church court proceedings, to bring shame and homelessness on a married cleric's family, to pay the legal costs involved, and wished to avoid the delays that often accompanied a full disciplinary process.[37]

As to the numbers of clergy discipline cases in the church courts: in the Exeter consistory court, for example, there were 8 cases in the 1760s and 21 in the 1830s. In London consistory court, in the 1760s there were 0 cases and in the 1830s, 2. And in the Court of Arches, in the 1760s there were 8 cases and in the 1830s, 4. Generally, the penalty imposed was lighter than we might assume or there was none: for instance, in *Wenham v Atham* (1779), no penalty was imposed as Atham was adjudged insane at the time he committed adultery; and in *Cox v Priest*, no penalty was imposed because the cleric was mentally unstable; sometimes the penalty is not known.[38]

Some ecclesiastical jurisprudence also developed with respect to clerical discipline. For example: in marriage preliminaries, a minister must enquire into

---

[32] Jacob (n 1) 108.
[33] ibid 100.
[34] F Knight, 'Did Anticlericalism Exist in the English Countryside in the Early Nineteenth Century?' in N Aston and M Cragoe (eds), *Anticlericalism in Britain c 1500-1914* (Stroud, Sutton, 2000) 159–78.
[35] Jacob (n 1) 101–03.
[36] A Burns, *The Diocesan Revival in the Church of England, c 1800-1870* (Oxford, Oxford University Press, 1999) 76–91.
[37] Jacob (n 1) 103.
[38] MG Smith, *Church Courts, 1680-1840*, ed P Smith (Lampeter, Edwin Mellen Press, 2006) 97–102; ibid 97–99, Smith provides tables of the number of cases and the matters they dealt with. Smith does not supply citations for *Wenham v Atham* (1779) and *Cox v Priest*.

the residence of the parties and may be subject to ecclesiastical censure for failure to do so (1801), but he will be excusable if he has been diligent or has been misled (1809); but the Arches Court declined to determine whether a cleric was bound to solemnise the marriage of a Dissenter, baptised or unbaptised, and thus whether a cleric who refused could be disciplined (1827); however, an unauthorised interference with the churchyard by an incumbent may constitute an offence under ecclesiastical law and may therefore be restrained by injunction (1830); and that conviction in the temporal courts is not required for the deprivation of a cleric (1837).[39]

III. Lay Officers and Lay Discipline in the Church Courts

The parish remains the most localised unit of the English Church – the focus of communal life, spiritual and civil, governed by its vestry, elected by householders, chaired by the parish priest, assisted by elected lay officers, and supervised in church matters by the bishop and his officers and in temporal administrative and financial matters by magistrates. Parish vestry officers include overseers of the poor, surveyors of highways, constables and those levying property rates to fund these. But as the period unfolds, the parish model was increasingly difficult to sustain – due to population growth in new mining and manufacturing towns in formerly large sparsely-populated areas remote from parish churches, particularly in the north and west midlands; and the growing numbers of Dissenters increasingly did not see the parish church as their spiritual home. However, in designing new towns, a new parish church was often made a focal point, and proprietary chapels increased to fund a cleric from pew-rents.[40]

The principal ecclesiastical officers in the parish remained the churchwardens, whose functions included maintaining the church fabric and churchyard. The period saw some notable judicial decisions about them. For example: the remedy for unlawful refusal to admit a churchwarden was mandamus (1763); churchwardens could not interfere with divine service for any impropriety by the minister, unless his conduct was riotous, violent or indecent – rather, they should complain to the ordinary, but in exceptional cases they or even private persons could intervene to preserve the decorum of worship (1792); aliens, Jews and persons convicted of prescribed offences could not be churchwardens (1798); a person

---

[39] *Priestly v Lamb* (1801) 6 Ves 421 (see also *Diddear v Faucit* (1821) 161 ER 1421; and *Wynn v Davies and Weaver* (1835) 1 Curt 69); *Nicholson v Squire* (1809) 16 Ves 259; *Jenkins v Barrett* (1827) 1 Hag Ecc 12; *Bennett v Bonaker* (1830) 3 Hag Ecc 17; *Taylor v Morley* (1837) 1 Curt 470, 163 ER 165.

[40] Jacob (n 1) 92–94. For the Vestries Acts 1818, 1819 and 1831, see Halsbury, *Ecclesiastical Law* (n 10) para 568; also *Halsbury's Statutes of England*, 4th edn, vol 34, *Ecclesiastical Law* (London, Butterworths, 1986) 220–42.

might be removed for disturbing the congregation at the time of divine service, even though no part of that service was actually proceeding at the time (1824); and churchwardens owned the movables of the church, and their authority extended to every consecrated church or chapel in the parish not provided with separate wardens, and the churchyard and its curtilage (1828).[41]

The laity continued to be subject to the jurisdiction of the church courts, which themselves continued to be active throughout the period. Most cases were brought by laypeople against laypeople, rather than to enforce clergy discipline. Women used them to defend themselves against defamation, sexual slander and gossip. In London, matrimonial jurisdiction was much in demand to grant judicial separations. Perhaps surprisingly, people were willing to accept the severest penalty, public penance, to be performed in their parish church at Sunday morning service; this often achieved the reconciliation of a person with the community. For example, in returns for 1764, the vicar of St Mary's, Nottingham, noted that 'many publick penances' had been performed in his church; but, by way of contrast, the vicar of Radcliffe-on-Trent stated that men seldom did penance for fornication or for fathering a child out of wedlock, and he added 'I cannot tell why they are excused, or what it may cost them.'[42]

However, change was in the air – and various changes to the church courts responded to a range of factors. By the eighteenth century, archdeaconry courts had ceased to function in some dioceses (such as Coventry and Lichfield); in Lancashire, sexual delinquency cases were heard mainly in deanery courts, but from the 1770s there seemed a general reluctance to proceed in such cases. Between 1760 and 1795, Nottingham archdeaconry court heard 154 suits for bastardy, but only two after 1774. An Act of 1787, 'to prevent frivolous and vexatious suits in Ecclesiastical Courts', prohibited any suit for pre-nuptial fornication to commence eight months after this was committed; it also prohibited any suit for pre-marital fornication after the parties concerned had married each other; for defamation, the statute required plaintiffs to begin their suit within six months of the date of the offending words; and a suit to recover tithes had to begin within six months of the date due for payment.[43]

These trends continued. The diocesan returns to the Royal Commission on the Ecclesiastical Courts in 1830 show fewer than 50 correction causes for all diocesan courts combined in 1827–29; many diocesan courts heard no such causes in these

---

[41] See respectively: *R v Dr Harris* (1763) 1 Wm Bl 430 (see also *R v Williams* (1828) 8 B & C 681); *Hutchins v Denziloe and Loveland* (1792) 1 Hag Con 170, 173, 174; *Anthony v Seger* (1798) 1 Hag Con 9; *Williams v Glenister* (1824) 2 B&C 699; *Mosey v Hillcoat* (1828) 2 Hag Ecc 30, 56, 57.

[42] Jacob (n 1) 108, which cites, eg, A Tarver, *Church Court Records: An Introduction for Family and Local Historians* (Chichester, Phillimore and Co Ltd, 1995); and S Waddams, *Sexual Slander in the Nineteenth Century: Defamation in the Ecclesiastical Courts* (Toronto, University of Toronto Press, 2000).

[43] RB Outhwaite, *The Rise and Fall of the English Ecclesiastical Courts, 1500–1860* (Cambridge, Cambridge University Press, 2006) 83–84, 91, 96, 98, 119–28, 138 (including the statute of 1787, 27 Geo III c 44).

three years; some reported that they had tried no causes at all – by 1830 the criminal side of their work had virtually gone.[44]

By the late 1820s, 61 per cent of all probates and administrations were being granted in the two provincial courts; only 150 cases a year were brought in all other diocesan courts combined.

Defamation causes also dropped: the London consistory court heard 24 a year in the decade 1735–45, but only 1 a year in 1827–29. Most diocesan courts had virtually no marriage cases; yet the London consistory court heard more than 10 cases a year in 1770–99, but by 1827–29, 14 a year; of 101 causes begun in all church courts in the years 1827–29, 58 cases were heard in the two courts at Doctors' Commons. So, the Royal Commission records that by 1830, 1,903 causes were begun in the church courts: testamentary, 947; matrimonial, 101; tithes, 184; church rates, 58; church seats (dealt with by faculty), 190; brawling, 22; defamation, 331; miscellaneous, 49; appeals, 21.[45]

The Ecclesiastical Courts Act 1813 maintained the church courts' power to excommunicate, but discontinued it for contumacy – the writ *de contumace capiendo* obtainable from the Chancery replaced the writ *de excommunicato capiendo*. The judge was empowered to use the writ within 10 days of the party's disobedience or contempt of the church court; it also empowered sheriffs to imprison offenders until they submitted to the courts' decision.[46]

Moreover, between 1815 and 1821, several royal commissions examined delays in the church courts and the duties, salaries and emoluments of their officers. Two commission reports in 1823 led to an Act of 1829; it provided, for instance, that only such holidays as were observed at the Stamp Office were permitted in the Prerogative Court of Canterbury.[47] Also, two cases of clerical misconduct – those of David Griffith Davies and Edward Drax Free – fuelled further criticisms of the church courts, which led to another royal commission – the Commission on Ecclesiastical Courts 1832. This led to the Privy Council Appeals Act 1832, which abolished the High Court of Delegates (which heard appeals from the Arches and Chancery Courts) and transferred its powers to the Privy Council. One criticism was that the Delegates were too young and experienced – often barristers or advocates of a year or so's standing were passing judgments in appeals against the decisions of 'the greatest luminaries of the Civil Law', such as Sir William Scott, Sir John Nicholl and Sir Christopher Robinson.[48] A further bill came to the Commons in 1835 that led to the controversial 1840 Act on clergy discipline.[49]

As well as these statutory reforms, there were also several, probably declaratory, judicial decisions from the period concerning the jurisprudence and jurisdiction

---

[44] ibid 84: Outhwaite links this to the failure at the Restoration to effect reforms in procedure.
[45] ibid 90–94.
[46] 53 Geo III c 127 (1813): Outhwaite (n 43) 103, 128; see also Smith (n 38) 117–18.
[47] Outhwaite (n 43) 130: statute 10 Geo IV c 53 (1829).
[48] Outhwaite (n 43) 131–44: 2 & 3 Will IV c 92 (1832). See also Judicial Committee Act 1833, s 3.
[49] That is 3 & 4 Vict c 86 (1840).

of the church courts. For example, that the decisions of the Arches Court bind only the courts of the Province of Canterbury (1804); that an action at common law may lie against a bishop or a chancellor and damages may be recovered for an unlawful excommunication (1812, 1815); and that a writ of prohibition at common law may not lie for error (rather than excess) of jurisdiction (1835).[50]

Also, further study is needed on whether the ecclesiastical lawyers saw the ecclesiastical law itself – as the common law was still conceived of in our period – as 'a system of remedies, deriving the substantive content of law from below largely out of cases' or, rather, as Blackstone and Bentham saw the common law, as a 'rule-based' system and science.[51]

IV. Doctrine and Education, Worship and Rites of Passage

Though the Enlightenment had a profound effect on the natural sciences, the period was one still characterised by superstitions, visions and belief in witchcraft. Most Church of England clergy, whether Whig or Tory in politics, were mainly orthodox in theology, with high views of the Church, apostolic succession and the sacraments; and they bought a growing literature defending orthodoxy against alleged 'atheists', 'deists' and 'Socinians' (who saw themselves as devout Protestants exploring the implications of faith). Successive governments from the 1720s sought to avoid public debate of theological issues as they feared arousing again the cry 'the Church in danger'. Even in 1771, when Francis Blackburne and Theophilus Lindsey petitioned Parliament to remove the clerical and lay-office-holder duty to subscribe to the Thirty-Nine Articles, only 250 signed it, of whom 200 were clergy. Clergy were orthodox.[52]

Changes were afoot, however, in the field of education. For example, in Wales, the Anglican cleric Griffith Jones started 'the circulating schools' movement – it spread throughout Wales, teaching children by day and adults by night to read the Bible, participate in liturgy, promote family and personal prayers, and catechise children each Sunday. At Jones's death in 1761, over 6,465 schools had been held

---

[50] For precedent, see *Stephenson v Langston* (1804) 1 Hag Con 379; for actions, see *Beaurain v Scott* (1812) 3 Camp 388; *Ackerley v Parkinson* (1815) 3 M&S 411; for prohibition, see *R v Judicial Committee of the Privy Council, ex parte Smyth* (1835) 2 CM&R 748.

[51] See Lobban (n 8) 251–89. It would also be instructive to identify the extent to which the church courts invoked natural law ideas, connecting ecclesiastical law and morals: see RH Helmholz, *Natural Law in Court: A History of Legal Theory in Practice* (Cambridge MA, Harvard University Press, 2015); and D Ibbetson, 'Natural law and common law' (2001) 5 *Edinburgh Law Review* 4-20.

[52] Jacob (n 1) 95–97. See also WM Jacob, *Laypeople and Religion in the Early Eighteenth Century* (Cambridge, Cambridge University Press, 2002) 112–20; and BW Young, *Religion and Enlightenment in Eighteenth-Century England: Theological Debate from Locke to Burke* (Oxford, Oxford University Press, 1998).

and over 200,000 people attended them.⁵³ In 1811, Joshua Watson (1771–1855) and the Hackney Phalanx set up the National Society for Promoting the Education of the Poor in the Principles of the Established Church, throughout England and Wales, aiming to establish a Church School in every parish – there were 12,000 by 1861.⁵⁴ Low-cost devotional, family prayer books and collections of sermons sold in large numbers; and many town churches had libraries whose registers show clergy and laity as borrowers.⁵⁵

By contrast, worship patterns changed little. The Canons of 1603 and Prayer Book 1662 on daily morning and evening prayer, and Sunday sermons, were generally fulfilled in towns and large villages, but not in smaller villages. While there was no duty to record it, attendance seemed buoyant: evidence from Weston Longville from the 1780s to 1790s, that on Sundays there were 'good congregations', is typical. Communion was usually monthly in towns, quarterly in villages, both with two or three Easter celebrations; but many did not receive outside Easter, thinking extensive preparation was required, and fearing divine punishment if they received unworthily. Some attended both the parish church and Dissenting meeting-house.⁵⁶

Clerical diaries suggest that people liked sermons that mostly avoided controversy.⁵⁷ But music in church was sometimes contentious. From the 1730s, bishops and clergy began to resist singers sitting together, especially in galleries, claiming that singers monopolised the music. Bishop Sherlock of Salisbury ordered his archdeacons to ensure that clergy suppressed anthems. In Exeter diocese in the 1730s, a clause was inserted in faculties for galleries barring their use by singers. There is considerable clerical diary evidence from 1772–1839 of music disputes.⁵⁸

Other disputes about worship were litigated. For example, it was held in 1814 and 1825 that no cleric might conduct divine service publicly in any benefice without the consent of its incumbent; in 1824, that no parishioner might interrupt a service to call a vestry meeting after the churchwardens had failed to do so; and in 1828, that a minister would be in neglect of duty for failing to use only the Book of Common Prayer 1662 – however, there was no liability if neglect was occasional or accidental, but a mistake as to his own rights would not excuse.⁵⁹ A notable statute

⁵³ RL Brown, 'The age of the saints to the Victorian church' in N Doe (ed), *A New History of the Church in Wales* (Cambridge, Cambridge University Press, 2020) 9–26, 18.
⁵⁴ L Louden, *Distinctive and Inclusive: The National Society and Church of England Schools 1811–2011* (London, The National Society, 2012).
⁵⁵ WM Jacob, 'Libraries for the Parish: Individual Donors and Charitable Societies' in G Mandelbrote and KA Manley (eds), *The Cambridge History of Libraries in Britain and Ireland 1640–1850* (Cambridge, Cambridge University Press, 2006) 65–82.
⁵⁶ Jacob (n 1) 97–98.
⁵⁷ M Stone (ed), *The Diary of John Longe (1765–1834), Vicar of Coddenham* (Woodbridge, Suffolk Records Society, 2008) 171; Jacob (n 1) 107–08.
⁵⁸ H Coombs and AN Bax (eds), *Journal of a Somerset Rector: John Skinner, AM, Antiquary, 1772–1839* (London, Murray, 1930) 8, 15, 238: Jacob (n 1) 107.
⁵⁹ *Carr v Marsh* (1814) 2 Phillim 198 at 206; *Farnworth v Bishop of Chester* (1825) 4 B & C 555 at 568; *Dawe v Williams* (1824) 162 ER 243; *Bennett v Bonaker* (1828) 2 Hag Ecc 25.

is the Parish Notices Act 1837: this prohibited the making of proclamations or giving of public notices concerning non-ecclesiastical matters at divine service; it enabled notices usually given in or after a service to be affixed to the church doors; and it forbade any decree relating to a faculty, or other decree, citation or proceeding in any ecclesiastical court, to be read or published in any church or chapel during or immediately after divine service.[60]

By way of contrast, the period saw some major legal changes with regard to rites of passage. First, the Parochial Registers Act 1812 required registers of public and private baptisms and burials in the Church of England to be kept in separate books by the clergy or officiating minister of every parish or other place (eg, a cathedral or a burial ground) where these ceremonies were performed. Provided at the expense of the parish, the registers belonged to the parish, and had to be preserved by the minister in a locked iron chest and secure place in his house of residence, if he was resident in the parish, or in the parish church. The registers could not be removed except to make entries, to inspect or to produce in court, or for some other lawful purpose. Copies had to be made annually by or under the direction of the minister of the parish, and be signed by him and sent every year to the diocesan registrar who was to file them. The Act also provided that the church registers of Nonconformists were not admissible in court as evidence of births, marriages and deaths. The Act was replaced in the 1970s.[61]

Second, there were a number of cases and statutes developing the law on the rites of passage. For example, it was held that a lay person could administer baptism (1809); that all the parts of a baptismal name should be read when publishing banns of marriage (1812); just before our period, that a parishioner had a right to be married in the parish church (1758); and that the divine law as to the marriage of persons within the prohibited degrees was immutable (1837).[62] The Marriage Act 1836 legalised civil marriages – and therefore relieved, for instance, Roman Catholics and Dissenters (Quakers and Jews were already exempt) from marriage in the parish church, and allowed marriages to be registered in buildings belonging to other religious groups; these groups could apply to register their buildings with the Registrar General and so could conduct weddings if a Registrar and two witnesses were present.[63]

Third, the Burial Ground Act 1816 enabled ecclesiastical corporations under prescribed circumstances to alienate lands for enlarging cemeteries or churchyards.[64] Also in our period, it was held by the courts that: parishioners have a right to burial in the parish churchyard (1794); a minister cannot in law

---

[60] Halsbury, *Ecclesiastical Law* (n 10) para 948.
[61] The statute was replaced by the Parochial Registers and Records Measure 1978.
[62] *Kemp v Wickes* (1809) 3 Phillimore 264 at 276; *Pouget v Tomkins* (1812) 2 Hag Con 236; *Argar v Holdsworth* (1758) 2 Lee 515; 161 ER 424; *Ray v Sherwood* (1837) 1 Moo PCC 353 on 5 & 6 Will IV c 54.
[63] 6 & 7 Wm IV c. 85. See also the Marriage Act 1823 (4 Geo. IV c. 76).
[64] 56 Geo III c 141; Halsbury, *Statutes* (n 40) 799–800.

be compelled to bury a person in a particular vault or part of the churchyard, but rather has the right to prescribe the location of a grave in the churchyard (1830); personal representatives do not have a right to insist on an unusual mode of burial, such as in an iron coffin (1819); and there is no common law or canonical right to burial in the church building without a faculty – as Lord Stowell stated, '[i]n our country, the practice of burying in churches is said to be anterior to that of burying in what are now called churchyards, but was reserved for persons of pre-eminent sanctity of life' (1820).[65] Also, it was held that: an exclusive right of burial may be limited to a particular family so long as it includes parishioners or inhabitants (1827); the request of an incumbent does not fetter the discretion of the consistory court to grant or refuse the exclusive right of burial (1827); and a grant for such right of burial in a churchyard must be made by deed and not orally (1828).[66]

V. Church Property and Finance

The greatest number of statutes enacted relate to church property and finance. First, church buildings. During the eighteenth century, dilapidation was a serious problem.[67] For instance, a visitation of 1791 in St Asaph diocese reveals dilapidated church buildings and a lack of clergy houses.[68] As to major work on church buildings, it was held in a case of 1793 that those charged with reordering should have regard to the church as a centre of worship and mission.[69] The Gifts for Churches Act 1803 enabled a person, by deed or by will executed, to give land not exceeding five acres, or goods and chattels not exceeding £500, towards a church or chapel, or a mansion house to be used as a clergy residence for the minister in that church or chapel, or any outbuildings, churchyard or glebe for it; and that property could be held without licence in perpetuity.[70] There followed a programme to build new churches.

To meet population increase and movement, the creation of new ecclesiastical parishes became necessary. This required statutory authority. In some cases

---

[65] *Maidman v Malpas* (1794) 1 Hag Con 205; *Blackmore, ex parte* (1830) 1 B & Ald 122 (location); *R v Coleridge* (1819) 2 B & Ald 806 (iron coffin); *Gilbert v Buzzard* (1820) 3 Phillim 348, 349.

[66] *Magnay v Rector, Churchwardens and Parishioners of the United Parishes of St Michael, Paternoster Royal and St Martin, Vintry* (1827) 1 Hag Ecc 48; *Rich v Bushnell* (1827) 4 Hag Ecc 164; *Bryan v Whistler* (1828) 8 B & C 288.

[67] For the law on dilapidations, see, eg, R Burn, *Ecclesiastical Law*, 3rd edn (1775) vol II, 127–35.

[68] Brown (n 53) 16–17.

[69] *Groves and Wright v Rector, Parishioners and Inhabitants of Hornsey* (1793) 1 Hag Con 188, 161 ER 521.

[70] Halsbury, *Ecclesiastical Law* (n 10) para 1057 (repealed by the Charities Act 1960); ibid paras 1058–69: the 1803 rules on Crown lands, manorial waste land (see also the Gifts for Churches Act 1811 for these) and grants by corporations, which still ran in the 1970s. See ibid para 1146 for the Glebe Exchange Act 1815.

this was effected by a local or special Act of Parliament. However, after the Church Building Act 1818 (repealed by the New Parishes Act 1843), the process was carried out by Orders in Council ratifying a scheme of the Church Building Commission; and £1 million was assigned to build new churches and a Church Building Commission was set up – by 1833, over 100 new churches were built, with about £6 million spent.[71] A series of Church Building Acts were enacted, which also dealt with patronage; for example, rights of patronage in these new districts and parishes vested by agreement and otherwise in various patrons, such as the patron of a parish out of which a new district was formed, and the incumbent and others were added, such as the Crown and the diocesan bishop.[72] And in 1830 it was held that the incumbent was custodian of the church keys.[73]

Second, tithes and related payments. The laity maintained the clergy by paying: tithes (sometimes commuted to a money payment under local custom); rents for pews in churches; (in towns) grants from borough funds to augment stipends and pay for curates; and donations to Queen Anne's Bounty to assist poor clergy. There were often disputes about paying tithes. But Dissenters, as well as continuing payment towards the cost of their own ministers and meeting-houses, mostly paid tithes (and church rates) without significant objection until the 1820s.[74] In turn, the Tithes Acts 1832, 1836, 1837, 1838 and 1839 deal with, for instance, commutation of tithes, and tithe rentcharges, as well as their extinguishment and compensation for this.[75]

Third, church rates. Each house owner or tenant had to pay church rates, used to maintain the church building and provide the necessities of worship, though disputes arose as to whether this included heating, lighting and music. As our period ends, Nonconformists opposed them: church rates supported a church they did not attend, and they had their own place of worship to support. For example, the Abergavenny Church Rate Abolition Association was formed in 1834, and Nonconformists, attending parish vestries, prevented church rates from being imposed in Swansea, Newport and Merthyr Tydfil in 1836. By 1864, half of Welsh parishes had ceased to levy compulsory church rates. Statute abolished them in 1868.[76]

Fourth, the Ecclesiastical Corporations Act 1832 authorised ecclesiastical corporations (eg, archbishops, bishops, deans and chapters) to enter agreements

---

[71] Church Building Acts 1818 to 1884: Halsbury, *Ecclesiastical Law* (n 10) para 537. See also MH Port, *Six Hundred New Churches: A Study of the Church Building Commission, 1818–1856, and its Church Building Activities* (London, SPCK, 1961).
[72] Halsbury, *Ecclesiastical Law* (n 10) para 788.
[73] *Lee v Matthews* (1830) 3 Hag Ecc 169, 162 ER 1119.
[74] Jacob (n 1) 99–100. See also D Cummins, 'The Social Significance of Tithes in Eighteenth-Century England' (2013) 128 *English Historical Review* 1129–54; Jacob, *Laypeople and Religion* (n 52) 36–39.
[75] Halsbury, *Ecclesiastical Law* (n 10) paras 1211–15.
[76] Brown (n 53) 23.

with their lessees to ascertain and settle unknown or disputed boundaries of leased land, and to summon and examine witnesses on oath, call for deeds and carry out associated tasks for these purposes.[77] There were also many cases about the charitable status of trusts to benefit religion, such as gifts for the erection of a bishopric, for the 'worship of God' and for the distribution of the Bible.[78]

Fifth, parsonages. The scourge of clerical non-residence was in part because parishes lacked a parsonage or funds to build one, or it was unsatisfactory; and clergy often lived in nearby towns within walking distance of their parishes.[79] The Clergy Residences Repair Act 1776 sought to remedy this, making provision to acquire a parsonage or a site for one, or to improve an existing one; it also dealt with mortgages and the exchanges of parsonages.[80] Clergy residences were also regulated by the Gifts for Churches Act 1803 (for which see above).

Finally, clergy income. As well as plurality, tithes, pew rents, grants and donations, clergy income came from cultivating or renting out the glebe land with which the parish was endowed. Improvements in agriculture, as when land was 'enclosed' in the late eighteenth and early nineteenth centuries, also increased clergy income.[81] Charities for clergy widows and children were important too.[82] In 1809, Parliament granted £100,000 to Queen Anne's Bounty, renewed annually, to augment the income of poor clergy. In the spirit of the great Reform Act 1832, in 1835 two commissions were appointed to consider reform of the dioceses of England and Wales: their revenues; a more equal distribution of episcopal duties; how cathedrals could be more efficient; and the best way to provide for the cure of souls, especially around clergy residence. It was enacted in 1835 that during the commission, the profits of offices without cure of souls (as in cathedrals) that became vacant should be paid over to Queen Anne's Bounty. A permanent commission was then appointed under the Ecclesiastical Commissioners Act 1836 to present to the Privy Council schemes to carry out the reforms suggested by the original commissions. It was constituted as a corporation with power to purchase and hold lands. The first members of the commission were the Archbishops of Canterbury and York, three bishops, the Lord Chancellor and the principal officers of State, and three laymen. The constitution of the commission was amended by the Ecclesiastical Commissioners Act 1840. The modern Church Commissioners were born.

---

[77] 39 & 40 Geo III c 41; Halsbury, *Statutes* (n 40) 793–97; see also ibid 806 for the Ecclesiastical Leases Act 1836.

[78] *Attorney-General v Bishop of Chester* (1785) 1 Bro CC 444; *Attorney-General v Pearson* (1817) 3 Mer 353; *Attorney-General v Stepney* (1804) 10 Ves 22.

[79] Jacob (n 1) 105.

[80] Halsbury, *Ecclesiastical Law* (n 10) para 1140 (for the preamble); see also the Clergy Residences Act 1780 and the Parsonages Act 1838.

[81] WM Jacob, *The Clerical Profession in the Long Eighteenth Century 1680–1840* (Oxford, Oxford University Press, 2006) 139–41.

[82] Jacob (n 1) 106.

VI. Conclusion

Norman Sykes famously argued that the Hanoverian Church of England was consensual, unified and moderate. It was, to a degree.[83] Its monopoly in Parliament was eroded – so much so that some scholars today might consider the period to yield evidence of a trend towards the secularisation of ecclesiastical law as a merely functional, rule-based system of law that had lost a clear 'Anglican' and distinctively religious character. However, the Church addressed new issues about its parochial ministry, new challenges from Evangelicalism within and Nonconformists without, and the novel impact of the Industrial Revolution and population growth. Anglicans also experimented with lay-led voluntary societies. The Church emerged from these changes more diverse than in the previous century.[84] Above all, from the 1780s the Church called for its own reform and renewal. The law played its part in all this. We see the creation of an established United Church of England and Ireland, the enactment of 299 statutes, an increase in commentaries on ecclesiastical law, the incorporation of Doctors' Commons and the rise of religious freedom legislation. Then there were new laws to clarify doubts about on the age for ordination, to prohibit clergy from being elected to the Commons, to limit pluralities and to enforce clergy residence on the benefice; and we see innovations in visitation practice, as well as a decline in clergy discipline litigation. For the laity, change came in the form of more case law on churchwardens, and criticisms and reviews of the church courts, which by the end of the period were more closely regulated by statute and slowly in decline in their business over the morals of the laity. There was little change in doctrinal and liturgical law, but church schools were further developed, as was case law on public order at the time of divine service, the administration of baptism and burial, the introduction of statutes on civil marriage, as well as on public notices and registers. Finally, there were further developments of the law on dilapidations, new law on the establishment of new parishes and churches, improvements in the law on clerical income, tithes and church rates, and new law to establish the Ecclesiastical Commissioners. In all this, the period 1760 to 1837 in the Church of England is one of legal continuity and change – law followed life.

---

[83] JCD Clark, 'Church, Parties, Politics' in Gregory (ed) (n 1) 289–313, 312–13.
[84] ibid; M Smith, 'The Anglican Churches, 1783–1829' in Gregory (ed) (n 1) 68–89.

8

The Victorian Church: Revival, Reform, Ritualism: 1837–1901

CHARLOTTE SMITH

The Church of England, planted in the soil of a non-documentary constitution, and drawing authority from the trinity of Scripture, church tradition and human experience, exists in a state of constant evolution and adaptation. We have seen this in the preceding chapter, exploring the relationship between the Church and the law in the period 1760 to 1837. Profoundly influenced by the Victorian historiography of the long eighteenth century, it is easy for us to view the Church in that period as being characterised by stability and continuity rather than change. Though the Victorian portrait of an unchanging and somnolent Church was in some respects true, this was a superficial picture of continuity, and masked considerable adaptation and evolution. As we have seen in chapters 6 and 7 of this volume, the Hanoverian era in fact gave birth to the seismic political, social, industrial and economic changes, which would do so much to shape the relationship between Church, law and people under Queen Victoria. It set in train the great changes to the confessional state, and reshaped ideas of the Church and its relationship with State and nation, which have ultimately evolved into the relationship between the two with which we are familiar today.

If the developments of the Hanoverian era set the stage for the many changes and reforms with which this chapter is concerned, then it was in the reign of Victoria that they progressed, if not to their logical conclusion then certainly to something more nearly related to the modern constitutional settlement. Legal and ecclesiastical reform proceeded apace throughout the nineteenth century, and the brush with which we paint our picture of the Church and the law in Victoria's reign is a necessarily broad one.[1] Inevitably, there is much that is missing or

---

[1] For the classic study of the period, see O Chadwick, *The Victorian Church*, 2 vols (London and Oxford, Adam and Charles Black, 1966 and 1970). More recently see G Evans, *Crown, Mitre and People in the Nineteenth Century: The Church of England, Establishment and the State* (Cambridge, Cambridge University Press, 2021).

mentioned only in passing, and no claim to completeness is even attempted.[2] The focus of this account is upon England, and much of significance that happened beyond its shores, and which played a role in shaping its fortunes, is omitted here. The chapter leaves for others a detailed treatment of Irish disestablishment and the Irish Church Act 1869, the birth of the worldwide Anglican Church, and legislation such as the Jerusalem Bishopric Act 1841, Colonial Bishops Act 1853 and Colonial Clergy Act 1874. Even a number of key domestic initiatives have been excluded. Despite their claims to our attention, for example, the Ecclesiastical Commissioners and the Ecclesiastical Commissioners Act 1840 are similarly largely ignored, as is the legislation that opened the Universities of Oxford and Cambridge to non-conformists,[3] and that which provided for the increase of the episcopate in England.[4]

Some readers will, no doubt quite justifiably, baulk at this, but in the midst of such an embarrassment of riches as that offered by the period in question, choices had to be made and a narrative crafted. Here that narrative is that of the metamorphosis of the Church of England from the established church of a theoretically or ideologically confessional state, to that of a state that had enthusiastically embraced not only pluralism, but also self-conscious ideas and identities of modernity and progress, expressed in extended programmes of political, legal and social reform that eventually changed the very fabric of the constitution within which the Church functioned. The resulting story is, in part, one of legal and constitutional change forced on the Church by the external pressures exerted by the State and nation to which she was bound. It is also, however, inescapably the story, as it has always been, of the Church's own spontaneous and self-willed responses to the spirit of the age. In what follows, this broad narrative is traced through the stories of litigation, judicature reform and provisions for the government of the Church.

I. Situating the Church of England in the Reign of Victoria

As chapter 7 has shown us, when Victoria ascended to the throne in 1837, the age of reform was already well underway, and many of the events and reforms that were to shape the legal history of the Church of England in her reign had already come to pass. The intellectual fruits of the Enlightenment were already being reaped; and the social, economic and technological reverberations and dislocations of the

---

[2] For a positively magisterial overview of ecclesiastical legal history in this period, see RE Rodes, *Law and Modernization in the Church of England: Charles II to the Welfare State* (Notre Dame, IN, University of Notre Dame Press, 1991).
[3] The University Tests Act 1871.
[4] Such as the Bishoprics Act 1878.

Industrial Revolution were already in full flow, reshaping the demographic make-up of England, remodelling its economy, and breaking and remaking the social bonds and institutional structures that had characterised England and English society in the pre-industrial era.

The Church was already part of this tide of change – sometimes proactively instigating reform, and sometimes grudgingly adapting perforce to its changed circumstances. The impetus for reform was already in play. Situated in a State and nation experiencing a radical period of intellectual, social, political, economic and religious change, the Church felt itself to be awakening from somnolence or quiescence to a state of renewed vigour and sensitivity. Whether shaken by the high-church cry of 'the Church in danger' or fired by a spirit of evangelistic zeal, it responded to the spirit of modernity, rationality and utilitarianism that did so much to shape the secular state, and to countervailing trends of romanticism and medievalism. It was, however, possessed of its own prophets. Its spiritual life and institutions were reshaped first, as we have already seen, by the evangelical revival's call to seriousness and to the personal experience of God at the Cross, and then by the calls of the evolving high-church tradition to revive, restate and reassert the spiritual claims and authority of the Church of England as an institution. Still another source of invigoration came from the efforts of the broad church, or liberal Anglicans, who, prompted by scientific advances, new Continental European trends in biblical criticism, religious pluralism and incipient doubt, turned their attention and energies to developing liberal, or perhaps scientifically informed, contributions to biblical and theological scholarship and church reform.[5]

The stage, then, was set for the legal agonies of the Victorian era. Having always been, of necessity and by design, a broad church seeking to encompass within itself the widest possible range of theological positions and ecclesiastical traditions, it was inevitable that the Church of England's adherents would respond to the clarion call of the age in differing ways, and draw on diverse sources of inspiration. In the white heat of self-identified spiritual awakening, of dislocation from past certainties and of uncertainty, it was, perhaps, inevitable that those diverse responses would be framed within the context of heightened partisan sensitivities and divisions – though, as chapter 7 shows, the idea of the Hanoverian Church as characterised by unity, moderation and consensus should not be pushed too far. In consequence, if one believes the self-proclaimed publicity of the Victorian commentators, the Victorian Church was characterised not only by renewed vigour and zeal, but also by the party spirit that set evangelicals against the heirs of the high church, and both against the liberal/broad/low churchmen whose heterodoxy or lack of proper religious feeling both despised. So it was that one of

---

[5] The literature here is voluminous but the classics include: B Hilton, *The Age of Atonement* (Oxford, Clarendon Press, 1988); P Nockles, *The Oxford Movement in Context* (Cambridge, Cambridge University Press, 1994); I. Ellis, *Seven Against Christ* (Leiden, E.J. Brill, 1980).

the most significant bequests of the Victorian Church to posterity was a tidal wave of litigation relating to its internal life, ordering, liturgy and doctrine.

II. Litigation: Battles in the Courts for the Soul of the Church

By virtue of the Church's Establishment, whatever their spiritual claims and character, its key formularies, its liturgy and its Articles of Religion, took legal form. Whereas in the preceding era the bishops and their supporters had largely eschewed the use of the courts as a means of enforcing clerical obedience to these legal forms, many of the crucial Victorian contests over the Church of England's doctrines and liturgy were fought through the medium of litigation, in both the ecclesiastical and secular courts. It seems, as we shall see, that the courts were not in the end an especially happy hunting ground for any of the various parties in the Church, but this did not prevent considerable resources from being ploughed into what became major set-piece battles between opposing forces. The resulting body of litigation is voluminous but can, for our purposes, be broken down into three parts.[6]

The earliest, and the least contentious, series of ecclesiastical suits arose out of renewed episcopal determination to impose and enforce heightened standards of clerical deportment and duty. The fruits of this reforming spirit were seen in what Arthur Burns has famously called the diocesan revival.[7] Its legislative harvest was evidenced, as Doe has already shown us, by the successive Pluralities Acts of 1838, 1850 and 1880, which cracked down on clerks in holy orders who held more than one living, who were not resident in their parish, who engaged in unsuitable occupations to supplement their income, or who neglected their pastoral duties. The most infamous legal battle centred on a morally lax, neglectful and unfit clergyman was that relating to the notorious Reverend Drax Free.[8] This concluded before our period of study but shaped earlier Victorian efforts to reform the ecclesiastical judicature.

The second body of litigation concerned the doctrine of the Church of England. Its focus changed over time – reflecting the evolving theological controversies of the day. No church party's doctrine was exempt from challenge. So, for example, the evangelical insistence on the individual and personal experience of conversion was most famously litigated in *Gorham v Bishop of Exeter*, a *duplex querela*

---

[6] For a study of discipline and the church courts, see N Patterson, *Ecclesiastical Law, Clergy and Laity: A History of Legal Discipline and the Anglican Church* (Abingdon, Routledge, 2019).

[7] See generally A Burns, *The Diocesan Revival in the Church of England, c 1800–1870* (Oxford, Oxford University Press, 1999).

[8] The story is best told in RB Outhwaite, *Scandal in the Church: Dr Edward Drax Free, 1764–1843* (London, Hambledon Press, 1997).

suit challenging the refusal of the high-church Bishop of Exeter to institute an evangelical clergyman who had denied the doctrine of baptismal regeneration.[9] The advanced Tractarian endeavour to rehabilitate Roman Catholic doctrines, and to hold them as being consistent with the Anglican Articles of Religion, was litigated in *Hodgson v Oakley*,[10] and the high-church eucharistic doctrine of the Real Presence was challenged in the *Denison*[11] and *Bennett*[12] cases. Most famously of all, perhaps, liberal Anglican attempts to engage with new biblical criticism were litigated in the infamous *Essays and Reviews* cases, as a result of which Anglicans were held to have been denied their 'hope' of eternal damnation, and dismissed with costs.[13] Even setting aside qualms about the character and authority of the final court of ecclesiastical appeal, which ultimately adjudicated upon these legal battles (see below), the outcome of litigation was universally unsatisfactory for the combatants who paid for it. The court resolutely declined to declare what the doctrine of the Church was and instead, resting its endeavours upon the evidence of the Thirty-Nine Articles and the Book of Common Prayer, determined to define the permissible range of doctrinal positions. In other words, it provided a legal ring-fence, within which diversity was permissible, at a time when those locked in dispute wanted absolute certainty and vindication.

The final group of cases, which took the form of both faculty and clergy discipline suits, was intertwined with the litigation regarding high-church sacramental doctrine and concerned the apparent outworking or manifestation of that doctrine in ritualist liturgy, vestments, ornaments and ceremonial. In these cases, the same court of final ecclesiastical appeal that had been roundly condemned for insisting on protecting an undesirable degree of doctrinal latitude, was vilified by the heirs of the high-church revival for insisting on, to them, an equally undesirable and unwarranted level of liturgical uniformity. So it was that both Parliament[14] and the courts grappled with the legality of stone altars, of candles, of incense, of vestments, communion wafers, the Eastward Position at the Eucharist, of altar crosses and of genuflecting or bowing to the altar.[15]

The ferocity and tenacity with which this litigation was pursued were underpinned and facilitated by the mobilisation of the party spirit at work in the Church, with each 'side' represented and organised by its own litigation

---

[9] *Gorham v Bishop of Exeter* (1850) 163 ER 1221.
[10] *Hodgson v Oakley* (1848) 1 Rob Ecc 322; 163 ER 1053; 1064.
[11] *R v Arches Court Judge, sub nom R v Dodson, Re Denison* (1857) 7 El & Bl 315, 119 ER 1264; *Ditcher v Denison* (1857) Dea & Sw 334, 164 ER 594; *Denison v Ditcher* (1857) 11 Moo PC 324, 14 ER 718.
[12] *Sheppard v Bennett* (1869-1872) LR 2 A & E 335, LR 2 PC 450, LR 4 PC 350, LR 3 A & E 167, LR 4 PC 371. Both this case and *Denison* demonstrate, like *Drax Free* before them, the extensive use of reference to the secular courts and multiple appeals as a means of delaying and impeding litigation.
[13] *Bishop of Salisbury v Williams* (1860-1864) 1 New Rep 196, 15 ER 943; *Fendall v Wilson* (1860-1864) 1 New Rep 213.
[14] See the four reports of the *Ritual Commission* (C 3951 of 1867; C 4016 of 1867-68; C 17 of 1870; C 218 of 1870).
[15] Key cases include *Liddell v Beale* (1860) 14 Moo PC 1, 15 ER 206; *Hebbert v Purchas* (1870-1872) LR 3 PC 605, LR 4 PC 301; *Ridsdale v Clifton* (1876-1877) 1 PD 383, 2 PD 276.

society – the English Church Union for the high church and the Church Association for the evangelicals. Ultimately, however, enthusiasm for litigation foundered on the rocks of the episcopal veto[16] under the Church Discipline Act 1840 and the Public Worship Regulation Act 1874, and of the spectacle of 'reverend rebels' imprisoned for their refusal to submit to the orders of the courts.[17] Almost its final flourish was the Church Association's prosecution of the moderate and universally admired Bishop Edward King of Lincoln before Archbishop Benson of Canterbury.[18] At the end of several decades of determined courtroom warfare, the Royal Commission on Ecclesiastical Discipline acknowledged that not only had the means of effective ecclesiastical discipline broken down, but the legally enshrined liturgy and ceremonial of the Church was 'too narrow for the religious life' of that generation of churchmen.[19] In fact, despite the lack of legal change, many of the liturgical innovations/revivals, ornaments and rituals adopted by the heirs of the high-church revival had become respectable and increasingly widely adopted.

III. Reforming Ecclesiastical Judicature, the Ecclesiastical Legal Profession and Its Literature

In such a litigious era, it will come as little surprise that there was enthusiasm for reform of the ecclesiastical courts. Such enthusiasm was not, however, rooted solely in ecclesiastical soil, for the reforms that reshaped ecclesiastical judicature at this time were no less the product of the same spirit of reform that moulded the secular courts into their modern form. In consequence, the efforts of would-be ecclesiastical court reformers were dogged by complexity and disagreement. Perpetually, they faced the conundrum of, and disagreement over, the proper values and character of the reformed ecclesiastical court system. Was that system to reflect the values of the reformed secular legal system, with its insistence on certainty, uniformity, efficiency and rationality; or was it to reflect the traditional pastoral structures, and renewed spiritual sensitivities and reasserted claims to spiritual autonomy, of the Church? The answer to that question was further complicated by the dual character of the law those courts were to apply, being both part of the general law of the land and enshrining the doctrine and liturgy of

---

[16] The secular courts would not review the right of the bishop to veto proceedings. See *Julius v Bishop of Oxford* (1879) 4 QBD 245; 4 QBD 525; *Allcroft v Bishop of London* [1891] AC 666.

[17] See the cases of the Reverends Tooth, Dale, Enraght, Cox and Green – (1877) 2 PD 125; (1877) 3 QBD 46; (1881) 6 QBD 376; (1882) 7 App Cas 240; (1881) 7 QBD 273; (1881) 6 App Cas 657. This was a consequence of Ecclesiastical Courts Act 1813, which had made imprisonment rather than excommunication the punishment for contumacy.

[18] (1888) 13 PD 221; (1889) 14 PD 88; (1889) 14 PD 148; [1891] P 9; [1892] AC 644.

[19] Royal Commission on Ecclesiastical Discipline, *Report and minutes of evidence* (Cd 3040, 1906).

a Church with, in certain quarters at least, a newly enhanced sense of its spiritual claims and character.

However vexed the nature of the exercise, reform was inevitable. The inexorable logic and practical consequences of secular court reform compelled it. The ecclesiastical courts were progressively shorn of their jurisdiction in non-spiritual causes. Discipline of the laity, which had previously sustained the archidiaconal courts, was, by our period, practically in abeyance, and the Court of Probate Act and Matrimonial Causes Act of 1857 transferred jurisdiction in probate and matrimonial suits to the secular courts. Gone was the mainstay of the ecclesiastical legal profession. Ecclesiastical court jurisdiction in defamation suits went the same way under the Ecclesiastical Courts Jurisdiction Act 1860, and all the work that was left could not sustain the extensive network of diocesan courts, nor the ecclesiastical courts in London.[20] Yet many of those courts remained in existence, as we shall see, beyond the end of our period.[21]

A. Reforming the Courts of First Instance

Three Victorian Acts of Parliament reshaped the lower ecclesiastical courts as they related to the worship, doctrine and discipline of the Church. Behind these three statutes, as a survey of the parliamentary papers for the period shows, lay the wreckage of almost yearly attempts to secure court reform, or to reverse the reforms that had been achieved.[22] In this wreckage is found one of the key differences between the experience of the Hanoverian and Victorian Church of England. Whereas the former was, as discussed in the previous chapter, the subject of extensive legislative intervention and reform,[23] the latter found that legislative action became effectively inaccessible to it. The expanding reach of the state into new areas of life, together with changing attitudes to parliamentary action in relation to the Church, increasingly diverted meaningful or productive parliamentary time away from church bills.[24]

The first statute relating to clergy discipline successfully secured under Victoria was the Church Discipline Act 1840, which might best be viewed as an attempt to address the defects in the ecclesiastical court system highlighted in the

---

[20] Most notably, the Court of Arches (which survived) and the High Court of Delegates and the Prerogative Court of Canterbury (which did not).

[21] On the decline of the ecclesiastical courts, see RB Outhwaite, *The Rise and Fall of the English Ecclesiastical Courts, 1500–1860* (Cambridge, Cambridge University Press, 2006).

[22] For the reforms discussed here, see Burns (n 7) ch 7; J Bentley, *Ritualism and Politics in Victorian Britain: The Attempt to Legislate for Belief* (Oxford, Oxford University Press, 1978); G Graber, *Ritual Legislation in the Victorian Church* (San Francisco, CA, Edwin Mellen Press, 1993); and, generally, S Waddams, *Law, Politics and the Church of England* (Cambridge, Cambridge University Press, 1992).

[23] A matter that draws adverse comment from Robert Phillimore in the preface to his book, *The Ecclesiastical Law of the Church of England* (London, Sweet & Maxwell, 1872) v.

[24] On this point, see C Smith, 'The Quest for an Authoritative Court of Final Appeal in Ecclesiastical Causes: A Study of the Difficulties, c 1830–76' (2011) 32 *Journal of Legal History* 189–213.

case of Dr Drax Free, cited in section II. This legislation classified all suits brought under it as office suits. So, though the leave of the bishop was required for such a suit to come to trial in court, anyone could seek leave to promote a suit (which was technically then prosecuted by the relevant church officer) under the Act, without the need to show a qualifying interest in the proceedings.[25] The bishop was empowered, at his discretion, to appoint a commission of inquiry[26] to investigate whether there was a case to answer.[27] If there was, then the bishop could, with the consent of the parties, dispose of the case without further hearing.[28] If the defendant pleaded guilty, then the bishop could require the parties to appear before him and pass sentence.[29] If a hearing was required, then the bishop could, sitting with three assessors,[30] hear the case himself, or he could delegate that task to his diocesan chancellor. Alternatively, he could use letters of request to send the case for hearing in the provincial court.[31]

The Church Discipline Act 1840 left substantially intact the traditional system of multiple diocesan courts, and letters of request and appeals, to the provincial court of the archbishop; but the second Act, the Public Worship Regulation Act 1874, drove a coach and horses through it. Passed as a direct response to the liturgical innovations/revivals of the Ritualist movement, the 1874 Act applied only to cases concerning the fabric and ornaments of the Church, the ornaments of the minister and the performance of public worship.[32] At the same time, though, it explicitly saved all existing jurisdictions,[33] meaning that litigants henceforth had a choice (depending on the nature or account of the case) between proceeding under faculty jurisdiction, the Church Discipline Act 1840, or the Public Worship Regulation Act 1874. The preservation of existing jurisdictions was fatally to undermine the aims of the 1874 Act, which Archbishop Tait had hoped would aid certainty, simplify and streamline ecclesiastical court proceedings.

It was with these objectives in mind that the Public Worship Regulation Act 1874 abolished the commission of inquiry and, subject to provisions enabling the bishop to veto further process,[34] or to dispose of the suit without further process with the consent of the parties,[35] substituted the multiplicity of diocesan

---

[25] This contrasts with instance suits, in which a litigant's case can be heard as of right, but only if they can first prove that they have an interest in the suit that gives them standing to bring it.

[26] Church Discipline Act 1840, s 4 – the commission was appointed at the discretion of the bishop and was to consist of five persons, one of whom was to be the archdeacon, rural dean or diocesan chancellor.

[27] ibid s 3.
[28] ibid s 6.
[29] ibid s 9.

[30] One was to be a lawyer (the diocesan chancellor if he was a lawyer) and then the diocesan chancellor, archdeacon, or rural dean and one other person. See ibid s 11.

[31] ibid s 17.
[32] Public Worship Regulation Act 1874, s 8.
[33] ibid s 5.
[34] ibid s 9.
[35] ibid. This was unlikely ever to happen.

courts with one unified court of first instance – a combined provincial court with jurisdiction over both York and Canterbury – presided over by a single legally qualified judge.[36] Like the provision saving existing jurisdictions, the provision relating to the appointment of a single judge in a combined provincial court was to prove problematic. Successive defendants rejected the authority of that court as being uncanonical, formed in breach of the principles of the Reformation and lacking in spiritual authority. The intransigence of Penzance, the first judge appointed under the 1874 Act, was matched only by that of his opponents. Contempt of court proceedings followed, along with the spectacle of priests imprisoned under *writs de contumace capiendo*.[37]

While the prevailing tone of the Public Worship Regulation Act was dictated by secular legal concerns with legal proficiency, efficiency, uniformity, certainty and due process, its final departure from tradition highlighted ecclesiastical concerns of quite another nature. Traditionally, the rules governing standing in the ecclesiastical courts reflected the general proposition that all people resident in England had legal rights in respect of the Church of England.[38] In office suits, which were brought to vindicate the law of the Church, a litigant required the permission of the bishop to bring his case to hearing, and technically he merely promoted the action of the relevant church officer who then brought the case to court. He did not have to prove any special status or interest in the suit, because all citizens, even dissenters,[39] were presumed to have an interest in enforcing the law of the Church. By contrast, in instance suits, the primary purpose of which was to vindicate individual rights, the litigant could proceed to hearing as of right, but to have standing they were required to demonstrate the requisite interest in, or connection to, the suit. That interest turned not on any claims of church membership, but rather on residence in the affected parish or possession of relevant property rights.[40] By contrast, the standing requirements of the 1874 Act, in so far as they related to proceedings initiated by lay persons who were not church officers, granted standing only to three male parishioners of full age who signed a declaration stating that they were members of the Church of England.[41]

---

[36] ibid s 7.

[37] In fact, the question of whether the court under the Public Worship Regulation Act was in fact the Chancery Court of York or the Court of Arches (depending on the province from which a suit came) served by a single judge, or in fact an entirely new court, was a hotly contested issue. See especially *Hudson v Tooth* (1877) LR 2 PD 125, 3 QBD 46; and C Smith, 'Martin v Mackonochie/Mackonochie v Penzance: A Crisis of Character and Identity in the Court of Arches?' (2003) 24 *Journal of Legal History* 36–58. For successive legislative attempts to deal with the embarrassment caused by the imprisonment of clergy for contempt of court, see, eg, Discharge of Contumacious Prisoners Bill 1881 (Bill No 250), Contumacy Imprisonment Abolition Bill 1887 (Bill No 157), Ecclesiastical Courts Regulation Bill 1888 (Bill No 201), Ecclesiastical Contumacy Bill 1888 and 1890 (Bill Nos 100 and 276 respectively).

[38] For an accessible general introduction, see C Chapman, *Ecclesiastical Courts, their Officials and their Records* (Lochin Publishing, 1992). For the absolute (except under certain statutes) distinction between office and instance suits, see *Fagg v Lee* (1873) 4 A & E 135 and (1874–5) 6 PC 38.

[39] *Escott v Mastin* (1842) 4 Moo PCC 104.

[40] See, eg, *Hansard v St Matthew Bethnal Green* (1878) 4 PD 46.

[41] See Public Worship Regulation Act 1874, s 8.

Here, for the first time, was a statutory requirement that only those positively asserting their membership of the Church of England should have an interest in vindicating the law as to its fabric and worship.[42] The insistence that the bishop had a discretionary right to veto proceedings, that only three parishioners acting together could bring proceedings, and that those parishioners had to declare themselves to be members of the Church of England, reflected the tangled reactions of the Church to its changed pastoral circumstances. Many within it clung stubbornly to the parochial system, and consequently to the legal rights of all parishioners in the worship of the Church. They defended zealously the assiduous enforcement of the principles of doctrinal breadth and liturgical uniformity, to ensure that the Church could comprehend the broadest possible range of beliefs consistent with biblical truth, and that believers of all types could meet on the common ground of a shared and uniform liturgy.[43] Yet others (and indeed sometimes the same churchmen) felt compelled to retreat from this position. They recognised that, in Victorian England, many parishioners rejected the services of their parish church. Further, even those who identified themselves as churchmen could often choose where they worshipped according to their tastes and temperament. As such, congregations were increasingly drawn, at least in urban areas, from outside the parish. Following the commutation of tithes in 1836, and the abolition of compulsory church rates in 1868,[44] these same congregations often voluntarily bore the cost of supporting the Church's ministry. Given this, though one might legitimately have worried about parishioners being driven out of their parish church by unlawful liturgical innovations, no less concerning were the potential consequences of prioritising parishioners' rights over those of congregations who were in fact voluntarily supporting and resourcing many of their church's activities.[45] Unwilling as yet either to abandon the principle of uniformity, or to deny the historic rights of parishioners, legislators had nevertheless to find some means of softening the blunt instrument of the law.

High Victorian efforts to reform the ecclesiastical courts of first instance could hardly be said to have been a success. Their authority was contested, and rather than simplifying things, the legislation bred complexity. The differences created were exploited by litigants, who framed their stories and chose their process according to their tactical objectives.[46] Faced with obdurate disputes over the authority of the courts, mounting costs and continued discord, the bishops, where they could, blocked proceedings, and so the appetite for litigation ultimately waned.

---

[42] Though it is noted that the Act also gave standing to churchwardens, who could have been dissenters.

[43] For arguments of this type see, eg, letter of John Gellibrand Hubbard published in the *Buckingham Express* (16 August 1871).

[44] See section IV for the two relevant statutes.

[45] See, eg, William Rogers' letter to the editor of *The Times* (4 June 1874).

[46] In essence, the availability of different processes meant that the complainants could 'forum shop' – choosing the process that best suited their purposes – for example, by framing their case as a faculty suit in order to avoid the bishop's veto under the Church Discipline Act 1840 and the Public Worship Regulation Act 1874.

The final attempt to reform jurisdiction at first instance, the Clergy Discipline Act 1892, addressed not worship and doctrine, but rather a revived concern to be able to deal effectively with clergy whose moral conduct fell short of the standards imposed upon them under canon law. It provided for the automatic vacation of a living, a bar on the holding of further ecclesiastical preferment without the express permission of the bishop, and the possibility of deposition from holy orders where a clergyman was sentenced by a secular court to imprisonment with hard labour, or where a cleric was the subject of a bastardy order or an adverse judgment in matrimonial proceedings.[47] Alternatively, where a cleric was tried in a secular court for an offence that did not attract the penalty of imprisonment with hard labour, but which did constitute an ecclesiastical offence, or where he was otherwise accused of an immoral act or habit, then the 1892 Act provided for him to be tried in the relevant diocesan consistory court.[48] In that court, presumably reinvigorated in 1892 as a belated response to oft-voiced concerns that clergy discipline should reflect canonical principles and adequately enshrine the pastoral and disciplinary role of a bishop in his diocese, an ecclesiastical judge (the diocesan chancellor) sitting alone determined questions of law, but he was assisted, in questions of fact, by three clergy and two justices of the peace sitting as assessors. Conviction in a secular court was accepted as conclusive proof of guilt.[49]

B. The Persistent Problem of the Court of Final Ecclesiastical Appeal

The first major reform to the court of final ecclesiastical appeal occurred before Victoria came to the throne. Under the Privy Council Appeals Act 1832 and the Judicial Committee Act 1833, the final appeal in ecclesiastical causes was transferred from the High Court of Delegates to the Judicial Committee of the Privy Council. These statutes apparently implemented a recommendation orchestrated by Lord Chancellor Brougham and put forward in the *Special Report* of the first Royal Commission on the Ecclesiastical Courts in 1830.[50] Although the transfer of ecclesiastical appeals to the Judicial Committee of the Privy Council was treated as being advantageous and unproblematic at that time, it soon became an on-going and apparently unresolvable source of difficulty and controversy within the Church.[51]

---

[47] Clergy Discipline Act 1892, s 1.
[48] Reflecting, in this respect, the recommendations of the Royal Commission on Ecclesiastical Courts 1883 (C 3760 of 1883).
[49] Clergy Discipline Act 1892, ss 2 and 3.
[50] House of Commons Parliamentary Papers, 1831–32 (199).
[51] This section draws on Smith (n 24).

Unlike the High Court of Delegates, which it replaced, and which consisted of both secular and ecclesiastical lawyers and bishops, the Judicial Committee of the Privy Council was composed of lay peers, who were predominantly senior judges and former judges in the secular courts. The only concession to the possible need for the Church to be represented in ecclesiastical appeals, and for the court of final ecclesiastical appeal to have access to theological learning, was found in the extra-legal constitutional convention that the Lord President would call one or more bishops who were Privy Councillors to attend such appeals.[52] This was neither a legal guarantee that the bishops would be present at such hearings, nor a means of enabling them to sit as judges. Further, the judges who did sit were not normally learned in ecclesiastical law and, following the logic that all Englishmen were prima facie churchmen, there was no requirement that they should be members of the Church of England.

The Church Discipline Act 1840 sought to address these difficulties, as they came to be perceived, by stipulating that, in appeals brought under that Act, at least one bishop should sit as a full judge on the Judicial Committee of the Privy Council.[53] This requirement, though, only applied to proceedings brought under the Act, and it did not apply to suits brought by other means.[54] As such, the composition of the Judicial Committee of the Privy Council in ecclesiastical appeals varied according to the procedure under which a suit was initially commenced. In actions under the 1840 Act, it had to include a bishop amongst its judges; but in actions brought under *duplex querela*, it might legally include no bishops amongst its number, or one or more bishops sitting by convention as assessors only. Following numerous failed bills, reports by the Church's Convocation, much pamphleteering and brief flirtations with the ideas of a court staffed entirely by ecclesiastics, or solely by lawyers, the composition of the Judicial Committee of the Privy Council in ecclesiastical appeals was finally standardised under the Appellate Jurisdiction Act 1876.[55] That Act abandoned the scheme under the Supreme Court of Judicature Act 1873, which would have transferred ecclesiastical appeals to the newly created Court of Appeal.[56] Rather, it provided that in all ecclesiastical appeals, the Judicial Committee of the Privy Council was to be staffed by lay and legally qualified judges, assisted at their discretion by a panel of three bishops acting as assessors and advising them on questions of theology and doctrine.[57]

---

[52] Judicial Committee Act 1833, s 5.
[53] Appellate Jurisdiction Act 1876, s 16.
[54] As, eg, in the famous *Gorham* case (n 9), which was brought under *duplex querela*.
[55] See s 3.
[56] Judicature Act 1873, ss 21, 22; Act Delaying Coming into Force of Supreme Court of Judicature Act 1873; Supreme Court of Judicature Amendment Act 1875, s 2.
[57] This mirrored the practice seen in admiralty appeals of this period, in which the judges of the Judicial Committee were often advised on matters of naval practice by two naval officers sitting as assessors. This is evidenced in the minute books of the Judicial Committee of the Privy Council in record series PCAP 9 at the National Archives, UK. See, eg, the volume for 1875.

The 1876 Act, though it settled the form and composition of the final court of ecclesiastical appeals until well beyond the reign of Queen Victoria, did not end disputes about how that court should be staffed, what its work was and whether it possessed the requisite authority to bind the clergy to obedience. Such disputes were, as in the case of the lower ecclesiastical courts, tied up in differing conceptions of the relationship between the Church and the State, and of the resulting nature of the Church of England and its law, partaking of both spiritual and temporal aspects.

On one level, the Church claimed temporal authority and access to coercive jurisdiction as a national institution and an established Church. On another level, it claimed spiritual authority as a doctrinally true and reformed branch of the Church of Christ. This duality carried through to its formularies and doctrines, which, though spiritual in content, were enshrined in prerogative acts issued by the Crown and in statute law passed by Parliament. The role of the Judicial Committee of the Privy Council itself was a clear example of the junction between Church and State, since it represented an appeal to the Crown as the temporal head of the Church.

Sometimes objections to the Judicial Committee of the Privy Council focused on the so-called Reformation Settlement, which was said to set the terms of the relationship between Church and State. On this basis, some of its detractors rejected the Judicial Committee of the Privy Council because it was not the mixed court provided for by the Reformation Settlement in the form of the High Court of Delegates, and because ecclesiastical appeals had been transferred to it by an unsupported act of the legislature, without consulting or obtaining the consent of the Church. They argued that the change could only properly have been made with the consent of the Church as expressed by its Convocations. For some, the lack of a spiritual mandate for its jurisdiction was fatal to its claims to possess authority over the clergy in spiritual matters. Once again, this was to give rise to embarrassing episodes of clerical contumacy.[58]

Even if concerns about its authority could be settled, arguments remained about the proper staffing of the final court of ecclesiastical appeal. Some conceptualised the Judicial Committee of the Privy Council as dealing with doctrine, and thus as needing the expertise of theologians. Others saw it as interpreting and applying laws, and thus as being most properly staffed by lawyers. In the heat of theological controversy, few, as noted above, were happy with what it did. The presence of bishops as assessors caused some to argue that it was making judgments based on policy rather than law.[59] Equally, when it applied rigorous legal rules to the evidence and pleadings before it, almost no one was satisfied

---

[58] This was dealt with at some length by the Royal Commission on Ecclesiastical Courts, which reported in 1883 (C (2nd series) 3760).

[59] For arguments about the nature and work of the court at play in litigation, see C Smith, 'Ridsdale v Clifton: Representations of the Judicial Committee of the Privy Council in Ecclesiastical Appeals' (2008) 19 *King's Law Journal* 551–74.

with its failure to condemn what many perceived to be unacceptable doctrinal positions or liturgical practices.

It was in the midst of these debates and difficulties that the Royal Commission on Ecclesiastical Courts 1883 was appointed and reported – the final Victorian effort to address the vexed question of ecclesiastical appeals. It attempted to clarify the nature of the appellate court's work, and its character and authority as a court dealing with cases relating to a spiritual body the membership of which was not now coterminous with that of the nation. To this end, it recommended that the final court of ecclesiastical appeal should be composed solely of a permanent body of lay judges who had declared themselves to be members of the Church of England. The court could, at the request of one or more of its judges, consult the bishops and archbishops in matters of worship and doctrine, but it was not bound to give effect to the advice received.[60] Ultimately, however, the recommendations of the 1883 report came to nothing and things remained as they had been settled in 1876.

C. The Impact of Reforms on the Ecclesiastical Legal Profession and its Literature

It was inevitable that the factors that drove ecclesiastical court reform would, in turn, impact decisively on the ecclesiastical legal profession, and on the careers of individual ecclesiastical lawyers. The inexorable decline in business in the diocesan and archidiaconal courts had meant that, even before Victoria came to the throne, that profession had been increasingly confined to London, and specifically to the College of Doctors Commons. The reforms of the Victorian era, however, prompted the demise of even this last bastion of the civilian legal profession. Discipline over the laity was no more, and jurisdiction over defamation, probate and matrimonial causes was transferred to the secular courts. Even in an era renowned for its enthusiasm for clergy discipline litigation, there was not enough work to sustain a separate ecclesiastical legal profession. Nor did the civilians have such business as had traditionally been theirs, or that was left to them, to themselves. Reforming legislation ensured that all advocates, proctors, barristers and attorneys would be able to carry out business in the courts to which jurisdiction was transferred. Even the High Court of Admiralty was opened to the non-civilians in 1859.[61]

The scions of the civilian profession, so long a tight-knit community bound by both family and professional ties, increasingly had to seek their fortunes, and to make their careers, within the wider legal world. In doing so, they were aided by extended rights of audience, and by the increasingly common practice of pursuing

---

[60] *Report of the Royal Commission on Ecclesiastical Courts* (C (2nd series) 3760, 1883) – see recommendations.

[61] See, eg, Matrimonial Causes Act 1857, s 1 and Probate Act 1858, s 2; High Court of Admiralty Act 1859, s 1.

legal training and practice at one of the Inns of Court. Less obviously, for some of that later generation of Victorian ecclesiastical lawyers, the reforms of the courts shaped their career path even within the secular courts. Walter Phillimore, for example, took preferment in Queen's Bench Division, rather than in the Probate, Divorce and Admiralty Division for which his professional expertise more obviously fitted him. Apparently, as a devout high churchman, he did not wish to sit as a judge in civil divorce proceedings.[62]

Though ecclesiastical lawyers remained bound, in many instances, by ties of family and affection, and though shared interests in matters of faith and the law often brought them together, the reforms of Victoria's reign spelled the end for the separate civilian profession located in the College of Doctors Commons. Under the Court of Probate Act 1857, the College was empowered to surrender its charter and to dispose of its assets.[63] The process of dissolution began in January 1858, and though its charter was never surrendered, its last meeting, and the sale of its buildings, took place in 1865.[64] This did not, however, signal the death of ecclesiastical law as a distinctive subject of study. The writing and publication of books on ecclesiastical law remained alive and well, even as the reach of ecclesiastical law dwindled.

Setting aside the myriad pamphlets in which arguments were advanced in respect of ecclesiastical appeals or particular points of the law relating to the worship of the Church,[65] the ecclesiastical law books of the period shared many of the characteristics or tropes common to legal publishing in England at that time. Reflecting, perhaps, the complications and confusions caused to parochial clergy and lay officers by extensive legislative reform of the ecclesiastical law, several of the most prominent texts published in the Victorian period, like *Burn* before them, were alphabetical abridgements – designed to be comprehensive and accessible handbooks for practitioners and clergy alike. Into this category fell books such as Francis Newman Rogers, *A Practical Arrangement of Ecclesiastical Law* (London, 1840) and Archibald John Stephens, *A Practical Treatise of the Laws Relating to*

---

[62] See C Smith, 'The disruptive power of legal biography: the life of Lord Phillimore – churchman and judge' (2020) 41 *Journal of Legal History* 164–85. It might otherwise have been thought that the Probate, Divorce and Admiralty Division would have been the obvious home for him – especially since the Matrimonial Causes Act 1857 very largely maintained the substantive law as previously applied by ecclesiastical courts and provided that ecclesiastical principles would be a continuing source of jurisprudence for the new courts. See H Kha and W Swain, 'The Enactment of the Matrimonial Causes Act 1857: The Campbell Commission and the Parliamentary Debates' (2016) 37 *Journal of Legal History* 303–30.

[63] Court of Probate Act 1857, ss 116, 117.

[64] See P Barber, 'The Fall and Rise of Doctors Commons?' (1996) 4 *Ecclesiastical Law Journal* 462–69.

[65] See, eg, C Burton, *Considerations on the Ecclesiastical Courts and Clergy Discipline* (London, James Parker & Co, 1875); W Finlason, *The History, Constitution, and Character of the Judicial Committee of the Privy Council, considered as a Judicial Tribunal, especially in Ecclesiastical Cases* (London, Stevens, 1878); J Joyce, *On the Court of Final Ecclesiastical Appeal as proposed by the Commissioners on Ecclesiastical Courts* (London, Rivingtons, 1884); R Phillimore, *Clergy Discipline: A Letter to His Grace the Archbishop of Canterbury* (London, 1872).

the Clergy (London, 1848), both published by barristers working primarily in the secular courts.

Others, however, though they still professed the desire to fulfil the role of author of a practical handbook, moved beyond this model and began to group related subjects together for developed and systematic treatment. The most notable such volumes included Henry William Cripps, *A Practical Treatise on the Laws relating to the Church and the Clergy* (London, 1845), written by a barrister of Lincolns Inn and Middle Temple who was a fellow of New College Oxford; and John Henry Blunt, *The Book of Church Law: Being an Exposition of the Legal Rights and Duties of the Parochial Clergy and the Laity of the Church of England* (London, 1873), written by an ecclesiastical historian and theologian whose interest in the subject was that of a parish clergyman. The most famous ecclesiastical law book of the period, however, was the fruit of Doctors Commons, and was written by one of the most eminent sons of one of its most illustrious civilian families: Robert Joseph Phillimore's[66] *Ecclesiastical Law of the Church of England* (London, 1872 and 1895) set out to 'promote a more continuous and scientific study of Ecclesiastical Jurisprudence than has for a very long period of time been prevalent in this country'. Moving beyond the merely practical, Phillimore desired to show how the ecclesiastical law of the Church of England was 'capable of being reduced to a system',[67] and embraced, albeit imperfectly,[68] broader developments in legal writing that saw English lawyers beginning to reinvigorate the art of legal treatise writing.[69]

IV. Adjusting to the Loss of the Confessional State: Developments in Church Government

Such is the tangled and protracted tale of Victorian attempts to reform the ecclesiastical courts, and of their consequences for the ecclesiastical legal profession. Lurking within the threads of this story, however, is a final theme that we need, albeit briefly, to bring to the fore. The legal history of representative church government, and of the Church's legal assertion of the means of spiritual autonomy from a state that had decisively abandoned the confessional principle in favour of

---

[66] See Norman Doe's biography of Phillimore in the *Oxford Dictionary of National Biography* (latest version 2007) at https://doi.org/10.1093/ref:odnb/22138.

[67] R Phillimore, *The Ecclesiastical Law of the Church of England* (London, Sweet & Maxwell, 1872; 2nd edn, 1895) preface, v.

[68] Baker describes Phillimore's two volumes rather as 'a typical Victorian practitioner's textbook than a work of intellectual coherence'. See JH Baker, 'Sir Robert Phillimore, QC, DCL (1885)' (1997) 4 *Ecclesiastical Law Journal* 709–19, 713.

[69] On this see, eg, C MacMillan, 'Stephen Martin Leake: A Victorian's View of the Common Law' (2011) 32 *The Journal of Legal History* 3–29; AWB Simpson, 'The Rise and Fall of the Legal Treatise: Legal Principles and the Forms of Legal Literature' (1981) 48 *University of Chicago Law Review* 632–79.

pluralism, more properly belongs to the Edwardian era. Its roots, however, were planted firmly in the high Victorian period. Its causes went back even further for, as chapter 7 has shown, the confessional state and its ideology had passed from view before Victoria had come to the throne. This reality, together with the Church's response to it, could not fail fundamentally to reshape the relationship between the Church of England and the State, and between the Church and the people.

By Victoria's time, dissenters and non-conformists were no longer content quietly to accept the status quo, nor to leave unchallenged the Church of England's claim to engage with, and to meet the spiritual needs of, most people in England. This led to the reform of Parliament, and to the admission of non-Anglicans, and ultimately non-Christians, to the full civic life of the nation.[70] In this changed political reality, as England embraced at least Christian pluralism rather than merely toleration, traditional models of church funding changed too. The Tithe Commutation Act 1836 and its successors addressed discontent with tithe payments for the support of the clergy of the Church of England, while the Compulsory Church Rate Abolition Act 1868 finally settled the grievance of dissenters who objected to paying compulsory church rates for the maintenance of the buildings and fabric of church buildings which they did not use. At the same time, by 1840 at the latest, it became clear that the Government would make no more grants, as it had in the early years of the nineteenth century, for the building of churches. If not before, then the disestablishment and disendowment of the Church of Ireland, and the dissolution of its constitutional union with the Church of England,[71] provided conclusive proof that henceforth the 'national' churches could expect to be reliant solely upon their own resources and efforts for the fulfilment of their core spiritual functions. This was not to say that considerable state money was not directed to the support of Church of England, for the Church of England (like other faith bodies) received considerable sums from the state to support its extensive network of schools,[72] but state funding directed explicitly to the support of the exclusively religious activities of the Church was no more. New methods of funding, including the offertory, pew rents and voluntary rates, had to be explored instead.

Turning back to the Church's relationship with Parliament, not only the changed composition of Parliament, and the Church's evolving sense of its own spiritual identity and authority, but also the heightened workload of Parliament demanded a reappraisal of Parliament's role as the legislature of the Church. As chapter 7 tells us, an average of four ecclesiastical statutes a year were passed in the Hanoverian period. The Victorian Church, too, was the subject of

---

[70] Repeal of the Test and Corporation Acts 1828, Roman Catholic Relief Act 1829, Religious Disabilities Act 1846; Jewish Relief Act 1858; Oaths Act 1888.
[71] Irish Church Act 1869.
[72] On elementary education, see Rodes (n 2) 135–40.

extensive parliamentary intervention, but despite the obvious need for reform, the desire for reform and the Church's continuing reliance upon Parliament for legislative reform, it became ever more difficult for the Church to secure the successful passage of legislation through Parliament. Successive prime ministers insisted on what appeared to amount to a new constitutional convention, that the Government would not introduce legislation without proof of consensus in the Church on the matter in question.[73] Even supposing that such consensus could be demonstrated, governments reliant on an increasingly diverse electorate, and with ever more packed parliamentary schedules, were reluctant to sponsor church legislation and insisted instead that it should come from the bishops.[74] While securing government support for a bill was not necessarily an unmixed blessing,[75] reliance upon private members' bills, especially where these were not granted government support, radically reduced the chances of ecclesiastical bills passing into law when parliamentary time was limited and parliamentary business was dominated by government bills.[76] Moreover, the difficulties of the Church did not end there. While the withdrawal of government support for its legislative initiatives increasingly denied it the effective means of securing its own legislative objectives, the lack of effective parliamentary safeguards around the process of initiating ecclesiastical legislation exacerbated the precarity of the Church's position. Whatever the conventions governing the introduction of government bills for exclusively ecclesiastical reform, it was, as Gathorne Hardy's amendment[77] to Lord Selborne's Judicature Bill in 1873 showed, perfectly possible for private members to secure profoundly important changes to the law and courts of the Church of England through amendments to bills otherwise concerned solely with secular matters.[78]

One response to this, and to the Church's growing sense of the need for the means of independent action, was the revival of the Church of England's convocations, and the birth of synodical government in the form of diocesan synods and conferences. The impetuses for such developments reflected the changed circumstances of the Church. Revival of the convocations of Canterbury and York,

---

[73] See, eg, Burns' discussion of Lord Derby's treatment of clergy discipline measures in A Burns, 'The Costs and Benefits of Establishment' (2000) 18 *Parliamentary History* 81–95, 85–86; see also statements by Gladstone and Disraeli during debates on the Public Worship Regulation Bill 1874 at HC Deb 8 July 1874, series 3, vol 220, col 1377; HC Deb 15 July 1874, series 3, vol 221, cols 76–77 respectively.

[74] See, eg, Selborne and Salisbury at HL Deb 11 May 1874, series 3, vol 219, cols 44 and 50–51 respectively; Disraeli at HC Deb 15 July, series 3, vol 221, cols 76–77, though note that up to 1856, a number of bills affecting clergy discipline were introduced by government law officers.

[75] As demonstrated in the passage of the Public Worship Regulation Act 1874 – see A Warren, 'Disraeli, the Conservatives and the National Church, 1837–1881' (2000) 19 *Parliamentary History* 96–117.

[76] For a useful overview spanning the whole period, see S Anderson, 'Parliament' in W Cornish et al (eds), *Oxford History of the Laws of England*, vol XI: *1820–1914 English Legal System* (Oxford, Oxford University Press, 2010) pt 2, ch I, 301–41, esp at 305–15.

[77] Transferring ecclesiastical appeals to Lord Selborne's new (secular) Court of Appeal.

[78] See Smith (n 24) 189–213.

in 1855 and 1861 respectively, reflected a heightened sense of the spiritual claims and identity of the Church, as did the development of diocesan synods, which was woven into the fabric of the diocesan revival.[79] So too, though, they reflected both the sense of a Church increasingly thrown upon its own resources, both in terms of financial support and governance, and a sense of growing alienation from a Parliament that could no longer, by any stretch of the imagination, be characterised as the lay synod of the Church of England.

This sense of alienation from Parliament and of reliance upon the voluntary efforts of active churchmen and women, together with the democratic spirit prevailing at the time, prompted initiatives to include lay adherents of the Church in its deliberative institutions, leading to their inclusion in diocesan conferences and the creation of the Houses of Laymen in the convocations of Canterbury (1886) and York (1892).[80] Yet for all these developments, for all the evidence of reinvigoration in the institutional life of the Church, and for all that the state seemed increasingly to set itself at odds with the Church's historic role in the life of the nation, the Church remained dependent upon it for the means of legislative action.

Not the least of the reasons for this continued reliance upon an ever less amenable Parliament was the apparent reluctance of the state, in the form of the Crown in Parliament, to relinquish any part of its control over the Church. Parliament's jealous defence of its powers in respect of the Church precluded it from assenting to any suggestion on the part of the high church[81] that there was, as a matter of law or constitutional convention, any requirement that it should consult the revived convocations on parliamentary initiatives touching the Church. Parliament could, and sometimes did, consult convocations, but it insisted that it was under no obligation to do so; nor was it bound to give effect to the views expressed in convocations. In the eyes of many high churchmen, as we have seen, this undermined the spiritual claims and authority of the resulting initiatives.[82] So it was that, in 1906, the Royal Commission on Ecclesiastical Discipline asserted that 'the Church has had to work under regulations fitted for a different condition of things, without that power of self-adjustment which is inherent in the conception of a living Church'.[83]

---

[79] See Burns (n 7) ch 9.

[80] The most complete account of these developments remains M Roberts, 'The Role of the Laity in the Church of England, c 1850–1885' (DPhil Thesis, University of Oxford, 1974).

[81] As in respect of the parliamentary treatment of the Public Worship Regulation Act 1874.

[82] On the activities of convocations and their relationship with Parliament at this time, see E Kemp, *Counsel and Consent* (London, SPCK, 1961) 172ff; S Anderson, 'The Church and the State' in W Cornish et al (eds), *The Legal System, Oxford History of the Laws of England*, vol XI: *1820–1914 English Legal System* (Oxford, Oxford University Press, 2010) pt 2, ch III, 385–400. The Church itself was divided on this point.

[83] See the conclusion to the *Report* (n 19). On the protracted and lingering death of the 'political Protestantism' that in many instances underpinned parliamentary reluctance to let go of its authority in church matters, see J Maiden, *National Religion and the Prayer Book Controversy, 1927–1928* (Woodbridge, Boydell Press, 2009); and J Maiden and P Webster, 'Parliament, the Church of England and the Last Gasp of Political Protestantism, 1963–4' (2013) 32 *Parliamentary History* 361–77.

V. Conclusion

The story told here has been one of a Church with a sense of being newly revived and reinvigorated, set apart from what it saw, perhaps rather unjustly, as the torpor of the long eighteenth century. It is a story of a diverse body of churchmen responding to both the promptings of religious zeal and a prevailing sense of dislocation and the unsettlement of past certainties. In both instances they were as much constrained by significant forces for continuity as they were liberated by a sense of new possibilities and the will to change. Within this context, ecclesiastical law was a powerful source of continuity. It remained part of the general law of the land, composed of an amalgam of prerogative, statute and canon, and the Crown in Parliament remained adamant in its determination to control its creation and modification. Ecclesiastical law was, though, also a source of perplexity and ambiguity in a rapidly changing social, political and constitutional context. Its essential nature and authority – whether spiritual or legal – was increasingly the subject of debate. So, too, was Parliament's role in respect of it. Whatever its general form and legal standing, its character was, in reality, that of the law governing a faith body that was ever more distinct from the nation to which it was constitutionally bound.

Even, then, while ecclesiastical law was a powerful source of continuity, it was also a no less powerful source of, or sometimes a mirror reflecting, change. So, for example, a significant part of the history of the Church of England in the reign of Victoria is told through stories of momentous litigation – both reflecting and reacting to change within the Church. This focused, as we have seen, on standards of clerical deportment, the place of distinctively high-church, evangelical and liberal theologies within accepted understandings of its doctrine, and the acceptability or otherwise of high-church revivals/innovations in the liturgy, ceremonial and ornaments of the Church. No less importantly, the centrality of law to the history of change within the Victorian Church is reflected in the story of Herculean legislative efforts to reform or reshape the means by which the Church was funded, the means by which it was to be governed and administered, and, most especially, to reform the courts through which its laws were enforced and given effect. The legacy of all this activity was, perhaps inevitably, a curate's egg – a compound of both continuity and change, of success and failure.

Theologically, the Church was throughout the period riven by a partisan spirit and heightened internal divisions, as different church parties responded to their times in diverse and not always mutually compatible ways. Despite this, it remained a theologically broad and inclusive Church, and one that was still defined chiefly by reference to its mission or purpose as an established Church. Its worship, though, was indelibly marked by the high-church revival of the Victorian era, with many high-church practices having been accepted, often in defiance of the substantive law, into the mainstream of church life by the turn of the century. So, too, the high-church emphasis upon the spiritual claims of the Church, the desire for the means of autonomous church government, and the practical growth and manifestation of quasi-democratic church councils, all left their mark. The Church succeeded, in some measure at least, in mobilising the voluntary efforts of the laity for its support, and in incorporating some sense of the democratic spirit into its governance. As it moved into the twentieth century, it managed not only to avoid disestablishment, but also to create a model of representative self-government that struck a balance, between the legal rights of citizens in an established Church and the interests and concerns of the active adherents upon whose efforts, finances and zeal its ministry increasingly depended.

If these developments could be characterised as signifying the importance of ecclesiastical law as a mirror of, or impetus for, change, then the legacy of Victorian ecclesiastical court reform was more ambiguous. It left to posterity a court of final appeal, the authority of which was fiercely contested, a complex morass of courts and process at first instance, unresolved questions about the right authority and character of the ecclesiastical courts (whether spiritual or legal), and an abiding fear of grasping the nettle of ecclesiastical court reform that hampered reform efforts going forward. The efforts and experiences of Victorian court reformers, and the consequences of their initiatives, cast a long shadow over the question of clergy discipline even quite late into the twentieth century. In all of this, of course, ecclesiastical lawyers played their part and navigated their own paths between continuity and change. Even while they continued to be bound by affinities of faith and education in the civilian legal tradition, and even while they continued to practise and advance the claims of ecclesiastical law as a separate and distinctive body of law, they increasingly had to seek their fortunes within the wider legal world and were subject to the forces and influences at play there. Like the Church of which they were a part, they had a distinctive character and vocation, but they were nevertheless inevitably influenced by the forces at work in the state and in society more broadly.

9

The 'New World' of Ecclesiastical Law: 1901–47

RUSSELL DEWHURST

> We are living in a new world: it is ours, if we are true to the faith that is in us, to seek to make it a better world. It is by prayer and service that we may hope to do it. But we dare not think that a Book of Common Prayer fitted for the seventeenth century can supply every want of the twentieth …
>
> *Preface, The Book of Common Prayer with the additions and deviations proposed in 1928*

This chapter continues the themes of ecclesiastical self-governance and the responses to revival, reform and ritualism that were explored in chapter 8 alongside changes to the system of ecclesiastical courts and the profession of ecclesiastical lawyers. In doing so, section I traces the development of the ecclesiastical law of the Church of England in the first half of the twentieth century, especially the Church's creation of the Church Assembly and its early legislation. Section II examines the causes of Prayer Book revision and the effects of its failure in Parliament. Section III describes some significant developments in ecclesiastical law that took place in Parliament, at the Lambeth Conferences and in the Convocations.

I. The Establishment and Work of the Church Assembly

Just as the ritual and ceremony of church services had been incendiary and pressing issues during the nineteenth century, so they continued well into the twentieth. It is estimated that 188 of the Members of Parliament returned to the House of Commons in the 1900 election had pledged to support anti-ritualist legislation, and the issue was eclipsed only by the Boer War.[1] Anti-ritualist

---

[1] N Yates, *Anglican Ritualism in Victorian Britain 1830–1910* (Oxford, Oxford University Press, 2000) 325.

legislation was brought to the House every year until 1908, although rarely passed the Second Reading.² Instead, the matter was committed to a Royal Commission, which was in 1904 charged to 'inquire into the alleged prevalence of breaches or neglect of the Law relating to the conduct of Divine Service in the Church of England ... and to make ... recommendation.'³

The Commissioners received extensive evidence from parishes and dioceses across the Church of England. As expected, they found a great many 'breaches or neglect of the law', which they categorised as insignificant, significant and 'illegal practices of a graver kind'.⁴ Three points made in the Report's conclusion touch upon the areas that would see significant activity and controversy in ecclesiastical law in the succeeding decades. First, the Commissioners found that 'the law of public worship in the Church of England is too narrow for the religious life of the present generation. It needlessly condemns much which a great section of Church people, including many of her most devoted members, value.'⁵ Prayer Book revision was, therefore, on the agenda. Second, the Commissioners confirmed that the 'machinery for discipline has broken down'.⁶ They believed this was unacceptable, and proper enforcement of a revised liturgical law was essential. Third, and perhaps most significantly, the Commissioners acknowledged that 'the Church has had to work under regulations fitted for a different condition of things, without that power of self-adjustment which is inherent in the conception of a living Church'.⁷ It is noteworthy that the Commissioners did not recommend the imposition of parliamentary legislation to rectify the illegal practices they catalogued, but saw the need for some degree of self-government as 'inherent' in what it was to be a Church. Accordingly, they proposed that the Convocations should embark upon Prayer Book revision.⁸

In directing the matter to the Convocations, the Commissioners acknowledged that there was a body within the Church that could, in theory, exercise a power of government and create legislation. However, where a change to the law

---

² G Machin, 'The Last Victorian Anti-Ritualist Campaign, 1895–1906' (1982) 25 *Victorian Studies* 277–302, 293.
³ Royal Commission on Ecclesiastical Discipline, *Report of the Royal Commission on Ecclesiastical Discipline* (London, 1906).
⁴ Perhaps inevitably this categorisation betrayed the Commissioners' own theological leanings and the political desire to target ritualism rather than law-breaking generally. The fact that 7,941 churches out of 12,532 reporting on the matter did not provide daily services was said to be 'non-significant' (although it might not have seemed so to parishioners who wanted to attend church on weekdays), whereas, remarkably, the practice obtaining in some places of large numbers of (non-communicant) children attending services of Holy Communion – which was not contrary to the law – was one of the principal headings in the section entitled 'illegal practices of a graver kind' ibid 14, 32.
⁵ ibid 75.
⁶ ibid 76.
⁷ ibid.
⁸ D Cruickshank, 'Debating the Legal Status of the Ornaments Rubric: Ritualism and Royal Commissions in Late Nineteenth- and Early Twentieth-Century England' (2020) 56 *Studies in Church History* 434–54, 452.

of the Church required the amendment of parliamentary statute, only Parliament had the power to legislate. There were two main reasons why this was no longer acceptable: one theoretical, and one practical.

The theory had been (so it was argued) that Parliament was the lay government of the Church, cooperating with the bishops and clergy who had their own distinctive roles and institutions. As a church report put it in 1902, 'We believe that there is a primitive distinction between the clergy and laity' and that 'this distinction is involved in the choice and commission of the Apostles', but nevertheless in the New Testament are found 'traces of the cooperation of clergy and laity ... and we cannot but conclude that this cooperation belongs to the true ideal of the Church.'[9] The Report goes on to argue that, historically, the Church had been co-extensive with nation, and so it had been justified for Parliament, including both bishops and representatives of the laity, to legislate for the Church. By the twentieth century, however, matters had changed, so that 'the constitution of Parliament no longer justifies such a claim'[10] – in other words, it was inappropriate for Parliament to legislate for the Church when so many MPs were not members of that Church. This question had been of course central to the concerns of the Oxford Movement,[11] although the Tractarians had not placed the same emphasis on the inclusion of the laity in church governance.

Even setting aside the ecclesiological arguments against the twentieth-century Parliament's enactment of legislation for the Church, it was in any case no longer practical for Parliament to supply all the legislation that was required. Between 1880 and 1913, only an average of one Church bill per year became law – 183 were dropped, usually because of a lack of parliamentary time.[12]

Since 1903, there had been a Representative Church Council for the Church of England, uniting the Convocations and the House of Laymen of each province (which had been elected by Diocesan Conferences since 1886 as consultative bodies) – but it remained purely deliberative and could not perform a legislative function. In 1916, the Archbishops' Committee on Church and State proposed a reconstituted Representative Church Council, which would have powers to legislate for the Church (subject to a parliamentary veto).[13] In another age, the Report might have vanished without trace, but this was the time of Home Rule

---

[9] *Report of the Joint Committee of the Convocation of Canterbury on the Position of the Laity: Presented April 29, 1902; with Appendix* (London, SPCK, 1902) 84.

[10] ibid 86.

[11] One of the movement's early leaders, Richard Froude, had written in 1833, 'Whenever it was that the Church of England lost her exclusive supremacy in the councils of this nation, then, at that very instant, a change took place in her internal constitution – a change, too, of no ordinary magnitude or importance, but a *down-right* revolution.' R Froude et al, *Remains of the Late Reverend Richard Hurrell Froude, Part 2* (Derby, JG and F Rivington, 1839) 1:192.

[12] C Podmore, 'Self-Government Without Disestablishment: From the Enabling Act to the General Synod' (2019) 21 *Ecclesiastical Law Journal* 312–28.

[13] Church of England and Archbishops' Committee on Church and State, *The Archbishops' Committee on Church and State: Report, with Appendices* (London, 1916).

for Ireland,[14] and a time when Roman Catholic social teaching was bringing the principle of subsidiarity to greater prominence.[15] The Welsh Church Act 1914 disestablished the Church of England in Wales, separating it from the State, provided that the ecclesiastical law ceased to exist as law in Wales, and enabled the foundation of a new institutional church that would be governed by its own constitution and regulations as a private voluntary religious association.[16] (And later, the Church of Scotland Act 1921 would recognise the Church of Scotland's independence as a national Church in matters spiritual.) In all these ways, the importance of self-governance was manifesting itself, and so the needs of the Church of England were perhaps more apparent than they would have been at another time: it was widely believed to be not just impractical for the State to govern all minutiae of Church life but wrong that it should even try. From 1917, the campaign for the self-governance of the Church grew rapidly in popularity, thanks to the work of the 'Life and Liberty' group and its spokesman, William Temple.[17]

In early 1919, the Representative Church Council adopted a slightly revised version of the proposals of the Committee on Church and State. If the proposed system of self-governance was to be truly the Church's own, the new governing body could not be a creation of Parliament. Therefore, the constitution of the Church Assembly (as it was now to be known) was determined by the Convocations, and Parliament was asked to confer powers on it as a body whose Measures could be adopted into statute law. Introducing a bill to this effect in the House of Lords, the Archbishop of Canterbury began: 'My Lords, I ask your Lordships to give a Second Reading to a Bill to enable the Church of England to do its work properly.'[18] His speech focused almost entirely on the practical issues – the lack of parliamentary time – that necessitated a Church Assembly, and played down any sense in which the bill would constitute a constitutional change or deprive non-conformists of

---

[14] This resulted in the Government of Ireland Act 1914.

[15] That is, the period between the papal encyclicals *Rerum Novarum* (1891) and *Quadragesimo Anno* (1931), although the word 'subsidiarity' was not frequently used before the end of this period. Among significant thinkers in the Church of England, John Neville Figgis was an early proponent – see his 1900 Birkbeck Lectures, JN Figgis, *Studies of Political Thought from Gerson to Grotius: 1414–1625* (Cambridge, Cambridge University Press, 2011) 207: 'It is not merely that [Althusius] allows rights to families and provinces; but he regards these rights as anterior to the State, as the foundation of it, and as subsisting always within it. He would no more deny or absorb them than a hive of bees would squash all the cells into a pulp.' And especially JN Figgis, *Churches in the Modern State, by John Neville Figgis* (London, Longmans, Green and Co, 1913).

[16] N Doe, 'The Welsh Church Act 1914: A Century of Constitutional Freedom for the Church in Wales?' (2020) 22 *Ecclesiastical Law Journal* 2–14. The date of disestablishment was deferred, due to the First World War, till 31 March 1920. The Archbishop of Canterbury declared the Welsh dioceses as separate from the province of Canterbury. However, 'vestiges of establishment' continued in, eg, the duty to marry and bury parishioners.

[17] 'Q. What is it we are seeking? A. Liberty. Q. How do we hope to gain it? By pressing with all the force we can amass for the passage of the Enabling Bill through Parliament without delay.' FA Iremonger, quoted in a report on the *Life and Liberty Movement's First Anniversary Meeting*, *Church Times* (19 July 1918).

[18] *Hansard*, HL Deb 3 June 1919, vol 34, col 974.

influence in the national church. He continued: 'What we want to do is to help the lives, the homes, the needs, the sorrows of the English people in the best and deepest way. That is a matter quite literally of life and death to us to do.'[19] Parliament gave its agreement in the form of the Church of England Assembly (Powers) Act 1919, which became known, simply, as the Enabling Act.[20]

There were parliamentary checks on this new form of church legislation, which became known as Measures. The Enabling Act required that any proposed Measure of the Church Assembly be forwarded to the newly formed Ecclesiastical Committee of both Houses of Parliament, which must present a report to Parliament on the Measure's expediency and its effect on the constitutional rights of individuals. If both Houses by resolution agreed to the Measure, it would have 'the force and effect of an Act of Parliament on the Royal Assent being signified thereto in the same manner as to Acts of Parliament'.[21] Measures, therefore, could amend and repeal Acts of Parliaments, and in their effects bind both clergy and laity, just as Acts of Parliament do. (Even today, substantially the same procedure applies to Measures passed by the General Synod, the body which has succeeded the Church Assembly.)

A couple of further points about the Church Assembly are worth noting. First, questions of doctrine were still primarily in the purview of the bishops and the Convocations. The constitution of the Church Assembly specified that it did not 'belong to the functions of the Assembly to issue any statement purporting to define the doctrine of the Church of England on any question of theology' and, furthermore, any Measures with a doctrinal element had to be proposed in terms agreed by the House of Bishops.[22] Second, the franchise (ie the qualification for membership of the electoral roll in each parish) was baptism, following revision to that effect by the Representative Church Council; elected lay representatives themselves had to be communicants and not members of other churches.[23] The baptismal franchise was controversial, as Anglo-Catholics in particular believed that it was wrong for Christians who were not fully initiated to be involved in

---

[19] ibid col 993.

[20] Does the Enabling Act confer powers? HW Cripps, *A Practical Treatise on the Law Relating to the Church and Clergy*, 8th edn (London, Sweet & Maxwell, 1937) 10 argues no: 'The [Enabling] Act 1919, neither constitutes as a statutory body, nor gives any express powers, statutory or otherwise, to the National Assembly of the Church; it recognises, however, that body, as constituted in accordance with the constitution set forth in the Appendix to the Addresses of the Convocations, as the only body whose measures are entitled to be considered under and treated in accordance with the provisions of the Act.' However, the 1919 Act describes itself as 'An Act to confer powers ...' and *does* give powers to the Church Assembly: eg, s 3(5), s 3(7) and, not least, the power to submit Measures to Parliament, which 'shall' (not 'may') be considered by the Ecclesiastical Committee, s 3(2).

[21] Church of England Assembly (Powers) Act 1919, s 4.

[22] 'Constitution of the Church Assembly set forth in the Appendix to the Addresses presented to His Majesty by the Convocations of Canterbury and York on the tenth day of May, nineteen hundred and nineteen, and laid before both Houses of Parliament', s 14, reproduced in Cripps (n 20) 10–12. Further discussion of the cause and effects of this restriction can be found in Podmore (n 12) 322.

[23] See *Rules for the Representation of the Laity* contained in the Schedule to the 'Constitution of the Church Assembly' (n 22) and, later, the like provisions of the Representation of the Laity Measure 1929.

the government of the Church.[24] Nevertheless, these qualifications have remained largely unchanged down to the present day, save for an eventual loosening of the restriction on membership of churches not in communion with the Church of England.

With the Church Assembly now able to submit Measures to Parliament, there followed a period of prodigious legislating. In the years 1920–47, 95 Measures received Royal Assent.[25] There follows a selection of Measures, giving a flavour of the topics addressed.

The Convocations of the Clergy Measure 1920 declared, for the avoidance of doubt, that the Convocations had the power to amend the constitution of their lower houses (ie the clerical houses), allowing the reform of those houses to proceed by means of Canon in 1921. Parochial Church Councils (PCCs) had been an integral part of the vision for church governance in the proposals from the Committee on Church and State,[26] and were duly included in the Constitution of the Church Assembly. Under the Parochial Church Councils (Powers) Measure 1921, certain powers, duties and liabilities of vestries, churchwardens and others were transferred to the PCC, and new powers and duties were created.[27] The PCCs continue to be central to parish church governance to this day.

The Union of Benefices Measure 1923 introduced more efficient and consolidated processes for the permanent union of benefices, intended primarily for use in small parishes.[28] Whereas in the past legislation had aimed to restrict and discourage the holding of benefices in plurality, the Pluralities Measure 1930 allowed pluralism given the consent of the patrons, bishop and the Ecclesiastical Commissioners. It was intended for use in cases where a permanent union of benefices was not desirable.[29] The Clergy Pensions Measure 1926 provided for a national pension scheme for the clergy for the first time.[30]

The Church of England had for centuries understood that parishioners had a right to be married in the parish church where they resided: the Marriage Measure 1930 extended that right to those who usually worshipped in a particular

---

[24] C Buchanan, *Confirmation – the Excluding Feature? A Study of Anglican Confirmation in Its Ecumenical Implications 1870–1920* (Leiden, Brill, 2019) 36–40.

[25] Podmore (n 12) 320.

[26] Church of England and Archbishops' Committee on Church and State (n 13) 43, 45–48.

[27] PCCs were made bodies corporate (s 3); some newly created powers reflected the understanding of the PCC as part of the government of the Church, eg the power to make representations to the bishop with regard to any matter affecting the welfare of the Church in the parish (s 6).

[28] The Union of Benefices Measure 1923 was one of the few Measures in this period that resulted in a number of cases tried in the courts. In *Re Union of the Benefices of Great Massingham and Little Massingham, Norfolk* [1931] UKPC 22 (JCPC), for example, the Judicial Committee of the Privy Council dismissed the scheme proposed for the union of benefices because, while the union might release surplus income for other benefices, the scheme would not accrue any benefit to the parishes that were themselves to be united.

[29] This Measure caused parts of the Pluralities Act 1838 and the Pluralities Act 1885 to cease to have any effect, and varied various provisions of the Pluralities Act 1838 and the Union of Benefices Measure 1923.

[30] Clergy aged 70 with 40 years' service would be eligible to receive £200 per annum.

church. The Cathedrals Measure 1931, drafted according to the recommendations of a Commission of Inquiry, provided for the appointment of Cathedral Commissioners, who could assist cathedrals in revising their statutes and similar instruments. This Measure also effected a compulsory transfer of all the cathedrals' landed property lying beyond their precincts, vesting it in the Ecclesiastical Commissioners.[31] The Faculty Jurisdiction Measure 1938 amended the law relating to faculties, making various improvements including the introduction of archdeacons' certificates. The Episcopal Endowments and Stipends Measure 1943 centralised the endowments and property of diocesan sees, and provided for the Ecclesiastical Commissioners to take over the payment of bishops' stipends and expenses.[32] The Church Commissioners Measure 1947 united the Queen Anne's Bounty Commissioners and the Ecclesiastical Commissioners. As well as these Measures of general applicability, there were Measures with narrower scope, relating to certain ecclesiastical corporations or new dioceses.[33]

Many of the Church Assembly's Measures made use of the power to amend or repeal Acts of Parliament that had been given in section 3(6) of the Enabling Act 1919. In particular, where a Measure consolidated an area of law that had been the subject of repeated parliamentary legislation, the repeal of numerous statutory provisions was usually required.[34] This demonstrates that the power to amend or repeal Acts of Parliament was essential for the Church Assembly to be able to legislate effectively. Moreover, in all the legislative examples listed above, Parliament gave its approval by resolution so that the Measures could become law.[35] In the case of Prayer Book revision, however, Parliament was not so cooperative.

---

[31] See N Doe, *The Legal Architecture of English Cathedrals* (Abingdon, Routledge, 2017) 7. The centralisation of assets would be a recurring theme of the ecclesiastical legislation later in the 20th century.

[32] This Measure used the power to legislate with the force and effect of an Act of Parliament in a general way, consequent upon schemes that would be introduced under the Measure. Therefore, rather than listing the Acts and other provisions repealed in a schedule, s 9 provides that 'Upon the coming into operation of a scheme, so much of any Act or Parliament, Measure, Order in Council, trust deed or other instrument as is inconsistent with any provision of the scheme shall cease to have effect in relation to the see to which the scheme relates.'

[33] Earlier in the century, Acts of Parliament had been used to create new dioceses: Bishoprics of Southwark and Birmingham Act 1904; Bishoprics of Sheffield, Chelmsford, and for the County of Suffolk Act 1913; Bishoprics of Bradford and Coventry Act 1918. Thereafter, Measures were used: Bishopric of Blackburn Measure 1923; Diocese of Southwell (Division) Measure 1923 (creating the diocese of Derby); Diocese of Winchester (Division) Measure 1923 (creating the dioceses of Portsmouth and Guildford); Bishopric of Leicester Measure 1925. Other Measures dealt with local matters that nevertheless required national legislation, such as the Brislington Parishes (Transfer) Measure 1926, providing for the transfer of certain parishes from one diocese to another.

[34] For example, the Parsonages Measure 1930 regulated and simplified the processes to buy and sell parsonages. It contained a formal schedule of repeals, repealing parts of the Parsonages Act 1838 and the Church Building Act 1839, and the whole of the Parsonages (Amendment) Act 1838 and the Parsonages Act 1911.

[35] RE Rodes, *Law and Modernization in the Church of England: Charles II to the Welfare State* (Notre Dame, IN, University of Notre Dame Press, 1991) 343, for occasions prior to 1927 when Parliament vetoed Measures of the Church Assembly.

II. Ritual, Discipline and Prayer Book Revision

As already seen, at the start of the century, the Royal Commission on Ecclesiastical Discipline had reported on ritual disobedience and proposed reform of the law of public worship. Up into the 1920s there remained a 'lack of general conformity' to the authorised liturgy.[36]

Nevertheless, in this period, bishops remained generally unwilling to allow the use of the legal processes provided for the enforcement of liturgical discipline (namely, the Clergy Discipline Act 1840 and the Public Worship Regulation Act 1874). For example, in 1917, it came to the attention of Arthur Winnington-Ingram, Bishop of London, that the church of St Saviour's in Hoxton was using the Latin rite mass and similar devotions. The bishop permitted no proceedings against the incumbent, but instead refused to license curates, to confirm in the parish or to permit diocesan grants to be used there. In 1919, John Watts-Ditchfield, Bishop of Chelmsford, disciplined Conrad Noel, the 'Red Vicar' of Thaxted, for holding a Corpus Christi procession in the parish, by refusing to confirm or license curates.[37]

The faculty jurisdiction continued to be used in cases of ritual conformity, generally ruling against ornaments in church that were not required by a strict reading of the Prayer Book.[38] There had been moves in Parliament to reduce the jurisdiction of the consistory courts, but the Church obtained an exception in the Ancient Monuments Consolidation and Amendment Act 1913, so that the faculty jurisdiction could continue much as before. In fact, the exercise of the faculty jurisdiction became very active following the Great War, as a large number of petitions were made for memorial monuments in churches and churchyards.[39]

The religious effects of the Great War also included a strengthening of the desire in many quarters for authorisation both of public prayer for the departed and of reservation of the Blessed Sacrament. This influenced the preparation of a proposed new Prayer Book, which was in part an attempt to answer the points made in the 1906 Report on Ecclesiastical Discipline and noted above. The provision of alternative services would broaden the liturgical possibilities allowed by law, and it might then be hoped general discipline could be restored. In the Church Assembly, the Church believed it now had the necessary 'power of self-adjustment'. The Church Assembly and the Convocations agreed to a proposed new Book in 1927.

---

[36] Archbishops' Commission on the Relations between Church and State, *Report* (London, 1935) 38.
[37] Yates (n 1) 342.
[38] eg, *Rector and Churchwardens of Capel St Mary, Suffolk v Frank Victor Packard* [1927] P 289. In this case, the Dean of the Arches on appeal confirmed the removal of illegal articles, including a holy water stoup, the Stations of the Cross, the censer, the sacring gong and the tabernacle; but permitted the retention of crucifixes, notices asking for prayers for the dead ('the Church of England nowhere forbids us to pray for the dead') and articles connected with the hearing of confessions.
[39] A Brook, 'The Chancellors' Dilemma: The Impact of the First World War on Faculty Jurisdiction' (2020) 56 *Studies in Church History* 471–86.

However, as Prayer Book revision required legislation by Measure,[40] the agreement of Parliament was required – but the revised Prayer Book did not obtain parliamentary agreement in 1927. Much opposition was focused on the new Prayer Book's permission for perpetual reservation of the Sacrament. Evangelicals especially worried that if reservation received so official an imprimatur, this would implicitly sanction devotional practices contrary to their understanding of Reformation theology.[41] To assuage these fears, regulations were added to the Proposed Book, and the Measure was brought again in 1928.[42]

There were many English people who rarely attended church yet who fervently wished the Prayer Book Measure 1928 to fail in Parliament. The authorisation of a new Book of Common Prayer seemed to them as unimaginable and as undesirable as a bill mandating that a brand-new version of Shakespeare be taught in the nation's schools. To the promoters of the Book, on the other hand, it seemed unconscionable that the Church could not determine its own worship: was the Church of England in bondage to a secular state?

The Church Assembly approved the Measure both in 1927 and 1928 (despite opposition from evangelicals who opposed reservation and from some Anglo-Catholics who did not like the regulations' restriction of the devotional use of the reserved sacrament). The Ecclesiastical Committee of Parliament said it 'would not recommend any interference with the decisions of the Church Assembly on matters so clearly lying within the province of that assembly as the doctrines and ceremonial of the Church,'[43] but Parliament in 1928 once again rejected the Measure. This seemed like an ecclesiological disaster. The Church of England did not, after all, have a 'power of self-adjustment' even on so doctrinal a matter as its own services.

In 1929, both (episcopal) upper houses of Convocation made a resolution to deal with the situation: 'For many years the Church of England has been engaged in an endeavour to amend the existing laws of public worship so as to make fuller provision for the spiritual needs of the Church and to bring order into the variety of

---

[40] The Act of Uniformity 1662 required that no form of service be used 'other than what is prescribed and appointed to be used in and by' the 1662 Book of Common Prayer (s 13). A Measure (which, as we have seen, has the force and effect of an Act of Parliament) was therefore needed to permit the use of the new alternative services contained in the proposed Book.

[41] Art XXVIII states that 'The Sacrament of the Lord's Supper was not by Christ's ordinance reserved, carried about, lifted up, or worshipped.' Many evangelicals understood this article to forbid the reservation of the Sacrament. One of the most influential commentators of the time, fairly representing the central churchmanship position, argued that it could be permitted: 'Reservation purely for the communion of the sick or absent is thoroughly primitive and natural': EJ Bicknell, *A Theological Introduction to the Thirty-Nine Articles* (London, Longmans, 1925) 504. Many Anglo-Catholics, however, wanted to go beyond that and permit extra-liturgical devotions to the reserved Sacrament.

[42] The new regulations in the proposed Book of 1928 would: empower the Bishop to license the parish priest to reserve the Sacrament, and if the Bishop refused licence, the incumbent or PCC could appeal to the Archbishop; forbid the use of the reserved Sacrament in any exposition, service or ceremony except for the communion of the sick; and regulate other matters, such as the position of the aumbry in which the sacrament was to be reserved.

[43] *Hansard*, HC Deb 14 June 1928, vol 218, c 1279.

usage which has become prevalent.' However, they continued, 'this endeavour has for the present failed. It is impossible and undesirable to bring back the conduct of public worship strictly within the limits of the Prayer Book of 1662.' Accordingly, 'the bishops, having failed to secure the statutory sanction which was desired and sought, are compelled in the present difficult situation to fulfil by administrative action their responsibility for the regulation of public worship'. Therefore, 'during the present emergency and until further order be taken the bishops ... cannot regard as inconsistent with loyalty to the principles of the Church of England the use of such additions or deviations as fall within the limits of [the proposed Book]'. Moreover, each diocesan bishop, 'in the exercise of that legal or administrative discretion which belongs to each bishop in his own diocese, will be guided by the proposals set forth in the Book of 1928'.[44]

In the years following, the bishops used the powers given to them in the Church Discipline Act 1840 and the Public Worship Regulation Act 1874 to prevent any prosecutions for ritual or ceremonial offences that would have been legal under the 1928 Book. From one point of view, this extraordinary situation meant that the bishops: were not discharging their duty to 'correct and punish' the 'disobedient and criminous' in their dioceses (as the 1662 Ordinal puts it); were, by means of this general policy, fettering their own statutory discretion to choose to allow or disallow disciplinary process; and were encouraging the clergy to act contrary to Act of Uniformity 1662.[45] On the other hand, the construction of section 9 of the Public Worship Regulation Act 1874, giving the diocesan bishop a power to stay proceedings not solely according to whether there had been an infraction of the law, had been upheld by the House of Lords.[46] Therefore, it is arguable that in preventing invocation of that Act against clergy who had used the proposed Book, bishops were properly exercising their statutory discretion to consider 'the whole circumstances of the case'.[47]

Some bishops still attempted to restrict devotions that went beyond those of the proposed Book. For example, in 1929, Bishop Winnington-Ingram directed his clergy in the diocese of London to desist from holding services of Benediction of the Blessed Sacrament (although the proposed Book permitted reservation, it forbad Benediction): 170 incumbents complied, but 21 refused. The bishop took no action against them beyond saying he would try to enforce his ruling on the next occasion a vacancy occurred in those parishes.[48]

---

[44] A Smethurst, H Riley and H Wilson (eds), *Acts of the Convocations of Canterbury and York 1921-1970* (London, SPCK, 1971) 65-6.

[45] In addition, under Canon XXXVI of the Canons of 1604, members of the clergy had also subscribed to the effect that they would 'use the Form in the said Book prescribed in publick Prayer, and Administration of the Sacraments, and none other'.

[46] *Allcroft v Bishop of London* [1891] AC 666, 675 (HL).

[47] Public Worship Regulation Act 1874, s 98. For consideration of this question at the legislative stage, see the debate in *Hansard*, HC Deb 28 July 1874, vol 221, cols 874-906.

[48] J Gunstone, *Lift High the Cross: The High Noon of the Anglo-Catholic Movement, 1919-1950* (Norwich, Canterbury Press, 2009) 214-15. For the contemporary question concerning the legality

The fallout from the Prayer Book controversy continued into the 1930s. A report of the Archbishops' Commission on the Relations between Church and State was published in 1935.[49] In this Report – remarkably – the Elizabethan settlement was described as effecting the 'subjection' of the Church to the State.[50] The Church Assembly was considered to have worked well in 'ordinary administrative matters', but 'the result with regard to spiritual questions has been less happy'. The report noted that because of the parliamentary veto over Measures, 'in law, spiritual liberty was not secured by the Church by the Enabling Act'.[51]

The Commission recognised, therefore, that 'the case for disestablishment is strong', and disestablishment was better than the prevailing situation. However, its Report did not ultimately recommend disestablishment as the way forward. Instead, the Report's recommendations, calling for a more democratic Assembly with unfettered control over doctrinal matters, sowed the seeds of what would later become the General Synod. Some thought the crisis over the abdication of Edward VIII in 1938 would further calls for disestablishment (fearing that the Church would be seen as partly to blame for that situation). In fact, support for establishment was strengthened in the 1930s, as both the Coronation and opposition to the totalitarianism that was threatening war in the European Continent brought the nation together, and the moment when disestablishment seemed a real possibility passed.[52]

The 1935 report made some other important proposals touching church law. For example, it agreed that the 'excessive rigidity' in observing the rubrics of the Book of Common Prayer 1662 required by *Martin v Mackonochie*[53] was not realistic: 'There is scarcely a church in which the strict letter of the law is complied with.'[54] The Report also recommended the appointment of a commission to revise canon law: this is dealt with in chapter 10 of this volume.

In 1946, the 'Shorter Prayer Book' was published on the initiative of the bishops.[55] This contained a simplified version of the 1662 Prayer Book and some

---

of Benediction of the Blessed Sacrament, see Law & Religion UK, 'Monstrances in the Church of England: Are They Legal?' at https://lawandreligionuk.com/2016/04/05/monstrances-in-the-church-of-england-are-they-legal/ (accessed 14 August 2021).

[49] Archbishops' Commission (n 36).
[50] ibid 18.
[51] ibid 35.
[52] M Chapman and W Whyte (eds), *The Established Church: Past, Present and Future* (London, T & T Clark, 2011).
[53] *Martin v Mackonochie* (1868) LR 2 A&E 116.
[54] The desire to move away from this rigidity would eventually find expression, on the basis of the Church of England (Worship and Doctrine) Measure 1974, in today's Canon B5. There are strong echoes of the 1935 report in modern judgments such as *Re St Thomas, Pennywell* [1995] Fam 50, stating that 'the Rubrics in all forms of service should in general be interpreted as directives rather than regulations', and *Re St John the Evangelist, Chopwell* [1996] 1 All ER 275, stating that 'the rigorist approach to the construction of the rubrics of the Book of Common Prayer or other authorised services no longer applies'.
[55] The Archbishop of Canterbury's Preface states that the book 'has no authority other than that which belongs to the sources from which it is derived', yet it was widely used.

material from the 1928 Book; although widespread, the use of the latter's alternative material was still unlawful.[56]

III. Beyond the Church Assembly: Parliament and Convocation

Parliament continued to legislate in many areas that affected the Church. Tithe legislation was still considered to be partially an ecclesiastical matter, not least because of the history of tithe ownership and its scriptural basis.[57] At the start of this period, the liability to pay tithe rentcharge could already be extinguished on payment of a lump sum under the Tithe Act 1846. The Tithe Acts 1918 and 1925 extended extinction by a terminable annuity of up to 50 and 60 years respectively. Following the report of the Royal Commission on Tithe Rentcharge 1934, the Tithe Act 1936 replaced all remaining rentcharges with redemption annuities payable to the state for 60 years, and it compensated the former tithe owners with government stock.[58]

Parliament also continued to legislate to amend the law of marriage. The question of whether a widower should be permitted to marry his late wife's sister continued to take up considerable parliamentary time. Heated public debate on this subject had been a perennial feature of national life since 1842. There existed a whole sub-genre of novels in which the plots hinged around the disasters that would occur if such legislation were (or were not) enacted.[59] Wealthier couples could circumvent the restriction by marrying overseas, as did, for example, William Holman Hunt and Edith Waugh, whose late sister had been married to the pre-Raphaelite painter. The Deceased Wife's Sister's Marriage Act 1907 eventually removed the prohibition, and thus the secular law permitted certain marriages that were forbidden by Canon 99 of 1604 (which referenced the Table of Kindred and Affinity of 1563).[60]

The Act included a proviso so that clergy would not be compelled to officiate at marriages between a man and his deceased's wife's sister, nor would they be liable for any act or omission for which they 'would not have been liable if [the] Act had not been passed'.[61] In 1907, a clergyman named Henry Thompson refused to administer Holy Communion to Alan Banister, who was married to his deceased wife's sister. Thompson argued that, in the eyes of the Church, the marriage was

---

[56] Many services from the 1928 Book would finally be authorised only in 1966 as 'Series One'.
[57] eg Genesis 14:20, Genesis 28:22, Deuteronomy 14:28, Numbers 18:28.
[58] The arrangements set up by the 1936 Act would eventually be brought to an end, earlier than planned, under the provisions of the Finance Act 1977.
[59] eg JB Middleton, *Love versus Law* (London, 1855); D Craik, *Hannah* (London, Harper and Bros, 1871).
[60] For a discussion of the authority of the 1563 Table, see ch 3 of this volume.
[61] Deceased Wife's Sister Marriage Act 1907, s 1.

not valid. Therefore, as he could lawfully refuse Holy Communion to any other couple who were living together as husband and wife but whose marriage was not recognised by the Church,[62] his refusal in this case was protected by the proviso in the Act. He could not, in other words, be liable for an omission that had arisen as a result of the Act allowing Mr Banister's marriage. The case came before Sir Lewis Dibdin in the Court of Arches, who found that the proviso only permitted clergy to refuse to conduct the relevant marriage ceremonies; it did not permit them to repel from Holy Communion those who were lawfully married.[63] The King's Bench Division, the Court of Appeal and finally the House of Lords upheld Dibdin's judgment.[64] This case was highly controversial because, to some, Anglo-Catholics especially, it appeared that the secular courts were deciding who was to be admitted to Holy Communion.[65]

The Deceased Brother's Widow's Marriage Act followed in 1921, and the Marriage (Prohibited Degrees) Relationship Act 1931 permitted a person to marry his or her nephews- and nieces-by-marriage; again, the Acts included clauses ensuring that the clergy would not be required to officiate at such marriages.[66] By the 1940s, however, the Church no longer objected to any of these categories of marriages. In 1946, the Convocations amended the canons to include a new Table of Kindred and Affinity that was adapted to the changes in the secular law.[67]

Divorce and remarriage presented another challenge for the Church.[68] The Matrimonial Causes Act 1937 permitted divorce on grounds wider than adultery. Clergy were permitted to refuse to solemnise the marriage of a person with a living former spouse, regardless of the reason for the divorce, and did not have to make their churches available for that purpose.[69] This contrasted with the Matrimonial

---

[62] See the introductory rubrics for the Order for Holy Communion in the Book of Common Prayer 1662; Canon 26 of 1604; and the Sacrament Act 1547.

[63] *Banister v Thompson* [1908] P 362.

[64] *Thompson v Dibdin* [1910] P 57; *Thompson v Dibdin* [1912] AC 533.

[65] B Bennet, 'Banister v Thompson and Afterwards: The Church of England and the Deceased Wife's Sister's Marriage Act' (1998) 49 *The Journal of Ecclesiastical History* 668–82.

[66] Archbishop of Canterbury Cosmo Gordon Lang welcomed in Parliament the 'conscience clause' while opposing the main principle of the 1931 bill and its two predecessors. He also warned, 'your Lordships will recognise that this Bill constitutes a still wider divergence between the principles of the Church and the law of the State – a problem which sooner or later must be faced and which is one of extreme gravity and difficulty. ... [T]he teaching and discipline of the Church of England ... remain and always will remain outside the sphere of Parliamentary enactment.' Hansard, HL Deb 7 July 1931, vol 81, cols 628–636 at 634.

[67] G Bray (ed), *The Anglican Canons, 1529–1947* (Woodbridge, Boydell Press, 1998) lxxxiv.

[68] The famous words used at the plighting of the troth in the form of Solemnisation of Matrimony in the Book of Common Prayer 1662, 'till death us do part', demonstrate the Church of England's understanding of marriage as indissoluble.

[69] The preamble to the 1937 Act listed among its purposes 'the relief of conscience among the clergy'. However, the right of clergy to refuse to officiate at certain categories of marriage was not restricted to occasions of conscientious objection. Section 12 simply enacted 'No clergyman of the Church of England or of the Church in Wales shall be compelled to solemnise the marriage of any person whose former marriage has been dissolved on any ground and whose former husband or wife is still living or to permit the marriage of any such person to be solemnised in the Church or Chapel of which he is the minister.'

Causes Act 1857, under which a clergyman had been able to refuse to marry someone with a living former spouse only if the person seeking marriage had been guilty of adultery; and if he did refuse, he had to permit another clergyman to officiate at the marriage in his church. The changes in 1937, therefore, indicated a 'loosening' of establishment: the gap between the state's view of marriage and that of the Church had widened.

Debate on the subject of divorce lasted for several years in the Convocations. In 1938, the Convocations resolved inter alia that they accepted some, but not all, of the new grounds for voidable marriage contained in the 1937 Act, and claimed as 'essential' the right to regulate the admission to the sacraments of re-married persons with a former spouse living.[70] Archbishop Cyril Garbett

> singled out the Matrimonial Causes Act 1937 ... as standing 'in a category of its own' among twentieth-century laws that adversely affected Church–State relations, because the Act ... 'made it clear beyond all misunderstanding that the laws of Church and State are not identical'.[71]

In line with the national ecclesiastical policy expressed by the Convocations, it continued to be the general practice of most clergy to refuse to solemnise the marriage of a divorced person with a former spouse still living.

The usual decennial pattern for the Lambeth Conference was disrupted by the two World Wars, and so the bishops of the Anglican Communion met in this period only in 1908, 1920 and 1930. Lambeth Conference resolutions did not create binding law yet carried significant authority, and are sometimes described as quasi-legislation.[72] Some Conference resolutions did influence the development of the law of the Church of England: for example, a 1908 resolution stated that Prayer Book revision would not be *ipso facto* a problem for the Communion, and so encouraged the Church Assembly in its plans for the proposed new Prayer Book of 1928; and a 1930 resolution establishing a doctrine commission with the Old Catholics led to an Act of Convocation in 1932 establishing intercommunion between the Church of England and the Old Catholics.[73]

Despite the creation of the Church Assembly in 1919, many matters still fell within the competence of the Convocations alone. Relatively minor revisions to the canons were made by the Convocations (as the official version of the Canons of 1604 were in Latin, these revisions were too) on the membership of the Convocations and their election (in 1921 and 1936), on marriage (in 1936), and on the Table of Kindred and Affinity (in 1946).[74] These changes aside, the canons remained substantially as they were in 1604, unfitted to the life of the Church as it

---

[70] Acts made in both Convocations June 1938, see Smethurst, Riley and Wilson (eds) (n 44) 117–22.
[71] Podmore (n 12) 322.
[72] N Doe, *Canon Law in the Anglican Communion: A Worldwide Perspective* (Oxford, Clarendon Press, 1998) 346–47.
[73] Agreed in all four Houses of the Convocations, January 1932, see Smethurst, Riley and Wilson (eds) (n 44) 176.
[74] Bray (n 67) lxxxiv.

was in the middle of the twentieth century. At the instigation of the Convocations, therefore, a Canon Law Commission was appointed in 1939, meeting eight times in the years 1943–47 and issuing a Report in 1947.[75] The Report, steeped in the historical study of canon law, was a conservative document, exhibiting a tendency perhaps exacerbated by a wartime desire to preserve precious heritage. Nevertheless, it represented a significant step forward on a journey that would in time lead to the wholesale revision of the canons.[76]

Much significant work was done in the form of Acts of Convocation, on subjects including ministry, deaconesses, liturgy and sacraments, marriage, doctrine and evangelism, education, moral and social questions, and relations with other churches. The majority of Acts recommended, commented, commended, affirmed or stated opinion. Some Acts of Convocation, however, did more than that. For example, in 1940, the Convocations regulated the nomination, examination, admission, licensing and duties of readers, with a schedule of forms and a liturgical office of admission.[77] Other Acts of Convocation resolved that bishops might approve in their dioceses certain additions or variations to the services authorised by the Act of Uniformity – although such forms of service were technically unlawful, as we have seen, the bishops had the tools to prevent the clergy from being disciplined for their use.[78] In all these cases, the Convocations chose to regulate by Act of Convocation as the best available path open to them following the failure of the Prayer Book Measure in 1928. Therefore, despite their uncertain legal status, Acts of Convocation could and did function effectively to enable and regulate developing areas of the Church's life.[79]

A particular example of this occurred in 1947, when the Convocation of York passed a resolution that referred to 'the present confusion between the civil laws of marriage and divorce and Church Law'.[80] What could be meant by 'Church Law', distinct from civil law, as regards divorce and marriage in 1947? In order to find out which grounds of divorce contained within the 1937 Act were accepted by the Church, one would have to examine the 1938 Act of Convocation. It appears, therefore, that the Convocations themselves considered their Acts to be a species of church law (yet not civil law).[81] For all the above reasons, Acts of Convocation

---

[75] *The Canon Law of the Church of England: Being the Report of the Archbishops' Commission on Canon Law, Together with Proposals for a Revised Body of Canons* (London, SPCK, 1947).

[76] The revision of the canons is considered in ch 10 of this volume.

[77] Smethurst, Riley and Wilson (eds) (n 44) 56–65.

[78] ibid 67–68; and for the approval for Services for Unction and the Laying-on of Hands, ibid 84–90.

[79] The term 'Act of Convocation' as used in this chapter indicates a formal resolution of Convocation. For most of the period covered by this chapter, it was not the practice of the President of Convocation to ratify and promulge such resolutions formally as Acts of Convocation, as happened in other periods.

[80] Smethurst, Riley and Wilson (eds) (n 44) 122.

[81] In discussing the legal status of Acts of Convocation, commentators usually refer to *Bland v Archdeacon of Cheltenham* [1972] Fam 157, *locus classicus* for the assertion that Acts of Convocation have only moral force. However, the Act of Convocation to which the Court of Arches' judgment refers in that case was a 1957 Act of Convocation entitled 'RECOMMENDATIONS concerning baptism …'. To make recommendation is clearly different from an intention to make law. The judgment in the Court

are an important, if often neglected, regulatory instrument for understanding the history of church law in this period.

IV. Conclusion

Since 1845, *Cripps on Church and Clergy* had been among the foremost reference works for ecclesiastical lawyers and clergy. Writing the Preface to the 8th edition in 1937, Kenneth MacMorran looked back over the first 15 years of the Church Assembly and noted the volume of legislative activity that had taken place by Measure over that period.[82] The large number of Measures passed was testament to the fact that the Church did – as it had argued – need the power to legislate for itself, and had made use of that power once granted. MacMorran went on to observe that the output of church legislation in the form of Acts of Parliament had correspondingly diminished. Yet over the 600 pages of *Cripps*, 8th edition of 1937, the Prayer Book controversy is not even mentioned; no comment is made on the bishops' statement on discipline in the wake of the controversy, despite its significant and widespread effect on the practice of clergy discipline and liturgy; Acts of Convocation are entirely and studiously ignored. Since the 7th edition of *Cripps* had been published in 1921, the Convocations had approved forms of service including the making of Deaconesses[83] and the use of Holy Unction,[84] services that were having a very significant effect on the life of the Church. Cripps does not mention them, not even to comment on whether the Convocations, in approving them, were acting ultra vires. It is tempting to suppose that the author of *Cripps* thought all of these matters were mere encouragement to law-breaking, and did not belong in a volume surveying the law of the Church. But the desire for self-government had not been wholly satisfied by the provisions of the Enabling Act 1919. As we have seen, in the 1930s the Church desired 'spiritual liberty' more than ever. Though Parliament had not been willing to approve the Prayer Book Measure, the Church nevertheless acted through the bishops' administrative discretion and through Acts of Convocation to develop its liturgical and doctrinal

---

of Arches repeatedly refers to the Convocations' 'Recommendations' in the case of baptism, eg 'The *recommendations* did not have the force of statute law but they had great moral force as the considered judgment of the highest and most ancient synod of the province.' (emphasis added) Of course, it would be contrary to reason to attempt to give 'recommendations' the force of law. Thus *Bland* only determines the unremarkable fact that when Convocation acts to recommend, that Act is merely one of 'great moral force'. The question as to what force an Act of Convocation may have in the domain of clergy discipline, on occasions when the Convocations have 'resolved' or 'regulated', has not been judicially determined. See also N Doe, *The Legal Framework of the Church of England* (Oxford, Clarendon Press, 1996) 21; Rodes (n 35) 345–46; S Hughes Carew, 'The Convocations of Canterbury and York' (2019) 21 *Ecclesiastical Law Journal* 41–42.

[82] Cripps (n 20) v.
[83] Smethurst, Riley and Wilson (eds) (n 44) 43–47.
[84] ibid 84–90.

life. This may not have been an altogether satisfactory situation for church lawyers, but it was a state of affairs that continued for decades, as the lawful authorisation of new liturgy and the wholesale revision of the canons would not occur until the second half of the century.

The Preface to the 1928 proposed Book of Common Prayer had stated 'we are living in a new world'. The Church's actions in the period, in campaigning for the Church Assembly, in legislation by Measure and in dealing with the fallout of the Prayer Book controversy, were each in their own way attempts to make the Church's law fit for that 'new world'.

10

The Post-War Church – Revision and Stability: 1947–94

NEIL PATTERSON

There are two reasons for the starting date of 1947 as a key juncture in the development of the post-war Church of England. The first is the Church Commissioners Measure 1947, finally bringing about the union of the Ecclesiastical Commissioners and Queen Anne's Bounty as a single central body to hold the historic endowments of the Church, and to exercise related administrative and legal functions. This indicates the strong theme of centralisation and modernisation of governance that runs throughout the ecclesiastical law of the period.

The second is that in 1947, the Archbishops' Commission on Canon Law, whose genesis and work have been described in chapter 9, concluded its exertions in a proposed complete new code of Canons.[1] The 1947 text is heavy with historical marginalia, identifying the sources of the draft Canons, including medieval authorities such as Gratian and Lyndwood (though I think the earliest reference is to the Council of Cloveshoo of 747),[2] the 1603 Canons and relevant statutes until the time of writing. Some of the more important of these are deciphered and explained in the footnotes of Gerald Bray's recent study of the development of the Canons.[3] The revision of these was to occupy the Convocations and the Church Assembly throughout Geoffrey Fisher's Canterbury archiepiscopate. Although his readiness to focus on this work has often been criticised, it is difficult to see how without it the Church of England could have had any workable canons today. The new code provided a basis for further amendment, 17 Amending Canons by 1994, and many more since.

If the first part of the period is characterised by administrative consolidation and the rather conservative process of canonical reform, the middle, roughly 1963–77, saw a number of major Measures, notably the Pastoral Measure 1968,

---

[1] The Archbishops' Commission on Canon Law, *Canon Law in the Church of England* (London, SPCK, 1947) (hereinafter '*Canon Law*').
[2] ibid 114.
[3] G Bray, *The Development of the Canons* (London, Latimer Trust, 2020).

the Synodical Government Measure 1969, the Church of England (Worship and Doctrine) Measure 1974, and the Endowments and Glebe Measure 1976. For good or ill, a Church that in the 1950s had still in many ways inhabited the clothes of the Middle Ages, or at least the *ancien regime* of the eighteenth century, was carried, not without some discomfort, into the modern world, and these Measures remain key pillars of the Church's legal constitution to this day.

By contrast, the period after about 1977 was one of comparative stability in overall legal structures, but dominated by the long debates and campaigns for the relaxation of the Church's position on remarriage after divorce and the ordination of women. At their conclusion, both of these issues involved court cases of lasting significance. Although not the end of the matter, as chapter 11 relates, the ordination of women in 1994 marks a key turning point in the modern life of the Church of England and so the end of this chapter.

I. Administrative Rationalisation: The Church Commissioners

The work of the Church Commissioners from their inception until the governance changes of the 1990s is ably covered in Chandler's history based on their archives,[4] and is a reminder that, although the specialist boards under the Church Assembly and General Synod covered some policy areas, the Commissioners *were* the central administrative body of the Church. This is surprising on the face of the 1947 Measure, which is notable for its conservatism in retaining a structure closely resembling that of the Ecclesiastical Commissioners who preceded it, with the unusually subtle governance of a widely elected Board, the influential but 'non-executive' Church Estates Commissioners, and the professional Secretary and staff.[5] The Measure provided that the new Church Commissioners should take over directly all the functions of both Queen Anne's Bounty and the Ecclesiastical Commissioners.[6] These included the important power of secondary legislation, in the form of Orders in Council, to make pastoral schemes reorganising parishes, an activity that saw a major increase in the post-war period.

The significance of the Commissioners emerges from the various Measures of the period providing for aspects of reorganisation of parishes and their endowments. These included the Pastoral Reorganisation Measure 1949, the Benefices (Stabilisation of Incomes) Measure 1951, the Union of Benefices (Disused Churches) Measure 1952 and the New Housing Areas (Church Buildings) Measure 1954. On top of the considerable range of responsibilities inherited from the parent bodies, these invariably conferred powers on the Commissioners to

---

[4] A Chandler, *The Church of England in the Twentieth Century* (Woodbridge, Boydell Press, 2009).
[5] Church Commissioners Measure 1947, ss 4–6.
[6] ibid s 2(a).

make schemes or approve schedules to effect whichever local reorganisation was required.[7]

Comprehensive reform of benefice finances would not take place until the 1970s, but two provisions towards the end of the first period fit into the pattern of rationalisation. The Clergy Pensions Measure 1961 made pensions available as of right to clergy who wanted to retire, removing the necessity for infirmity or for the income to come from the benefice, though retirement was not yet compulsory. The Cathedrals Measure 1963, whilst preserving the strong distinction between dean and chapter cathedrals and parish church cathedrals, gave permission for amendment of many aspects of cathedral governance, and provided that in each cathedral two canons, paid by the Commissioners, were to be engaged exclusively on cathedral duties.[8] The law of cathedrals is a whole book in itself,[9] and it is perhaps debatable whether the provisions of the 1963 Measure, by providing so extensively for cathedral constitutions and statutes, rendered them effectively secondary legislation under Measure. Certainly subsequent Cathedrals Measures have continued that trend, as did the Care of Cathedrals Measure 1990, establishing the Cathedrals Fabric Commission.[10]

II. A New Code of Canons

An oddity of the legal history of the Church of England is that the modern Canons, though generated within living memory by a fairly transparent process, are very much under-studied. This may be simply because not many people are interested in them; a widespread view has been that revision of Canons was the wrong priority for the post-war Church. Faced with the challenge of the modern world, Paul Welsby was dismissive: 'It is doubtful whether many people were able to see how the revision of canon law would contribute significantly to this task.'[11] Supported by contemporaries, this view has been widely influential. It seems that when Archbishop Fisher described the introductory debate on Canon Law Revision at the Church Assembly as 'an extraordinarily useful debate and also one of the most enjoyable to which he had ever listened',[12] he was speaking only for himself. A subsidiary factor in the neglect of study of the revision of the Canons must be the comparative unavailability of the *Chronicle of Convocation* and the proceedings

---

[7] eg Pastoral Reorganisation Measure 1949, s 5(1) directs the Commissioners to consult and draft the Order in Council for the holding of benefices in plurality, or the New Housing Areas (Church Buildings) Measure 1954, s 1(1) authorises the Commissioners to make grants or loans to provide new church buildings.
[8] Cathedrals Measure 1963, s 9.
[9] Specifically, N Doe, *The Legal Architecture of English Cathedrals* (Abingdon, Routledge, 2018).
[10] Care of Cathedrals Measure 1990, s 3.
[11] PA Welsby, *A History of the Church of England, 1945-1980* (Oxford, Oxford University Press, 1984) 42.
[12] *Proceedings of the Church Assembly*, XXXI.2, 20 June 1951, 225-26.

of the Church Assembly as resources for researchers; the new library at Lambeth Palace, opened in 2021, may alleviate this.

Fortunately, the under-studied road has clear waymarks. Between the 1947 Report of the Archbishops' Commission and the Canons made by the Convocations and promulged in 1964 and 1969, and published by the Society for Promoting Christian Knowledge in the latter year,[13] two interim texts of draft Canons exist from 1954 and 1959.[14] Combined with the records of the assemblies concerned, it is possible to reconstruct the process by which each Canon was revised in Convocation, sent for consideration to the House of Laity of the Church Assembly for approval or suggested amendment ('Stage I'), returned to the Convocations for further revision and finally approved again by the Laity ('Stage II') before final revision in the Convocations. By the 1959 edition, the Canons had been divided into the lettered sections familiar from all versions since promulgation in the 1960s, the reason being given in the Preface as 'to facilitate the addition of a Canon or Canons at any future time to any of the sections without interfering with the general numbering of the Canons'.[15] Let us consider as an example the Canon on the vesture of the clergy, a topic of perennial fascination and historic controversy.

The objective of those proposing the new Canon seems to have been to legitimise a diversity of liturgical attire of clergy in the Church of England, from the plain black and white of surplice and scarf, through various options to the vestments, including the chasuble, used before the Reformation and revived by the Ritualists amid great controversy (always carefully referred to in the text simply as 'the customary vestments'). The 1947 Canon XVII set this out and so provided a path to lay to rest the contested court judgments of the nineteenth century.[16] By 1954 the Convocations had rearranged the text, adding a new clause disavowing any doctrinal claims for allowing vestments to be worn, which had been devised to assuage Evangelicals, who remained concerned by the claims made by the Victorian ritualists that vestments were needed as a sign of reverence for the sacraments.[17]

This text is recorded in the 1954 book as 'Sent to the House of Laity'; it had been the subject of a long debate in May 1952, where Mr Wallace's amendment – to require the surplice for all services on the grounds that vestments were and should remain illegal (this assertion drawing cries of 'No' from the floor) – was defeated.[18] The 1959 revision saw the division of the draft Canons into lettered

---

[13] Canons Ecclesiastical promulged by the Convocations of Canterbury and York in 1964 and 1969, *The Canons of the Church of England* (London, SPCK, 1969) (hereinafter '*The Canons*').
[14] The Archbishops' Commission on Canon Law, *The Revised Canons of the Church of England Further Considered* (London, SPCK, 1954) (hereinafter '*Revised Canons*'); and The Archbishops' Commission on Canon Law, *Canon Law Revision 1959* (London, SPCK, 1960) (hereinafter '*Canon Law Revision*').
[15] ibid xi.
[16] *Canon Law* (n 1) 115. For court cases about vestments, see N Patterson, *Ecclesiastical Law, Clergy and Laity* (Abingdon, Routledge 2019) ch 4.
[17] *Revised Canons* (n 14) 16.
[18] *Proceedings of the Church Assembly*, XXXII.1, 23 May 1952, 212ff.

themed sections, this Canon being assigned to the 'B' section on Divine Service. The main change is a new clause 6, providing for consultation with the Parochial Church Council (PCC) on any change to vesture – this was part of a wider move from the House of Laity for consultation with the PCC across several Canons, such as Canons B2 and B3 providing for the authorisation and trial of new liturgies.[19]

This text is then marked as 'Approved by both Convocations and by the House of Laity at Stage II', and the Preface to the 1959 revision explains that this meant it was passed to 'the appropriate Committee'[20] (presumably of the Convocations, though this is not actually stated) for final drafting and consideration as to whether the proposed legislation was actually required. Stage II had seen a repetition of the attempt to prevent the legalisation of vestments, with an amendment by a Mr McQueen to replace all the garments mentioned with the ambiguous 'vesture consistent with the maintenance of the Protestant Reformed Religion established by law', but this evocation of the Coronation Oath was voted down 88:51 after a long debate.[21] This resulted in a final version with only cosmetic changes, except that the requirement to provide surplices was removed from draft Canon B8 and placed among the F Canons ('Things Appertaining to Churches'), and the question of *who* would provide and clean them was left curiously unanswered.

In the extensive history of legal controversy over vesture, frequent recourse had been made to the Ornaments Rubric before the order for Morning Prayer in the Book of Common Prayer 1662, which provides that 'such ornaments of the Ministers at all times of their ministrations shall be retained and be in use as were in the Church of England by the authority of Parliament in the Second Year of the reign of King Edward the Sixth',[22] with no certain answer as to what these were. This meant it was possible that some interpretations of the Ornaments Rubric, which as part of the Prayer Book had the statutory authority of the Act of Uniformity 1662, might be invoked to challenge the new Canon. The solution was the Vestures of Ministers Measure 1964, which refers back to the Ornaments Rubric (as quoted above) and declares that the rubric should be interpreted to fit the draft canon, except adding separate provision for Public Baptism alongside Holy Communion in order to recognise the latter as the second dominical sacrament. The Church Assembly debate rehearsed the whole history of vestiarian controversy at length before passing the Measure.[23] Only in the notes of the 1969 edition of Halsbury is there an admission that in the Appendix to the Report, on the draft Measure, of the Ecclesiastical Committee of Both Houses of Parliament it was revealed that 'customary vestments' of course means a chasuble (and admittedly dalmatic and tunicle where relevant). This means that by 1969, Parliament

---

[19] *The Canons* (n 13) 7–8.
[20] *Canon Law Revision* (n 14) xii.
[21] *Proceedings of the Church Assembly*, XXXVIII.3, 13 July 1959, 336ff.
[22] Book of Common Prayer, cited in the Vestures of Ministers Measure 1964, s 1.
[23] *Proceedings of the Church Assembly*, XLII.3, 9 November 1962, 823ff.

was willing to recognise the existence of 'customary vestments' as a legal category, only 95 years after the Public Worship Regulation Act.[24]

I offer such thorough treatment of what became Canon B8 because it provides an example of success, though the trial and error of the lengthy process in the Convocations, House of Laity and Church Assembly in canonical revision. An issue with a long history, painfully contested in the courts in the nineteenth century, was resolved into a permissive Canon using characteristically subtle language to defuse tension and allow the co-existence of different practices. In this case it was also possible to pass a Measure that modified, or at least clarified, the law in order decisively to close the hoary debate. Some of the Canons had simpler passages through their various stages. But the only extended study of canonical revision, by Peter Boulton in the 1990s (published posthumously and in part), draws attention to the interaction of Church and State in the formation of the Canons, which is important to the overall shape of the final product.[25]

Roughly speaking, those Canons that dealt with the rights of the laity, or which had been intended to settle some of the vexed 'constitutional' questions – notably the authority of the Canons themselves (the original draft Canons VII–IX and XIII)[26] or the proposal to introduce an Anglican process of annulment after civil divorce (original draft Canon XXXVI.2)[27] – fell foul of a Home Office committee under Sir Thomas Barnes, established to approve the process of revision.[28] Augur Pearce explains further how Barnes continued to be involved throughout the process, and was decisive in ensuring that any Canons that might imperil the essentially Erastian nature of the Church of England were either dropped or replaced by aspirational texts, usually devised by Archbishop Fisher.[29] Not included in the Canons was a definition of the requirements of lay membership of the Church, although sought by the two Convocations in 1948. In 1953 they adopted as an Act of Convocation, 'at the request of the House of Laity', a six-point statement subsequently published in 1954 as *The Duties of Church Membership*.[30] This was probably inspired by the similar, though not identically worded, Resolution 37 on *The Church and the World – The Church Militant* of the 1948 Lambeth Conference.[31]

By contrast, the revision process enabled some regulations, hitherto embodied in Acts of Convocation, to be taken into the Canons. A good example is the provision for Reader ministry, in existence since the nineteenth century but only

---

[24] Yonge, AD (ed), *Church Acts and Measures* (London, Butterworth & Co, 1969) 955, note.
[25] P Boulton, 'Twentieth-Century Revision of Canon Law in the Church of England' (2000) 5 *Ecclesiastical Law Journal* 353–68.
[26] *Canon Law* (n 1) 107–09, 112–13.
[27] ibid 125–26.
[28] Boulton (n 25) 362.
[29] A Pearce, 'Episcopacy and the Common Law' (2003) 7 *Ecclesiastical Law Journal* 195–209, 205–06.
[30] A Smethurst, H Riley and H Wilson (eds), *Acts of the Convocations of Canterbury and York* (London, SPCK, 1961) 172–73.
[31] See www.anglicancommunion.org/media/127737/1948.pdf (accessed 17 August 2022).

given a national set of Regulations by resolution of the two Convocations in 1939–40.[32] These formed the basis of Canons E4, E5 and E6.

III. The Reform of the Church Courts

The other reform that ran concurrently with that of the Canons, though in the end it was not to be closely related to them in practice, was that of the ecclesiastical courts, following a Report of 1954, and which took the eventual form of the Ecclesiastical Jurisdiction Measure 1963. This modernised and simplified what the Report referred to as 'a jungle of courts', including 'four courts and five quasi-courts for each diocese' and 'six courts for each province',[33] due to the introduction of successive, usually two-tier, court structures for different matters. In place of these, the new Measure provided a simple structure with one, consistory, court for each diocese, with appeals to the Arches Court of Canterbury and Chancery Court of York.[34] The simplification was considerable, the schedule of repeals running to three pages in Halsbury,[35] starting with the Statute of Circumspecte Agatis of Edward I and down to the Incumbents (Discipline) and Church Dignitaries (Retirement) Amendment Measure 1953. Most significant were the repeals of the Privy Council Appeals Act 1832, which had caused such controversy in *Gorham* and later cases,[36] the Church Discipline Act 1840 and the Public Worship Regulation Act 1874. This simplified structure has enabled the modern flourishing of the faculty jurisdiction as a process to oversee changes to church buildings, as discussed further below.

Less successful has been the provision in the Ecclesiastical Jurisdiction Measure 1963 for clergy discipline, which was based on the formalisation of a distinction between cases that do, or do not, involve 'doctrine ritual or ceremonial'. Those that did were to be tried, after examination by a commission drawn from the relevant Convocation, by the Court of Ecclesiastical Causes Reserved, consisting of a formidable three bishops and two senior judges. Also passed to the new court were the remotely possible causes of *duplex querela* and *quare impedit*, which although actually about the right of a priest to receive institution to a benefice from the bishop if presented by a legitimate patron, and the right of a patron to have their presentee instituted respectively, had also become associated with doctrinal controversy.[37] Significantly, the Court has almost never met, and I have argued that this constitutes a tacit agreement in the Church that doctrinal and liturgical

---

[32] Smethurst, Riley and Wilson (eds) (n 30) 53–61.
[33] The Archbishops' Commission on the Ecclesiastical Courts, *The Ecclesiastical Courts: Principles of Reconstruction* (London, SPCK, 1954) 38.
[34] Ecclesiastical Jurisdiction Measure 1963, pt 1 (ss 1–13).
[35] ibid Fifth Schedule.
[36] Patterson (n 16) ch 4; *Gorham v Bishop of Exeter: The Judgment of the Judicial Committee of the Privy Council* (as published by Seeleys, London, 1850).
[37] ibid 45–48, 111.

matters are not amenable to settlement in court.[38] By contrast, non-reserved cases were to be tried by the consistory courts, but this process was discredited by the 1972 case of *Bland v Archdeacon of Cheltenham*, where an initial judgment of deprivation by Garth Moore as Chancellor was overturned on appeal at the Court of Arches.[39] The later *Tyler* disciplinary cases, of 1990–94,[40] did nothing to improve this image, and contributed to the need after this period to produce a new clergy discipline process.

IV. Pastoral Reorganisation and the State of the Clergy

As noted, several Measures in the 1940s made provision for reorganisation in the post-war church, with eyes on bombed churches and new housing estates. A different perspective emerged in the 1960s following the publication of the 1963 Paul Report,[41] with its critique of the structure of individual freehold and the uninspiring flat career paths open to most priests. After much debate and criticism, the legislative child of Paul was the Pastoral Measure 1968. This consolidated previous legislation on pastoral reorganisation, repealing a series of acts from 1938–65, though without greatly simplifying the process.[42] More significantly, however, it introduced to law the concepts of team and group ministries,[43] offering different structures and roles as recommended by Paul. Yet like all such preceding Measures, it operated by providing for schemes to be drafted, meaning that whilst many teams and groups were created, the individual freehold incumbency remained the default.[44]

The most significant change to the clergy on a personal basis was the Ecclesiastical Offices (Age Limit) Measure 1975, which introduced universal retirement at 70 with only very limited exceptions. This was followed in short order by the Endowments and Glebe Measure 1976, transferring historic parish endowments (mostly managed by dioceses for some time) to diocesan ownership. At the time, these major reforms might have seemed naturally completed by the Incumbents (Vacation of Benefices) Measure 1977. This was devised in the wake of the disastrous decision in *Bland v Archdeacon of Cheltenham*, in 1972, to provide

---

[38] ibid 116–17.
[39] *Bland v Archdeacon of Cheltenham* [1972] Fam 157; see S Pix, 'Archdeacon of Cheltenham v Bland: a sledgehammer to crack a nut' (2001) 6 *Ecclesiastical Law Journal* 35–49.
[40] The cases went to the European Commission of Human Rights: *Tyler v United Kingdom* App no 21283/93 (ECmHR, 5 April 1994); cf M Hill, *Ecclesiastical Law*, 2nd edn (Oxford, Oxford University Press, 2001) 653–54, 677–81.
[41] L Paul, *The Deployment and Payment of the Clergy* (London, Church Information Office, 1964).
[42] Pastoral Measure 1968, sch 9.
[43] ibid ss 19–21.
[44] For an overview of the historic 'parson's freehold', see RH Bursell, 'The Parson's Freehold' (1992) 2 *Ecclesiastical Law Journal* 259–67.

a response to failing incumbencies better than that of trial under the Ecclesiastical Jurisdiction Measure 1963. But the 1977 Measure, though occasionally used, seems to have failed, like so many others, to resolve the persistent challenge of ineffective clergy at loggerheads with their parishioners.

The provisions of the Pastoral Measure 1968 were largely replicated in the Pastoral Measure 1983, the main changes being a statutory role for the Council for Church Buildings and the Redundant Churches Fund. The powers of the Commissioners to make a pastoral scheme on the recommendation of the bishop, even against the opposition of an incumbent directly affected, was upheld shortly after the period of this chapter in *Cheesman v Church Commissioners*.[45] A more significant change was introduced by the Patronage (Benefices) Measure 1986, which provided for the selection of parish representatives by the PCC of a benefice, with a right to participate in the process leading to the appointment of incumbents and with a power of veto. Although the independent rights of the patron to present, the bishop to institute and the parish representatives to refuse a presentee are carefully preserved in the Measure, in most vacancies this has led to the widespread practice of a joint appointment by bishop, patron (where not the bishop) and parish representatives, working together to draw up a statement of needs and interviewing as a panel before agreeing on the appointment.

V. Ecumenism

Most histories of Christianity in the later twentieth century contain large sections on the importance of the ecumenical movement, which seeks greater visible unity between separated churches. Sometimes it can seem from within the legal world of the Church of England that the Erastian assumption that the Established Church exists for all people and need acknowledge no other prevails, but this is not wholly so. The Sharing of Church Buildings Act 1969 made provision for the first time for shared use of buildings, under a sharing agreement containing terms that are either required or permitted by the statute. As to parties, the statute requires the diocesan board of finance, the incumbent and the PCC to enter the agreement on behalf of the Church of England, and, as to another Church, 'such persons as may be determined by the appropriate authority of that Church'.[46] Notably, as a provision made between Churches, this was passed as a public Act rather than as a Measure of the Church Assembly. The accompanying Sharing of Church Buildings Measure 1970 made some amendments to the Pastoral Measure 1968 and the powers of the Church Commissioners, which, as affecting only the Church of England and changing existing Measures, were deemed inappropriate for amendment

---

[45] *Cheesman v Church Commissioners* [2000] 1 AC 19, [1999] 3 WLR 603.
[46] Sharing of Church Buildings Act 1969, s 1(3)(b). See N Doe, *The Legal Framework of the Church of England* (Oxford, Clarendon Press, 1996) 434–39.

by a public Act.⁴⁷ However, as ownership of consecrated parish churches remains exclusively within the Anglican legal framework, it has been argued that these arrangements limit real ecumenical partnership.⁴⁸

An important provision from within the Church was made by the revision of the Canons on admission to Holy Communion, debated in the last days of the Church Assembly, passed in the new Synod and promulged as Canon B15A in 1972.⁴⁹ This admitted to communion baptised members of all mainstream Trinitarian Churches, removing a major barrier to common working and shared life.⁵⁰ In 1989, Synod promulged two new Canons – B43 and B44 (both since replaced). Canon B43 set out in great detail the rules for when ministers of other Churches might officiate and preach in churches of the Church of England, and for Church of England clergy invited to other Churches. Canon B44 set out the process for forming Local Ecumenical Projects, specifying carefully the high levels of agreement to set up such a Project and the rules around the (limited) interchangeability of ministers and communion rites.⁵¹ Local Ecumenical Projects are also of course sometimes found in church buildings shared under the Sharing of Church Buildings Act 1969. In their considerable detail these provide a strong example of the way in which some later Canons have needed to move from the spare and elegant form generally adopted in the post-war drafting to something much more closely resembling secular statutory and secondary legislation.

VI. Synodical Government

At the beginning of the period, the building blocks of both local and national representative church government were established in the form of PCCs and the Church Assembly respectively. The Parochial Church Councils (Powers) Measure 1956 consolidated the former and slightly modified their abilities with respect to property. More significant were the range of references, discussed in section II, in the new Canons giving the Council powers with respect to decisions about liturgy and (as above) vesture. The Measures for pastoral reorganisation in the period also established the rights of PCCs as formal consultees in the drafting of pastoral schemes.⁵² Between parishes and the national Church, the 1919 Enabling Act had provided for Diocesan Conferences and (optional) Ruri-Decanal Conferences,

---

⁴⁷ Report of the Sharing of Churches Committee (CA 1696, 1968, s 5) and Sharing of Church Buildings Measure 1970, as presented for Final Approval at the Church Assembly in 1968 (CA 1697).
⁴⁸ Doe (n 46) 434–39.
⁴⁹ Bray (n 3) 44–45.
⁵⁰ Patterson (n 16) 118–19.
⁵¹ Bray (n 3) 67–74, 83–90.
⁵² eg Pastoral Reorganisation Measure 1949, s 5(2); Pastoral Measure 1968, s 3(2)(c).

but these did not have substantial powers or functions, or a direct relationship to Diocesan Boards of Finance.[53] The financial significance of dioceses grew steadily from about the 1960s, with voluntary income from parishes making up a larger proportion of church income. This has been given various names in different dioceses at different times (quota, parish share, parish offer, common fund) and calculated by varying formulae. The Synodical Government Measure 1969 (referring to it as 'quota') specifically authorises diocesan synods to delegate allocation to deanery synods.[54] However, the strict law around what is effectively a voluntary tax is limited.[55] In 1976, the Endowments and Glebe Measure gave the dioceses landholdings of varying size to manage and draw on as an endowment.

With respect to the constitutional position, however, the shadow cast by the 1927–28 Prayer Book crisis lasted well into the 1950s. In his 1950 volume, *Church and State in England*, Archbishop of York Cyril Garbett lamented the 'dramatic expression of the supremacy of Parliament over the Church' and (clearly not appreciating the post-war Labour Government) was alarmed that 'the State is steadily moving towards totalitarianism', leading him to feel 'profound disquiet of soul. I find it impossible to regard the present relationship between the Church and State without grave heart-searching and discomfort.'[56] The Church Assembly responded to this post-war mood by commissioning another Report, published in 1952 and entitled, confusingly, *Church and State*, as had been that of 1935. This 1952 Report (sometimes called the 'Moberley Report' after the chairman) preferred to temporise on the alarm of Garbett. Indeed, the 1952 Report, unlike that of 1935, saw Parliament as a guarantor of moderation in church life, and asserted hopefully, 'it is arguable that, however paradoxically, the House of Commons represents the mind of the inarticulate mass of laymen[!] more closely than does the House of Laity'.[57]

Deliverance from the constitutional deadlock about how to revise the Prayer Book came, in some ways, not from any of the proposals of the 1935 or 1952 Reports, but from the experience of canon law revision described in Section II above, with the draft Canons being passed back and forth between the Convocations and House of Laity over several years, so that many of the divisive issues were settled. Against this, some clergy maintained the more Catholic view that the Convocations were, as wholly ordained bodies, possessed of a unique spiritual authority. However, this had been undermined by the insistence of the Barnes Committee, in the 1940s, as discussed in section II, that the Ecclesiastical Committee would not allow the

---

[53] Church of England Assembly (Powers) Act 1919, appendix, schedule, 'Rules for the Representation of the Laity', rr 2, 16, 17.
[54] Synodical Government Measure 1969, s 5(4).
[55] For a fuller discussion, see Doe (n 46) 478–82.
[56] C Garbett, *Church and State in England* (London, Hodder & Stoughton 1950) 139–40.
[57] *Church and State, being the Report of a Commission appointed by the Church Assembly in June 1949* (London, Church Information Board, 1952) 23.

passage of Canons on which the laity had not been properly consulted.[58] During the process of canon law revision this had been framed as an inclusion of the laity by grace, not right,[59] but there had been many arguing that the laity should have equal rights. And the readiness of the Church to cooperate with Barnes developed a confidence that wise decisions could be made in future. If the laity were to be involved in all future canonical revision, it would make more sense for a single body of all three houses to make Canons. Eric Kemp's *Counsel and Consent* offered a clear Catholic voice for this option.[60] Further delay was caused by the reluctance of the York Convocation, as one of the few institutions to embody the Northern Province, to surrender its separate identity. In the end, a typical compromise was worked out and incorporated in the Synodical Government Measure 1969. The key concession to the historic Convocations was that in the case of 'a provision touching doctrinal formulae or the services or ceremonies of the Church of England or the administration of the Sacraments or sacred rites thereof'[61] ('Article 7 Business'), not only was a two-thirds majority required in each house but each house of Convocation, or the single House of Laity, should have the power to ask to sit separately and agree, or not, the provision in question.[62]

This renamed and reconstituted[63] the Church Assembly, with a revised and reduced membership, as the General Synod, and (save for the seldom-used right of the Convocations to claim reference of certain matters) transferred the powers of the Convocations to the Synod, creating a single, national legislative body for the Church of England with respect to both Measures and Canons. The barriers of the separate Convocations and the inconsistent role for the laity, identified as long ago as the 1860s by some of the first revivers of Convocation, were finally broken down. The fundamental legislative role, however, remained that conferred by the Church of England Assembly (Powers) Act 1919, and section 1(3) of the Measure reaffirmed the necessity (under the Submission of the Clergy Act 1533) for royal licence for Canons, as well as their subordination to statute and measure. In the same year, the Statute Law (Repeals) Act 1969 repealed all other clauses of the 1533 Act, including the long-debated section 7 providing for pre-Reformation canon law to remain in force unless superseded. It therefore seems clear since 1969 that such canon law is only applicable where it can be shown to have operated with the force of custom since 1533, if at all.[64]

---

[58] Boulton (n 25) 362–63.
[59] Speech of Mr P Goyder opening the 1951 Church Assembly debate on Canon Law Revision, alluding to an (unpublished) address by Archbishop Fisher to the House of Laity on the day before the Assembly had opened. *Proceedings of the Church Assembly*, XXXI.2, 20 June 1951, 201.
[60] E Kemp, *Counsel and Consent* (London, SPCK 1961) 217–31.
[61] Synodical Government Measure 1969, s 7(1).
[62] ibid s 7(2).
[63] ibid s 2(1).
[64] See further at N Doe, 'Pre-Reformation Roman Canon Law in Post-Reformation English Ecclesiastical Law' (2022) 24 *Ecclesiastical Law Journal* 273–94.

Perhaps more of a change was the introduction of Diocesan and Deanery Synods by the 1969 Measure, especially in places where a Ruri-Decanal Conference had never been constituted. The actual powers conferred on the lower Synods were however modest, and for all the excitement of getting together, they swiftly earned a reputation as tedious talking-shops in many places. The innovation in synodical governance was the consultative process introduced under Article 8 of the Constitution of the General Synod, providing that business 'providing for permanent changes in the services of Baptism or Holy Communion or in the Ordinal, or for a scheme for a constitutional union or a permanent and substantial change of a relationship between the Church of England and another Christian body ... in Great Britain'[65] must be referred to the Diocesan Synods, and the agreement of a majority required before the General Synod could proceed to legislate or make the relevant Canon. I believe the first use of this procedure was for the 1971–72 consideration of the proposals for unity between the Church of England and the Methodist Church, which found approval in 39 out of 43 diocesan synods[66] but in the end failed to reach the necessary two-thirds majority in the House of Clergy in General Synod. It was, however, used successfully to endorse the Worship and Doctrine Measure 1974 and those for women deacons and priests.

The Constitution of the General Synod, enacted as schedule 2 to the 1969 Measure, also sets out clearly[67] the four categories of 'provision' that the Synod may make, and it is worth listing and explaining their different natures:[68]

1. Measures, the full legislative function inherited from the Church Assembly, with the force of statute and able to amend previous legislation concerning the Church of England.
2. Canons, taking on the power previously exercised by the Convocations, and which are as ever binding only on the clergy.
3. To make 'order, regulation or other subordinate instrument or proceeding as may be appropriate' under a Measure or Canon, the latter defining who has the authority to make and amend the regulation. This function was used comparatively little in the period of this chapter but, as chapter 11 relates, has become more common, in imitation of secular use of statutory instruments.
4. Acts of Synod, which express the mind of the Church on matters that for some reason it is not possible or appropriate to legislate, for example international ecumenical declarations like support for the Meissen and Porvoo Declarations.[69] Much the best-known has been the controversial Episcopal

---

[65] Synodical Government Measure 1969, s 8(1).
[66] *Church Times* (28 April 1972) 1.
[67] Synodical Government Measure 1969, sch 2, para 6(a).
[68] Further analysis may be found in Doe (n 46) 55–84.
[69] See S Slack, 'Synodical Government and the Legislative Process' (2012) 14 *Ecclesiastical Law Journal* 43–48, 51–52.

Ministry Act of Synod 1993, which established the Provincial Episcopal Visitors. Acts of Synod have inherited the ambiguous authority of the preceding Acts of Convocation. They are not strictly law, but all sources refer to the somewhat overburdened citation of the 1972 *Bland* case that those had 'great moral force, as the considered judgment of the highest and ancient synod of the province'.[70] It is unclear whether the General Synod's lack of ancientry adds or subtracts from the moral force of its Acts.

The coming of General Synod, on top of successful canonical revision, meant that the proposals of the committee chaired by Owen Chadwick and presented in the 1970 Report entitled, again, *Church and State*,[71] could finally achieve a breakthrough in the deadlock over the Prayer Book crisis 1927–28. As well as liturgy and doctrine (see section VII), this largely removed the selection of diocesan bishops from the direct choice of the Prime Minister to what was at first called the Crown Appointments Commission (now Crown Nominations Commission), which included representation of the diocese concerned through the convening of a Vacancy-in-See Committee. Although ultimately arising from an unwritten agreement between Government and the Church, the worked-out rules for this process were embodied as an appendix to the Standing Orders of General Synod, where they are amendable by Synod.[72]

VII. Liturgical and Doctrinal Reform

The issues to be resolved in the post-war era about the reform of public worship and the definition of doctrine were subtle and complex. Many significant questions of doctrine, such as the status of the eucharist or baptismal theology, were at least in theory defined by nineteenth-century judgments based mostly on sixteenth-century texts, but widely contested or defied.[73] Older clergy and laity sitting in the Convocations and the Church Assembly, notably Archbishop Michael Ramsey, recalled clearly from their youth the painful failure of the 1928 Prayer Book after so many years of work. Some matters (such as vestments, discussed in section II) had been settled in the revision of the Canons, and where necessary by Measures to remove possible legal challenges based on historic interpretations of the law or the Prayer Book. The Prayer Book (Miscellaneous Provisions) Measure 1965 and the Prayer Book (Further Provisions) Measure 1968 continued this process by, inter

---

[70] *Bland* (n 39) 1018.
[71] The Archbishops' Commission on Church and State, *Church and State* (London, Church Information Office, 1970).
[72] Synodical Government Measure 1969, sch 2, para 11.
[73] Patterson (n 16) 45–52.

alia, amending the Communion and Baptism rubric respectively[74] to conform to the draft Canons enabling the final promulgation of the new Canons in 1969.

More important for the future was the Prayer Book (Alternative and Other Services) Measure 1965, which conferred on the Convocations the power to authorise alternative forms of service for experimental use, re-opening the door to authorised liturgical change that had been so firmly closed in 1928. This enabled the publication of the successive Series 1, 2 and 3, providing a (limited) variety of possible new service patterns. However, the power under the 1965 Measure and the original Canons B2 and B3[75] covered temporary authorisation only.

Pressure to revise liturgy in the 1960s ran in parallel with pressure to revise doctrine, in the form of the Clerical Subscription Act 1865, which still required clergy at ordination to subscribe to the Thirty-Nine Articles of Religion and Book of Common Prayer, and at induction to read out the Articles in full. Anecdotes of Anglo-Catholic clergy respectfully doffing their birettas at mention of 'the Bishop of Rome' in Article 37, before muttering that he 'hath no jurisdiction in this Realm of England', suggest one aspect of the problem. The carefully worked out response was the Church of England (Worship and Doctrine) Measure 1974, famously introduced in the House of Lords by Michael Ramsey on the verge of his retirement.

The Measure offers a balance between assurance that the Book of Common Prayer will continue to be available and that any doctrinal provision requires special majorities under Article 7 of the Constitution of General Synod as described in section VI, and is in fact a remarkably permissive provision. General Synod is enabled to authorise orders of service for permanent use for all rites provided for in the Prayer Book. The Convocations, Archbishops and Bishops are given power to make canons, under which they may authorise services – incorporated into the revised Canons B3–B5 by Amending Canon 3 in 1975. This power has largely come to be used in the commendation of forms under Canon B5 by the House of Bishops, beginning with *Lent, Holy Week and Easter* in 1987. And Synod also acquired power to define the terms of clerical assent to church doctrine in Canon, taking effect as the new Declaration of Assent in Canon C15 by Amending Canon 4, also in 1975.

Striking from a legal perspective is the transfer of matters that had been governed by Measure (or to a large extent earlier Acts of Parliament) into Canon, arguably a significant step of disestablishment. This is emphasised by section 4 of the 1974 Measure[76] and by section 6 (disapplying the Submission of the Clergy

---

[74] See respectively Prayer Book (Miscellaneous Provisions) Measure 1965, s 3; and Prayer Book (Further Provisions) Measure 1968, s 3.
[75] *The Canons* (n 13) 7–9.
[76] Church of England (Worship and Doctrine) Measure 1974, s 4(2): 'The final approval by the General Synod of any such Canon [ie amending worship or assent] or regulation or form of service

Act 1533 in relation to matters covered by the Measure). The latter provision ensured that no new liturgical provision could be challenged by reference to statutes of whatever period. Other Measures passed to ensure the conformity of the 1964/69 Canons to statute, including the Holy Table Measure 1964 and the aforementioned Vestures of Ministers Measure 1964, were repealed, removing these matters from law to Canon.

Adrian Hastings identifies this as a period when the State became increasingly uninterested in the major events of the Church. A minor exception that proves the rule was the rejection of the draft Appointment of Bishops Measure (which would have abolished the symbolic election of diocesan bishops by their cathedral chapter) by the House of Commons in 1984. A group of reactionary MPs, including Enoch Powell, mischievously alluding to the York Minster fire, mounted a successful rearguard action late one night in the Commons,[77] but the fact that they required only 32 votes (to defeat 17) to achieve victory says a good deal about the lack of concern in Westminster for the state of the Church.[78]

The principle that the Church had freedom to determine its own doctrinal and liturgical life was tested towards the end of our period by two significant cases concerning controversial issues: the ordination of remarried divorcees in *Brown v Runcie* (1991)[79] and the ordination of women priests in *R v Ecclesiastical Committee of Both Houses of Parliament, ex parte the Church Society* (1993),[80] the Court of Appeal and Divisional Court respectively confirming that they had no authority to change the legislative will of Synod. Whereas the former judgment on appeal focuses on the technical question of whether special majorities were required, the latter, given the day before the House of Commons was to debate the Measure, established the more fundamental position that the power of the Synod to determine 'any matter concerning the Church of England'[81] could not be limited by way of judicial review. In Parliament too, the 1984 rebellion noted above and the controversies discussed in section VIII look like exceptions to a predominant acceptance that the role of the Ecclesiastical Committee is limited to assessing Measures by a narrow test of their expediency within the wider law of the land, rather than acting as 'a kind of select committee'[82] for spiritual matters in themselves.

---

or amendment thereof shall conclusively determine that the Synod is of such opinion as aforesaid [ie that it is no departure from the doctrine of the Church of England] with respect to the matter so approved.'

[77] According to RE Rodes, *Law and Modernisation in the Church of England* (Notre Dame, IN, University of Notre Dame Press, 1991) 345: the debate began at 10.40 pm, and the division was at 12.21 am.

[78] A Hastings, *A History of English Christianity 1920–1990* (London, SCM Press, 1991) 606–08.

[79] *Browne v Runcie*, *The Times* (20 February 1991) (CA).

[80] *R v Ecclesiastical Committee of Both Houses of Parliament, ex parte the Church Society* (1994) 6 Admin LR 670.

[81] Church of England Assembly (Powers) Act 1919, s 3(6).

[82] I Slaughter, 'Functions of the Ecclesiastical Committee under section 3(3) of the Church of England Assembly (Powers) Act 1919' (unpublished), cited in Doe (n 46) 65, fnn 68 and 69.

VIII. The Long Road to Remarried and Women Priests

The close of our period is marked by changes in the important areas of divorce and women's ministry that had been the subject of long previous debate, continuing in different forms to the present day. Both are good examples of the manner in which legal change often happens in the Church of England: slowly, with extensive safeguards for those who do not support it.

With the exception of the loss of a controversial proposal in the 1947 Report to allow diocesan chancellors to declare (some) marriages ending in divorce to be null, the Canons had embodied the resistance of the Church to remarriage after divorce, already stated in resolutions of the Convocations in 1938 and 1957.[83] Canon C4 reflected this in the discipline of the clergy, forbidding ordination to all those remarried after divorce or married to divorcees. This was mirrored for the avoidance of doubt by section 9 of the Clergy (Ordination and Miscellaneous Provisions) Measure 1964, though careful reading of the Church Assembly debates in 1962–63 reveals much argument about the holiness of marriage, and nothing about why this needed to be in a Measure. The Explanatory Memorandum simply states that 'This Clause contains two new impediments to Orders which are contained in paragraph 3 of Canon C4.'[84] It is possible that further research will reveal the legal advice as to why inclusion in the Measure was judged necessary.

By the 1980s, the question of divorce and remarriage had been a matter of vigorous debate for some time, with motions passed in General Synod against the remarriage of divorcees in 1973, 1978 and 1985,[85] though with a motion of 1981 calling for processes to allow remarriage in church passed. Because the Matrimonial Causes Act 1937 had placed the power to refuse remarriage in the hands of individual clergy (either for themselves as officiants or for their churches as incumbents), the debate allowed for what earlier editions of Hill's *Ecclesiastical Law* call 'an unfortunate variety of practice from diocese to diocese and from parish to parish.'[86] But at least some who were remarrying did so in church where clergy were willing, and others made use of the Service of Prayer and Dedication after Civil Marriage commended by the House of Bishops in 1985.[87]

Those wishing to be ordained, however, were subject to the absolute bar of Canon C4, a situation made more awkward by inconsistent treatment of those who remarried after ordination, who by the late 1980s included members of the episcopate. The result was the Clergy (Ordination) Measure 1990 and Amending Canon 9 in 1991. This dual provision (the key text being replicated verbatim)

---

[83] Smethurst, Riley and Wilson (eds) (n 30) 90–95, 170–72.
[84] *Clergy (Ordination and Miscellaneous Provisions) Measure 1964. Explanatory Memorandum* (CA 1389X, 1962).
[85] Hastings (n 78) 610.
[86] Hill (n 40) 140.
[87] P Bradshaw, *A Companion to Common Worship* (London, SPCK, 2006) 192.

marks a shift from the enabling provisions of, for example, the Church of England (Worship and Doctrine) Measure 1974, requiring the same double action to amend in future. Former Chief Legal Officer Stephen Slack attributes this to the drafting preferences of his predecessor Brian Hanson,[88] though it may also reflect the high-tension status of remarriage as a subject at the time. It would have been possible, and simpler, to repeal section 9 of the Clergy (Ordination and Miscellaneous Provisions) Measure 1964, which contained the ban, and leave the process only in Canon.

I am grateful for an error in Gerald Bray's newest work for revealing what must have been a draft form of the Amending Canon, replacing the prohibition in Canon C4.3 with permission for the bishop to ordain.[89] However, in the event this proved too permissive, and a compromise was adopted, drawing on the existing provision for archiepiscopal faculties for ordination below the canonical age. Under the new Canon C.4.3A, bishops wishing to ordain remarried divorcees are required to obtain a faculty from the archbishops to do so, and the archbishops are given joint power to provide regulations to direct this process. A Question at General Synod in February 2019 by the author revealed that 108 such faculties had been sought in the previous year, against a pool of some 500–600 candidates (faculties not necessarily corresponding to their selection year).[90]

The journey to the ordination of women priests is much-charted, and this is not the place to retell the full story of theological debate and division. It is interesting, however, that from a legal viewpoint, it was assumed as early as 1972 that 'because for centuries it has been the custom that men only can be ordained for the ministry, this is as much part of the law as if it had been the subject of legislation … [I]t would seem therefore that a Measure would be needed …'[91] In other words, a change in the Canons (where there were many gender-specific references to clergy as men) would not be sufficient.

From a legislative viewpoint, the meaningful start was the passing of a diocesan synod motion (one of eight tabled by that time),[92] in 1984, calling for legislation to be brought forward. In the period when the legislation was being prepared, two related Measures progressed through Synod: the Women Ordained Abroad Measure (which would have allowed them to celebrate legally in England); and the remarkably uncontentious Deacons (Ordination of Women) Measure. All three reached a crux in the same sessions in 1986: the proposals for women priests moved on to further complex debate; the draft Women Ordained Abroad Measure

---

[88] In conversation with the author, 28 January 2022.
[89] Bray (n 3) 95.
[90] General Synod February 2019, Questions, Q81, at www.churchofengland.org/sites/default/files/2019-02/General%20Synod%20February%202019%20Questions.pdf (accessed 25 November 2022).
[91] *The Ordination of Women to the Priesthood (GS104)* (London, Church Information Office, 1972) 82–83.
[92] M Webster, *A New Strength, A New Song: Journey to Women's Priesthood* (London, Mowbray, 1994) 118.

fell, having been determined to be Article 7 business (as described in section IV) and not reaching the required majorities; and the Deacons Measure passed.[93] Although it may not have seemed that significant to allow deaconesses to be ordained deacon from 1987, the appointment of experienced former deaconesses as deacons-in-charge of parishes sharpened the sense of 'when, not if' women would become priests.

The narrow final approval (by 169:82 in the House of Laity,[94] 67.3 per cent with two-thirds required) of what became the Priests (Ordination of Women) Measure 1993 at Synod on 11 November 1992 is one of the famous moments of modern Church of England history; the culmination of years of campaigning for many, and perhaps a decisive point of doctrinal definition in doing a new thing. From a legal perspective, however, the simplicity of the core decision is almost obscured by the breadth and depth of provision for those unable to receive women's ordained ministry, developed both before and after the decisive vote. The Measure itself provides for parishes, cathedrals and bishops to refuse to receive (in the case of bishops, to ordain) women as priests, and the accompanying Ordination of Women (Financial Provisions) Measure 1993 provided financial compensation for those stipendiary clergy who determined that in conscience they must leave the Church of England.

The more remarkable structure was created after the passage of the Measure in the quasi-legislative form of the 1993 Episcopal Ministry Act of Synod, which provided for the work of the provincial episcopal visitors, bishops consecrated especially to minister to those parishes no longer able to accept the ministry of their own diocesan on account of his ordaining women. Much ink has been spilt on the sacramental logic of this arrangement: from a legal angle, provincial episcopal visitors are technically suffragans of the dioceses of Canterbury and York, operating by agreement of relevant diocesan bishops across sections of the Church of England; however, 'the bishop of each diocese continues as ordinary of his diocese'.[95] Thus, whilst by 1994 it might reasonably have been asked whether the Church of England was in communion with itself, we were still, precariously, one Church by Law Established.

IX. Conclusion

Between 1947 and 1994, the Church of England undertook a decisive revision of its Canons (which before revision were those contained in the Canons Ecclesiastical 1603 with only minor amendments): decisive especially for being largely internal

---

[93] ibid 124.
[94] *Church Times* (13 November 1992) 1 at www.ukpressonline.co.uk/ukpressonline/view/pagview/ChTm_1992_11_13_001 (accessed 25 November 2022).
[95] General Synod (1993) Episcopal Ministry Act of Synod 1993, para 1(2).

in motivation and accomplishment, though limited, as related in this chapter, by Erastian pressure from Parliament through the Barnes Committee. Especially in liturgical practice (eg, service patterns, furnishings, vestments) these replaced the norms of the Jacobean area with those of the second Elizabethan. Alongside organisational consolidation, the painstaking revision of the Canons laid to rest many hoary controversies, and provided at least some frameworks of expectation for the twentieth century. The law enabled the Church Commissioners to work as the agent of financial and structural reform, moving the clergy away from finance by local endowment to standardised stipends with reliable pensions, and reorganising parishes into more sustainable groupings. A phase of partial disestablishment and liberalisation, marked especially by the Church of England (Worship and Doctrine) Measure 1974 and other responses to the Chadwick Report, was achieved whilst retaining many benefits of establishment and tradition. New liturgies were introduced, leading to the Alternative Service Book of 1980, and the Church gained the main voice in the choice of bishops. This gave way to a slower pace of change in the 1980s. Against this backdrop the campaign for the ordination of women priests, whilst successful in the end, revealed deep cultural divisions that required great legal and structural ingenuity to manage.

11

Change and Decay – The Twilight Years of an Established Church: 1994–2023

MARK HILL

This final chapter brings our journey to the present day. Inevitably, our perceptions of a period through which we have lived and continue to live will differ significantly from the earlier periods viewed through the prism of history and at arm's length. Authors can examine primary and secondary sources from those earlier periods with detachment, and consider how the reflections of previous scholars and commentators have been refined, reviewed and revised. The old adage that journalism is the first draft of history suggests that my reflections may be illusory, porous and less durable that those of the chapters that precede them. The fact remains that in analysing the current era, we ourselves are part of the narrative. And I feel that particularly strongly. In 1994, I had completed the LLM in Canon Law at Cardiff University and written the manuscript for my textbook *Ecclesiastical Law*, published by Butterworths in 1995, little knowing that it would be absorbed into the stable of Oxford University Press and be the subject of successive editions in 2001, 2007 and 2018. Having been Editor of the *Ecclesiastical Law Journal* (2002–13) and Chairman of the Ecclesiastical Law Society (2015–21), a member of the Legal Advisory Commission of the General Synod of the Church of England and a Diocesan Chancellor, this is a story being told from the inside. For present purposes, I intend to look at several short themes that emerge from my review concerning the law of the Church of England from 1994 until today. They may not be unique to this period, but collectively they define it and are worthy of further discussion and consideration.

I. The Speed of Change

The earlier chapters of this book will have written of continuity and change in its various guises, but the three short decades in my custodianship evidence an unusual period of constant revision, both of substance and of form. Take, for example, the discipline of clergy, for which a so-called criminal jurisdiction had long existed, procedurally framed within the procedures of the Ecclesiastical Jurisdiction Measure 1963. This had never been a wholly satisfactory piece of legislation, being slow, cumbersome and costly to enforce. Following a report published under the title *Under Authority*, an entirely new system was introduced in the Clergy Discipline Measure 2003.[1] Undoubtedly it had some advantages over the previous system, but it failed to achieve its potential and was not the panacea intended by its drafters.[2] In particular, with reference to issues of safeguarding, Archbishop Justin Welby declared it unfit for purpose.[3] Its days were numbered from that point on. We now await a revised Clergy Conduct Measure to reset the systems that deal with allegations of misconduct on the part of bishops, priests and deacons.[4] This represents a major reform in church law, which came and went in less than 20 years, something for which there is little by way of precedent in previous eras.

Others will have spoken of canon law in its strict sense: the Canons Ecclesiastical of the Church of England – their medieval origins, their continuance through the Reformation and their substantial revision in the 1960s. In contradistinction with the wholesale revision of the type carried out in the 1960s by a highly expert commission,[5] the last few decades have been dominated by a succession of Amending Canons, tinkering with the current suite of canonical provision with sequential changes, some minor and some of greater consequence.[6] Whereas once the canons were published as a book, strong, proud and durable, the change to a loose-leaf publication in a flimsy ring-binder was redolent of their ephemeral nature, and now they are online, floating in the ether, sometimes updated, sometimes not.[7]

Brief mention might be made of the Covid-19 pandemic, which brought restrictions on individual liberty across the globe: devastating but passing.

---

[1] General Synod Working Party reviewing Clergy Discipline and the Working of the Ecclesiastical Courts, *Under Authority* (London, Church House Publishing, 1996). The Ecclesiastical Law Society can rightly claim credit for the title of the 2003 Measure (though not its content) as its draft had the more prosaic working title 'Ecclesiastical Jurisdiction (Discipline) Measure'. A representative of the Society's Working Party suggested that the titles of the draft measure (both short and long) should more clearly convey its purpose.

[2] Two noteworthy changes were that the hearings are generally in private, whereas formerly they were in public, and that the standard of proof was changed from beyond reasonable doubt (the norm for secular criminal allegations) to the balance of probabilities, the secular civil standard, which is adopted in employment tribunal cases. See section V.

[3] *Church Times* (23 March 2018) at www.churchtimes.co.uk/articles/2018/23-march/news/uk/i-am-ashamed-of-the-church-archbishop-of-canterbury-justin-welby-admits-to-iicsa.

[4] Expected to come into force in 2024.

[5] During the Covid pandemic in 2021/22, the Ecclesiastical Law Society initiated several reading groups, under the leadership of Russell Dewhurst and Stephen Coleman, to examine how the current Canons might be reformed. Their study and recommendations have yet to be published.

[6] See G Bray, *The Development of the Canons: A Historical Study and Summary of the Church of England's Canons 1969 to 2020* (London, Latimer Trust, 2022).

[7] The same might be said of the Church Representation Rules. Although there was a major revision and reordering achieved by the Church Representation and Ministers Measure 2019, they continue to be tinkered with and the version on the Church of England website is slow to be updated.

Churchgoers were affected by the closure of places of worship. Restrictions were placed on the use of the common cup. The lifespan of General Synod was extended. Chancellors waived public notice of proposed petitions. Hearings were conducted online. The proposed Church of England (Miscellaneous Provisions) Measure 2023, however, seeks to put on a permanent basis a number of ad hoc changes introduced during the pandemic.[8]

II. Simplification

There has been something of a change of culture within General Synod during the period under discussion. There seems to have been a recognition that ecclesiastical law is the servant of the Church, not its master, and there is therefore an obligation on Synod, as a legislative body, to ensure that the law is clear, comprehensible, relevant and accessible. In 2013, the Archbishops' Council and Church Commissioners[9] established a body whose terms of reference were to consider concerns about the constraints caused to the mission and growth of the Church of England by existing canons, legislation, regulations and procedures.[10]

The Simplification Task Group, as it became, considered that church legislation had hitherto been predicated on building in detailed provision for all possible eventualities, which led to legislative complexity which the group considered to be a barrier to experiment and innovation, frustrating the Church's missionary calling. Two significant measures deserve special mention. The Statute Law (Repeals) Measure 2017 brought about the wholesale repeal of provisions of ecclesiastical law that are no longer of practical utility.[11] Slightly more controversial was the Legislative Reform Measure 2017, which provided a mechanism for removing burdens[12] from ecclesiastical legislation[13] by way of an order approved by General Synod, thereby avoiding the cumbersome Synodical legislative process. The Measure made provision for the establishment of a committee to scrutinise

---

[8] eg remote meetings of General Synod (cl 1); live broadcast of hearings of ecclesiastical courts (cl 13).

[9] They were responding to General Synod, *Challenges for the New Quinquennium – New Steps* (2011, GS 1815).

[10] See the *Report of the Simplification Task Group* (2015, GS 1980).

[11] This Measure was long overdue: it implements a reform for which the Ecclesiastical Law Society had been lobbying for the better part of 30 years: see the various reports of the Society's Working Party on the Repeal of Ecclesiastical Statute Law in (1990) 2 *Ecclesiastical Law Journal* 42–44 and (1992) 2 *Ecclesiastical Law Journal* 305–14 and 388–418.

[12] For examples of the type of burden that might be addressed by order, see Appendix II to the report of the Revision Committee of the Legislative Reform Measure (2017, GS 2027Y). Section 1(2) of the Measure defines 'burden' as '(a) financial cost, (b) an administrative inconvenience, or (c) an obstacle to efficiency'.

[13] This applies to Measures and those Acts of Parliament that form part of the ecclesiastical law of the Church of England.

draft orders,[14] and for a so-called 'sunset' clause, giving this innovative fast-track procedure a five-year lifespan.[15] However, the sunset clause has itself now been repealed.[16]

Mention might also be made of certain provisions of the Civil Partnership Act 2004, which effectively reverse the principle established by the formation of the Church Assembly under the Enabling Act in 1919, whereby a high degree of autonomy was given to the Church of England to legislate for itself.[17] The intriguing power, hidden away in the high-numbered ephemera sections of the Act, provides that a Minister of the Crown may by order amend, repeal or revoke 'Church legislation'. This term is defined so as to include Measures of the Church Assembly or General Synod and any orders, regulations or other instruments made by virtue of such Measures. Section 259 is very widely drafted and empowers a Minister by order to make 'such further provision as he considers appropriate for the general purposes, or any particular purpose, of the Civil Partnership Act, or for giving full effect to the Act or any provision of it'. Whilst hitherto the exercise of this provision has been benign, the words of the statute are broad, giving power to the Executive to legislate for the Church of England. Reliance must be placed on the continuance of the constitutional convention that the Government does not legislate for the Church of England without its consent.[18] Recent administrations have shown distinct enthusiasm for defying parliamentary convention.[19]

III. Women Priests and Bishops: Mutual Flourishing

It is no exaggeration to identify the admission of women to the order of priests as the most significant change to the doctrine of the English Church. The jurisdictional issue of the Henrician reformation, whose focus was on royal supremacy over papal authority, somewhat pales in comparison. Although the Priests (Ordination of Women) Measure 1993 pre-dates the allotted era for this final

---

[14] Legislative Reform Measure 2017, s 6.

[15] ibid s 10. There is provision for the Archbishops' Council to extend its period of operation beyond five years from the making of the first order.

[16] Church of England (Miscellaneous Provisions) Measure 2023, s 2. The section includes in its heading the expression 'removal of sunset', suggestive of a departure from scripture: Genesis 1:16.

[17] See ch 9 of this volume.

[18] In the course of parliamentary debate on 19 July 2005 concerning the proposed Civil Partnership Act 2004 (Overseas Relationships and Consequential, etc Amendments) Order, a Minister stated, 'by convention the Government do not legislate for the Church of England without its consent. I stress that the provisions in the order amending Church legislation have been drafted by Church lawyers, consulted on internally within the Church, and finally have been approved by the Archbishops' Council and the House of Bishops. The Church has asked that we include the amendments in the order, which we are content to do' (Grand Chamber, 19 July 2005, GC192–193). A cynic might suggest that the church hierarchy preferred to give to a government minister the power to amend legislation on pension provisions for same-sex couples, rather than have a potentially awkward debate on the floor of General Synod.

[19] See, by way of illustration only, *R (on the application of Miller) v Prime Minister* [2019] UKSC 41.

chapter, it is properly included because the first ordinations did not take place until March 1994 at Bristol Cathedral.[20] Ordaining women as priests has had various consequences, some anticipated and others not. For many it was a simple matter of gender equality; while for others it marked an enduring obstacle to ecumenism, the pursuit of greater visible unity, irreconcilably departing from the practice of Christendom and the Latin Church in particular.

It is not the purpose of this chapter to enter into the merits of the doctrinal dispute,[21] merely to consider its impact as a matter of ecclesiastical law. It placed the Church of England out of alignment with much of the Anglican Communion, in also making provision for those who in conscience could not accept women priests. General Synod, the Westminster Parliament (in approving the draft Measure) and the Supreme Governor (in giving royal assent) effectively legislated for division.[22] Two irreconcilable 'integrities' were to be held in tension with nuanced provisions such as the Episcopal Ministry Act of Synod 1993, allowing for alternative episcopal oversight. This was new and unknown territory. The conscience clause, providing clergy with relief from the duty to marry in the case of divorcees (and later those within the prohibited degrees or who had undergone gender reassignment), was a simple and workable solution of narrow application. The Act of Synod was pragmatic and practical, but thin on theology and doctrinally questionable.[23] However, its provisions (particularly those that gave opponents to the ordination of women an assured place within the Church of England)[24] were sufficient to get the legislation across the line, achieving the special majorities required. The package of compensation for those who resigned from stipendiary ministry due to their opposition to the ordination of women, was also an essential part of the composite arrangement.[25]

No such financial provision was made when the law was changed again to permit women to be consecrated as bishops,[26] and the Act of Synod was

---

[20] The memorial to the event has recently been removed, because, incongruously, it bore the names of the male cathedral dignitaries but not of the women ordained. See www.theguardian.com/world/2022/mar/06/bristol-cathedral-plaque-first-female-priests.

[21] Indeed, there are many who would say that the dispute is not doctrinal but related to practice and discipline. See *Brown v Runcie* The Times, 20 February 1991 (CA); *R v Ecclesiastical Committee of the Houses of Parliament, ex parte The Church Society* (1994) 6 Admin LR 670. The judgments are reproduced in M Hill, *Ecclesiastical Law*, 1st edn (London, Butterworths, 1995) 68 and 72 respectively.

[22] The provision was conceptually and practically very different from the conscience clause attendant on the re-marriage of divorcees (Matrimonial Causes Act 1965, s 8(2)(a)); and in other circumstances: see the Marriage (Prohibited Degrees of Relationship) Act 1986 and the Gender Recognition Act 2004.

[23] See J Maltby, 'The Act of Synod and Theological Seriousness' in M Furlong (ed), *Act of Synod – Act of Folly?* (Norwich, Canterbury Press, 1998) 42–58.

[24] The Priests (Ordination of Women) Measure 1993 entitles Parochial Church Councils (PCCs) to pass Resolution A (not accepting the sacramental ministry of women priests) and/or Resolution B (not accepting a woman priest as incumbent, priest-in-charge or team vicar). The Act of Synod enabled parishes that had passed these resolutions to petition the diocesan bishop, seeking alternative episcopal oversight.

[25] Ordination of Women (Financial Provisions) Measure 1993.

[26] Bishops and Priests (Consecration and Ordination of Women) Measure 2014, amending Canon 33.

withdrawn to be replaced with more informal arrangements, binding in honour only,[27] stimulated by the *Five Guiding Principles*,[28] particularly principle four designed to promote the concept of mutual flourishing:

> Since those within the Church of England who, on grounds of theological conviction, are unable to receive the ministry of women bishops or priests continue to be within the spectrum of teaching and tradition of the Anglican Communion, the Church of England remains committed to enabling them to flourish within its life and structures.

The fallout from the withdrawal of the acceptance of Bishop Philip North to his nomination as Bishop of Sheffield has exposed the legal, conceptual and practical fragility of the current arrangements.[29] At least two ecclesiological anomalies have been recognised[30] in the 2014 Settlement, and the absence of a firm legal underpinning is apparent. A Standing Commission on the House of Bishops' Declaration and the Five Guiding Principles was established in 2022. The creation of such a Commission was a key recommendation of the Implementation and Dialogue Group, a temporary body that reviewed the arrangements originally put in place in 2014.[31]

IV. The Lords Spiritual

The Equality Act 2010 offers no definition of positive discrimination; the term is generally taken to mean the favouring, without proper consideration of merit, of under-represented individuals from minority groups over individuals in majority groups: giving preferential treatment to a group of people over another because those people possess a protected characteristic.[32] Treating one person more favourably than another purely because of a protected characteristic is generally prohibited, unless a strict occupational requirement applies. However, and fortuitously, the Bishops and Priests (Consecration and Ordination of Women) Measure

---

[27] The Act of Synod is properly categorised as ecclesiastical quasi-legislation, whereas the informal procedure that superseded it lacked that status.

[28] *House of Bishops' Declaration on the Ministry of Bishops and Priests* (GS Misc 1076).

[29] *Independent Reviewer's Report on the Nomination to the See of Sheffield and Related Matters* (September 2017).

[30] P Avis, 'Bishops in Communion' (2017) 13 *Ecclesiology* 299–323.

[31] See generally section VII on soft law. The role of the Standing Commission is stated on the Church of England website to include: (i) to receive and disseminate good practice in relation to the implementation of the House of Bishops Declaration at all levels within the Church; (ii) to consider how effectively the Declaration, including the Five Guiding Principles, is being promoted throughout the Church; (iii) to receive and comment on reports published by the Independent Reviewer; and (iv) to provide an annual report to the House of Bishops. See www.churchofengland.org/media-and-news/press-releases/standing-commission-house-bishops-declaration-and-five-guiding. It has yet to publish its first annual report.

[32] The nine protected characteristics as defined under the 2010 Act are: age; disability; gender reassignment; marriage and civil partnership; pregnancy and maternity; race; religion or belief; sex; or sexual orientation.

2014 expressly provides that the office of a diocesan or suffragan bishop is not a public office under the Equality Act.

Though little noted outside the rarefied world of scholars of constitutional establishment, this wide restriction was successfully navigated when royal assent was given to the Lords Spiritual (Women) Act 2015.[33] It stipulates that whenever a vacancy arises among the Lords Spiritual during the 10 years following the coming into force of the Act, it has to be filled by a woman, if there is one who is eligible.[34] The Act has a sunset provision, whereby its provisions will cease to have effect after 10 years. Although the Explanatory Notes asserted that thereafter, pre-existing arrangements would be restored, it is understood that the Church of England is reviewing whether the Government might be invited to extend the life of the Act.[35]

In December 2022, the leader of His Majesty's Opposition indicated that the Labour manifesto at the next general election would include proposals for the House of Lords to be replaced with a wholly elected second chamber. Reform of the Upper House, and in particular the inclusion of Anglican bishops, has never been far from the public consciousness in recent years. As I have noted elsewhere, there are likely to be a number of challenges to the privileges enjoyed by the established Church of England under the constitution. Opinions that were hitherto muted in deference to the devoted service of Her Late Majesty will be expressed vocally and with greater force under the new King. The Memorandum on the compatibility of the Lords Spiritual (Women) Act 2015 with the European Convention on Human Rights was robust and unambiguous: 'As to whether the presence of Church of England bishops in the House of Lords generally is discriminatory, the government is not aware of any Strasbourg case-law as to requirements for the composition of the second chamber of a member state of the Council of Europe'.[36]

---

[33] Notably a statute of the Westminster Parliament, as opposed to a Measure of the Church of England. The Explanatory Notes to the Bill, prepared by the Cabinet Office record 'the Archbishop of Canterbury, after consultation with the Lords Spiritual and others, requested on behalf of the Church of England that amendments be made to the arrangements under the Bishoprics Act 1878 to enable the accelerated entry of female bishops to the House of Lords. The Government welcomed the decision by the Church of England to enable women to become bishops and wishes to see female bishops represented in the House of Lords as soon as possible.' The Bishops and Priests (Consecration and Ordination of Women) Measure 2014 expressly provides that the office of a diocesan or suffragan bishop is not a public office under the Equality Act.

[34] The Act supersedes s 5 of the Bishoprics Act 1878, which would otherwise require 'the issue of a writ of summons to that bishop of a see in England who having been longest bishop of a see in England has not previously become entitled to such writ'. The Act does not apply to the sees of Canterbury, York, London, Durham or Winchester, each of which carries *ex officio* membership of the Upper House.

[35] There are arguments both ways: there is still a statistical under-representation of women bishops in the House of Lords (although their selection is now almost entirely a matter for the church authorities). The burdens of office for a diocesan bishop are considerable, and the additional weight of parliamentary duties, which are imposed immediately upon appointment to episcopal office in the fast tracking of women bishops, is a heavy responsibility.

[36] See https://assets.publishing.service.gov.uk/government/uploads/system/uploads/attachment_data/file/388755/LORDS_SPIRITUAL__WOMEN__BILL_-_ECHR_MEMO_VF.pdf, para 6.

But the mere fact that the retention of the Lords Spiritual does not constitute a violation of human rights norms is an insufficient answer when there is a growing appetite for disestablishment generally and a secularisation of the constitution.[37]

V. The Ecclesiastical Courts

Earlier chapters have revealed the waning of the reach and influence of the consistory court, with its jurisdiction gradually being transferred to the secular courts, particularly during the nineteenth century in the area of probate and family law.[38] That trend persisted with the removal of the court's jurisdiction over clergy discipline, formerly exercised under the Ecclesiastical Jurisdiction Measure 1963,[39] the creation of the Clergy Discipline Commission, and the establishment of bishop's disciplinary tribunals drawn from national panels of clergy and laity with a legally qualified chair.[40] There had been very few cases brought under the 1963 Measure, in part due to the cumbersome procedure and its attendant cost, and in part due to the standard of proof that was applied, namely, the criminal standard of proof beyond reasonable doubt. The new process was designed to be simpler and cheaper, and allegations were subject to the civil standard of proof, namely, the balance of probabilities. The last case under the 1963 Measure concerned the Very Reverend John Methuen, then Dean of Ripon: it was compromised at the court door. At the core of the system introduced in 2003 is a procedure whereby a complaint is initially investigated by the diocesan registrar, who then reports to the bishop on whether the complaint has any substance.[41] If the bishop decides not to dismiss the complaint, a range of options may be pursued: no further action, conditional deferral, conciliation, penalty by consent and, finally, formal investigation, which can then lead to a hearing before an independent disciplinary tribunal consisting of two members of the clergy, two members of the laity and a legally qualified chair.[42] A similar process is provided for the discipline of bishops and archbishops.

---

[37] See, by way of example, J Chaplin, *Beyond Establishment: Resetting Church State Relations in England* (London, SCM Press, 2022). See also M Hatcher, 'Bishops in the House of Lords – Fit for the Future?' (LLM in Canon Law, Cardiff University, 2023).

[38] See ch 8 of this volume.

[39] Matters of doctrine, ritual and ceremonial continue to be justiciable.

[40] Clergy Discipline Measure 2003: see M Hill, *Ecclesiastical Law*, 4th edn (Oxford, Oxford University Press, 2018) ch 8.

[41] In 2006 and 2007 there were 66 and 71 complaints, respectively (of some 22,500 clergy); with 92 and 94, respectively, in 2020 and 2022: see the Annual Reports of the Clergy Discipline Commission.

[42] Under the former regime, the chancellor sat in the Consistory Court with four assessors, replicating the functions respectively of judge and jury in the Crown Court. Since the assessors were drawn from within the diocese, care had to be taken to ensure they were not acquainted with the respondent cleric, the complainant or any witnesses: see *Burridge v Tyler* [1992] 1 All ER 427. Under the Clergy Discipline Measure, panellists are now drawn from provincial panels of clergy and laity.

There have also been inroads into what is generally described as the inherent jurisdiction of the consistory court. Traditionally, by custom, chancellors had been at liberty to disseminate *de minimis* provisions, or lists of minor works, identifying classes or categories of proposals that were considered to be of such triviality that they might be carried out without the need to secure the prior grant of a faculty. It was considered that the variation of practice from one diocese to another was not conducive to good administration, particularly where clergy tend to be more mobile and likely to officiate in several dioceses during their ministry. The Ecclesiastical Jurisdiction and Care of Churches Measure 2018 brought about a sea change, with national, as opposed to diocesan, control of minor works. Section 77 allows for Rules to be made by the General Synod's Rule Committee, specifying categories of works that may be undertaken without the authority of faculty. These now appear in the Faculty Jurisdiction Rules 2015 (as amended). Anything not within List A or List B requires a faculty.[43] A subsequent enlargement of the preamble to the schedule empowered chancellors to give directions as to matters not included in List A or List B that are of such a minor nature that they may be undertaken without a faculty. The consistory court no longer has an inherent *de minimis* jurisdiction.[44]

Earlier chapters will have made reference to the jurisdiction previously exercised by archdeacons, particularly in relation to the faculty jurisdiction, where in some respects they had formerly shared in the work of the consistory court. More recent clarifications have properly made plain that the archdeacon's role in this regard is chiefly pastoral and certainly not judicial. The Faculty Jurisdiction Rules 2015 (as amended), are explicit in rule 7.1: 'The jurisdiction of the consistory court is to be exercised by the chancellor (except as otherwise provided by these Rules).' In only three instances is jurisdiction expressed to be exercised by an archdeacon: (i) the issuing of archdeacon's licences for temporary minor reorderings;[45] (ii) the authorisation of works under List B that do not require a faculty; and (iii) the making of a place of safety order under section 53 of the Ecclesiastical Jurisdiction and Care of Churches Measure 2018. All other archidiaconal jurisdiction has lapsed, archdeacons' courts having fallen into desuetude in the eighteenth century.

---

[43] This can be the only legitimate reading. There would be no need for the statutory power to issue Additional Matters Orders under s 78 if the *de minimis* jurisdiction had survived.

[44] A working party established by the Ecclesiastical Judges Association is currently reviewing the self-claimed inherent jurisdiction of chancellors to issue Churchyard Regulations. It is examining the legal basis for such regulations, as well as their content, with a view to minimising the difference in content between dioceses.

[45] Faculty Jurisdiction Rules 2015 (as amended), r 8. Despite the recent revision enlarging the duration of such licences to two years, parishes and archdeacons can easily fall foul of some of the technical provisions outlined in *Re Christ Church, Armley* [2017] ECC Lee 5. The Church of England's online faculty system unhelpfully speaks of 'TMRO' rather than 'Licence', which is the more readily comprehensible terminology of the Rules.

The centuries-old trend of reducing the jurisdiction of the consistory court[46] was recently reversed (to a very modest extent) with an obscure provision conferring new power upon diocesan chancellors. Section 12 of the Diocesan Boards of Education Measure 2021 gives to chancellors a new and unprecedented jurisdiction. It permits diocesan boards of education and school authorities to refer to the consistory court a question on whether the school is prevented by law from providing information to assist the board in carrying out its functions. The matter is to be determined on written representations and the chancellor's decision is final.[47] To the best of this author's knowledge, this provision has yet to be invoked.

In relation to the jurisprudence of the ecclesiastical courts, the period under consideration has seen several changes and developments. The Court of Arches and Chancery Court of York, which traditionally transacted their business by a single judge sitting alone,[48] now sit as panels. In faculty cases, the other two judges are diocesan chancellors.[49] The Court of Arches is now empowered to determine matters on written representations, without the need for a hearing.[50] The Covid pandemic also compelled new ways of working, which included the conduct of hearings online and the live-streaming of appeals.[51] When hearing appeals on clergy discipline matters, the Dean or Auditor sits with four panellists, two ordained and two lay.[52] The Vicar General's court, for each of the provinces of Canterbury and York, had been assumed to have fallen into desuetude, retaining only the somewhat archaic jurisdiction for the confirmation of election of diocesan bishops. The Clergy Discipline Measure 2003 conferred on the Vicar General's court a new first-instance jurisdiction in respect of disciplinary hearings in respect of bishops and archbishops.[53]

The decision of a consistory court of one diocese does not bind that of another, but the majority of chancellors seek to ensure that generally accepted practices and norms are followed unless there is good reason to do otherwise. In consequence

---

[46] Whilst their reduction may be reduced, the functioning of the judiciary is to be professionalised in consequence of the introduction of compulsory judicial training for ecclesiastical judges: s 21A of the Ecclesiastical Jurisdiction and Care of Churches Measure 2018, inserted by s 11 of the Church of England (Miscellaneous Provisions) Measure 2023.

[47] Diocesan Boards of Education Measure 2021, s 12(3).

[48] The Dean of Arches and Auditor respectively.

[49] See now the Ecclesiastical Jurisdiction and Care of Churches Measure 2018, s 15. The first appeal determined on the papers under the new rules was *Re St Michael and All Angels, Berwick* [2022] EACC 2.

[50] Ecclesiastical Jurisdiction and Care of Churches Measure 2018.

[51] As, eg, in the case of *Re Holy Trinity, Hurstpierpoint* [2020] ECC Chi 7. The Court of Arches authorised live-streaming of its proceedings in *Re St Giles Exhall* [2021] EACC 1, a procedural note annexed to the judgment setting out the Court's reasoning and the mechanics for streaming. Routine live-streaming has not endured beyond the pandemic, an application for it being refused in *Re St Michael and All Angels, Berwick* [2022] ECC Chi 3.

[52] Ecclesiastical Jurisdiction Measure 1963, s 3; Clergy Discipline Measure 2003, s 20(2), (3).

[53] Clergy Discipline Measure 2003, ss 6(2), 23. The Vicar General sits with two lay and two clerical members, each drawn from provincial panels. At least one of the clerical members must be in holy orders.

of a statutory deeming provision in section 14A of the Ecclesiastical Jurisdiction and Care of Churches Measure 2018,[54] the somewhat sterile question[55] of whether appellate decisions in one province are binding precedents in the other has been conclusively determined:

14A Decisions treated as taken by each Court

(1) A decision of the Arches Court of Canterbury or the Chancery Court of York is to be treated by the other Court, and by the lower ecclesiastical courts in the province of the other Court, as if it were a decision which the other Court had itself taken.

Where there are conflicting decisions in the Court of Arches and the Chancery Court of York, the later in time will prevail, unless it can be convincingly argued that the earlier decision was not brought to the attention of the later court.[56]

VI. Case Law

Various chapters of this book include reference to the state (civil) courts' determination of matters concerning the Church of England. This one is no exception. In 2004, the Law Lords were provided with an opportunity to consider the constitutional status of the Church of England in determining the appeal in *Parochial Church Council of Aston Cantlow v Wallbank*.[57] Although the presenting issue was the enforceability of obligations under the Chancel Repair Act 1932,[58] the importance of the case lies in its detailed consideration of the juridic nature of the Church of England,[59] distinguishing its public and private aspects.[60] Lord Hope of Craighead declared that 'the Church of England as a whole has no legal status or personality'.[61] Instead, legal personality is dispersed amongst various office-holders

---

[54] Inserted by the Church of England (Miscellaneous Provisions) Measure 2018.
[55] The suggestion in *Re Sam Tai Chan (sub nom Re St Chad's, Bensham)* [2017] Fam 68, that the outcome of a case for exhumation would have been different depending on whether the court followed the test in *Re Christ Church, Alsager* [1999] Fam 142 (Chancery Court of York) or that in *Re Blagdon Cemetery* [2002] Fam 299 (Court of Arches), is unconvincing and confected.
[56] Somewhat heavy weather was made of this straightforward proposition in *Re Lambeth Cemetery (sub nom Re Armstrong)* [2020] PTSR 2130.
[57] *Aston Cantlow and Wilmcote with Billesley Parochial Church Council v Wallbank* [2004] 1 AC 546, [2003] 3 WLR 283, [2003] 3 All ER 1213 (HL).
[58] Baker described the liability as 'One of the more unsightly blots on the history of English jurisprudence': JH Baker, 'Lay Rectors and Chancel Repairs' (1984) 100 *Law Quarterly Review* 181–85.
[59] At issue, although perhaps not immediately apparent from the papers filed by the parties, was whether the Church of England might be uniquely disadvantaged in enjoying the right to freedom of religion, guaranteed by Article 9 of the European Convention on Human Rights.
[60] See M Hill, 'Aston Cantlow v Wallbank: Defining the Public and Private Functions of the Establishes Church of England' in P Babie et al (eds), *Landmark Cases in Law and Religion* (Oxford, Hart Publishing, 2022) ch 9.
[61] *PCC of Aston Cantlow v Wallback* (n 57) [61] (HL) per Lord Hope of Craighead. Lord Rodger of Earlsferry (ibid [154]) put the matter as follows: 'The juridical nature of the Church is, notoriously, somewhat amorphous.'

and bodies that exist within its overall structure.⁶² The House of Lords ruled⁶³ that a PCC was not a core public authority for the purposes of the Human Rights Act 1998. As Lord Rodger of Earlsferry remarked:

> The key to the role of the PCC lies in the first of its general functions: cooperation with the minister in promoting in the parish the whole mission of the Church. Its other more particular functions are to be seen as ways of carrying out this general function. The mission of the Church is a religious mission, distinct from the secular mission of government, whether central or local. Founding on scriptural and other recognised authority, the Church seeks to serve the purposes of God, not those of the government carried on by the modern equivalents of Caesar and his proconsuls.⁶⁴

Lord Hope similarly identified the relevant act as the enforcement of a civil liability, and noted that the liability is one that arises under private law, enforceable by the PCC as a civil debt by virtue of the 1932 Act.⁶⁵ Nor, the majority found, is the PCC is a hybrid public authority, since the enforcement of chancel repair liability is a private act as opposed to the discharge of a public function. Lord Nichols dealt with this matter very shortly:

> [W]hen a parochial church council enforces, in accordance with the provisions of the Chancel Repairs Act 1932, a burdensome incident attached to the ownership of certain pieces of land: there is nothing particularly 'public' about this. This is no more a public act than is the enforcement of a restrictive covenant of which church land has the benefit.⁶⁶

The civil courts have also had occasion to consider the employment status of ministers of religion. In *President of the Methodist Conference v Preston*,⁶⁷ the Supreme Court ruled that a Methodist minister was not an employee and, accordingly, could not bring a claim for unfair dismissal in the employment tribunal.⁶⁸ The juridical tide had ebbed and flowed on office holders,⁶⁹ but the Supreme Court found that the spiritual character of the ministry did not give rise to a presumption against contractual intentions. The correct approach was to examine the rules and practices of the particular religious community in question. So far as freehold clergy of the Church of England were concerned, the opportunity to do so came in

---

⁶² ibid [84] (HL) per Lord Hobhouse of Woodborough.
⁶³ Lord Scott of Foscote dissenting, although agreeing that the enforcement of chancel repair liability did not amount to a public function.
⁶⁴ *PCC of Aston Cantlow v Wallback* (n 57) [156] (HL).
⁶⁵ ibid [63].
⁶⁶ ibid [16].
⁶⁷ *President of the Methodist Conference v Preston* [2013] UKSC 29.
⁶⁸ Lady Hale disagreed (ibid [49]): 'Everything about this arrangement looks contractual ...'.
⁶⁹ Lord Templeman, in *Davies v Presbyterian Church of Wales* [1986] 1 All ER 705, 709h, had previously said 'A pastor is called and accepts the call. He does not devote his working life but his whole life to the church and his religion. His duties are defined and his activities are dictated not by contract but by conscience. He is the servant of God.'

Sharpe v Bishop of Worcester,[70] where the Court of Appeal unanimously reversed the decision of the Employment Appeal Tribunal and held that the office of an incumbent was 'governed by a regime which is a part of ecclesiastical law. It is not the result of a contractual arrangement.'[71] As Lewison LJ put it, [i]n my judgment there are no features of the method of Rev Sharpe's [*sic*] appointment, the duties imposed upon him by law or the means by which he could be deprived of his benefice which would support the existence of a contract between him and either the bishop or the diocesan board of finance'.[72] Whether these and other decisions will need to be revisited in the light of common tenure remains to be see, but on its face the new regime under the Ecclesiastical Offices (Terms of Service) Measure 2009 does not create a contractual relationship, still less a impose a contract of employment. In sector ministry, such as hospital and military chaplaincies, the employer is the health authority or prison service, as appropriate. Similarly, college and school chaplains are employees of the institution they serve. In these circumstances, the relationship will be governed by a contract of employment. However, it is was held lawful for a bishop to withhold a licence, without which the priest concerned could not function in the institution, on the basis of a failure to comply with the Church's teaching on human sexuality.[73] The issue of the

---

[70] *Sharpe v Bishop of Worcester* [2015] EWCA Civ 399. While in previous generations, the senior judiciary were familiar with the proper form of address for clergy, the Court of Appeal judges (in common with some ecclesiastical judges) referred to the appellant as 'Reverend Sharpe' or 'Rev Sharpe'. Those familiar with Cluedo will have encountered 'Reverend Green', and Postman Pat receives the ministrations of 'Reverend Timms'. However, *Crockford's Clerical Directory* is clear: 'The form "Reverend Smith" or "The Reverend Smith" should never be used this side of the Atlantic. If the Christian name or initials are not known, the correct forms are (a) The Reverend – Smith, or The Reverend Mr/Mrs/Miss/Ms Smith (b) Mr/Mrs/Miss/Ms Smith and (c) The Reverend Mr/Mrs/Miss/Ms Smith at the first mention, and Mr/Mrs/Miss/Ms Smith thereafter.' This solecism has become a common place, unfortunately, in both civil and ecclesiastical case law.
[71] *Sharpe* (n 70) per Arden LJ [108]. Interestingly, in the year of the 800th anniversary of its sealing at Runnymede, Arden LJ (ibid [110]) made reference to the continuing relevance of Magna Carta; whilst Lewison LJ commented (ibid [135]) 'The right to appoint to an ecclesiastical office may seem a dry subject; but it was a hot topic throughout Europe in the Middle Ages.' The earlier chapters of this book should not be consigned to history. Contemporary judges still go back as far as the medieval period in their reasoning. The long reach of the ecclesiastical common law should not be underestimated. The legal historian, FW Maitland, claimed in 1898 that '[w]hen in any century, from the thirteenth to the nineteenth, an English lawyer indulges in a Latin maxim, he is generally, though of this he may be profoundly ignorant, quoting from the Sext' [a canon law text of 1298]: F Pollock and FW Maitland, *The History of English Law before the Time of Edward I*, vol 1 (Cambridge, Cambridge University Press, 2nd edn, 1898; repr Indianapolis, IN, Liberty Fund, 2010) 196.
[72] *Sharpe* (n 70) [182].
[73] *Pemberton v Inwood* [2018] EWCA Civ 564. The priest concerned had married his former civil partner following the coming force of the Marriage (Same Sex Couples) Act 2013. Reliance was placed on the House of Bishops' *Pastoral Guidance on Same Sex Marriage* (15 February 2014), which stated, at para 27, 'The House … considers that it would not be appropriate conduct for someone in holy orders to enter into a same sex marriage, given the need for clergy to model the Church's teaching in their lives.' Whether such a statement can still be considered declaratory of a universal opinion shared by the House of Bishops is questionable, as several, notably the Bishops of Oxford and Worcester, have publicly called for the Church of England to solemnise and to bless same-sex marriages: see https://oxford.anglican.org/news/same-sex-marriage-in-cofe.php.

employment status of ministers has developed to the extent that an entire book has been devoted to the topic.[74]

VII. Soft Law

Quasi-legislation or 'soft law' has come into greater prominence as a source of governance and regulation in the Church of England.[75] It comprises policy documents, regulations, directions, codes of practice, circulars, guidance and guidelines. Some of these are issued nationally, some at the provincial level and others by individual dioceses or bishops. Often their provenance and authority are obscure. They are interstitial in their nature, filling legislative lacunae, supplementing, clarifying and interpreting formal law. Of particular interest are Acts of Convocation and Statements by the House of Bishops. Such pronouncements are not law per se, nor do they have the force of a statute, but they have 'great moral force as the considered judgment of the highest and ancient synod of the province'.[76]

It is not uncommon for consistory courts to place reliance on quasi-legislation.[77] Further, quasi-legislation may have ramifications in the field of judicial review: it may create rights and duties, and may foster a legitimate expectation whereby disregard of its content might give rise to redress by way of a public law remedy in the Administrative Court.[78]

The weight to be given to guidance (in this instance on church seating) provided by the Church Buildings Council under the Dioceses, Mission and Pastoral Measure 2007, section 55(1)(d), was discussed in *Re All Saints West Burnley*.[79] The guidance includes a footnote suggesting that it should not be departed from unless the departure is justified by reasons that are spelled out clearly, logically and convincingly. A similar *in terrorem* enjoinder is highlighted in the *A Brief Guide to Contested Heritage in Cathedrals and Churches*.[80] Whilst the guidance will be

---

[74] J Duddington, *The Church and Employment Law: A Comparative Analysis of The Legal Status of Clergy and Religious Workers* (Abingdon, Routledge, 2022).

[75] See N Doe, 'Ecclesiastical Quasi-Legislation' in N Doe, M Hill and R Ombres (eds), *English Canon Law* (Cardiff, University of Wales Press, 1998) 93–103.

[76] This quotation is from the judgment in *Bland v Archdeacon of Cheltenham* [1972] Fam 157, 166; [1972] 1 All ER 1012, 1018, Court of Arches, and relates to an Act of Convocation, although the principle is of general application.

[77] See, by way of example, *Re St James, Shirley* [1994] Fam 134, where effect was given to a *Response by the House of Bishops to Questions Raised by Diocesan Chancellors* dated June 1992.

[78] See *R v Bishop of Stafford, ex parte Owen* (2000) 6 Ecclesiastical Law Journal 83 (CA).

[79] *Re All Saints West Burnley* [2017] ECC Bla 6.

[80] Cathedrals Fabric Commission for England, *A Brief Guide to Contested Heritage in Cathedrals and Churches* (2021). The warning reads: 'This guidance is issued by the Cathedrals Fabric Commission for England pursuant to its powers under section 3(3)(a) of the Care of Cathedrals Measure 2011, and by the Church Buildings Council pursuant to its powers under section 55 (1)(d) of the Dioceses, Mission and Pastoral Measure 2007. As it is statutory guidance, it must be considered with great care. The standards of good practice set out in the guidance should not be departed from unless the departure is justified by reasons that are spelled out clearly, logically and convincingly.'

given due weight by consistory courts having regard to its provenance, and the considerable collective expertise of the Council, its prescriptive tone is overstated and wrong at law. The guidance is only statutory to the extent that the Council[81] has a duty under section 55(1)(d) of the 2007 Measure 'to promote, in consultation with such other persons and organisations as it thinks fit, by means of guidance or otherwise, standards of good practice in relation to the use, care, conservation, repair, planning, design and development of churches'. There is no corresponding duty on third parties, such as diocesan chancellors, to follow such guidance as it thinks fit to issue,[82] and it is unfortunate that the Council has misstated the status of its guidance.[83]

Reference might also be made to the *Guidelines for the Professional Conduct of the Clergy* (2003, revised 2015). These guidelines were part of the reform involving clergy terms and conditions of service, linked with capability procedures. Their purpose was to create a common statement of expectation in relation to the behaviour of clergy. Their introduction coincided with the coming into force of the Clergy Discipline Measure 2003. Any complaint must allege 'misconduct' under section 8 of the Measure, which generally invokes section 8(1)(d), namely, 'conduct unbecoming or inappropriate to the office and work of a clerk in Holy Orders'. The detailed provisions of the Professional Conduct Guidelines now provide a yardstick by which any allegation may be measured. The Guidelines feature prominently in registrar's preliminary scrutiny reports, the designated officer's investigation reports and the President's determinations. It is rare for a bishop's disciplinary tribunal not to make reference to them in its written reasons. Accordingly, by repeated deployment in the well-documented clergy discipline jurisdiction, the soft law of the Guidelines is hardening.

VIII. Principles of Anglican Canon Law

The ecclesiastical law of and concerning the Church of England is *sui generis*. It is replicated nowhere else in the Anglican Communion. No other Anglican province is established, has representatives in the state legislature, is beholden to the Crown in relation to senior appointments, or is required to submit its laws for parliamentary approval. Yet the Anglican Communion claims a shared inheritance of doctrine and ecclesiology, and what the Latin Church refers to as Anglican

---

[81] And Cathedrals Fabric Commission.

[82] Note, eg, the Safeguarding and Clergy Discipline Measure 2016, which imposes a duty on bishops to have 'due regard' to safeguarding guidance issued by the House of Bishops.

[83] That said, a prospective amendment to the law may well impose a duty on diocesan chancellors to follow such advice on issues of contested heritage, unless there is a compelling countervailing reason for not doing so.

patrimony.[84] This is in marked contradistinction to the Latin Church itself, which enjoys a universal Code of Canon Law, reissued in 1983 and revised subsequently thereafter. This structural asymmetry[85] presented a difficulty for the groundbreaking work of the Colloquium of Anglican and Roman Catholic Canon Lawyers.[86]

This difficulty was ameliorated to a considerable degree by a project that had its origins in 2001, when the Primates' Meeting decided to explore whether there is an unwritten common law (or *ius commune*) shared by all the Provinces of the Anglican Communion, the principles of which may be induced from the profound similarities between the laws of those Provinces. A scoping study recognised the unwritten law common to the Churches of the Communion, and the Primates concluded that these shared principles of canon law may be understood to constitute a fifth instrument of unity.

A Network of Legal Advisers formed a Drafting Group that produced *The Principles of Canon Law Common to the Churches of the Anglican Communion*, launched at the Lambeth Conference in 2008.[87] In 2009, the Anglican Consultative Council commended the Principles for study in every Province, and invited each of them to submit comments on the document.[88] A second edition was launched at the Lambeth Conference in 2022 and commended for use in the Communion by the Anglican Consultative Council in 2023.[89] The *Principles* have a strong persuasive authority and are fundamental to the self-understanding of the Anglican Communion. They have a living force and contain the possibility of further development. Provincial independence is unaffected: Provinces remain entirely free to depart from any or all of them. However, the fact that different legal systems converge in shared principles of canon law is a concrete expression of the very character of Anglicanism, and, in so far as each Province contributes to the *Principles*, they are collectively responsible for shaping and maintaining Anglican identity.[90]

---

[84] In November 2009, Pope Benedict released the apostolic constitution *Anglicanorum coetibus*, creating a permanent home for Anglicans who wish to be reconciled to the Catholic Church but hoped to retain portions of their Anglican patrimony.

[85] For an authoritative study, see N Doe, *Canon Law in the Anglican Communion: A Worldwide Perspective* (Oxford, Clarendon Press, 1998).

[86] See M Hill et al, 'A Decade of Ecumenical Dialogue: A Report on the Proceedings of the Colloquium of Anglican and Roman Catholic Canon Lawyers 1999–2009' (2009) 11 *Ecclesiastical Law Journal* 284–328.

[87] The principles project was suggested by Norman Doe on the basis of his book (n 85); Doe then drafted candidate principles for consideration, revision and adoption by the Network. For the process and methodology used by the Network, see N Doe, 'The common law of the Anglican Communion' (2003) 7 *Ecclesiastical Law Journal* 4–16.

[88] ACC-14, Resolution 14.20 (5 May 2009).

[89] *The Principles of Canon Law Common to the Churches of the Anglican Communion*, 2nd edn (London, Anglican Consultative Council, 2022); ACC-18, Resolution 3(d) (February 2023): Legal Advisers' Network.

[90] They were invoked in a property dispute by the Supreme Court of British Columbia in the case of *Bentley v Anglican Synod of the Diocese of New Westminster* [2009] BCSC 1608, and have been cited with approval in secular litigation in a number of jurisdictions.

The *Principles* are not a 'top-down' global legal system imposed by a central Anglican authority but a 'grass-roots' development growing from the exercise by each Province of its own legislative autonomy. The *Principles* evidence just how much Anglicans share in common, using canon law as the medium for so doing. They also provide an accessible resource for ecumenical partners in understanding the nature of Anglicanism.[91] The coherent statement of *Principles* gives an ecclesial density to Anglican canon law, hitherto lacking in the disparate particular laws of the component Provinces. Notably, they assisted the Colloquium of Anglican and Roman Catholic Canon Lawyers to explore ways in which the respective laws of each tradition reveal profound similarities.[92]

IX. Safeguarding and the Seal of the Confessional

The period in question has been dominated by issues of historic sexual abuse and institutional cover up, not just within the Church of England but within other Churches, within the scout movement and other youth organisations, and within children's homes and local authority care. Church law has responded, though arguably too slowly and not far enough. The Safeguarding and Clergy Discipline Measure 2016 has imposed stricter requirements in relation to children and vulnerable adults, as has an entirely new Canon C30. Diocesan safeguarding staff are now obligatory for each diocese, as are designated officers in parishes. There is compulsory safeguarding training for clergy and volunteers, together with regular updating.

The Independent Inquiry into Child Sexual Abuse (IICSA) had a wide remit, which included the practices of the Church of England. It was established in March 2015 and published its final report in October 2022.[93] Its recommendations included the mandatory reporting of disclosures of child sexual abuse in certain cases,[94] and consideration of its application to the seal of the confessional.[95] In paragraph 109, the report concludes:

> Some core participants and witnesses argued that a mandatory reporting law ought to provide exemptions for some faith-based settings or personnel and, in particular, in

---

[91] See N Sagovsky, 'The contribution of canon law to Anglican-Roman Catholic ecumenism' (2011) 13 *Ecclesiastical Law Journal* 4–14.

[92] See Hill et al (n 86).

[93] See www.iicsa.org.uk/key-documents/31216/view/report-independent-inquiry-into-child-sexual-abuse-october-2022_0.pdf. It had previously published several interim reports, including a Case Study regarding Bishop Peter Ball and one on the Diocese of Chichester. The costs of the inquiry ran to some £186 million.

[94] Recommendation 13 would criminalise breaches of the duty: 'It should be a criminal offence for mandated reporters to fail to report child sexual abuse where they: are in receipt of a disclosure of child sexual abuse from a child or perpetrator; or witness a child being sexually abused.'

[95] The interim report on the Church of England deliberately left to the final report its recommendations in this regard: see www.iicsa.org.uk/reports-recommendations/publications/investigation/anglican-church/part-d-conclusions-and-recommendations/d1-conclusions-respect-church-england.

the context of sacramental confession. As the Inquiry has already noted, the respect of a range of religions or beliefs is recognised as a hallmark of a liberal democracy. Nonetheless, neither the freedom of religion or belief nor the rights of parents with regard to the education of their children can ever justify the ill-treatment of children or prevent governmental authorities from taking measures necessary to protect children from harm. The Inquiry therefore considers that mandatory reporting as set out in this report should be an absolute obligation; it should not be subject to exceptions based on relationships of confidentiality, religious or otherwise.[96]

Shortly before the publication of the final report, the Church of England announced the establishment of a working party, inter alia, to assist the House of Bishops and the Archbishops' Council in responding to the recommendations of IICSA concerning the seal of the confessional, including considering legal options.[97] Whether the Church of England will voluntarily change its doctrine and practice in relation to the sacrament of penance, as the Anglican Church of Australia has done, remains to be seen. If it declines to act, it may be that Parliament might consider enacting primary legislation disapplying the seal of the confessional, although it may be argued that this would constitute governmental overreach and a violation of the Article 9 rights of those Churches for whom the inviolability of the seal is a canonical duty, binding on priests.

X. The Future

Nearly 20 years on from the decision of the House of Lords in *PCC of Aston Cantlow v Wallbank*, defining and describing the cleavage between the public and private functions of the Church of England remains problematical. It is difficult to overstate the significance of the death of Her Late Majesty Queen Elizabeth II and the accession of King Charles III.[98] The Church of England is judicially recognised as essentially a religious organisation, not an organ of government. Whilst there may be some enduring symbolism in the retention of vestiges of establishment, the judgment seems to reinforce the prevalent mood of modern

---

[96] See www.iicsa.org.uk/key-documents/31216/view/report-independent-inquiry-into-child-sexual-abuse-october-2022_0.pdf.

[97] For a compilation of commentary on this complex issue, see M Hill and AK Thompson (eds), *Religious Confession and Evidential Privilege in the Twenty-first Century* (Sydney, Shepherd Street Press, 2021) esp M Hill and C Grout, 'The seal of the confessional, the Church of England and English Law' (ibid, ch 5).

[98] The deference owed to the late Queen following her 70 years of devoted service as monarch and Supreme Governor has been a powerful restraint on disestablishment. Her words, spoken on her 21st birthday in 1947, speak volumes: 'I declare before you all that my whole life whether it be long or short shall be devoted to your service and the service of our great imperial family to which we all belong.' Such deference and restraint died with her. For a prospective discussion, see the papers delivered at the Ecclesiastical Law Society Conference, *Church and State in the Post-Elizabethan Age* (March 2018).

secularism, side-lining religion into little more than a hobby or leisure pursuit.[99] Those agitating for disestablishment might well place reliance on the results of the 2021 Census, which indicate a declining number of British people who identify as Christian (47 per cent) and an increase in those who claim to be of no faith (37 per cent).[100] Humanists UK have invoked these statistics to justify disestablishment, removal of bishops from the House of Lords, and the end of compulsory religious education and acts of worship in schools.

The solemnisation of marriage was recognised in *PCC of Aston Cantlow v Wallback* as a public function of priests of the Church of England. In the two decades that have followed the judgment, the nature of marriage has changed almost beyond recognition. We have witnessed the introduction of civil partnerships,[101] and subsequently same-sex marriage.[102] Neither of these changes permitted the clergy of the Church of England to solemnise such unions. Further, a document issued by the House of Bishops indicated that it would not be appropriate to authorise a public liturgy to follow the solemnising of a same-sex marriage, or for clergy to provide a service of blessing.[103] But the mood of the nation, and perhaps also the Church of England,[104] seems to be changing.

On 20 January 2023, the House of Bishops published its Response to *Living in Love and Faith* (GS 2289). That response, in summary, comprised several elements: (i) a letter welcoming, accepting and affirming every person in Christ, and apologising for the way many LGBTQI+ people have been treated in the past; (ii) joyful affirmation of committed same-sex relationships and the provision of a resource in the form, *Prayers of Love and Faith*; (iii) re-affirmation that '[t]he Church of England continues to hold the received understanding of Holy Matrimony as between one man and one woman, as set forth in its canons and authorised liturgies'; and (iv) a pledge to publish new Pastoral Guidance to replace *Issues in Human Sexuality*. A separate document, *Prayers of Love and Faith: a note from the Legal Office*, sought to draw a clear distinction between civil marriage on the one hand and holy matrimony.[105] General Synod approved and adopted this report during its February 2023 group of sessions.[106] It was expected that draft liturgies and revised guidance would be tabled for consideration in July 2023, but further progress was deferred to a subsequent group of sessions. The Church of England is

---

[99] See J Rivers, 'The Secularisation of the British Constitution' (2012) 14 *Ecclesiastical Law Journal* 371–99.
[100] See www.ons.gov.uk/peoplepopulationandcommunity/culturalidentity/religion/bulletins/religionenglandandwales/census2021.
[101] Civil Partnership Act 2004, creating a legal union for same-sex couples, subsequently extended to opposite-sex couples in consequence of a decision of the Supreme Court in *R (on the application of Steinfeld and Keidan) v Secretary of State for International Development* [2017] UKSC 32.
[102] Marriage (Same Sex Couples) Act 2013.
[103] The *House of Bishops' Pastoral Guidance on Same Sex Marriage* (15 February 2014).
[104] See the Living in Love and Faith project.
[105] GS Misc 1339, 25 January 2023, para 3.
[106] The voting figures were decisive, but did not reach the two-thirds majority that would have been required had the proposal amounted to a change of doctrine.

divided, and confidence in the Archbishop of Canterbury as *primus inter pares* for the Anglican Communion has been openly questioned.[107]

XI. Conclusion

In terms of the legal history of the Church of England as an established Church, many believe we have now entered the end game. Centuries of church law – in the sense of the law of the state as it applies to the Church of England – are drawing to a close. As we enter the new Carolean era, the nature of the Church of England as the established Church in England is under question. The coronation of King Charles III on Saturday, 6 May 2023, contained many, though not all, of the religious trappings of those of previous monarchs, and the realm and commonwealth joined in the celebration. But with the growth of secularism and religious pluralism, and with constitutional reform threatening the presence of bishops in the legislature, many see the Church of England as increasingly irrelevant, both at home and overseas, as its status of primacy is diminished throughout the Anglican Communion. It is hard to conceive of the Church of England remaining a state church when its practice on equal marriage is discriminatory. Establishment is a rope of many threads. Those threads may be broken individually with no perceivable impact on establishment. But when a critical number of threads are severed, the rope can no longer hold. Some form of disestablishment or re-establishment is inevitable in the next decade, and it is likely that the historic nexus between the Church of England and the State will be lost in a generation. The Church of England will not cease to exist, but it will morph into a voluntary association: a members club, governed by its internal regulations. This will be by way of quasi-contract and not, as the preceding chapters of this volume so vibrantly demonstrate, as the law of the realm. And why not? Every other faith group operates in this manner, and has done so for centuries.

---

[107] See https://anglican.ink/2023/02/21/global-south-anglicans-no-longer-recognize-canterbury/.

Conclusion

NORMAN DOE AND STEPHEN COLEMAN

The periodised chapters in this book provide a comprehensive analysis of the principal legal landmarks in the evolution of the law of the established Church of England since the Reformation to the present day. They have disclosed that ecclesiastical law has played a significant part in the life of the Church of England over the centuries. It has been the focus of innumerable controversies, political and practical, spiritual and sacramental. The chapters depict an historical narrative, often much contested, that has directly conditioned the nature, identity and mission of the Church as it has played out its role as a national church.

The studies have also underscored the pervasiveness of the law in the life of the Church, nation and society – in governance and ministry, in doctrine and liturgy, in the rites of passage and in the administration of the temporal patrimony of the Church. In turn, the studies reveal a multifaceted understanding of the law itself, found, as it has been over the centuries, in a multiplicity of regulatory instruments – from parliamentary statutes, to canons ecclesiastical, through the decisions of the temporal and spiritual courts, to the learned discourses of common lawyers, civilians and clerical jurists. The contributors have made every effort to describe the law accurately, to explain it not least on the assumptions of the stakeholders involved (sometimes clear, sometimes obscure) and to evaluate it in accordance with the wide range of criteria operative as the centuries unfolded as well as in retrospect.

This short conclusion draws together reflections on the discussions in each of the chapters in the contexts of their purpose, content, angle and relevance to an understanding of the legal history of the Church of England over the centuries. Above all, this conclusion summarises the principal findings through the lens of juridical and wider ecclesial continuity and change.

Sarah White provides an expert treatment of the medieval antecedents of the ecclesiastical law as it was to develop at the Reformation. Before the Reformation, the Roman Church in England was regulated by 'foreign' law made by the pope and 'domestic' law made by archbishops and papal legates in England – it was administered by church courts, and it was studied and commented upon by jurists such as Lyndwood. Dr White shows how canon law brought order to the Church, how it necessitated in the Church the professionalisation of its lawyers, how its courts asserted spiritual authority (though there were secular mechanisms to police it) and how canon law expanded into the lives of ordinary people in a wide range of areas. All in all, church law was a reality in England before the Reformation. The scene is set.

Michelle Johnson, with Will Adam, helps us understand the legal complexities of the first phase of the Reformation itself in the critical period 1533–58. The study proposes that the Reformation included a legal revolution. The law played a fundamental role in the break from Rome when we see the rise of 'the King's Ecclesiastical Law'. Acts of Parliament under Henry VIII terminate papal jurisdiction in England and effect the legal establishment of the Church of England as a national church under the royal supremacy. Statute declares that clerical Convocations may make Canons with royal assent. The political factors in legal change are clear: parliamentary statutes transfer papal powers to the Crown; this legal 'revolution' stimulated the development of the idea of parliamentary supremacy (over religion, in nationalising the Church); and pre-Reformation Roman canon law continued to apply in England on the basis of statute and its reception, provided that law was not repugnant to the law of the realm and until reviewed by a royal commission. There were changes to the structure of the church courts (ending appeals to Rome), the rise of polemical works with a high juridical content (like those of Christopher St German), and the demise of the canon law faculties at Oxford and Cambridge – and Doctors Commons is a civilian monopoly. 'Protestantism' and uniformity of worship come under Edward VI – and the law is the medium. However, using parliamentary statute, England returns to Rome under Mary – the reforming statutes are repealed. But Elizabeth reverses the Marian reform in a new Anglican settlement. In the space of these 50 years, change is the dominant force: the Church is established under Henry, disestablished under Mary and re-established under Elizabeth.

Taking the period 1558–1603, Paul Barber and Morag Ellis explore how Elizabeth I and her government used law to convert an ecclesial and legal 'revolution' (under Henry, reversed under Mary) into a 'settlement'. The law was used to steer a course between the radical puritans and the recusant Catholics – who both were a threat to the endeavour – a course clothed in constitutional propriety and articulated juristically and theologically in Hooker's influential book, *The Laws of Ecclesiastical Polity*. Parliamentary statutes re-establish the Church of England, revive legislation made under Henry VIII and Edward VI, and impose uniformity in worship throughout the realm (with a single Book of Common Prayer). *Cawdrey's Case* confirms the continuing applicability of Roman canon law, provided that law has been received. The church courts thrive, over clergy and laity, over marriage, wills and much else. Hooker is not the sole contributor to ecclesiastical jurisprudence – there is also, for example, the great Swinbourne. The period also sees the use of 'soft law', such as Articles (on doctrine), Admonitions (on marriage) and Advertisements (on church order); Parliament rejected the *Reformatio Legum Ecclesiasticarum* in 1571, but there were piecemeal Canons in 1571, 1575, 1585 and 1598, which heralded the canonical codification under James.

Ian Blaney explores the years 1603 to 1660. What extraordinary years these were. He argues that they were largely preoccupied with controversy about the source and limit of the king's ecclesiastical law. The tumultuous years of the first two Stuarts saw conflict about the nature of ecclesiastical authority, the demise of the king's ecclesiastical law after the Civil War, and the new 'law on religion' in the Commonwealth. A new code of Canons was promulged 1603/04 under James I. Archbishop Laud tightened ecclesial discipline under Charles I. Soft law continued to be used with archiepiscopal 'instructions'. The Canons of 1640 were rejected. Conflict between king and Parliament resulted in the abolition of episcopacy and the (Tudor) High Commission and, after the Civil War, of monarchy itself, with the royal supremacy in ecclesiastical causes terminated. The Republic enacted 'ordinances' on a wide range of subjects and 'established' a presbyterian church government. Lawyers contributed much to the development of ecclesiastical jurisprudence – such as Coke, the common lawyer under the Stuarts, Matthew Sheppard in the Republic, and the civilians Zouche, Cowell and Ridley across the period. The period also saw developments in the limited legal protection of religious conscience, the birth pangs of the idea of 'religion law' in the keeping of the state, and it demonstrates vividly the provisionality of a legal establishment for the English Church.

But change was in the air. The Restoration of the monarchy meant the re-establishment of the Church of England in 1660. Russell Sandberg guides us through the development of the re-established king's ecclesiastical law through to 1701. He shows how law is used to erase the 'juridical memory' of the Commonwealth, to enable Parliament to assert its dominance over the Crown in religious matters, and to effect a sea-change from 'Anglican monarchy' to a consolidated parliamentary supremacy in religion. The Restoration statutes include the 'Clarendon Code' on the limits of religious dissent, a new Book of Common Prayer in 1662, and the rise of a greater religious toleration with the Bill of Rights 1689 and the securing of the Protestant succession under the Act of Settlement 1701. The period is also significant for its case law and the works of jurists such as Simon Degge, William Watson and John Godolphin. The period may be summed up as reflecting the durability of the principle of ecclesiastical establishment, but with new freedoms and limitations associated with its scope.

However, the Whig legal principle of toleration of dissent opened a new fear for the Tory faction: the Church was in danger. And so, for the years 1701–60, Stephen Coleman explores the impact on ecclesiastical law of the transition from the Stuarts to the Hanoverians. Laws were created to protect 'the church in danger', to combat Jacobitism and its tendency towards Roman Catholicism, and to mediate over patronage, which was important as a political tool for ecclesial identity. There was a boom in commentaries on ecclesiastical law, such as those of Nelson (common lawyer), Ayliffe and Oughton (civilians), and Gibson (clerical jurist) – they all developed a juridical conception of the Church. But there were reforms: the statutory Queen Anne's Bounty for the maintenance of clergy; the adjustment of patronage legislation; and, for the law of marriage, Lord Hardwicke's Marriage Act 1753. The Church and its clergy are less active in the creation of canon law (with the demise of the Convocation in this period). The church courts begin to show signs of decline, and the courts of the common law flex their muscles, particularly in the momentous the case of *Middleton v Crofts* (1736), which held that the Canons Ecclesiastical 1603/04 did not bind the lay people – they were simply creatures of the clerical Convocation, and not approved by Parliament. The case may also be seen as significant in the development of the idea of religious freedom.

The reign of the last four Hanoverians, 1760–1837, saw the Anglican monopoly in Parliament eroded, resulting in a trend towards the secularisation of ecclesiastical law as a merely functional rule-based system of law that had lost a clear 'Anglican' and distinctively religious character. Parliament's legislative output, however, was prolific: 299 statutes on ecclesiastical law. The legal landmarks were the creation of an established United Church of England and Ireland; the incorporation of Doctors Commons; the emergence of Richard Burn as a leading commentator on ecclesiastical law; and a subtle shift away from the idea of religious toleration to the rise of that of religious freedom, including Roman Catholic emancipation. New laws were made for the clergy, on ordination, on membership of the House of Commons (which was forbidden), and on pluralities and residence. There was a decline in clergy and lay discipline litigation, but an increase in case law on public order at divine service, baptism and burial, as well as new statutes on civil marriage, new parishes, improvements in the law on clerical income, tithes, church rates and the Ecclesiastical Commissioners. A study of the period also demonstrates the benefits of a sociological approach to the legal history of the Church of England as it faces: new issues about its parochial ministry; new challenges from Evangelicalism within and Nonconformists without; and the impact of the Industrial Revolution and population growth – pluralism is a key factor.

Charlotte Smith casts an expert and analytical eye over the law in the age of Victoria (1837–1901). Whatever the general form and status of the ecclesiastical law (as the law of the land), its character was, in reality, that of law applicable to one faith body among many – the Church of England was ever more distinct from the nation to which it was constitutionally bound. The law reflects this as an expression of revival and reform, typified in the Oxford Movement, and experiments in church governance. Litigation in the spiritual and temporal courts saw a fight for the soul of the Church with an abundance of ritualist legislation and cases. The church courts were reformed at all levels, and parliamentary statute transferred matrimonial and probate matters from them to secular courts. One by-product was the end of the ecclesiastical law profession centred on Doctors' Commons, though commentaries (such as those by Rogers, Cripps, Stephens and Phillimore) continued to find a market. While portrayals of the Victorian Church as unchanging and somnolent are in part accurate, they mask considerable adaptation and evolution in the law of the Church. Moreover, ecclesiastical law was in this period a source of perplexity and ambiguity in a rapidly changing social, political and constitutional context, and its essential nature and authority – whether spiritual or legal – was increasingly debated, as was Parliament's role in it as its principal legislator.

The two World Wars provide the wider political setting for the development of English ecclesiastical law in the years 1901–47. The 'new world' explored by Russell Dewhurst opens with debate about the time spent by, and the fitness of, an increasingly otherwise-occupied and non-Anglican Parliament to continue as the principal legislator for the Church. And this debate results in the creation by the Church itself of a new legislature for the Church of England – the Church Assembly, empowered by Parliament in the shape of the Church of England Assembly (Powers) Act 1919 to legislate for the Church by way of Measures. This 'Enabling Act' gave to Measures the same force as Acts of Parliament once approved by Parliament and given the royal assent; and it enabled, for the first time, the laity as part of the Church Assembly to legislate at the highest ecclesial level. In 1920, pursuant to the Welsh Church Act 1914, the Church of England in Wales was disestablished; the Act was opposed by the House of Lords and the Parliament Act 1911 was used, for the first time, to enact it. The 1920s saw the Church Assembly flex its legislative muscles with the first of an ever increasing new body of ecclesiastical law in the form of Measures. Ritual and ceremonial continued to be problematic, not least when Parliament rejected the proposed Prayer Book revision in 1928 and permitted remarriage of divorced persons in church in 1937, provided no cleric with a conscientious objection was compelled to solemnise such a marriage. Landmark cases include that of *Thompson v Dibdin* (1910): clergy could not refuse Holy Communion to a person whose marriage was valid under the law of the state. The period also saw the rise of Halsbury as the dominant practitioner commentary on ecclesiastical law. Crucially, the shift in ecclesiastical legislative activity from Parliament (profuse in Victoria's reign) to the Church's own legislature (the Church Assembly) is a further piece in the jigsaw that portrays the ecclesiastical law more fully as law made by the Church for its own mission.

Change continued after the Second World War, as Neil Patterson explains for the years 1947–94. There was administrative rationalisation in the fields of property and finance with the creation of the Church Commissioners. Canonical revision led to a new code of Canons Ecclesiastical. The church courts were restructured by the Ecclesiastical Jurisdiction Measure 1963. The Church Assembly was reconstituted as the General Synod under the Synodical Government Measure 1969. Doctrinal and liturgical development were put more firmly in the keeping of the Church itself with the Worship and Doctrine Measure 1974. New ecumenical laws were passed in the 1980s. The ordination of women priests came in 1994. Halsbury continued to be the principal commentary, but the Ecclesiastical Law Society was set up in 1987, which stimulated the study of church law. Throughout, political and theological forces play their part: the law is the battleground. Moreover, some of these changes may be seen as effecting a form of 'partial disestablishment' and 'liberalisation' when viewed from the perspective of pressures from secular culture and society on the evolving ecclesiastical law.

These and other pressures are, according to Mark Hill, especially evidence from 1994 to 2022, years he suggests in which secularism and globalism impact on the ecclesiastical law. Moreover, the speed of legal change quickens. This is evidenced by new Measures on: the establishment of a secular cabinet-style executive, the Archbishops' Council (1998); clergy discipline (2003), itself undergoing reform today; the ordination of women bishops (2014); cathedrals (1999 and 2022); the faculty jurisdiction of church courts over consecrated property (2018); and facilitating easier legislative reform by the (executive) Archbishops' Council but with synodical safeguards (2018). There has also been a dramatic increase in ecclesiastical soft law (with a host of new codes of practice and the like). The monopoly of Halsbury as *the* commentary was broken with the appearance of Hill on ecclesiastical law in 1995 (and to a lesser extent Doe in 1996 and Leeder in 1997). The Covid-19 pandemic tested the efficacy of legal rules in the Church and their relaxation on the basis of necessity. Case law with regard to the exercise of the faculty jurisdiction continued to develop apace. Though an initiative of the non-established Church in Wales, English ecclesiastical law contributed a great deal to the global statement of principles of canon law common to churches of the Anglican Communion (2008, revised 2022). The period is also important for the impact on ecclesiastical law of secular forces such as the Equality Act 2010, Human Rights Act 1998 and, till Brexit, European Union law (in areas such as data protection). In all this, Mark Hill rightly asks whether the established status of the Church of England will be sustainable in the future.

However, in the meantime, the Church of England still exists as the established Church in England. Its ecclesiastical law still exists. That law is still the site of political and theological debate about its purposes as a servant of the Church – to facilitate and to order church life. Its makers have changed: what began life in the Middle Ages as the law of the Church made by the Church for the Church, at the time of the Reformation became law made by the state, to maintain the autonomy of the Church to the exclusion of its religious rivals. The historic legal trajectory is characterised by this tension between the legal maintenance of the established nature and position of the Church of England to the legal regulation of an ever-decreasing Anglican minority within the context of an ever-increasing religious pluralism in England. The role of the state in making church law has diminished, but not disappeared, as evidenced in the process to make Measures. But the renaissance in the creation of Canons, following the dormancy of the Convocations from the eighteenth to the nineteenth centuries, and the central role in Canon-making played today by the General Synod, means that English ecclesiastical law has in many ways returned to its original function – as the law of a faith community made by that community for that community as it discharges its mission to wider society.

While historically the law of the Church has undergone profound changes over the centuries since the Reformation, to address mischiefs faced by the Church – to right wrongs – and to adapt the Church to the ever-changing circumstances to which its law applies, there is equally profound continuity in the fundamentals that underlie that law, and which it seeks to articulate. Namely: the royal supremacy; representative government for the Church; a threefold ordained ministry of deacons, priests and bishops; lay office-holding at all levels; doctrine grounded in Scripture; an adaptable liturgy; the accessibility of the rites of passage; and the stewardship of church property – and all this for a national Christian ministry under the law in a changing world, as the Church of England moves towards its 500th anniversary.

BIBLIOGRAPHY

A Gentleman of Doctors Commons, *The Clerk's Instructor in the Ecclesiastical Courts* (Dublin, 1766).
Adams, N, 'The Writ of Prohibition to Court Christian' (1936) 20 *Minnesota Law Review* 272–93.
Adams, N and Donahue, C (eds), *Select Cases from the Ecclesiastical Courts of the Province of Canterbury, c 1200-1301* (London, Selden Society, 1981).
Aklundh, J, 'The Church Courts in Restoration England, 1660–c 1689' (PhD Thesis, University of Cambridge, 2008).
Alvarez de las Asturias, N, *La 'Collectio Lanfranci': Origine e Influenza Di Una Collezione Della Chiesa Anglo-Normanna* (Milan, Giuffrè Editore, 2008).
Anderson, S, 'Parliament' in W Cornish et al (eds), *Oxford History of the Laws of England*, vol XI: *1820-1914 English Legal System* (Oxford, Oxford University Press, 2010) pt 2, ch I, 301–41.
——, 'The Church and the State' in W Cornish et al (eds), *Oxford History of the Laws of England*, vol XI: *1820-1914 English Legal System* (Oxford, Oxford University Press, 2010) pt 2, ch III, 385–400.
Anglican Communion Legal Advisers Network, *The Principles of Canon Law Common to the Churches of the Anglican Communion*, 2nd edn (London, Anglican Consultative Council, 2022).
Ashley, M, *The Glorious Revolution of 1688* (London, Hodder & Stoughton, 1966).
Austin, G, *Shaping Church Law Around the Year 1000: The Decretum of Burchard of Worms* (Aldershot, Ashgate Publishing Ltd, 2009).
Avis, P, 'Bishops in Communion' (2017) 13 *Ecclesiology* 299–323.
Avis, P, 'Polity and Polemics: The Function of Ecclesiastical Polity in Theology and Practice' (2016) 18 *Ecclesiastical Law Journal* 2–13.
Ayliffe, J, *Parergon Juris Canonici Anglicani* (1726).
Aylmer, GE, 'Introduction: the Quest for Settlement 1646–1660' in GE Aylmer (ed), *The Interregnum: The Quest for Settlement* (London, Macmillan, 1972) 1–28.
—— (ed), *The Interregnum: The Quest for Settlement* (London, Macmillan, 1972).
Baker, JH, *An Introduction to English Legal History*, 5th edn (Oxford, Oxford University Press, 2019).
Baker, JH, 'Lay Rectors and Chancel Repairs' (1984) 100 *Law Quarterly Review* 181–85.
—— (ed), *Reports from the Lost Notebooks of Sir James Dyer* (London, Selden Society, 1994).
——, 'Sir Robert Phillimore, QC, DCL (1885)' (1997) 4 *Ecclesiastical Law Journal* 709–19.
——, *Monuments of Endlesse Labours: English Canonists and their Work 1300-1900* (London, Hambledon Press, 1998).
——, 'Some Elizabethan Marriage Cases' in TL Harris (ed), *Studies in Canon Law and Common Law in Honor of RH Helmholz* (Berkeley, CA, The Robbins Collection, 2015) 181–211.
Barber, P, 'The Fall and Rise of Doctors Commons?' (1996) 4 *Ecclesiastical Law Journal* 462–69.
Barnes, AS, *Bishop Barlow and Anglican Orders* (London, Longmans, 1922).
Barrister, *The Ecclesiastical Legal Guide* (1839).
Barton, J and Plucknett, T (eds), *Christopher St German: Doctor and Student* (London, Selden Society, 1975).
Behrens, B, 'A note on Henry VIII's divorce project of 1514' (1934) 11 *Bulletin of the Institute of Historical Research* 163–64.
Bellomo, M, *The Common Legal Past of Europe, 1000-1800* (Washington, DC, Catholic University of America Press, 1995).
Bennet, B, 'Banister v Thompson and Afterwards: The Church of England and the Deceased Wife's Sister's Marriage Act' (1998) 49 *Journal of Ecclesiastical History* 668–82.

242 Bibliography

Bentley, J, *Ritualism and Politics in Victorian Britain: The Attempt to Legislate for Belief* (Oxford, Oxford University Press, 1978).

Bernard, GW, *The King's Reformation: Henry VIII and the Remaking of the English Church* (New Haven, CT, Yale University Press, 2005).

——, *The Late Medieval English Church: Vitality and Vulnerability before the Break with Rome* (New Haven, CT, Yale University Press, 2012).

Bertram, M, 'The Late Middle Ages: Four Remarks Regarding the Present State of Research,' in A Winroth and JC Wei (eds), *The Cambridge History of Medieval Canon Law* (Cambridge, Cambridge University Press, 2022) 108–21.

Best, GFA, *Temporal Pillars : Queen Anne's Bounty, the Ecclesiastical Commissioners, and the Church of England* (Cambridge, Cambridge University Press, 1964).

Bicknell, EJ, *A Theological Introduction to the Thirty-Nine Articles of the Church of England* (London, Longmans, 1925; 3rd edn, 1955).

Boulton, P, 'Twentieth-Century Revision of Canon Law in the Church of England' (2000) 5 *Ecclesiastical Law Journal* 353–68.

Boyle, LE, 'The Beginnings of Legal Studies at Oxford' (1983) 14 *Viator* 107–32.

——, 'Canon Law before 1380' in JI Catto (ed), *History of the University of Oxford*, vol I: *The Early Oxford Schools* (Oxford, Oxford University Press, 1984) 1–36.

Bradshaw, P, *A Companion to Common Worship* (London, SPCK, 2006).

Brand, P, *The Origins of the English Legal Profession* (Oxford, Blackwell, 1992).

——, 'The Common Lawyers of the Reign of Edward I and the Canon Law' in TL Harris (ed), *Studies in Canon Law and Common Law in Honor of RH Helmholz* (Berkeley, CA, The Robbins Collection, 2015) 27–40.

Brasington, B, *Order in the Court: Medieval Procedural Treatises in Translation* (Leiden, Brill, 2016).

Bray, G (ed), *The Anglican Canons 1529–1947* (Woodbridge, Boydell Press, 1998).

——, 'The Strange Afterlife of the *Reformatio Legum Ecclesiasticarum*' in N Doe, M Hill and R Ombres (eds), *English Canon Law* (Cardiff, University of Wales Press, 1998) 36–47.

—— (ed), *Tudor Church Reform: The Henrician Canons of 1535 and the Reformatio Legum Ecclesiasticarum* (Woodbridge, Boydell Press, 2000).

—— (ed), *Records of Convocation* (Woodbridge, Boydell Press, 2006).

——, 'Canon Law and the Church of England' in A Milton (ed), *The Oxford History of Anglicanism*, vol 1: *Reformation and Identity c 1520–1662* (Oxford, Oxford University Press, 2017) 168–85.

——, *Canon Law and the Anglican Church* (Martlesham, Boydell & Brewer, 2018).

—— (ed), *Documents of the English Reformation* (Cambridge, James Clarke & Co, 1994 and 2019).

—— (ed), *The Development of the Canons: A Historical Study and Summary of the Church of England's Canons 1969 to 2020* (London, Latimer Trust, 2022).

Brook, A, 'The Chancellors' Dilemma: The Impact of the First World War on Faculty Jurisdiction' (2020) 56 *Studies in Church History* 471–86.

Brooke, CNL, 'The Archdeacon and the Norman Conquest' in DE Greenway, CJ Holdsworth and JE Sayers (eds), *Tradition and Change: Essays in Honour of Marjorie Chibnall Presented by Her Friends on the Occasion of Her Seventieth Birthday* (Cambridge, Cambridge University Press, 1985) 1–19.

Brown, RL, 'Pastoral Problems and Legal Solutions' in N Doe (ed), *Essays in Canon Law: A Study of the Law of the Church in Wales* (Cardiff, University of Wales Press, 1992) 9–12.

——, 'The Age of the Saints to the Victorian Church' in N Doe (ed), *A New History of the Church in Wales: Governance and Ministry, Theology and Society* (Cambridge, Cambridge University Press, 2020) 9–26.

Brundage, JA, *Medieval Canon Law* (London, Longman, 1995).

——, 'The Calumny Oath and Ethical Ideals of Canonical Advocates' in *Proceedings of the Ninth International Congress of Medieval Canon Law: Munich, 13–18 July 1992* (Vatican City, 1997) 793–805.

——, *The Medieval Origins of the Legal Profession: Canonists, Civilians, and Courts* (Chicago, IL, University of Chicago Press, 2008).

——, 'The Practice of Canon Law' in W Hartmann and K Pennington (eds), *The History of Courts and Procedure in Medieval Canon Law* (Washington, DC, Catholic University of America Press, 2016) 55–56.
Bryson, WH, *The Equity Side of the Exchequer* (Cambridge, Cambridge University Press, 1975).
—— (ed), *Miscellaneous Reports of Cases in the Court of Delegates: From 1670 to 1750* (Richmond, VA, Centre for Law Reporting, 2016).
Buchanan, C, *Confirmation – the Excluding Feature? A Study of Anglican Confirmation in Its Ecumenical Implications 1870–1920* (Leiden, Brill, 2019).
Bullard, JV and Bell, HC (eds), *Lyndwood's Provinciale: The Text of the Canons Therein Contained, Reprinted from the Translation Made in 1543* (London, Faith Press, 1929).
Bullingbroke, E, *Ecclesiastical Law* (1770).
Burden, J, 'Reading Burchard's Corrector: Penance and Canon Law' (2019) 46 *Journal of Medieval History* 77–97.
Burn, R, *Ecclesiastical Law* (1763; 3rd edn, 1775).
Burns, A, *The Diocesan Revival in the Church of England, c 1800–1870* (Oxford, Oxford University Press, 1999).
——, 'The Costs and Benefits of Establishment' (2000) 18 *Parliamentary History* 81–95.
Bursell, RH, *Liturgy, Order and the Law* (Oxford, Clarendon Press, 1996).
——, 'Consecration, *Ius Liturgicum*, and the Canons' in N Doe, M Hill and R Ombres (eds), *English Canon Law* (Cardiff, University of Wales Press, 1998) 71–81.
——, 'The Parson's Freehold' (2008) 2 *Ecclesiastical Law Journal* 259–67.
Burton, C, *Considerations on the Ecclesiastical Courts and Clergy Discipline* (London, James Parker & Co, 1875).
Bush, G, 'Dr Codex Silenced: *Middleton v Crofts* Revisited' (2003) 24 *Journal of Legal History* 23–58.
Bush, ML, 'The Tudor Polity and the Pilgrimage of Grace' (2007) 80 *Bulletin of the Institute of Historical Research* 47–72.
Canons Ecclesiastical promulged by the Convocations of Canterbury and York in 1964 and 1969, *The Canons of the Church of England* (London, SPCK, 1969).
Cardwell, E, *Documentary Annals of the Reformed Church of England* (Oxford, Oxford University Press, 1844).
Carlson, EJ, 'Marriage Reform and the Elizabethan High Commission' (1990) 21 *The Sixteenth Century Journal* 437–52.
Carlson, LH, 'The Court of High Commission: A Newly Discovered Elizabethan Letters Patent, 20 June 1589' (1982) 45 *Huntingdon Library Quarterly* 295–315.
Chadwick, O, *The Victorian Church*, 2 vols (London, Adam and Charles Black, 1966 and 1970).
Chandler, A, *The Church of England in the Twentieth Century* (Woodbridge, Boydell Press, 2009).
Chaplin, J, *Beyond Establishment: Resetting Church State Relations in England* (London, SCM Press, 2022).
Chapman, C, *Ecclesiastical Courts, their Officials and their Records* (Dursley, Lochin Publishing, 1992).
Chapman, M and Whyte, W (eds), *The Established Church: Past, Present and Future* (London, T & T Clark, 2011).
Child, GW, *Church and State under the Tudors* (New York, Lennox Hill, 1974).
Chrimes, SB, 'Richard II's Questions to the Judges, 1387' (1956) 73 *Law Quarterly Review* 365–90.
Church Assembly Commission (appointed in June 1949), *Church and State: Report* (London, Church Information Board, 1952).
Church of England and Archbishops' Committee on Church and State, *The Archbishops' Committee on Church and State: Report, with Appendices* (London, SPCK, 1916).
Churchill, IJ, *Canterbury Administration: The Administrative Machinery of the Archbishopric of Canterbury Illustrated from Original Records*, 2 vols (London: SPCK for the Church Historical Society, 1933).
Clark, JCD, 'Church, Parties, Politics' in J Gregory (ed), *The Oxford History of Anglicanism*, vol II: *Establishment and Empire, 1662–1829* (Oxford, Oxford University Press, 2017) 289–313.

Clavering, H, *The New and Complete Parish Officer … A Complete Library of Parish Law*, 8th edn (London, W and J Stratford, 1808).
Cobban, AB, 'Theology and Law in the Medieval Colleges of Oxford and Cambridge' (30 September 1982) 65 *Bulletin of the John Rylands Library* 57.
Cockburn, W, *The Clerk's Assistant in the Practice of the Ecclesiastical Courts* (2nd edn 1756; 4th edn, 1792).
Collins, JR, 'The Church Settlement of Oliver Cromwell' (2002) 87 *History* 18–40.
Collinson, P, *Archbishop Grindal 1519-1583: The Struggle for a Reformed Church* (London, Jonathan Cape 1979).
——, 'The Prophesyings and the Downfall and Sequestration of Archbishop Edmund Grindal 1576-1583' in M Barber, S Taylor and G Sewell (eds), *From the Reformation to the Permissive Society* (Woodbridge, Boydell Press, 2010) 1–41.
Collinson, P, Craig, J and Usher, B (eds), *Conferences and Combination Lectures in the Elizabethan Church, 1582-1590* (Woodbridge, Boydell Press, 2003).
Commission appointed by His Grace the Archbishop of Canterbury, Report: *Kindred and Affinity as Impediments to Marriage* (London, SPCK, 1940).
Commission into the Constitution and Working of the Ecclesiastical Courts, Report: *Ecclesiastical Courts* (1883).
Coombs, H and Bax, AN (eds), *Journal of a Somerset Rector: John Skinner, AM, Antiquary, 1772-1839* (London, Murray, 1930).
Coquillette, DR, 'Legal Ideology and Incorporation I: The English Civilian Writers, 1523–1607' (1981) 61 *Boston University Law Review* 1–89.
Cowell, J, *The Interpreter* (Oxford, John Legate, 1607).
Craik, D, *Hannah* (London, Harper and Bros, 1871).
Cripps, HW, *A Practical Treatise on the Law Relating to the Church and Clergy*, 8th edn (London, Sweet & Maxwell, 1937).
Cromartie, A, *Sir Matthew Hale 1609-1676: Law, Religion and Natural Philosophy* (Cambridge, Cambridge University Press, 1995).
Cross, C, 'The Church in England 1646-1660' in GE Aylmer (ed), *The Interregnum: The Quest for Settlement 1646-1660* (London, Macmillan, 1972) 99–120.
——, *Church and People, 1450-1660: The Triumph of the Laity in the English Church* (London, Wiley & Sons, 1976).
Cruickshank, D, 'Debating the Legal Status of the Ornaments Rubric: Ritualism and Royal Commissions in Late Nineteenth- and Early Twentieth-Century England' (2020) 56 *Studies in Church History* 434–54.
Cummins, D, 'The Social Significance of Tithes in Eighteenth-Century England' (2013) 128 *English Historical Review* 1129–54.
Cunningham, T, *The Law of Simony* (London, His Majesty's Law Printers, 1784).
Daniell, D, *William Tyndale: A Biography* (New Haven, CT, Yale University Press, 1994).
——, *The Bible in English: its history and influence* (New Haven, CT, Yale University Press, 2003).
Davies, J, *The Caroline Captivity of the Church* (Oxford, Oxford University Press, 1992).
Dawson, I and Dunn, A, 'Seeking the Principle: Chancels, Choices and Human Rights' (2002) 22 *Legal Studies* 238–58.
Degge, S, *The Parson's Counsellor* with *The Law of Tithes or Tithing* (1676; 7th edn, 1703).
De Haas, E and Hall, GDG, *Early Registers of Writs* (London, Selden Society, 1970).
Denton, JH, 'The Making of the Articuli Clerici of 1316' (1986) 101 *Ecclesiastical History Review* 564–89.
Dickens, A, *The English Reformation* (London, Batsford, 1964).
Dixon, RW, *History of the Church of England*, vol V: *1558–1563* (Oxford, Clarendon Press, 1902).
Doe, N, *Fundamental Authority in Late Medieval English Law* (Cambridge, Cambridge University Press, 1991).
——, *The Legal Framework of the Church of England* (Oxford, Clarendon Press, 1996).

——, *Canon Law in the Anglican Communion: A Worldwide Perspective* (Oxford, Clarendon Press, 1998).
——, 'Ecclesiastical Quasi-Legislation' in N Doe, M Hill and R Ombres (eds), *English Canon Law: Essays in Honour of Bishop Eric Kemp* (Cardiff, University of Wales Press, 1998) 93–103.
——, 'The common law of the Anglican Communion' (2003) 7 *Ecclesiastical Law Journal* 4–16.
——, 'Richard Hooker, Priest and Jurist' in M Hill and RH Helmholz (eds), *Great Christian Jurists in English History* (Cambridge, Cambridge University Press, 2017) 115–37.
——, *The Legal Architecture of English Cathedrals* (Abingdon, Routledge, 2017).
——, 'Rediscovering Anglican Priest-Jurists II: Samuel Hallifax (1735–90)' (2020) 22 *Ecclesiastical Law Journal* 48–66.
——, 'The Welsh Church Act 1914: A Century of Constitutional Freedom for the Church in Wales?' (2020) 22 *Ecclesiastical Law Journal* 2–14.
——, 'Pre-Reformation Roman Canon Law in Post-Reformation English Ecclesiastical Law' (2022) 24 *Ecclesiastical Law Journal* 273–94.
——, 'Rediscovering Anglican Priest-Jurists IV: Robert Sanderson (1587–1663)' (2022) 24 *Ecclesiastical Law Journal* 68–86.
——, 'Rediscovering Anglican-Priest-Jurists V: Ralph Lever (c 1530–1585)' (2023) 25 *Ecclesiastical Law Journal* 66–80.
——, '"Legalists and Moralists" in the Historic Portrayal of the Constitution of the Church of England' (2023) 25 *Ecclesiastical Law Journal* 1–25.
——, 'Juridifying Ecclesiology and Moralizing Law in Enlightenment Anglicanism: The Ecclesiastical Lawyers' in *History of European Ideas*, forthcoming.
Doe, N and Nikiforos, D, 'Rediscovering Anglican-Priest Jurists III: William Beveridge (1637–1708)' (2021) 23 *Ecclesiastical Law Journal* 82–99.
Dolezalek, G, 'Roman Law: Symbiotic Companion and Servant of Canon Law' in A Winroth and JC Wei (eds), *The Cambridge History of Medieval Canon Law* (Cambridge, Cambridge University Press, 2022) 230–61.
Donahue, C, 'Roman Canon Law in the Medieval English Church: Stubbs vs. Maitland Re-Examined after 75 Years in the Light of Some Records from the Church Courts' (1974) 72 *Michigan Law Review* 647–716.
——, 'Proof by Witnesses in the Church Courts of Medieval England: An Imperfect Reception of the Learned Law' in MS Arnold et al (eds), *On the Laws and Customs of England: Essays in Honor of Samuel E Thorne* (Chapel Hill, NC, North Carolina University Press, 1981) 127–58.
——, '*Ius Commune*, Canon Law and Common Law in England' (1992) 66 *Tulane Law Review* 1745–80.
——, *The Records of the Medieval Ecclesiastical Courts*, Part II: England. Reports of the Working Group on Church Court Records(Berlin, Duncker u Humblot, 1994).
——, 'Gerard Pucelle as a Canon Lawyer: Life and the Battle Abbey Case' in RH Helmholz et al (eds), *Grundlagen Des Rechts: Festschrift Für Peter Landau Zum 65. Geburtstag* (Paderborn, Schöningh, 2000) 333–48.
——, *Law, Marriage, and Society in the Later Middle Ages: Arguments about Marriage in Five Courts* (Cambridge, Cambridge University Press, 2007).
——, 'Ethical Standards for Advocates and Proctors of the Court of Ely (1374–1382) Revisited' in TL Harris (ed), *Studies in Canon Law and Common Law in Honor of RH Helmholz* (Berkeley, CA, Robbins Collection, 2015) 41–60.
Drossbach, G, 'Decretals and Lawmaking' in A Winroth and JC Wei (eds), *The Cambridge History of Medieval Canon Law* (Cambridge, Cambridge University Press, 2022) 208–29.
Duddington, J, *The Church and Employment Law: A Comparative Analysis of the Legal Status of Clergy and Religious Workers* (Abingdon, Routledge, 2022).
Duggan, C, 'The Reception of Canon Law in England in the Later-Twelfth Century' in S Kuttner and JJ Ryan (eds), *Proceedings of the Second International Congress of Medieval Canon Law* (Città del Vaticano: Bibliotheca Apostolica Vaticana, 1965) 378–82.

Duncan, GIO, *The High Court of Delegates* (Cambridge, Cambridge University Press, 1971).
Edwards, J, *Mary I: England's Catholic Queen* (New Haven, CT, Yale University Press, 2011).
Ellis, I, *Seven Against Christ* (Leiden, Brill, 1980).
Elton, GR, *The Tudor Constitution* (Cambridge, Cambridge University Press, 1968).
——, *Policy and Police: The Enforcement of the Reformation in the Age of Thomas Cromwell* (Cambridge, Cambridge University Press, 1972).
——, *Reform and Renewal: Thomas Cromwell and the Common Weal* (Cambridge, Cambridge University Press, 1973).
——, *Reform and Reformation England 1509-1558* (London, Edward Arnold Ltd, 1977).
Emden, AB, *A Biographical Register of the University of Oxford to A.D. 1500* (Oxford, Clarendon Press, 1957).
——, *A Biographical Register of the University of Cambridge to 1500* (Cambridge, Cambridge University Press, 1963).
Eppley, D, *Defending Royal Supremacy and Discerning God's Will in Tudor England* (Aldershot, Ashgate, 2007).
Evans, G, *Crown, Mitre and People in the Nineteenth Century: The Church of England, Establishment and the State* (Cambridge, Cambridge University Press, 2021).
Figgis, JN, *Churches in the Modern State, by John Neville Figgis* (London Longmans, Green and Co, 1913).
——, *Studies of Political Thought from Gerson to Grotius: 1414-1625* (Cambridge, Cambridge University Press, 2011).
Figueira, RC, 'Ricardus de Mores at Common Law – The Second Career of an Anglo-Norman Canonist' in L Kolmer and P Segl (eds), *Regensburg, Bayern Und Europa. Festschrift Für Kurt Reindel Zu Seinem 70. Geburtstag* (Regensburg, Universitätsverlag, 1995) 281-89.
Fincham, K, 'Annual Accounts of the Church of England, 1632-1639' in M Barber and S Taylor with G Sewell (eds), *From the Reformation to the Permissive Society: A miscellany in celebration of the 400th anniversary of Lambeth Palace Library, Church of England Record Society, xviii* (Woodbridge, Boydell Press, 2010) 79-81.
Fincham, K (ed), *Visitation Articles and Injunctions of the Early Stuart Church* (Woodbridge, Boydell Press, 1994).
Fincham, K and Taylor, S, 'Vital statistics: episcopal ordination and ordinands in England, 1646-1660' (2011) 126 *English Historical Review* 319-44.
Finlason, W, *The History, Constitution, and Character of the Judicial Committee of the Privy Council, considered as a Judicial Tribunal, especially in Ecclesiastical Cases* (London, Stevens, 1878).
Firth, CH and Rait, RS (eds), *Acts and Ordinances of the Interregnum, 1642-1660* (London, HMSO, 1911).
Flahiff, GB, 'The Use of Prohibitions by Clerics against Ecclesiastical Courts in England' (1941) 3 *Mediaeval Studies* 101-16.
——, 'The Writ of Prohibition to Court Christian in the Thirteenth Century' (1944) 6 *Mediaeval Studies* 261-313.
——, 'The Writ of Prohibition to Court Christian in the Thirteenth Century. Part II' (1945) 7 *Mediaeval Studies* 229-90.
Fowler-Magerl, L, *Ordines Iudiciarii and Libelli de Ordine Iudiciorum* (Turnhout, Brepols, 1994).
Fox, A and Guy, J, *Reassessing the Henrician Age: Humanism, Politics and Reform 1500-1550* (Oxford, Blackwell, 1986).
Frere, WH (ed), *Visitation Articles and Injunctions of the Period of the Reformation* (London, Longmans Green & Co, 1910).
Froude, R et al, *Remains of the Late Reverend Richard Hurrell Froude* (London, JG and F Rivington, 1838).
Gairdner, J et al (eds), *Letters and Papers, Foreign and Domestic, of the Reign of Henry VIII* (London, Longman, 1862-1932).
Garbett, C, *Church and State in England* (London, Hodder & Stoughton, 1950).

Gee, H and Hardy, WJ, *Documents illustrative of English Church History*, 4th edn (London, MacMillan and Co, 1921).
General Synod Working Party reviewing Clergy Discipline and the Working of the Ecclesiastical Courts, *Under Authority* (London, Church House Publishing, 1996).
General Synod, *Challenges for the New Quinquennium – New Steps* (2011, GS 1815).
Gentiles, IJ and Sheils, WJ, *Confiscation and Restoration: the Archbishopric Estates and the Civil War*, Borthwick Paper no 59 (York, University of York, 1981).
Gibson, E, *Codex Juris Ecclesiastici Anglicani* (1713).
Gibson, W, *James II and the Trial of the Seven Bishops* (London, Palgrave Macmillan, 2009).
Graber, G, *Ritual Legislation in the Victorian Church* (San Francisco, CA, Edwin Mellen Press, 1993).
Graves, EB, 'Circumspecte Agatis' (1928) 43 *The English Historical Review* 1–20.
Gray, J, 'Conscience and the Word of God: Religious Arguments against the *Ex Officio* Oath' (2003) 64 *Journal of Ecclesiastical History* 494–512.
Grey, R, *A System of English Ecclesiastical Law* (1730).
Gunn, SJ and Lindley, PG, *Cardinal Wolsey: Church, State and Art* (Cambridge, Cambridge University Press, 1991).
Gunstone, J, *Lift High the Cross: The High Noon of the Anglo-Catholic Movement, 1919–1950* (Norwich, Canterbury Press, 2009).
Guy, J (ed), *St German on Chancery and Statute* (London, Selden Society, 1985).
Gwyn, P, *The King's Cardinal: the rise and fall of Thomas Wolsey* (London, Barrie & Jenkins, 1990).
Haigh, C, 'Anticlericalism and the English Reformation' in C Haigh (ed), *The English Reformation Revised* (Cambridge, Cambridge University Press, 2000) 56–74.
—— (ed), *The English Reformation Revised* (Cambridge, Cambridge University Press, 2000).
——, 'Where was the Church of England, 1646–1660' (2019) 62 *The Historical Journal* 127–47.
Halsbury's Laws of England, 4th edn, vol 14: *Ecclesiastical Law* (London, Butterworths, 1975).
Halsbury's Laws of England, 5th edn, vol 14: *Ecclesiastical Law* (London, LexisNexis, 2011).
Halsbury's Statutes of England, 4th edn, vol 34: *Ecclesiastical Law* (London, Butterworths, 1986).
Harris, TL, 'The Work of the English Ecclesiastical Courts, 1725–1745' in TL Harris (ed), *Studies in Canon Law and Common Law in Honor of RH Helmholz* (Berkeley, CA, The Robbins Collection, 2015) 251–79.
Hasler, PW (ed), *The History of Parliament: the House of Commons 1558–1603* (Martlesham, Boydell & Brewer, 1981).
Hastings, A, *A History of English Christianity 1920–1990* (London, SCM Press, 1991).
Hatcher, M, 'Bishops in the House of Lords – Fit for the future?' (LLM in Canon Law Dissertation, Cardiff University, 2023).
Helmholz, RH, 'Ethical Standards for Advocates and Proctors in Theory and Practice' in *Proceedings of the Fourth International Congress of Medieval Canon Law* (Vatican City, Biblioteca Apostolica Vaticana, 1976) 283–99.
——, 'Writs of Prohibition and Ecclesiastical Sanctions in the English Courts Christian' (1976) 60 *Minnesota Law Review* 1011–33.
——, 'The Writ of Prohibition to Court Christian before 1500' (1981) 43 *Medieval Studies* 297–314.
——, 'The Early History of the Grand Jury and the Canon Law' (1983) 50 *The University of Chicago Law Review* 613–27.
——, *Roman Canon Law in Reformation England* (Cambridge, Cambridge University Press, 1990).
——, 'The Canons of 1603: The Contemporary Understanding' in N Doe, M Hill and R Ombres (eds), *English Canon Law* (Cardiff, University of Wales Press, 1998) 23–35.
——, 'Richard Hooker and the European *Ius Commune*' (2001) 6 *Ecclesiastical Law Journal* 4–11.
——, *The Ius Commune in England: Four Studies* (Oxford, Oxford University Press, 2001).
——, *The Canon Law and Ecclesiastical Jurisdiction from 597 to the 1640s* (Oxford, Oxford University Press, 2004).
——, 'University Education and English Ecclesiastical Lawyers 1400–1650' (2011) 13 *Ecclesiastical Law Journal* 132–45.

—, 'Richard Zouche (1590–1661)' (2013) 15 *Ecclesiastical Law Journal* 204–07.
—, 'Ecclesiastical Lawyers V: Sir Daniel Dun (c 1545–1617)' (2014) 16 *Ecclesiastical Law Journal* 205–10.
—, 'William of Drogheda (c 1200–1245)' (2014) 16 *Ecclesiastical Law Journal* 66–71.
—, *Natural Law in Court: A History of Legal Theory in Practice* (Cambridge, MA, Harvard University Press, 2015).
—, 'Ecclesiastical Lawyers XIV: William Somner (c 1598–1669)' (2017) 19 *Ecclesiastical Law Journal* 224–29.
—, *The Profession of Ecclesiastical Lawyers: An Historical Introduction* (Cambridge, Cambridge University Press, 2019).
Herman, PC, 'Hall, Edward (1497–1547), lawyer and historian' in *Oxford Dictionary of National Biography* (2012) at www.oxforddnb.com/.
Hill, M, et al, 'A Decade of Ecumenical Dialogue: A Report on the Proceedings of the Colloquium of Anglican and Roman Catholic Canon Lawyers 1999–2009' (2009) 11 *Ecclesiastical Law Journal* 284–328.
—, *Ecclesiastical Law*, 1st edn (London, Butterworths, 1995); 2nd edn (Oxford, Oxford University Press, 2001); 4th edn (Oxford: Oxford University Press, 2018).
—, 'Aston Cantlow v Wallbank: Defining the Public and Private Functions of the Established Church of England' in P Babie et al (eds), *Landmark Cases in Law and Religion* (Oxford, Hart Publishing, 2022) ch 9.
Hill, M, and Grout, C, 'The seal of the confessional, the Church of England and English Law' in M Hill and AK Thompson (eds), *Religious Confession and Evidential Privilege in the Twenty-first Century* (Sydney, Shepherd Street Press, 2021) ch 5.
Hilton, B, *The Age of Atonement* (Oxford, Clarendon Press, 1988).
Hirschberg, DR, 'The Government and Church Patronage in England, 1660–1760' (1980–81) 20 *Journal of British Studies* 109–39.
Hobbes, T, *The Elements of Law* (1650).
—, *Leviathan* (London, Penguin Classics, Reprinted 1986).
Homfray, K, 'Sir Edward Coke Gets It Wrong? A Brief History of Consecration' (2009) 11 *Ecclesiastical Law Journal* 36–50.
House of Bishops, *Declaration on the Ministry of Bishops and Priests* (GS Misc 1076).
House of Bishops, *Pastoral Guidance on Same Sex Marriage* (15 February 2014).
Hudson, J, 'Constitutions of Clarendon, Clause 3, and Henry II's Reforms of Law and Administration' in C Whittick, S Jenks and J Rose (eds), *Laws, Lawyers and Texts: Studies in Medieval Legal History in Honour of Paul Brand* (Leiden, Brill, 2012) 1–19.
Hudson, J, *The Oxford History of the Laws of England*, vol II: *817–1216* (Oxford, Oxford University Press, 2012).
Huels, JM, *Liturgy and Law* (Ottawa, Wilson & Lafleur, 2006).
Hughes Carew, S, 'The Convocations of Canterbury and York' (2019) 21 *Ecclesiastical Law Journal* 19–49.
Hughes, P, *The Reformation in England* (London, Hollis and Carter, 1954).
Hughes, PH and JL Larkin, *Tudor Royal Proclamations* (New Haven, CT, Yale University Press, 1964–69).
Hurstfield, J, *Elizabeth I and the Unity of England* (West Drayton, Harmondsworth, 1960).
Hylson-Smith, K, *The Churches in England from Elizabeth I to Elizabeth II*, vol II: *1689–1833* (London, SCM Press, 1997).
Ibbetson, D, 'Natural law and common law' (2001) 5 *Edinburgh Law Review* 4–20.
Independent Reviewer, *Report on the Nomination to the See of Sheffield and Related Matters* (September 2017).
Ingram, RG, 'The Church of England, 1714–1783' in J Gregory (ed), *The Oxford History of Anglicanism*, vol II: *Establishment and Empire, 1662–1829* (Oxford, Oxford University Press, 2017) 49–67.

Jacob, WM, *Laypeople and Religion in the Early Eighteenth Century* (Cambridge, Cambridge University Press, 2002).
——, 'Libraries for the Parish: Individual Donors and Charitable Societies' in G Mandelbrote and KA Manley (eds), *The Cambridge History of Libraries in Britain and Ireland 1640-1850* (Cambridge, Cambridge University Press, 2006) 65-82.
——, *The Clerical Profession in the Long Eighteenth Century 1680-1840* (Oxford, Oxford University Press, 2006).
——, 'England' in J Gregory (ed), *The Oxford History of Anglicanism*, vol II: *Establishment and Empire, 1662-1829* (Oxford, Oxford University Press, 2017) 90-120.
James, MR, *The Ancient Libraries of Canterbury and Dover* (Cambridge, Cambridge University Press, 1903).
Johnson, ML, 'Christopher St German's "Discourse of the Sacramentes Howe Many There Are": a reflection on St German's ideas in the context of Law and the Reformation' (2018) 181 *Law and Justice* 189-206.
Johnson, ML, 'The Works of Christopher St German' (PhD Thesis, University of Reading, 2019).
Jones, G, *History of the Law of Charity 1532-1827* (Cambridge, Cambridge University Press, 1969).
Jones, WJ, *The Elizabethan Court of Chancery* (Oxford, Clarendon Press, 1967).
Jones, WR, 'Bishops, Politics, and the Two Laws: The Gravamina of the English Clergy, 1237-1399' (1966) 41 *Speculum* 209-45.
Joyce, J, *On the Court of Final Ecclesiastical Appeal as proposed by the Commissioners on Ecclesiastical Courts* (London, Rivingtons, 1884).
Kemp, EW, *Counsel and Consent* (London, SPCK, 1961).
Kenyon, JP (ed), *The Stuart Constitution 1603-1688: Documents and Commentary* (Cambridge, Cambridge University Press, 1986; repr 1993).
Kéry, L, *Canonical Collections of the Early Middle Ages (ca 400-1140): A Bibliographical Guide to the Manuscripts and Literature* (Washington, DC, Catholic University of America Press, 1999).
Kha, H and Swain, W, 'The Enactment of the Matrimonial Causes Act 1857: The Campbell Commission and the Parliamentary Debates' (2016) 37 *Journal of Legal History* 303-30.
Klerman, D, 'Was the Jury Ever Self-Informing?' (2003) 77 *Southern California Law Review* 123-49.
Knight, F, 'Did Anticlericalism Exist in the English Countryside in the Early Nineteenth Century?' in N Aston and M Cragoe (eds), *Anticlericalism in Britain c 1500-1914* (Stroud, Sutton, 2000) 159-78.
Kuttner, S and Rathbone, E, 'Anglo-Norman Canonists of the Twelfth Century: An Introductory Study' (1949) 7 *Traditio* 279-358.
Lambarde, W, *The Duties of Constables* (1601).
Lehmberg, SE, 'Supremacy and Vicegerency: A Re-examination' (1966) 81 *The English Historical Review* 225-35.
——, *The Reformation Parliament 1529-1536* (Cambridge, Cambridge University Press, 1970).
Levack, B, *The Civil Lawyers in England, 1603-1641: A Political Study* (Oxford, Oxford University Press, 1973).
Little, D, 'God v Caesar: Sir Edward Coke and the Struggles of His Time' (2016) 18 *Ecclesiastical Law Journal* 292.
Lobban, M, *The Common Law and English Jurisprudence 1760-1850* (Oxford, Clarendon Press, 1991).
Logan, FD, *Excommunication and the Secular Arm in Medieval England: A Study in Legal Procedure from the Thirteenth to the Sixteenth Century* (Toronto, Pontifical Institute of Mediaeval Studies, 1968).
——, *The Medieval Court of Arches* (Woodbridge, Canterbury and York Society, 2005).
Louden, L, *Distinctive and Inclusive: The National Society and Church of England Schools 1811-2011* (London, The National Society, 2012).
Lyon, A, *Constitutional History of the United Kingdom*, 2nd edn (Abingdon, Routledge, 2016).
MacCulloch, D, 'Richard Hooker: Invention and Reinvention' (2019) 21 *Ecclesiastical Law Journal* 137-52.
MacCulloch, D, *The Later Reformation in England, 1547-1603* (New York, St Martin's, 1990).

——, *The Boy King: Edward VI and the Protestant Reformation* (Berkeley, CA, University of California Press, 2002).
——, *Thomas Cranmer: A Life* (New Haven, CT, Yale University Press, 1996)
——, *Thomas Cromwell: A Life* (London, Allen Lane, 2018).
Machin, G, 'The Last Victorian Anti-Ritualist Campaign, 1895–1906' (1982) 25 *Victorian Studies* 277–302.
MacMillan, C, 'Stephen Martin Leake: A Victorian's View of the Common Law' (2011) 32 *Journal of Legal History* 3–29.
MacNair, M, 'Vicinage and the Antecedents of the Jury' (1999) 17 *Law and History Review* 537–90.
Maiden, J, *National Religion and the Prayer Book Controversy, 1927–1928* (Woodbridge, Boydell Press, 2009).
Maiden, J and Webster, P, 'Parliament, the Church of England and the Last Gasp of Political Protestantism, 1963–4' (2013) 32 *Parliamentary History* 361–77.
Maitland, FW, *Roman Canon Law in the Church of England* (London, Methuen and Co, 1898).
——, 'William of Drogheda and the Universal Ordinary' in FW Maitland, *Roman Canon Law in the Church of England: Six Essays* (London, Methuen & Co, 1898) 110–31.
——, *The Constitutional History of England* (Cambridge, Cambridge University Press, 1941 [1908]).
——, *Equity: A Course of Lectures* (Cambridge, Cambridge University Press, 1969 [1936]).
Maitland, FW, and FC Montague, *A Sketch of English Legal History* (New York, GP Putman's Sons, 1915).
Maltby, J, 'The Act of Synod and Theological Seriousness' in M Furlong (ed), *Act of Synod – Act of Folly?* (Norwich, Canterbury Press, 1998) 42–58.
Marchant, RA, *The Church under the Law: Justice, Administration and Discipline in the Diocese of York 1560–1640* (Cambridge, Cambridge University Press, 1969).
Matthews, NL, *William Sheppard, Cromwell's Law Reformer* (Cambridge, Cambridge University Press, 1984).
McCoy, R, '"The Wonderfull Spectacle": the Civic Progress of Elizabeth I and the Troublesome Coronation in Coronation Studies, Past, Present and Future' in JM Bak (ed), *Coronations: Medieval and Early Modern Monarchic Ritual* (Berkeley, CA, University of California Press, 1989) 217–25.
McNicoll, M, 'Henry VIII: Conciliarist?' 5 *Journal of Early Modern Christianity* (2018) 109–49.
Meyer, A, 'The Late Middle Ages: Sources' in A Winroth and JC Wei (eds), *The Cambridge History of Medieval Canon Law* (Cambridge, Cambridge University Press, 2022) 122–41.
Middleton, JB, *Love versus Law* (London, Thomas Cautley Newby, 1855).
Millon, D, 'Circumspecte Agatis Revisited' (1984) 2 *Law and History Review* 105–27.
Millon, D, 'Ecclesiastical Jurisdiction in Medieval England – A Symposium in Legal History: Medieval and Early Modern Law: The Birth of Modern Jurisprudence' [1984] *University of Illinois Law Review* 621–38.
Milton, A (ed), *The Oxford History of Anglicanism*, vol I: *Reformation and Identity c 1520–1662* (Oxford, Oxford University Press, 2019).
——, 'The Cromwellian Church' in A Milton (ed), *England's Second Reformation: The Battle for the Church of England 1625–1662* (Cambridge, Cambridge University Press, 2021) 335–78.
Moorhouse, G, *The Pilgrimage of Grace: The Rebellion That Shook Henry VIII's Throne* (London, Weidenfeld & Nicolson, 2002).
Müller, WP, 'Procedures and Courts' in A Winroth and JC Wei (eds), *The Cambridge History of Medieval Canon Law* (Cambridge, Cambridge University Press, 2022) 327–42.
——, 'The Reinvention of Canon Law in the High Middle Ages' in A Winroth and JC Wei (eds), *The Cambridge History of Medieval Canon Law* (Cambridge, Cambridge University Press, 2022) 79–95.
Mullett, CF, 'The Legal Position of English Protestant Dissenters, 1689–1767' (1937) 23 *Virginia Law Review* 389–418.
Nelson, W, *The Rights of the Clergy of Great Britain, as established by the Canons, the Common Law, and the Statutes of the Realm* (1709).
Nockles, P, *The Oxford Movement in Context* (Cambridge, Cambridge University Press, 1994).

Orme, N, *Going to Church in Medieval England* (Newhaven, CT, Yale University Press, 2021).
Oughton, T, *Ordo Judiciorum* (1728), ed JT Law, *Forms of Ecclesiastical Law* (London, Saunders and Benning, 1831).
Outhwaite, RB, *Scandal in the Church: Dr Edward Drax Free, 1764-1843* (London, Hambledon Press, 1997).
——, *The Rise and Fall of the English Ecclesiastical Courts, 1500-1860* (Cambridge, Cambridge University Press, 2006).
Owen, DM, *The Medieval Canon Law: Teaching, Literature and Transmission* (Cambridge, Cambridge University Press, 1990).
Palmer, B, *Serving Two Masters: Parish Patronage in the Church of England since 1714* (Lewes, The Book Guild Ltd, 2003).
Patterson, N, *Ecclesiastical Law, Clergy and Laity: A History of Legal Discipline and the Anglican Church* (Abingdon, Routledge, 2019).
Paul, L, *The Deployment and Payment of the Clergy* (London, Church Information Office 1964).
Pearce, A, 'Episcopacy and the Common Law' (2003) 7 *Ecclesiastical Law Journal* 195-209.
Pennington, K, 'The Decretalists 1190-1234' in W Hartmann and K Pennington (eds), *The History of Medieval Canon Law in the Classical Period, 1140-1234 from Gratian to the Decretals of Pope Gregory IX* (Washington, DC, Catholic University of America Press, 2008) 211-45.
——, 'The Jurisprudence of Procedure' in W Hartmann and K Pennington (eds), *The History of Courts and Procedure in Medieval Canon Law* (Washington, DC, Catholic University of America Press, 2016) 125-59.
Phillimore, R, *The Ecclesiastical Law of the Church of England* (London, Sweet & Maxwell, 1872; 2nd edn, 1895).
Philpott, M, 'Archbishop Lanfranc and Canon Law' (DPhil Thesis, University of Oxford, 1993).
Pix, S, 'Archdeacon of Cheltenham v Bland: a sledgehammer to crack a nut' (2001) 6 *Ecclesiastical Law Journal* 35-49.
Podmore, C, 'Self-Government Without Disestablishment: From the Enabling Act to the General Synod' (2019) 21 *Ecclesiastical Law Journal* 312-28.
Pollock, F and Maitland, FW, *The History of English Law before the Time of Edward I* (Cambridge, Cambridge University Press, 2nd edn, 1898; repr Indianapolis, IN, Liberty Fund, 2010).
Port, MH, *Six Hundred New Churches: A Study of the Church Building Commission, 1818-1856, and Its Church Building Activities* (London, SPCK, 1961).
Poser, NS, *Lord Mansfield: Justice in the Age of Reason* (Montreal and Kingston, McGill-Queen's University Press, 2013).
Prall, SE, *The Bloodless Revolution: England 1688* (Madison, WI, University of Wisconsin Press, 1985).
Probert, R, *Marriage Law and Practice in the Long Eighteenth Century: A Reassessment* (Cambridge, Cambridge University Press 2009).
Proctor, F and Frere, WH, *A New History of the Book of Common Prayer* (London, Macmillan, 1910).
Report of the Joint Committee of the Convocation of Canterbury on the Position of the Laity: Presented April 29, 1902; with Appendix (London, SPCK, 1902).
Report of the Simplification Task Group (2015, GS 1980).
Rex, R, 'Swynnerton [Swinnerton], Thomas (d 1554), evangelical preacher' in *Oxford Dictionary of National Biography* (2008) at www.oxforddnb.com/.
Rex, R, *Henry VIII and the English Reformation* (Hong Kong, MacMillan, 1994).
Richardson, HG, 'The Oxford Law School under John' (1941) 57 *Law Quarterly Review* 319-38.
Richardson, HG, 'The Schools of Northampton in the Twelfth Century' (1941) 56 *The English Historical Review* 595-605.
Ridley, T, *A View of the Civil and Ecclesiastical Law* (1607).
Ritchie, CIA, *The Ecclesiastical Courts of York* (Arbroath, The Herald Press, 1956).
Rivers, J, 'The Secularisation of the British Constitution' (2012) 14 *Ecclesiastical Law Journal* 371-99.
Roberts, M, *The Role of the Laity in the Church of England, c 1850-1885* (DPhil Thesis, University of Oxford, 1974).

Rodes, RE, *Law and Modernization in the Church of England: Charles II to the Welfare State* (Notre Dame, IN, University of Notre Dame Press, 1991).

Rolker, C, *Canon Law and the Letters of Ivo of Chartres* (Cambridge, Cambridge University Press, 2010).

Rolker, C, *Canon Law in the Age of Reforms (ca 1000 to ca 1150)* (Washington, DC, Catholic University of America Press, 2023).

Royal Commission on Ecclesiastical Discipline, *Report of the Royal Commission on Ecclesiastical Discipline* (London, SPCK 1906).

Rule, J, *Albion's People: English Society 1714–1815* (Abingdon, Routledge, 1992).

Russell, C, 'Whose Supremacy? King, Parliament and the Church 1530–1640' (1997) 4 *Ecclesiastical Law Journal* 700–08.

Ryan, R, *The Irish Incumbent's Guide or Digest of the Ecclesiastical Law of Ireland* (1825).

Ryrie, A, 'Book Review of R Rex (ed), *A Reformation Rhetoric: Thomas Swynnerton's The tropes and figures of Scripture* (Cambridge, RTM Publications, 1999)' (2001) 52 *Journal of Ecclesiastical History* 745–46.

——, *The Gospel and Henry VIII: Evangelicals in the Early English Reformation* (Cambridge, Cambridge University Press, 2003).

Sagovsky, N, 'The contribution of canon law to Anglican-Roman Catholic ecumenism' (2011) 13 *Ecclesiastical Law Journal* 4–14.

——, 'Hooker, Warburton and Coleridge and the "Quadruple Lock": State and Church in the Twenty-first Century' (2014) 16 *Ecclesiastical Law Journal* 140–46.

Sandberg, R, *Law and Religion* (Cambridge, Cambridge University Press, 2011).

——, *Subversive Legal History: A Manifesto for the Future of Legal Education* (Abingdon, Routledge, 2021).

——, *A Historical Introduction to English Law: Genesis of the Common Law* (Cambridge, Cambridge University Press, 2023).

Saul, N, *Richard II* (New Haven, CT, Yale University Press, 1999).

Sayers, JE, 'Canterbury Proctors at the Court of "Audienta Litterarum Contradictum"' (1966) 22 *Traditio* 311–45.

——, 'William of Drogheda and the English Canonists' in P Linehan (ed), *Proceedings of the Seventh International Congress of Medieval Canon Law, Cambridge, 23–27 July 1984* (Città del Vaticano, Biblioteca Apostolica Vaticana, 1988) 205–22.

Sayers, JE and Watkiss, L (eds), *Thomas of Marlborough: History of the Abbey of Evesham* (Oxford, Clarendon Press, 2003).

Scarisbrick, JJ, 'Clerical Taxation in England, 1485–1547' (1960) 11 *Journal of Ecclesiastical History* 41–54.

——, *Henry VIII* (Berkeley, CA, University of California Press, 1968).

——, *The Reformation and the English People* (Oxford, Blackwell, 1984).

Shahan, E, 'The Emergence of the Church of England 1520–1533' in A Milton (ed), *The Oxford History of Anticlericalism*, vol 1: *c 1520–1562* (Oxford, Oxford University Press, 2017) 28–44.

Sharpe, RJ, *The Law of Habeas Corpus* (Oxford, Clarendon Press, 1976).

Shaw, J, *Parish Law*, 9th edn (1755).

Sheehan, MM, *The Will in Medieval England: From the Conversion of the Anglo-Saxons to the End of the Thirteenth Century* (Toronto, Pontifical Institute of Mediaeval Studies, 1963).

Sheils, WJ, *Ecclesiastical Cause Papers at York: Files Transmitted on Appeal 1500–1883* (York, University of York, Borthwick Institute of Historical Research, 1983).

——, '"The right of the Church": the clergy, tithe and the courts at York, 1540–1640' in WJ Sheils and D Wood (eds), *The Church and Wealth* (Woodbridge, Boydell & Brewer, 1987) 231–55.

Sheppard, S (ed), *The Selected Writings and Speeches of Sir Edward Coke* (Indianapolis, IN, Liberty Fund, 2003).

Simpson, AWB, 'The Rise and Fall of the Legal Treatise: Legal Principles and the Forms of Legal Literature' (1981) 48 *University of Chicago Law Review* 632–79.

Slack, S, 'Synodical Government and the Legislative Process' (2012) 14 *Ecclesiastical Law Journal* 43–81.

Slaughter, I, 'Functions of the Ecclesiastical Committee under section 3(3) of the Church of England Assembly (Powers) Act 1919' (unpublished).
Smethurst, A, Riley, H and Wilson, H (eds), *Acts of the Convocations of Canterbury and York* (London, SPCK, 1961).
Smith, C, 'Martin v. Mackonochie/Mackonochie v Penzance: A Crisis of Character and Identity in the Court of Arches?' (2003) 24 *Journal of Legal History* 36–58.
——, 'Ridsdale v Clifton: Representations of the Judicial Committee of the Privy Council in Ecclesiastical Appeals' (2008) 19 *King's Law Journal* 551–74.
——, 'The disruptive power of legal biography: the life of Lord Phillimore – churchman and judge' (2020) 41 *Journal of Legal History* 164–85.
——, 'The Quest for an Authoritative Court of Final Appeal in Ecclesiastical Causes: A Study of the Difficulties, c 1830–76' (2011) 32 *Journal of Legal History* 189–213.
Smith, DC, *Sir Edward Coke and the Reformation of the Laws: Religion, Politics and Jurisprudence, 1578–1616* (Cambridge, Cambridge University Press, 2014).
Smith, M, 'The Anglican Churches, 1783–1829' in J Gregory (ed), *The Oxford History of Anglicanism*, vol II: *Establishment and Empire, 1662–1829* (Oxford, Oxford University Press, 2017) 68–89.
Smith, MG, *Pastoral Discipline and the Church Court: The Hexham Court, 1680–1730* (York, Saint Anthony, 1982).
——, *The Church Courts, 1680–1840: From Canon to Ecclesiastical Law*, ed P Smith (Lampeter, Edwin Mellen, 2006).
Snow, VF, 'The Evolution of Proctorial Representation in Medieval England' (1963) 7 *American Journal of Legal History* 319–39.
Southern, RW, 'Master Vacarius and the Beginning of an English Academic Tradition' in JJG Alexander and MT Gibson (eds), *Medieval Learning and Literature: Essays Presented to Richard William Hunt* (Oxford, Clarendon Press, 1976) 257–86.
Spalding, JC, 'The *Reformatio Legum Ecclesiasticarum* of 1552 and the Furthering of Discipline in England' (1970) 39 *Church History* 162–71.
——, *The Reformation of the Ecclesiastical Laws of England, 1552* (Kirksville, MO, Sixteenth Century Journal Publishers, 1992).
Spraggon, J, *Puritan Iconoclasm During the English Civil War* (Martlesham, Boydell & Brewer, 2012).
Spurr, J, *The Restoration Church of England 1646–1689* (New Haven, CT, Yale University Press, 1991).
Squibb, GD, *Doctors' Commons: A History of the College of Advocates and Doctors of Law* (Oxford, Clarendon Press, 1977).
Stein, P, 'Vacarius and the Civil Law' in CNL Brooke, DE Luscombe, GH Martin and D Owen (eds), *Church and Government in the Middle Ages: Essays Presented to CR Cheney on His 70th Birthday* (Cambridge, Cambridge University Press, 1976) 119–37.
——, 'The Vacarian School' (1992) 13 *Journal of Legal History* 23–31.
——, *Roman Law in European History* (Cambridge, Cambridge University Press, 1999).
Stephens, AJ, *A Practical Treatise of the Laws Relating to the Clergy* (London, W Benning and Co, 1848).
Stone, L, *Road to Divorce* (Oxford, Oxford University Press, 1990).
Stone, M (ed), *The Diary of John Longe (1765–1834), Vicar of Coddenham* (Woodbridge, Suffolk Records Society, 2008).
Stoughton, J, *Ecclesiastical History of England*, vol II (London, Walford and Hodder, 1867).
Strype, J, *Annals of the Reformation and Establishment of Religion: and other various occurrences in the Church of England, during Queen Elizabeth's happy reign* (Oxford, Clarendon Press, 1824).
Strype, J, *The History of the Life and Acts of The Most Reverend Father in God Edmund Grindal* (Oxford, Clarendon Press, 1821).
——, *The Life and Acts of Matthew Parker* (Oxford, Clarendon Press, 1821).
——, *The Life and Acts of John Whitgift DD* (Oxford, Clarendon Press, 1822).
Sullivan, T, *Benedictine Monks at the University of Paris, AD 1229–1500: A Biographical Register* (Leiden, Brill, 1995).

Taliadoros, J, *Law and Theology in Twelfth-Century England: The Works of Master Vacarius (c 1115/20–c 1200)* (Turnhout, Brepols Publishers, 2006).
Tanner, JR, *Constitutional Documents of James I* (Cambridge, Cambridge University Press, 1930).
Tapsell, G, 'The Church of England, 1662–1714' in J Gregory (ed), *The Oxford History of Anglicanism*, vol II: *Establishment and Empire, 1662–1829* (Oxford, Oxford University Press, 2007) 25–48.
Tarver, A, *Church Court Records: An Introduction for Family and Local Historians* (Chichester, Phillimore and Co Ltd, 1995).
The Archbishops' Commission on Canon Law, *The Canon Law of the Church of England: Being the Report of the Archbishops' Commission on Canon Law, Together with Proposals for a Revised Body of Canons* (London, SPCK, 1947).
The Archbishops' Commission on Canon Law, *The Revised Canons of the Church of England Further Considered* (London, SPCK, 1954).
The Archbishops' Commission on Canon Law, *Canon Law Revision 1959* (London, SPCK, 1960).
The Archbishops' Commission on the Ecclesiastical Courts, *The Ecclesiastical Courts: Principles of Reconstruction* (London, SPCK, 1954).
Thompson, AH, *Diocesan Organization in the Middle Ages: Archdeacons and Rural Deans* (Oxford, Humphrey Milford, 1943).
Thomson, A, *Church Courts and the People in Seventeenth Century England* (London, UCL Press, 2022).
Till, B, *The Church Courts, 1660–1720: Revival of Procedure* (York, Borthwick Institute, 2006).
Trapp, J (ed), *The Complete Works of St. Thomas More* (London, Yale University Press, 1979).
Trevelyan, GM, *The English Revolution, 1688–1689* (Oxford, Oxford University Press, 1963).
Tyler, P, *The Ecclesiastical Commission for the Province of York* (DPhil Thesis, University of Oxford, 1965).
Usher, R, *The Rise and Fall of the High Commission* (Oxford, Clarendon Press, 1913).
Waddams, S, *Law, Politics and the Church of England* (Cambridge, Cambridge University Press, 1992).
——, *Sexual Slander in the Nineteenth Century: Defamation in the Ecclesiastical Courts* (Toronto, University of Toronto Press, 2000).
Walker, G, *Writing under Tyranny: English Literature and the Henrician Reformation* (Oxford, Oxford University Press, 2005).
Walsh, J, Haydon, C and Taylor, S (eds), *The Church of England c 1689–c 1833* (Cambridge, Cambridge University Press, 1993).
Walter, J, '"Abolishing Superstition with Sedition"? The Politics of Popular Iconoclasm in England 1640–1642' (2004) 183 *Past & Present* 79–123.
Warren, A, 'Disraeli, the Conservatives and the National Church, 1837–1881' (2000) 19 *Parliamentary History* 96–117.
Watts, MR, *The Dissenters: From the Reformation to the French Revolution* (Oxford, Oxford University Press, 1978).
Webster, M, *A New Strength, A New Song: Journey to Women's Priesthood* (London, Mowbray, 1994).
Welsby, PA, *A History of the Church of England, 1945–1980* (Oxford, Oxford University Press, 1984).
White, SB, 'The Procedure and Practice of Witness Testimony in English Ecclesiastical Courts, c 1193–1300' (2020) 56 *Studies in Church History* 114–30.
Williams, R, 'Richard Hooker: The Laws of Ecclesiastical Polity Revisited' (2006) 8 *Ecclesiastical Law Journal* 382–91.
Winroth, A, 'III. The Two Recensions of Gratian's Decretum' (1997) 83 *Zeitschrift Der Savigny-Stiftung Für Rechtsgeschichte. Kanonistische Abteilung* 22–31.
Winroth, A, *The Making of Gratian's Decretum* (Cambridge, Cambridge University Press, 2000).
——, 'III. Where Gratian Slept: The Life and Death of the Father of Canon Law' (2013) 99 *Zeitschrift Der Savigny-Stiftung Für Rechtsgeschichte. Kanonistische Abteilung* 105–28.
——, 'Gratian and His Book: How a Medieval Teacher Changed European Law and Religion' (2021) 10 *Oxford Journal of Law and Religion* 1–15.
Winroth, A, 'Law Schools and Legal Education' in A Winroth and JC Wei (eds), *The Cambridge History of Medieval Canon Law* (Cambridge, Cambridge University Press, 2022) 262–84.

Winroth, A and Wei, JC (eds), *The Cambridge History of Medieval Canon Law* (Cambridge, Cambridge University Press, 2022).
Witte, J, *Law and Protestantism: The Legal Teachings of the Lutheran Reformation* (Cambridge, Cambridge University Press, 2004).
Woodcock, BL, *Medieval Ecclesiastical Courts in the Diocese of Canterbury* (Oxford, Oxford University Press, 1952).
Yates, N, *Anglican Ritualism in Victorian Britain 1830–1910* (Oxford, Oxford University Press, 2000).
Yonge, AD (ed), *Church Acts and Measures* (London, Butterworth & Co, 1969).
Young, BW, *Religion and Enlightenment in Eighteenth-Century England: Theological Debate from Locke to Burke* (Oxford, Oxford University Press, 1998).

INDEX

Abolition of High Commission Court Act 1640, 92
Act against the Authority of Rome 1536, 36–37
Act Concerning Absolute Restraint of Annates, *see* Annates Act 1532
Act Concerning Ecclesiastical Appointments, *see* Appointment of Bishops Act 1533
Act for the confirming and restoration of ministers 1660, 92–93
Act of Settlement 1701, 3, 104, 107, 115–16, 235
Act of Submission 1533, 128
Act of Succession 1534, 35
Act of Supremacy 1534, 35–36
Act of Supremacy 1558, 51, 64, 75
Act of Treasons 1534, 36
Act of Uniformity 1549, 45, 55–56
Act of Uniformity 1552, 46, 52
Act of Uniformity 1558, 51, 52
  repeal, 77, 89
Act of Uniformity 1662, 100–1, 184, 197
Act to Take Away all Positive Laws against the Marriage of Priests 1549, 46
Act of Union between England and Scotland 1706, 116–17
Act of Union between England and Ireland 1800, 135–36
Advertisements for Due Order 1566, 58
advowsons, 58
  sale of, 124, 125–26
American Revolutionary War (1775–83), 139
Annates Act 1532, 33–34, 51
Anne (Queen of England), 115
Appointment of Bishops Act 1533, 33–34, 51, 53, 123
Archbishops' Commission on Canon Law, 129–30, 193, 196
Articles:
  Articles of Religion, 54
  definition and role, 53–54
  visitation articles, 54
Articles devised by the whole consent of the king's most honourable council (1533), 40

Articles for Ecclesiastical Government 1563, 57–58
Articles for the Clergy 1583, 61–62
Audley, Thomas, 32
Augmentation of Benefices Act 1665, 100
Ayliffe, John, 118–19, 121, 122, 133, 235

Bancroft, Richard (Archbishop of Canterbury), 69, 71, 90–91
Baptists, 97–98
Bentham, Jeremy, 145
Bill of Rights 1688:
  authority of the King, 103
  religious toleration, 235
  succession of the Crown, 103, 115
Bishops and Priests (Consecration and Ordination of Women) Measure 2014, 217, 218–19
Blackstone, William, 118, 136, 145
blasphemy:
  state legislation, 87
    blasphemy and heresy Acts, 89
    denial of Holy Trinity, 106–7, 138
Blessed Sacrament, 44, 50, 182, 184
Boer War, 175–76
Book of Common Prayer, 52, 68
  abolition, 84–85, 86, 89–90
  Latin version, 55–56
  proposed revisions 1928, 191
  reinstatement, 100, 146–47, 157, 185–86, 197, 207, 235
  Welsh version, 56
Brexit, 238
buildings, *see* church buildings
burial grounds, 131–32, 147–48
Burial Ground Act 1816, 147–48
Burn, Richard, 55, 76, 77, 93, 132, 136–37, 236

Cabal, 107
Campeggio, Lorenzo (cardinal protector of England), 31, 33
Canon Law Commission, 188–89
Canons:
  Archbishops' Commission on Canon Law, 193
  Canons of 1571, 57, 58, 59–60, 61, 234

Canons of 1584, 62
Canons of 1597, 63
Canons of 1603, 70–71
  marriage, 129
  non-binding effect, 129–30
Canons of 1640, 78, 97
new code of Canons, 193, 195–96, 198–99
  vesture of the clergy, 196–98
cathedrals:
  abolition of cathedral office holders, 83
  appropriation of cathedral lands, 82–84, 88
  Care of Cathedrals Measure 1990, 195
  Cathedral Commissioners, 180–81
  Cathedrals Fabric Commission, 195, 227
  Cathedrals Measure 1931, 180–81
  Cathedrals Measure 1963, 195
  compulsory transfer of lands, 180–81
  contemporary reforms, 238
  governance reforms, 195, 238
  ordination of women, 211, 216–17
Catholicism:
  civil marriages, 147
  emancipation, 236
    oath of allegiance to the Crown, 135, 137–38
    Roman Catholic Charities Act 1832, 138
    Roman Catholic Relief Act 1829, 138
  Glorious Revolution, 113, 116
  Home Rule for Ireland, 177–78
  papal supremacy, 28–29
  Parliamentary Test Act 1678, 99–100
  patronage rights, 124–25
  persecution of, 73, 99–100, 107, 116–17
  rehabilitation of doctrines, 157, 188
  religious toleration, *see* religious toleration
  reserved sacrament, 183, 187
  succession crisis, 28, 47, 101–2, 116
  Test Act 1673, 99–100
  threat of, 49, 101–2, 235
Cave, William, 110–11
cemeteries, *see* **burial grounds**
Chancery, Court of, 95, 108, 222–23
  excommunication and contumacy, 144
  jurisdiction, 63
  writs of prohibition, 23
Chancery Court of York, 63, 130, 144
charity law, *see* **social legislation**
Charles I (King of England), 69–70
  execution, 78, 96
Charles II (King of England), 96–97
  tensions with Parliament, 98
Church Assembly:
  constitution, 178
  doctrine, questions of, 179

franchise, 179–80
jurisdiction, 188–89, 216, 237
Measures of the Church Assembly, 179–81, 183, 191, 216
Moberley Report, 203
new Code of Canons, 195–96, 198
new Prayer Book, proposals for, 188
power of self-adjustment, 182–83
reform, 202–4
  General Synod, creation of, 204–6
vestiarian controversy, 197–98
see also General Synod
church buildings, 148–49, 194–95, 199
  Council for Church Buildings, 201
  ecumenism, 201–2
  Redundant Churches Fund, 201
Church Commissioners, 124, 150, 194–95, 201, 212, 237–38
  Church Commissioners Measure 1947, 181, 193–94
Church Discipline Act 1840, 158, 159–60, 164, 184, 199
"Church in Danger" discourse, 112, 120, 139, 145–46, 155, 235–36
Church of England Assembly (Powers) Act 1919, 178–79, 204, 237
Church of Scotland, 77, 80, 178
  Church of Scotland Act 1921, 178
church rates, 106–7, 138, 144, 149, 162, 169, 236
  see also tithes
civil partnerships, 231
  state legislation, 216
Civil War, 77, 84, 96, 98, 100–1, 235
clandestine marriages, 126–27, 129–30
  legislation, 127–28
Clarendon Code, 98–99, 235
classical canon law, *see* **pre-Reformation Roman canon law**
Clement V (Pope), 9–10, 30
clergy:
  appointment, 139–40
  functions, 141
  income, 150
  patronage, 140–41
  pensions, 12, 123–24, 180–81, 195, 212
clergy discipline, 69, 143, 173, 222, 238
  Clergy Discipline Commission, 220
  Clergy Discipline Measure 2003, 214, 222, 227
  ecclesiastical court reforms, 199–200
  litigation, 141–42, 151, 157, 166–67

legislation, 144, 182
  Church Discipline Act 1840, 159–60, 182
  Clergy Discipline Act 1892, 163
  failures of, 213–14, 222
  Prayer Book controversy, 190
  Safeguarding and Clergy Discipline
    Measure 2016, 229
Clergy Act 1661, 100
Clergy Pensions Measure 1926, 180–81
Clergy Pensions Measure 1961, 195
Clerical Disabilities Act 1640, 78
clerical subsidies, 76
Coke, Edward (Chief Justice), 65, 72–73,
    88–89, 91, 235
College of Doctors Commons, 18, 91, 117–19,
    136, 144, 151, 166–68, 234, 236–37
**Colloquium of Anglican and Roman Catholic
    Canon Lawyers,** 227–29
Colonial Bishops Act 1853, 154
Colonial Clergy Act 1874, 154
commentaries, 118–20
**common law and ecclesiastical law, relationship
    between,** 18–20, 24–25, 144–45
  conflict of laws, 71–72
  Convocations, 128–30, 236
  testament doctrine, 20–21
  witnesses, 22–23
  writs of prohibition, 23–24
Commonwealth, 78, 79–81, 96
  church structure reforms, 85–86
  liturgical reformation, 84–85
  property reformation, 82–84
  republican church law, 82–88, 235
  Restoration, 97, 113
communion, *see* **Holy Communion**
*Concordia discordantium canonum
    (Decretum)*, 6–7
  commentaries, 7–8
  Luther, 29
confessional principle, 168–69
  seal of the confessional, 229–30
consanguinity, 56–57
consent of the people principle, 121–22
consistory courts, 3–4, 11–12, 73–74, 88, 130,
    220, 226–27
  defamation cases, 144
  discipline cases, 141
  jurisdiction, 182, 221–22
contumacy, 144, 165
Conventicle Act 1664, 99, 138
Convocations, 60–61, 72
  authority, 128–30, 188–90, 204
  Canon revision, 195–96, 198–99, 203–4

Constitution of Church Assembly, 178–80
marriage
  degrees of affinity, 187
  divorce, 188
  Prayer Book revision, 176–77, 182–83, 206–7
  revival of, 170–71
  taxation of clergy, 76
  vesture controversy, 197
Convocations of the Clergy Measure 1920, 180
Convention Parliament, 98–99, 102
Coronation Oath Act 1688, 103–4
coronavirus, 44–45, 214–15, 222, 238
Corporation Act 1661, 99, 105, 138
Corpus iuris canonici, 6, 9–10, 13
  Luther, 29
Corpus iuris civilis, 8, 10–11
Council for Church Buildings, 201
Council of Lambeth 1281, 16–17
Court of Arches, 17, 130, 137, 141–42, 145
  common law and precedent, 132
  Eleven Articles, 54–55
  jurisdiction, 199–200, 222–23
**Court of Commissioners for Ecclesiastical
    Causes,** 101–2
Court of Delegates, 34, 64, 127, 130, 132–33
Court of Ecclesiastical Causes Reserved, 199
Court of Final Ecclesiastical Appeal,
    157, 163–66
**Court of High Commission (Commissioners
    for Causes Ecclesiastical),** 64, 75
  abolition, 78, 97–98, 108
Court of Star Chamber, 75
  abolition, 108, 111
Courts of First Instance, 159–63
Cowell, John, 90–91
**Cranmer, Thomas (Archbishop of
    Canterbury),** 33, 35–36
  excommunication reforms, 45
  Forty-Two Articles, 46, 54
  injunctions, 52–53
  Prayer Book, 46
  reformation of ecclesiastical law, 45–46
Cromwell, Oliver, 77–78, 82, 86, 87–88
  death, 78, 92
Cromwell, Thomas, 29, 36, 52–53

**Deceased Brother's Widow's Marriage
    Act 1921,** 187
**Deceased Wife's Sister's Marriage
    Act 1907,** 186
Declaration of Breda, 98–99
Declarations of Indulgence 1662 and 1672,
    100, 101–2, 105

260 Index

Decretum, see Concordia discordantium canonum (Decretum); **Gratian**
Directory for the Public Worship of God, 84–85
disciplinary action:
  clergy discipline, 69, 143, 173, 222, 238
    Church Discipline Act 1840, 159–60, 182
    Clergy Discipline Act 1892, 163
    Clergy Discipline Commission, 220
    Clergy Discipline Measure 2003, 214, 222, 227
    ecclesiastical court reforms, 199–200
    failures of, 213–14, 222
    legislation, 144, 159–60, 163, 182, 213–14, 222
    litigation, 141–42, 151, 157, 166–67
    Prayer Book controversy, 190
    Safeguarding and Clergy Discipline Measure 2016, 229
  lay officers, 142–45
disestablishment, 86, 172–73, 185, 207–8, 211–12, 230–31, 232, 234
  Church of England in Wales, 178, 237
  Church of Ireland, 154, 169
  Liberation Society, 135–36
  partial disestablishment, 237–38
dissenters:
  increasing numbers, 142
  religious freedom, 137–39
  religious toleration, 104–5, 113
  repression, 100–1
  tithes, 138, 149, 169
dissolution of the monasteries, 67, 83–84
divine law, 42, 132–33
  human law, relationship with, 133
  marriage
    degrees of affinity, 56–57, 147
  moral law, relationship with, 133
divorce:
  Henry VIII, 28–30
    Great Matter, 40
    papal legatine court, 31
  jurisdiction, 12, 187–88, 189–90
  remarriage of divorcees, 209–10, 217, 237
Doctors' Commons, *see* **College of Doctors Commons**
doctrine, 145–48, 156–58, 179–80, 206–7, 208, 237–38
Doctrine of the Trinity Act 1813, 138
Dun, Daniel, 66
Durantis, William, 7–8, 12

ecclesiastical appeals, 167
  Ecclesiastical Appeals Act 1532, 51
  jurisdiction, 163–66

Ecclesiastical Commissioners, 180, 193, 236
  cathedral property, 181
  Ecclesiastical Commissioners Act 1836, 150
  Ecclesiastical Commissioners Act 1840, 150, 154
  jurisdiction, 51
ecclesiastical corporations, 147–48, 181
  Ecclesiastical Corporations Act 1832, 149–50
ecclesiastical courts:
  Anglicanisation, 64–65
    Dun, 66
    Hooker, 65–66
    Swinburne, 66
  Canons Ecclesiastical of 1603, 62
  clergy discipline, 199–200
  court business, 130–31
  Court of Commissioners for Ecclesiastical Causes, 101–2
  Court of Delegates, 34, 64, 127, 130, 132–33
  Court of Ecclesiastical Causes Reserved, 199
  Court of Final Ecclesiastical Appeal, 157, 163–66
  Court of High Commission (Commissioners for Causes Ecclesiastical), 64, 75
    abolition, 78, 97–98, 108
  jurisdiction, 63, 221–22
  lay discipline, 142–45
  post-WWII reforms, 199–200, 220–21
  pre-Reformation ecclesiastical courts
    civil and criminal procedure, 12–13
    English Church, 10–13
  proliferation of litigation, 63–64, 73–75
  Victorian reforms, 158–59
    Courts of First Instance, 159–63
    Court of Final Ecclesiastical Appeal, 163–66
    legal profession, impact on, 166–68
Ecclesiastical Courts Act 1813, 144
Ecclesiastical Jurisdiction Act 1531, 51
Ecclesiastical Jurisdiction Act 1546, 51
Ecclesiastical Jurisdiction Act 1661, 92–93, 97
Ecclesiastical Jurisdiction Measure 1963, 92, 199, 200–1, 213–14, 220, 237
Ecclesiastical Licences Act 1533, 34, 51
Ecclesiastical Licences Act 1536, 51
Ecclesiastical Offices (Age Limit) Measure 1975, 200–1
Ecclesiastical Offices (Terms of Service) Measure 2009, 225–26
ecclesiology, 133, 134, 227–28
ecumenical movement, 201–2
Edward VI (King of England), 28, 43–44
  election of bishops, 45
  excommunication, 45
  Forty-Two Articles, 46

reformation of ecclesiastical law, 45–46
sacrament, 44–45
uniformity in worship, 45
Edward VIII (King of England):
abdication crisis, 185
Election of Bishops Act 1547, 45
Eleven Articles 1559/60, 54–55
Elizabeth I (Queen of England), 28, 35, 49, 68, 234
Archbishop Grindal, 60–61
Archbishop Parker, 53–54
Advertisements for Due Order, 58
Articles for Ecclesiastical Government, 57–58
Canons of 1571, 59–60
Eleven Articles, 54–55
Latin Prayer Book, 55–56
Reformatio Legum Ecclesiasticarum, 58–59
Table of Impediments to Marriage, 56–57
Welsh Prayer Book, 56
Archbishop Whitgift, 61
Articles for the Clergy 1583, 61–62
Canons of 1584, 62
Canons of 1597, 63
legislative programme, 1583–1603, 62–63
Book of Common Prayer, 52
coronation, 50
early reforms, 50–51
social legislation
Poor Relief Acts 1597 and 1601, 67–68
Statutes of Charitable Uses 1597 and 1601, 67
supremacy reforms, 51–52
uniformity reforms, 51–52
employment status of ministers of religion, 224–25
Enabling Act 1919, *see* Church of England Assembly (Powers) Act
endowments, 200–1
litigation, 109–10
Enlightenment, 145, 154–56
episcopal incomes, 139
episcopacy, 69, 93
abolition, 78, 80–81, 82–83, 235
restoration of, 96, 98
Equality Act 2010, 218–19
ethical standards
advocates and proctors, 16
Evangelicalism, 139, 151, 236
ex officio **oaths,** 75
abolition, 78, 92, 97–98
excommunication, 18–19, 45, 62, 62–63, 73, 98, 128, 144–45
An Exhortation to the People instructing them to Unity and Obedience **(1536),** 41, 42

failing incumbencies, 200–1
First Lateran Council (1123), 46
First Statute of Repeal 1553, 47
Five Mile Act 1665, 99, 138
foreign canon law, 131
formal instruction, 117–18
Forty-Two Articles, 46, 54
French Revolution (1789), 139

General Synod, 179, 204–5, 215–16, 221, 237
Constitution of the General Synod, 205–6
ordination of women, 217
Prayer Book, 207
right to marry, 128
remarriage of divorcees, 209–10
same-sex marriage, 231–32
George I (King of England), 115–16
George II (King of England), 115
George III (King of England), 136
George IV (King of England), 136
Gibson, Edmund, 55, 133, 235–36
Codex Juris Ecclesiastici Anglicani, 51–52, 59, 119–20, 120–21
Glorious Revolution, 97, 102–3, 107, 111–12, 112–13, 116
Godolphin, John, 110, 119, 235
Gratian, 12, 65, 193
Concordia discordantium canonum (Decretum), 6–7, 9, 15
commentaries, 7–8
Luther, 29
Roman law, 9
"Great Matter", 30, 38, 40
Reformation Parliament, 31, 32–33
Gregory IX (Pope), 9, 119
Grey, Richard, 120–21
Grindal, Edmund (Archbishop of Canterbury), 49
sequestration, 60–61

Habeas Corpus Act 1679, 101, 111
Hale, Matthew, 109–10
Hampton Court Conference 1604, 69–70
Heath, Nicholas (Archbishop of York/Lord Chancellor), 50
Henry VIII (King of England), 27–28, 48, 234
accession, 28
divorce, 28–30
Great Matter, 30, 31, 32–33, 38, 40
papal legatine court, 31
propaganda, 37–43
Reformation Parliament, 31–37, 86
royal supremacy, 33, 36–37, 73

Tyndale, 29–30
see also Reformation; Reformation Parliament
heresy, 25, 32, 38
   blasphemy and heresy Acts, 89
   burning of heretics, 100
   sacrament, 44
   Tyndale, 29–30
High Court of Delegates, 144, 163–64, 165
historic sexual abuse, 229–30
Hobbes, Thomas, 110
Holy Communion, 44–45, 186–87, 197, 202, 205, 237
Home Rule for Ireland, 177–78
Hooker, Richard, 43, 65–66, 234
House of Lords (Appeals Court), 108
human law, 38, 42, 132–33
   divine law, relationship with, 133
   moral law, relationship with, 133
Human Rights Act 1998, 224, 238
humanism, 89, 230–31
Humble Petition and Advice 1657, 78

independence of the judiciary, 107–8
injunctions, 52–53, 54, 60, 75–76
   First Henrician Injunctions, 37
   Marian injunctions, 47
instructions, 75–76
Instrument of Government 1653, 77–78, 82
Interregnum, see **Commonwealth; Cromwell, Oliver**
inter-war years:
   Church Assembly, 178–81
   Convocations, 188–90
   marriage
      degrees of affinity, 187–88
      divorce, 188
   memorial monuments, 182
   power of self-adjustment, 171, 176, 182–83
   Prayer Book revision, 176–77, 182–83
   public prayer, 182
   Representative Church Council, 178–79
   reservation of Blessed Sacrament, 182
Ireland:
   Act of Union between England and Ireland 1800, 135–36
   disestablishment of the Church of Ireland, 154, 169
   home rule, 177–78

Jacobite rebellions, 116–17
James I (King of England), 69–70, 73, 75, 90–91, 235

James II (King of England), 99–100, 101–2, 102, 104, 105–6, 116
James III (King of England), 97
Jerusalem Bishopric Act 1841, 154
Judicial Committee of the Privy Council, 163–65
judiciary:
   independence of the judiciary, 72, 107–8, 111
   remuneration of judiciary, 107–8
   separation of powers, 111
jurisdictional matters, 63–64
   Chancery Court, 63
   Church Assembly, 188–89, 216, 237
   consistory courts, 182, 221–22
   divorce, 12, 187–88, 189–90
   ecclesiastical appeals, 163–66
   Ecclesiastical Commissioners, 51
   ecclesiastical courts, 63, 221–22
   Ecclesiastical Jurisdiction Act 1531, 51
   Ecclesiastical Jurisdiction Act 1546, 51
   Ecclesiastical Jurisdiction Act 1661, 92–93, 97
   Ecclesiastical Jurisdiction Measure 1963, 92, 199, 200–1, 213–14, 220, 237
   marriage, 81
   papal jurisdiction, 13
      Act in Restraint of Appeals 1533, 27–28
      termination in England, 5, 27–28
   probate, 81
jury trials, 21–23
   independence of jurors, 101

Katherine of Aragon, 28
   Great Matter, 30
   see also Henry VIII
King-in-Parliament's supremacy, 32–33, 39, 42–43
King James Bible, 69

Lambeth Conferences, 175, 188–89, 198, 228
land and property:
   abolition of episcopacy, 82–83
   administrative rationalisation, 237–38
   advowsons, 58
      sale of, 124, 125–26
   cathedral property, 181
   church buildings, 148–49, 194–95, 199
      Council for Church Buildings, 201
      ecumenism, 201–2
      Redundant Churches Fund, 201
   dissolution of the monasteries, 67, 83–84
   see also patrons and patronage
Laud, William (Archbishop of Canterbury), 69–70, 79, 235
   execution, 78

law as morality, 132–33
lay officers, 143–45
legal personality, 223–24
legal profession:
  advocates, 13–15
    educational requirements, 16–17
    regulation, 17
    requirements, 16
  emergence of a legal profession, 14–18
  iuris periti, 14
  judges, 17
  legal representation in court, 14–15
  proctors, 13
legal scholarship, 28–29, 37–43, 64–66
  Great Matter, 40–41
legislation, proliferation of, 106–7, 136–37
Leo X (Pope), 29
Liber extra, 9, 10, 24
Life and Liberty Movement, 178
Little Treatise against the Muttering of Some Papists in Corners (**1534**), 40
liturgy, 52, 85, 206–8, 212, 237–38
Long Parliament, 77, 82, 88
Lords Spiritual, 51, 219
  women, 219–20
Luther, Martin, 29
Lutheran Church, 59–60
Lyndwood, William, 10, 13, 193, 233

marriage law:
  clandestine marriages, 126–27, 129
  degrees of affinity, 56–57, 147, 187–88
  divorce:
    Henry VIII, 28–30, 31, 40
    jurisdiction, 12, 187–88, 189–90
    papal legatine court, 31
    remarriage of divorcees, 209–10, 217, 237
  Fleet marriages, 127
  Marriage Act 1540, 51
  Marriage Act 1836, 147
  marriage banns, 126
  Marriage Measure 1930, 180–81
  Matrimonial Causes Act 1937, 187–88, 209
  Matrimonial Causes Act 1957, 159, 187–88
  parishioners' right to marry, 127–28, 180–81
  parliamentary legislation, 186–87
  regulation of marriage licenses, 126
  solemnising marriage, 127–28
Mary I (Queen of England), 28, 35, 45–46, 47
  death, 50
Mary II (Queen of England), 97
Matrimonial Causes Act 1937, 187–88, 209
Matrimonial Causes Act 1957, 159, 187–88

Measures of the Church Assembly, 179
Methodism, 115, 137, 139, 205, 224
Millenary Petition 1603, 69
moral law, 132–33
  divine law, relationship with, 133
  human law, relationship with, 133
More, Thomas (Lord Chancellor), 31
Mustre of Schismatic Bishops of Rome (**1534**), 40–41

Napoleonic Wars (1803–15), 139
natural law, 132–33, 145
Nelson, William, 118, 120–22, 133, 235
next presentations, 124, 126
Nonconformism, 104–5, 137, 147, 149
  see also Dissenters, Quakers
Nonconformist Relief Act 1779, 138

ordinances:
  civil marriage, 81
  episcopacy, 80–81
  felonies, 81
  idolatry and superstition, 80
  Laud, 79
  "Presbyterianising" the Church of England, 79–80
Ordination of Women (Financial Provisions) Measure 1993, 211
ordination of women:
  bishops, 217–18
  priests, 210–11, 216–17
ornaments, 80, 157–58, 160, 172, 182, 197
Oughton, Thomas, 119, 121, 133, 235

papal decretals, 9, 24
papal jurisdiction:
  Act in Restraint of Appeals 1533, 27–28
  termination in England, 5, 27–28
papal legatine court:
  Henry VIII/Katherine of Aragon divorce, 31
papal supremacy, 28–29, 41–42
Papist Acts (**1715–57**), 116–17
Papists Act 1778, 137–38
Parker, Matthew (Archbishop of Canterbury), 53–54
  Advertisements for Due Order, 58
  Articles for Ecclesiastical Government, 57–58
  Canons of 1571, 59–60
  Eleven Articles, 54–55
  Latin Prayer Book, 55–56
  Reformatio Legum Ecclesiasticarum, 58–59
  Table of Impediments to Marriage, 56–57
  Welsh Prayer Book, 56

Parliamentary Test Act 1678, 99, 100
Parochial Church Councils (PCCs), 180, 197, 201–2, 202–3, 223–24
Parochial Registers Act 1812, 147
parsonages, 83, 88, 122, 124, 150
patrons and patronage, 124–25
  Church Patronage Act 1737, 125
  clergy, 140–41
Paul III (Pope), 29
penance, 73, 143, 230
  commutation of penance, 62
pensions, 212
  national pension scheme for clergy, 180, 195
persecution, *see* religious persecution
Places of Religious Worship Act 1812, 138
pluralism, *see* religious pluralism
Pole, Reginald (Cardinal), 47
  death, 50
poor clergy, 139
  Queen Anne Bounty, 123–24, 149–50
Poor Relief Acts 1597 and 1601, 67–68
post-WWII reforms:
  Church Assembly
    Constitution of the General Synod, 205–6
  General Synod, creation of, 204–5
  ecclesiastical courts, 199–200
  liturgical and doctrinal reform, 206–8
  ordination of women priests, 210–11
  pastoral reorganisation, 200–1
  remarried priests, 209–10
poverty, 16, 32
  poor clergy, 139
    Queen Anne Bounty, 123–24, 149–50
  Poor Relief Acts 1597 and 1601, 67–68
power of self-adjustment, 171, 176, 182–83
prayer books:
  Book of Common Prayer, 52, 68
    abolition, 84–85, 86, 89–90
    Latin version, 55–56
    proposed revisions 1928, 191
    reinstatement, 100, 146–47, 157, 185–86, 197, 207, 235
    Welsh version, 56
  new Prayer Book, proposals for, 182–85, 205–6
  Prayer Book controversy, 182–86, 203
  Shorter Prayer Book, 185–86
precedent, 72, 74–75, 108, 132, 134, 223
prerogative courts, 81, 95, 107, 137, 144
Presbyterianism:
  Church of Scotland, 77, 80, 178
  Presbyterian Church in England, 77
    Church of England, impact on, 79–80, 82

Presentation of Benefices Act 1688, 106
Presentation of Benefices Act 1713, 124–25
Priests (Ordination of Women) Measure 1993, 211, 216–17
Principles of Canon Law Common to the Churches of the Anglican Communion, 228–29
principles of ecclesiastical law, development of, 131–32, 227–29
Privy Council, 52, 54–55, 78, 107
  appeals, 163–66
  Judicial Committee of the Privy Council, 163–65
  Privy Council Appeals Act 1832, 144, 163, 199
  Victorian reforms, 144–45, 163–64
property, *see* land and property
prosecutions for ritual or ceremonial offences, 183–84
Public Acts:
  proliferation of, 106–7
public worship, 56, 84–85, 100, 176, 182–84
  post-war reform, 206–7
  Public Worship Regulation Act 1874, 158, 160–61, 182–84, 197–98
Puritans, 49, 58, 100, 124, 234
  Grindal, relationship with, 60–61
  Whitgift, relationship with, 61–62, 65
  persecution, 61–62, 65

Quakers, 97–98, 106–7, 138, 147
Queen Anne's Bounty, 84, 122–24, 181, 193

re-establishment of the Church of England, 135–36
  litigation, 157–58
  doctrine, 156–57
  faculty and clergy discipline suits, 157
  standards of clerical deportment and duty, 156
  Parliamentary legislation, 136–39
Redundant Churches Fund, 201
Reformatio Legum Ecclesiasticarum (1551–52), 45–46, 48, 58–59, 131, 234
Reformation, 27–28
  Act against the Authority of Rome 1536, 36–37
  Edward VI, 43–44
    election of bishops, 45
    excommunication, 45
    Forty-Two Articles, 46
    reformation of ecclesiastical law, 45–46
    sacrament, 44–45
    uniformity in worship, 45

European influences, 29–30
Great Matter, 30
   Reformation Parliament, 31–33
Henry VIII, 28–29
   Great Matter, 30
   propaganda, 37–43
   Reformation Parliament, 31–36
Reformation Parliament, 31
   Act Concerning Ecclesiastical Appointments and Absolute Restraint of Annates 1533, 33–34
   Act for the Submission of the Clergy 1533, 34
   Act in Restraint of Appeals 1532, 33
   Act of Succession 1534, 35
   Act of Supremacy 1534, 35–36
   Act of Treasons 1534, 36
   Ecclesiastical Licences Act 1533, 34
   King's supremacy, declaration of, 32–33
   role of Parliament, 33
   "six great causes", 32
   propaganda, 37–43
Reformation Parliament, 31
   Act Concerning Ecclesiastical Appointments and Absolute Restraint of Annates 1533, 33–34
   Act for the Submission of the Clergy 1533, 34
   Act in Restraint of Appeals 1532, 33
   Act of Succession 1534, 35
   Act of Supremacy 1534, 35–36
   Act of Treasons 1534, 36
   Ecclesiastical Licences Act 1533, 34
   King's supremacy, declaration of, 32–33
   role of Parliament, 33
   "six great causes", 31–32
religious education, 145–46
religious persecution:
   Restoration, 99–100, 104–5, 113
religious pluralism, 3, 104, 135–39, 151, 155, 168–69, 232, 236, 238
religious toleration, 70, 99–100, 235–36
   Cromwell
      Instrument of Government 1653, 77–78, 82, 87, 89–90
      patronage, 124–25
      Toleration Act 1689, 104–6, 109, 113, 138
      Toleration Act 1711, 116
Representative Church Council for the Church of England, 177–79
Restoration, 92–93, 95–97, 235
   case law, 108–9
   House of Lords (Appeals Court), 108
   judiciary, 107–8

   jurists, 109–11
   legislative reform, 100–2
      Public Acts, proliferation of, 106–7
   religious persecution, 99–100
   religious toleration, 104–5
   schisms within the Church of England, 104–6, 113
   tensions with Parliament, 98
   William III, 97, 102–3
      Convention Parliament, 102
      Glorious Revolution, 102–3, 111–12
Restraint of Appeals Act 1533, 27–28, 33, 35
retirement:
   clergy
      age of retirement, 200–1
Revolt of the Northern Earls 1569, 58–59
Ridley, Thomas, 91
rites of passage, 1, 147, 233, 239
ritualism, 157–58, 160, 236–37
   ritual conformity, 182
   vestments, 196
Roman law, development of, 8–9
   Corpus iuris civilis, 10–11
   pre-Reformation ecclesiastical courts
      civil and criminal procedure, 12–13
      English Church, 10–13
Royal Commission on the Ecclesiastical Courts (1830), 143–44, 163
Royal Commission on Ecclesiastical Discipline (1906), 158, 171, 182
royal prerogative, 18–19, 37, 111, 128, 172
   Henry VIII, 72–73
   James II, 101–2
   Reformation Parliament, 34, 42, 45, 48, 90–91
   Restoration, 95–96
   William and Mary, 103–4
royal proclamations:
   Declarations of Indulgence, 101–2
Rump Parliament 1650, 77

St German, Christopher, 28, 37–43, 234
Sabbath Act 1657, 78
sacraments, 12, 25, 29, 39, 59, 62, 99, 189, 196, 204, 229–30
   Advertisements for Due Order, 58
   Canons of 1603, 70–71
   reservation of the Blessed Sacrament, 182–83, 184
   Sacrament Act 1547, 44–45, 48, 51
Safeguarding and Clergy Discipline Measure 2016, 229–30
saints, 42
same-sex marriage, 231–32

Schism Act 1714, 116
schisms within the Church of England, 104–6, 113, 116
Scotland:
  Act of Union between England and Scotland 1706, 116–17
  Church of Scotland, 77, 80, 178
  Church of Scotland Act 1921, 178
  Solemn League and Covenant with Scotland 1643, 77, 100
seal of the confessional, 229–30
Second Statute of Repeal 1555, 47
Second Treason Act 1696, 104
secularisation, 151, 219–20, 230–32, 236, 238
sedition, 45–46
Sheppard, William, 83, 88, 89–90, 235
simony law, 106, 125–26
Simplification Task Group, 215–16
"six great causes" (Reformation Parliament), 31–32
social legislation:
  Poor Relief Acts 1597 and 1601, 67–68
  Statutes of Charitable Uses 1597 and 1601, 67
soft law, 226–27, 234, 235, 238
Solemn League and Covenant with Scotland 1643, 77, 84–85, 100
solemnisation of marriage, 61, 92–93, 126, 127–28, 142, 187–88, 231, 237
Sophia (Electress of Hanover), 115–16
Statute Law (Repeals) Act 1969, 92, 204
Statute Law (Repeals) Measure 2017, 215–16
Statute of Praemunire 1392, 37
Statutes of Charitable Uses 1597 and 1601, 67
Submission of the Clergy Act 1533, 34, 51, 58–59, 131
Succession to the Crown Act 1536, 50
Suffragan Bishops Act 1534, 51
sui generis nature of ecclesiastical law, 227–28
superstition, 42, 80, 145
supremacy of Parliament, 111, 203, 234–35
Swinburne, Henry, 65–66
synodical government, 93, 170–71, 193–94, 202–6, 237

Table of Impediments to Marriage 1560/63, 56–57
Tancred of Bologna, 7–8, 12–13
temporal power of the Church, 5, 39, 42–46, 71–79, 100, 118, 132, 142–45, 165, 233
tenure:
  Archbishops, 49
  common tenure, 88, 225

termination of papal jurisdiction, 5
  Act in Restraint of Appeals 1533, 27–28
Test Act 1673, 99, 100
testament doctrine, 20–21
Thirty-Eight Articles 1563, 54
tithes 83–84, 122, 141, 149–50, 162
  dissenters, 138
  Quakers, 106–7
toleration, *see* religious toleration
Toleration Act 1689, 104–5, 109, 113, 138
Toleration Act 1711, 116
Trinitarian Protestants, 104
Tudor's Act 1563:
  Welsh Prayer Book, 56
Tyndale, William, 29–30

Union of Benefices Measure 1923, 180
Unitarian Relief Act 1813, 138

Vacarius, 8
vestments, 137–38, 157
  new code of Canons, 196–98
  Puritans, 58
  vestiarian controversy, 197–98
Vicegerent of Spirituals, 36
Victoria (Queen of England), 153–56, 236–37
  confessional principle, 168–71
  judicature reforms, 158–59, 172–73
    Court of Final Ecclesiastical Appeal, 163–66
    Court of First Instance, 159–63
    legal profession, 166–68
  litigation, 156–58
  vestments, 196
visitation articles, 53–54

Wales:
  disestablishment of Church of England in Wales, 178, 237
  religious education, 145–46
  Welsh Church Act 1914, 178
  Welsh Prayer Book, 56
Warham, William (Archbishop of Canterbury):
  "six causes" of Reformation Parliament, 32
Watson, William, 110, 235
Welsh Church Act 1914, 178
Whitgift, John (Archbishop of Canterbury), 61
  Articles for the Clergy 1583, 61–62
  Canons of 1584, 62
  Canons of 1597, 63
  legislative programme, 1583–1603, 62–63

William III (King of England), 97, 102–3
　Convention Parliament, 102
　Glorious Revolution, 102–3, 111–12
William IV (King of England), 136
witnesses, 21–23
Wolsey, Thomas (Cardinal Archbishop of York), 30
　papal legatine court, 31
　"six causes" of Reformation Parliament, 32
women:
　Bishops and Priests (Consecration and Ordination of Women) Measure 2014, 217, 218–19
　Lords Spiritual, 219–20
　Ordination of Women (Financial Provisions) Measure 1993, 211
　ordination of women, 238
　　bishops, 217–18
　　General Synod, 217
　　priests, 210–11, 216–17
　Priests (Ordination of Women) Measure 1993, 211, 216–17
Worcester House Declaration, 98
world wars, impact on ecclesiastical law, 237–38
writs of prohibition, 23–24, 71, 129, 144–45

Zouche, Richard, 90, 235

Milton Keynes UK
Ingram Content Group UK Ltd.
UKHW032227130224
437752UK00003B/42